Bakhtin
and Religion

Jesus and the Grand Inquisitor (1948), wood engraving by Fritz
Eichenberg (copyright © by Fritz Eichenberg Trust/licensed by
VAGA, New York, N.Y.)

BAKHTIN AND RELIGION

A Feeling for Faith

Edited by

Susan M. Felch and Paul J. Contino

Northwestern University Press
Evanston, Illinois

Northwestern University Press
Evanston, Illinois 60208-4210

Copyright © 2001 by Northwestern University Press. Published 2001.
All rights reserved.

Printed in the United States of America

10 9 8 7 6 5 4 3 2 1

ISBN 0-8101-1824-6 (cloth)
ISBN 0-8101-1825-4 (paper)

Library of Congress Cataloging-in-Publication Data

Bakhtin and religion : a feeling for faith / edited by Susan M. Felch and Paul J. Contino.
    p.   cm. — (Rethinking theory)
  Includes bibliographical references and index.
  ISBN 0-8101-1824-6 (cloth : alk. paper) — ISBN 0-8101-1825-4 (pbk. : alk. paper)
  1. Bakhtin, M. M. (Mikhail Mikhaĭlovich), 1895–1975—Religion. I. Felch, Susan M., 1951–
II. Contino, Paul J. III. Series.
PG2947.B3 B327 2001
801'.95'092—dc21   2001001907

The paper used in this publication meets the minimum requirements of the American National
Standard for Information Sciences—Permanence of Paper for Printed Library Materials, ANSI
Z39.48-1984.

Not faith (in the sense of a specific faith in orthodoxy, in progress, in man, in revolution, etc.) but a feeling for faith, *that is, an integral attitude (by means of the whole person) toward a higher and ultimate value. Atheism is often understood by Dostoevsky as a lack of faith in this sense, as indifference toward an ultimate value which makes demands on the whole human being, as a rejection of an ultimate position in the ultimate whole of the world.*

—M. M. Bakhtin "Toward a Reworking
of the Dostoevsky Book"

Contents

Illustrations

Acknowledgments

The editors would like to thank the Calvin Center for Christian Scholarship for its generous financial support of this project. When the contributors to this volume met at Calvin College in the summer of 1997 for a week of intense discussion, the Center, and especially its director, Ronald A. Wells, provided warm hospitality and a wonderful space to think and converse. We are also deeply grateful to Caryl Emerson, who offered invaluable suggestions from the very beginning and led our discussions at Calvin with characteristic brilliance and generosity. We also thank Vitaly Makhlin for his help in securing permissions from Russia. Charity Houston, our research assistant, cheerfully performed numerous tasks. And we are very grateful to our colleagues—at Christ College and Valparaiso University, and Calvin College—for sustaining the stimulating academic environment in which we do our work.

Abbreviations

A&A	Mikhail Bakhtin, *Art and Answerability: Early Philosophical Essays by M. M. Bakhtin*. Edited by Michael Holquist and Vadim Liapunov. Translation and notes by Vadim Liapunov. Austin: Univ. of Texas Press, 1990.
"A&A"	"Art and Answerability," in *Art and Answerability*, 1–3.
"A&H"	"Author and Hero in Aesthetic Activity," in *Art and Answerability*, 4–208, 231–54.
"A&H (FFC)"	"Author and Hero in Aesthetic Activity (Fragment of the First Chapter)," in *Art and Answerability*, 208–31, 254–56.
"BiK"	"M. M. Bakhtin i M. I. Kagan (Po materialam semeinogo arkhiva)," published by K. Nevel'skaia in *Pamiat': Istoricheskii sbornik* 4 (1981): 259–81.
DI	Mikhail Bakhtin, *The Dialogic Imagination: Four Essays by M. M. Bakhtin*. Edited by Michael Holquist. Translated by Caryl Emerson and Michael Holquist. Austin: Univ. of Texas Press, 1981.
"PCMFVA"	"The Problem of Content, Material, and Form in Verbal Art," in *Art and Answerability*. Translation of "PCMFVA" by Kenneth Brostrom, 257–325.
PDP	Mikhail Bakhtin, *Problems of Dostoevsky's Poetics* [1963]. Edited and translated by Caryl Emerson. Minneapolis: Univ. of Minnesota Press, 1984.
RAHW	Mikhail Bakhtin, *Rabelais and His World*. Translated by Hélène Iswolsky. Cambridge: MIT Press, 1968.
RSV	Revised Standard Version of the Bible
SpG	Mikhail Bakhtin, *Speech Genres and Other Late Essays*. Translated by Vern W. McGee. Austin: Univ. of Texas Press, 1986.
TPA	Mikhail Bakhtin, *Toward a Philosophy of the Act*. Translation and notes by Vadim Liapunov. Austin: Univ. of Texas Press, 1993.
"TRDB"	"Toward a Reworking of the Dostoevsky Book," in *Problems of Dostoevsky's Poetics*, 283–302.

BAKHTIN
AND RELIGION

Introduction: A Feeling for Faith

Paul J. Contino and Susan M. Felch

Among the questions that have arisen over the work of Mikhail Mikhailovich Bakhtin, perhaps none has been more fiercely contested by some, or more ignored by others, than the religious dimension of his life and work. Clark and Holquist, his first biographers, declared unambiguously in 1984 that "Bakhtin was a religious man,"[1] but this is a statement both they and others have come to qualify, if not repudiate.[2] As Caryl Emerson comments in her recent *The First Hundred Years of Mikhail Bakhtin:* The jury is still out on "the role of truth and faith in Bakhtin's thought."[3]

This collection moves a bit closer to a verdict. As its subtitle—and the longer quotation from which it is taken—suggests, Bakhtin was careful to distinguish between "faith," which he identified as an abstract codification of a belief system, and "a feeling for faith."[4] The latter involves both the preparation for personal encounters—the adoption of a proper attitude—and the actual living engagement of persons, human and divine. Bakhtin himself comments upon such a feeling in Dostoevsky: it is "an integral attitude (by means of the whole person) toward a higher and ultimate value" ("TRDB" 294). As Robert Louis Jackson notes of Dostoevsky, one leans toward this value and stands "in a positive relation to it."[5]

Examinations of Bakhtin's own "feeling for faith," his leaning toward the religious, have tended to divide into the biographical and the textual. The essays in this volume take the latter path, investigating the religious dimensions of his thought as these shape and frame his writings. But the biographical evidence, which is both suggestive and disputed, should not be entirely overlooked, if for no other reason than Bakhtin's own emphasis on the answerability for one's life.

The Biographical Evidence

In their 1984 seminal intellectual biography, Katerina Clark and Michael Holquist offer what is still the best sketch of Bakhtin's religious activities and associations. They emphasize Bakhtin's immersion in the Russian tradition of kenosis that highlighted Christ's descent to earth, his Incarnation as a common man, and his death on the cross. Their claim that Bakhtin was "a highly religious man" was bolstered in the 1990s with the publication of reminiscences from Bakhtin's literary executors.

Vadim Kozhinov (born 1930), chief among those Russian scholars who, in the early 1960s, rediscovered Bakhtin, sought him out in Saransk, rescued him from obscurity, and saw that his work came back into print, insists in a 1992 interview with Nicholas Rzhevsky that "his religious convictions were apparently noncanonical," but "Mikhail Mikhailovich was a deeply religious person."[6] In particular, Kozhinov recalls Bakhtin's statement that "there was never a great human being who was not a believer" because "only religion truly gives human beings freedom of spirit."[7] In a later article, Kozhinov argues that while Holquist and Clark may have been the first to state in print that "all Bakhtin's ideas had a Russian Orthodox axis. . . . The people who were close to Bakhtin understood this after the first frank conversation with him."[8] Such religious convictions, however, could not be publicly expressed during the Soviet era. Kozhinov admits that "Mikhail Mikhailovich did not discuss religious issues very often," but

> several times he spoke at length about the most intimate [beliefs]. I recall that, still in the 1960s in Saransk, he spoke to me about God and Creation for several hours, finishing long after midnight. He spoke with such inspiration that I came back to my hotel, literally in a state of astonishment and could not fall asleep, remaining in a spiritual state which I had never experienced before.[9]

In this article, as in the previous interview, Kozhinov repeats that Bakhtin believed "the human being in communion with Russia could confess only and exclusively Orthodox Christianity."

Kozhinov's colleague in the project of reviving Bakhtin's reputation, Sergey Bocharov (born 1929), recalls his "Conversations with Bakhtin" in an essay published in Russia in 1993 and claims: "The religious aspect of Bakhtin's aesthetics is deep but concealed, an unspoken, implicit theme, evidently because of the external conditions of writing in the Soviet period."[10] Indeed, Bocharov remarks on the penitential tone in Bakhtin's voice as he recalled the "moral flaws" in his Dostoevsky book:

> "After all, in that book, I severed form from the main thing. I couldn't speak directly about the main questions."
> "What main questions, M. M.?"
> "Philosophical questions. What Dostoevsky agonized about all his life—the existence of God. In the book I was constantly forced to prevaricate, to dodge backward and forward. I had to hold back constantly. The moment a thought got going, I had to break it off. Backward and forward" (he repeated this several times during the conversation). "I even misrepresented the church."[11]

Finally, Vladimir Turbin (1927–93), Bakhtin's personal aide for his final decade in Saransk, in an article published posthumously, also recalls conversations with Bakhtin and records one comment in particular that was highly suggestive of Bakhtin's "feeling for faith." "'A cross and a prayer,' he told me simply and with conviction, 'a cross and a prayer are the most important.'" Turbin comments: "The words about a cross and a prayer are a clear result of Mikhail Mikhailovich's dialogue with the Gospels which continued throughout his whole life."[12]

One difficulty with these personal accounts (on which the Clark and Holquist biography is also based) is their late publication date—some twenty years after the conversations took place. As a result, some scholars in the West have regarded these reports with misgivings, suspecting that devotion to a master may have colored the memories of the disciples. The notes of L. V. Pumpiansky on Bakhtin's 1924–25 lectures, which are included in the appendix to this volume and are contemporaneous with Bakhtin's early works, do lend credence, however, to these memoirs. In his lecture on "The Problem of Grounded Peace," Bakhtin argues not only for the necessary engagement of the self and the other in the creation of meaning, but for the presence of the "incarnated Third One." God's activity in the world is even more clearly articulated in Bakhtin's response to a paper delivered by M. I. Tubiansky. Against Tubiansky's dismissal of miracle and revelation on the grounds that such supernatural intrusions would render morality and even faith meaningless, Bakhtin argues that the world itself is constituted by revelation as well as natural laws.[13] Furthermore, revelation is always personal, "the relationship of two consciousnesses." So it is not science, or reason, or intellectual maturity that causes people to deny the reality of revelation, but fear—fear of an encounter with a personal God, "of receiving a gift, and thereby obligating oneself too much." Against such fear, with its resulting cultural immanentism, Bakhtin posits a world that is meaningful *because* God has revealed himself, thus enabling human beings to enter into a face-to-face encounter with the divine person: "a personal relationship to a personal God—that is the distinguishing feature of religion." Such a relationship frees humans from the "attempt to enact an event with only one participant," an attempt that, for Bakhtin, is always doomed to failure.

Religious Dimensions in Bakhtin's Works

The Pumpiansky notes are a valuable contemporary witness to Bakhtin's early thought and also point us along the second path of exploring Bakhtin's relationship to religion through a close study of his own writings. The essays in this volume follow Pumpiansky's lead. Russian commentators on Bakhtin have been particularly sensitive to this approach. As Alexandar Mihailovic notes, "[T]he theological subtext of Bakhtin's work . . . has become a given in Russian interpretations of him."[14] Thus Rzhevsky concludes from his interview with Kozhinov:

> The issue, given the biographical data, is not whether Bakhtin was religious—the evidence is too strong to suggest he was not—but to what extent religion entered his philosophical concerns. . . . To define Bakhtin as a thinker who stood outside religion is to reduce the writer to ahistorical abstractions, to place him beyond the cultural dimensions of his own intellectual context, and, of course, to reduce religion itself from the role it actually plays in intellectual history.[15]

Similarly, Kozhinov remarks that Bakhtin's religious convictions "are present under various guises in any of Bakhtin's texts: one only needs to treat his texts without prejudice and in depth."[16]

Writers in the West have been slower to realize the religious significance of Bakhtin's writings. Julia Kristeva's 1970 introduction to the French edition of *Problems of Dostoevsky's Poetics* discounted Bakhtin's religious language as "the unrecognized influence of Christianity in a humanist terminology."[17] As early as 1982, however, Anthony Ugolnik noted the congruence between Bakhtin's sense of materiality and that of the Orthodox tradition, but few scholars until the 1990s picked up on this clue.[18] In her 1990 essay, "Russian Orthodoxy and the Early Bakhtin," Caryl Emerson affirms Bakhtin's qualifications as a thinker in the Russian Orthodox tradition not by way of his biography but by noting his adaptation of the relational aspects of Trinitarian theology, his iconic emphasis upon the vitality of seeing, and his rejection of the Cartesian split between body and mind.[19] In Bakhtin's *Toward a Philosophy of the Act* and his "Author and Hero in Aesthetic Activity," proper seeing of the other entails love in its "willingness to concentrate attention," and here the incarnate Christ emerges as exemplary: "If there is an Ideal in Bakhtin's otherwise passionately quotidian philosophy, it is here in the intimate individuating reciprocity promised by the embodied image of Christ."[20]

Embodiment is also the theme of Charles Lock's 1991 essay, "Carnival and Incarnation: Bakhtin and Orthodox Theology," which emphasizes the holiness of matter in the Orthodox imagination—and in Bakhtin's. In the eighth century, for example, St. John of Damascus, in his defense of icons, insisted that paint, wax, wood, and gold were fitting materials with which to image the Divine, above all because God "[took] up His abode in matter, and [accomplished] my salvation through matter. 'And the Word became flesh and dwelt among us.' "[21] The event of the Incarnation means that matter matters, that it is sacramental in its capacity to mediate divine grace. Thus, as Lock insists, drawing on *Toward A Philosophy of the Act*, "the realization of one's 'singular irreplaceable involvement in being' is to be achieved through the body, through the opposite of what Bakhtin rejects as 'non-incarnated thought, non-incarnated action, non-incarnated accidental life as an empty possibility.' "[22] So, too, is the body affirmed in *Rabelais and His World*, its "foods, banquets and ingestions" suggesting the Eucharist and the Paschal Feast of Easter.[23]

More recently, Alexandar Mihailovic's *Corporeal Words* (1997) draws especially upon the Gospel of John and the Chalcedonian formulation of the Fourth Ecumenical Council (A.D. 451) in their understanding of Christ as both human and divine, his two natures present "without change, without confusion, without separation." As Mihailovic demonstrates, terms that recall the Christological (and Trinitarian) notions of unity in diversity and interpenetration "emerge in almost every essay in Bakhtin's long and varied career."[24] Furthermore, as Mihailovic notes, "We cannot dismiss his interest in theology as simply terminological because the interaction among Christological motifs saturates his critical lexicon of dialogue, carnival, and polyphony and is in fact crucial in defining the interrelatedness of those latter concepts."[25]

Although these readers locate Bakhtin primarily within the particular Russian Orthodox tradition, Ruth Coates understands his religious subtexts within, one might say, the broadly orthodox and biblical tradition of the Christian faith. In *Christianity in Bakhtin: God and the Exiled Author*, Coates argues for a "coherent theistic framework to Bakhtin's aesthetic theory," based upon the biblical doctrines of God, persons, creation, fall, and incarnation. This framework is clearly established in his early works such as "Author and Hero" and modified, but not abandoned, in his middle and later writings.[26]

The essays in this volume build on these earlier textual studies and focus on works from the entire span of Bakhtin's scholarly life, progressing in roughly chronological order from his early to his later writings. With their explicit references to Christ and religious experience, the works of the 1920s, however, receive special attention. Indeed, Bocharov claims that "Author and Hero in Aesthetic Activity" is a treatise "which one could call Bakhtin's theology in the form of aesthetics or his aesthetics resolved in theological terms."[27]

In the first essay, "Bakhtin and the Hermeneutics of Love," Alan Jacobs draws from "Author and Hero" as well as *Toward a Philosophy of the Act* to present a convincing explanation of the ways in which Bakhtin might be taken to extend and enrich Augustine's notion of charitable interpretation. Jacobs does not situate Bakhtin exclusively within Russian Orthodoxy, but rather thinks through the implications of his thought in a broader Christian context. For Bakhtin, aesthetic creation—and by extension, hermeneutical responses to works of art—are marked by "lovingly interested attention" (*TPA* 64). In his discussion of this loving attentiveness, Jacobs provides an illuminating gloss on two of Bakhtin's most fertile reflections on Christ. The first is from *Toward a Philosophy of the Act*:

[S]elf-renunciation is a performance or accomplishment that encompasses *Being-as-event.* A great symbol of self-activity, the descending [?] of Christ. The world from which Christ departed will no longer be the world in which he had never existed; it is in its very principle, a different world. (*TPA* 16)

One might immediately connect this passage with Christ's act of kenosis, the emptying of self that St. Paul writes of in his Letter to the Philippians, and that has played such a formative role in Orthodox spirituality. And rightly so, argues Jacobs, who sees it as Bakhtin's commentary on the Philippians passage. But Jacobs insists that the self-renunciation of which Bakhtin (and St. Paul) speaks cannot be equated with the utter self-emptying, even self-annihilation, that an author like Simone Weil seems to advise. As the context of the passage from *Toward a Philosophy of the Act* makes clear, "losing oneself . . . [has] nothing in common with the *answerable act/deed* of . . . self-renunciation" (*TPA* 16). For Bakhtin, self-evacuation evades the authentic ethical deed that only I can accomplish. Indeed, it evades incarnation itself, as I fail to embody my own singular deed of attention, fail to undersign it as my own (*TPA* 51). Christ is the exemplar of such embodiment, as becomes clearer in the second passage, this time from "Author and Hero," which Jacobs cites:

[T]he Christ of the Gospels. In Christ we find a synthesis of unique depth, the synthesis of *ethical solipsism* (man's infinite severity toward himself, i.e., an immaculately pure relationship to oneself) with *ethical-aesthetic kindness* toward the other. For the first time there appeared an infinitely deepened *I-for-myself*—not a cold *I-for-myself,* but one of boundless kindness toward the other; an *I-for-myself* that renders full justice to the other as such, disclosing and affirming the other's axiological distinctiveness in all its fullness. ("A&H" 56)

In his explication of kenosis that is not self-annihilating, Jacobs presents an implicit response to the Russian critic K. G. Isupov, who, in his 1995 essay, "The Death of the Other," also links Bakhtin's ideas with those of Russian Orthodoxy.[28] According to Mihailovic, however, Isupov sees kenosis as "the complete purging of consciousness" and "explicitly links Eastern Orthodoxy's annihilation of the other with political authoritarianism in general and Stalinism in particular, implicitly suggesting that the purges were possible precisely because of the particular kind of spirituality that operated on the level of the Russian collective unconscious."[29]

But what does appropriate self-renunciation have to do with reading? Extending Bakhtin, we see how we might bring attention and loving kindness to our encounter with the text. Wayne Booth's golden rule of hermeneutics applies: "Read as you would have others read you; listen as you would have others listen."[30] But the golden rule operative here necessitates an intentional, attentive love. If I totally give myself up to the text I am reading, or lazily allow its words to roll over me, I fail ethically in that I bring nothing of myself to the encounter. As Bakhtin insists in one of his final essays, "The event of the life of the text, that is, its true essence, always develops *on the boundary between two consciousnesses, two subjects*" (*SpG* 106). Even as I attend in loving contemplation to the text I am interpreting, I retain my unique and irreplaceable outsideness in relation to it. And yet, Jacobs suggests at the end of his essay, Bakhtin hints in his early writing that the answerable deed of charitable interpretation is not necessarily only shared by two. According to Bakhtin, Christ not only serves as exemplar in the "I-for myself" he brings to the encounter with the other, he remains as a presence, a third, for "[w]hat I must be for the other, God is for me" ("A&H" 56). As Jacobs writes: "the suggestion here is first that God's 'I-for-myself' and 'I-for-the-other' finds its perfect expression in the kenosis of Christ: 'the Word become flesh' (John 1:14) is God's signature, in Bakhtin's sense, of his love for us. But second, the divine signature, once recognized by me, provides the ground for, or source of, my own determination to act answerably, to 'undersign' and 'incarnate' my love for the other." Jacobs identifies a kinship here between Bakhtin and the philosopher Vladimir Solovyov, but one recalls, too, Bakhtin's own late notion of the "superaddressee," the third present in every dialogue, "whose absolutely just responsive understanding is presumed" (*SpG* 126).

Jacobs's Bakhtinian gloss on Augustinian hermeneutics reminds us that when St. Augustine first encountered the Gospels he resisted them because of their low style. St. Ambrose helped him to see that the *sermo humilis*—the low and humble style—may not only be the bearer of the divine word, but is indeed most apt because the union of elevated and low evokes the Incarnation itself. As Erich Auerbach has written, "the Incarnation, as it actually happened on earth, could only be narrated in a lowly and humble style."[31]

Graham Pechey, in his essay "Philosophy and Theology in 'Aesthetic Activity,'" rehearses the links between Bakhtin and Auerbach in his elucidation of a related paradox: for Bakhtin "the novel is our gospel, and (like the Gospels themselves) it offers at every turn a direct route from the everyday into the most elevated." Bakhtin works toward this position in "Author and Hero," which is Pechey's primary focus. In a further paradox, Bakhtin "sacralizes the novel"—and modernity itself—by embracing and exploring the problematics of faith within a genre that stands as one of modernity's signature achievements. The novel has often been seen as rising out of the development of Cartesian consciousness,[32] with all of its destructive capacities for isolated rationalization and objectifying instrumentalization. The novel images modern thought in its celebration of the autonomous hero. Bakhtin affirms the autonomy of the hero, but grounds the hero's freedom within the authority of the author, thus reinscribing a communalism and intersubjectivity that many trends in modern thought had banished to the realm of theology. For Bakhtin, Dostoevsky's authority emerges in his willingness to grant his characters their freedom. As Pechey writes, "Dostoevsky matters so much for Bakhtin because his writing keeps faith with modernity's promise of freedom while resisting its will to totality."

A literary image from Dostoevsky—pictorially represented on the frontispiece—might make more concrete the dynamic that Pechey explores.[33] In Christ's response of "lovingly interested attention" toward the Grand Inquisitor, Christ kenotically resists any imposition of power and sustains the Inquisitor's freedom. The Inquisitor, with his totalitarian blueprint for the future, could very well stand for what Pechey calls the "sinful hubris of modern reason [that] produces in the twentieth century the terroristic heresies of its characteristic politics." But although the Inquisitor "adheres to his idea," Christ's graceful kiss upon his lips glows in his heart, and opens up his chance to exit his solipsism. Indeed, Eichenberg's woodcut suggests that the door leading from imprisonment is now open to the Inquisitor. On the one hand, the Inquisitor's last word to Christ—"Go!"—suggests willful refusal of the grace-bestowing other, and the utterance could stand for modern epistemology writ large. But "Go!" also comprises his release of the One whom he had willfully determined to destroy. The Inquisitor seems here to recognize that he is not his own author but, rather, is authored by an authoritative, grace-bestowing Other. To borrow Pechey's terms, the moment suggests a movement from sin toward faith: "Sin in Bakhtin's ethical-aesthetic sense is the absurd presumption that I can, as it were, 'rhythmicize' [give form to] my own life. Faith is the rightfully insane belief against all odds that I do not coincide with myself, the desperate refusal of the last word which spurs on my life-as-it-is-lived." The fact that in this episode Christ chooses a tactile kiss to communicate his loving authorial authority recalls Bakhtin's own embrace of figures like St. Bernard of Clairvaux and St. Francis of Assisi who celebrate embodiment and who, as Pechey writes, "might be seen as the saints who preside over" Bakhtin's "Author and Hero." Further, the Inquisitor's experience at this moment is one of paradoxical "passive activity" in his acceptance of Christ's kiss, an experience "of at once encompassing and being encompassed," and the moment might be read as emblematic of Bakhtin's sophianic dance, which Pechey explicates in the conclusion of his essay.

In "The First and the Second Adam in Bakhtin's Early Thought," Ruth Coates also observes Bakhtin's critique of—and hope for—the modern world in his early writings. In both *Toward a Philosophy of the Act* and "Author and Hero," human pride takes the form of claiming a false autonomy and, thus, a falling away from God, other, and the world. Coates looks closely at Bakhtin's choice of specific words that "strongly connote the bid of Adam and Eve for autonomy as they eat the fruit of the Tree of Knowledge of Good and Evil in the Garden of Eden." In *Toward a Philosophy of the Act*, such bids take the form of human thought detaching itself from life and refusing personal responsibility; in "Author and Hero," they comprise refusals of the form the other offers me as gift and "prideful attempts of the self to pursue his or her own form." Bakhtin, however, envisions redemption from this fall into the sin of pride, and, as in Christian theology, reconciliation and healing come through the process of incarnation. Like Jacobs, Coates calls up Bakhtin's kenotic example of Christ, and the virtue of humility embodied there. Just as Christ embraced the limits of time and place, so must we embrace our own "unique *situatedness*" and "develop humility to the point of participating in person and being answerable in person" (*TPA* 52). I must also have the humility to accept the gift of form the other offers, and offer that form to others with the "kindness" and "loving mercy" that Christ exemplifies ("A&H" 56).

Five years later, however, with *Problems of Dostoevsky's Art* (1929; revised and expanded as *Problems of Dostoevsky's Poetics*, 1963), Bakhtin no longer celebrates the redemptive capacities of form, nor is he so sanguine that all authors will approach their characters with loving kindness and not exploit their position of outsideness. To finalize through form is to reify—and thus the author may fall into the sin of a monologizing pride and violence toward his creation. Here again Christ's kenosis emerges as the model of redemption, of which Dostoevsky is the authorial exemplar in his respect for his character's unfinalizability. But, Coates wonders: Is this scenario of redemption in fact an illusion, "a new and impossible utopia of authorial-heroic equality?"

Perhaps not, Coates suggests, and she finds hope in Bakhtin's focus upon a particular type of dialogue between characters, namely his emphasis upon the penetrative word. As Coates observes, Bakhtin defines the penetrative word twice: "the first time as 'a word capable of actively and confidently interfering in the interior dialogue of the other person, helping that person to find his own voice' (*PDP* 242), and later on as 'a firmly monologic, undivided discourse, a word without a sideward glance, without a loophole, without internal polemic' (*PDP* 249)." The characters who utter such penetrative words—Myshkin, Tikhon, Alyosha—"offer a model for responsible, embodied authority in which, as before, their 'otherness' is absolutely essential to the 'hero,' and yet who kenotically assist the latter to approach a finalized image of themselves . . . rather than doing the finalizing for them."

One might extend Coates's analysis and say that the penetrative word respects the unfinalizability of the other, yet calls that other toward incarnating his wish into a deed, often a deed of public confession. Sonia speaks such a word to Raskolnikov; Zosima does the same with Mikhail, his mysterious visitor. In doing so, such confessors integrate the open and closed dimensions of Bakhtin's thought and give novelistic witness to the possibility of practicing loving, authoritative authoring in everyday life.[34] Furthermore, such a word suggests a third presence, to return to a point that emerged in our discussion of Jacobs's essay. Caryl Emerson has corrected the translation of "the penetrative word" to "the penetrated word,"[35] which suggests both its horizontal dimension—it penetrates the other, assisting that one to find his or her own voice—and its vertical dimension: it is itself penetrated by the Divine presence. This notion of the penetrated word recalls one of Bakhtin's favorite lines from Scripture: "For where two or three are gathered in my name, there am I in the midst of them" (Matt. 18:20, *RSV*).

As Coates points out, the speakers of the penetrated word are invariably Christlike. They are kind, charitable, and authoritative in their kenotic self-denial—yet they are cheerful, indeed joyous. But S. S. Averintsev's essay, "Bakhtin, Laughter, and Christian Culture," causes us to pause and ask, do they ever laugh? The young, ecstatic Alyosha does with the boys at the end of *The Brothers Karamazov*, and Zosima does in his youth, at the moment of his liberating discovery of vocation. But in his old age as an elder, Zosima hardly ever laughs (though he always smiles). Why might this be?

Averintsev's essay turns our focus to one of Bakhtin's middle works, *Rabelais and His World*, and considers "the possibility of combining Bakhtin's theory of the 'culture of laughter' and its subordinate internal categories—'carnivalization' and the 'menippea'—with Christian culture and, in particular, with that old tradition according to which Christ never laughed." Averintsev asks, could this tradition be true? And if so, how might it be significant? These questions lead Averintsev to a trenchant critique of carnival laughter as Bakhtin celebrates it in *Rabelais*, one akin to criticisms leveled by Michael André Bernstein and Konstantin Isupov.[36] Averintsev begins, however, with an appreciation of laughter. Laughter's dynamic, impulsive, explosive quality often liberates us from fear and anxiety. But what of the person who is already free from such constricting emotions? Such a person has no need or desire to laugh, and thus the tradition of Christ's never laughing: "[T]he God-man Jesus Christ, as he has always been imagined and conceived by Christian tradition . . . is absolutely free, and not from the moment of some liberation . . . but before the beginning of his earthly life, before the creation of the world, from the very pre-temporal depth of his 'pre-eternity.' . . . *At the point of absolute freedom, laughter is impossible because it is superfluous.*" Averintsev recognizes that there is laughter that might be understood as Christian, namely laughing at oneself, and links such laughter with a prayer, "I believe; help my unbelief" (Mark 9:24, *RSV*), that Bakhtin saw as exemplary of "the penitent and petitionary tones of confessional self accounting" ("A&H" 144). One is reminded here of the etymology of the English word "humor," which, like "humility," finds its roots in the Latin *humus*, "soil," or "earth." Such laughter can bring us "down to earth." But the Russian Orthodox spiritual tradition, as Averintsev explains, is not so sanguine about the virtuous potential in laughter, and uses the word "joker" as a "common Russian euphemism for the devil." And rightfully so. Historically there are more instances of demonic laughter than examples of Bakhtin's reductively benevolent carnival. Bakhtin claims that "violence never hides behind laughter"; Averintsev points to Ivan the Terrible, Condorcet, Mussolini, and Stalin, and insists that "all of history, literally, screams against" such a claim.

V. N. Turbin recollects a conversation with Bakhtin:

"The Gospels are also carnival!" said Bakhtin, half whispering, wincing as if a [wire] spring had contracted inside of him. This was in Saransk in the 1960s. He spoke about the Gospels like a conspirator speaking to his accomplice.[37]

Averintsev would agree, but in a different tone: "The Gospel episode in which Christ is jeered at seems to throw us back to the very sources of the popular culture of laughter, to the age-old procedure of the ambivalent crowning-decrowning. But this procedure overshadows the bitter seriousness of the innocent man's torment, which is followed by his execution immediately after the end of the mock ceremony."[38]

Near the end of his essay, Averintsev imagines a scene redolent of Dostoevsky in its tones of penitence. An English soldier has just been mocking Joan of Arc as she burns at the stake. He has "engag[ed] in the culture of laughter at the victim's expense." He faints, revives, and "hurries to repent of his guilt." One might imagine the soldier's confession, and the peace, which Bakhtin calls "grounded peace," that follows: "this time liberation coincides not with laughter, but with the end of laughter, with the sobriety that comes after laughter."

Although Averintsev presents a pointed critique of Bakhtin's "absolutized laughter," he movingly avows his respect and gratitude to Bakhtin, and recognizes that Bakhtin's celebration of the foul-mouthed folk comes from his genuine love for the Kustanai peasants with whom he worked. And Bakhtin himself, in the "Notes" he wrote three years before his death, seems to anticipate—and respond to— Averintsev and others when he declares, first, that "[e]verything that is truly great must include an element of laughter," but then distinguishes between two kinds: "The joyful, open, festive laugh. The closed, purely negative, satirical laugh. This is not a laughing laugh" (*SpG* 135).

As noted earlier, Charles Lock has written on carnival in a more celebratory vein. In his 1991 essay, he reads Bakhtin's Rabelais book within the Christian context that affirms matter's goodness; such an affirmation is grounded in and required by the confession that "the Word became flesh." Here, in "Bakhtin and the Tropes of Orthodoxy," Lock reflects again on what he calls the central paradigm of Bakhtin's thinking, that of the Incarnation, as it shapes his essays on the novel, especially those collected in *The Dialogic Imagination*. As Lock writes: "Two natures, divine and human, in the one hypostasis of Christ. The formula affirmed at the Council of Chalcedon in 451 serves Bakhtin as a paradigm for the dialogical: two voices in the hypostasis of one word." Unlike Pechey, who stresses, in part, Bakhtin's Kantian dimension—his love of Dostoevsky's novels for their autonomous, free, modern heroes—Lock emphasizes Bakhtin's project "of resistance to dualistic models of thinking and being" such as Kant's, which maintain the split between the sensible material world and the immutable intelligible world. Like Pechey, however, Lock suggests ways in which Bakhtin's thinking on the novel offers an exit from destructive dualisms by affirming the bond between the ordinary and the holy. Bakhtin's notion of the "chronotope," for example, bears affinities to Gregory of Nyssa's notion of *diastēma*—the extension in time and space characteristic of creation, but not of God—"and to the theological argument that time and space and intelligibility all belong to creation . . . and must therefore all be subject to change and variation."[39]

Gregory of Nyssa emphasizes the asymmetrical relation that exists between Creator and creature: although creation is limited, it does not limit the Creator, but neither does it completely separate the Creator from creation. From this, the twentieth-century émigré theologian Georges Florovsky develops "an asymmetrical Christology." Lock links Florovsky's understanding of Christ to Bakhtin's central notion of outsideness: "In making Himself circumscribable, God—inaccessible, essential, transcendent—rendered himself as an outside, took on outsideness." Indeed, God's circumscribing of Himself in the Incarnation becomes, as we saw earlier with St. John of Damascus, a central defense for the circumscribing of God's image in the icon. Both Incarnation and iconography give witness to the tropic nature of all creation. In Christ, the human is revealed to be like the divine: we are made in God's image and likeness; after the Fall, and through Christ, we are called to restore that image. Thus, in Christ, "two natures—human and divine—[are] joined together, without confusion, without separation." And although the icon is not the same as Christ, the image participates in the holiness of the prototype.[40] This asymmetrical relation is, perhaps, best imaged in the icon reprinted at the end of this introduction.[41] One of the earliest known icons, painted in Sinai in the sixth century, probably less than one hundred years after Chalcedon, it shows the face of Christ—especially His eyes—as clearly asymmetrical. The countenance suggests both human and divine, accessibility and omnipotence, tender mercy and powerful judgment, flesh and Logos: each is represented without confusion or separation. Or, to borrow Caryl Emerson's paradoxical paraphrase of Bakhtin's position, "separation and connection happen simultaneously, in a complementary way, without contradictory aims."[42]

This icon provides a trope for Bakhtin's understanding of the novel. For, as Lock writes, "What is not possible in speech is possible in writing: a Chalcedonian, two-voice, double-natured discourse." Indeed, Lock points out that the "classical" arguments against the novel are very much like the claims of the iconoclasts— that God cannot be circumscribed in an image. The novel dispenses with clear markers between self-contained and singular voices, and, especially in free indirect discourse, "insists . . . on the incarnation of language, and therefore on its representability." Language is represented in all of its double-voicedness, and such dialogism renders the novel "a text [that is] readable without being readable aloud."

In his discernment of likeness between the silent reading the novel invites and the hesychast practice of bodily silence, Lock looks ahead to the apophatic dimension in Bakhtin's work that Randall Poole will develop further.

For Lock, Bakhtin discovers in the novel "the Chalcedonian trope of the Logos incarnate: the double-nature and double-voice of Word-play." Alexandar Mihailovic emphasizes this Chalcedonian pattern throughout Bakhtin's work, both in his groundbreaking *Corporeal Words*, and here, in his essay "Bakhtin's Dialogue with Russian Orthodoxy and Critique of Linguistic Universalism." In this essay, Mihailovic sees Bakhtin's "theology of discourse" as determinative in his disagreement with the Soviet linguist Nikolai Marr and with Stalin, who declared Marr's theories anathema in the 1950s, but whose own foray into linguistics reveals thinking much akin to Marr's. Both Marr and Stalin prove exemplary of what Bakhtin understands as *faith*: that which rigidly adheres to frozen dogma and objectifies and reduces the vitality of human experience. Marr asserted both the existence of a single originary language and, with the inevitable triumph of world communism, the ultimate convergence and synthesis of all languages. Such ideas "could not be farther from Bakhtin's reverence for the individual utterance" and for "the actual process of cultural development." Bakhtin's reverence here suggests his "feeling for faith" and his engagement with three central Christian ideas: the Chalcedonian formula of "coexisting yet separate twin natures of Christ"; the notion of *perichoresis* or Trinitarian interpenetration; and the Johannine word become flesh. Bakhtin's employment of these doctrines as structural paradigms evinces both his indebtedness to and idiosyncratic attitude toward the Orthodox tradition he inherited.

In "The Problem of Speech Genres"—written during the Marr controversy of the early 1950s, but not published until twenty years later—Bakhtin uses these doctrines to present a covert critique of both Marr and Stalin. For example, "Bakhtin's concept of the primacy of speech genres underscores a coexistence and a conditional merging of opposites that would be unthinkable to Marr. This conflation of synchronicity and diachronicity goes deeply against the grain of Marrist linguistics." Ultimately, "[f]or Bakhtin, the Marrist and Stalinist positions are flip sides of the same double-faced coin in their frozen ideological versions of the liquidation of all discourses into a single language." Bakhtin rejects both versions through the "theoretical constructs" provided him by the Johannine Logos, Trinitarian interpenetration, and Chalcedonian unity within diversity.

By the end of Mihailovic's essay, however, one wonders whether these doctrines are functioning *only* as "theoretical construct[s]," "expressive metaphor[s]," or "structural paradigms." After all, Mihailovic points to Bakhtin's "ultimate underscoring of [the doctrines'] spiritual provenance and content by using them as tools of political criticism." But then, as Lock's essay emphasizes, the power of metaphor, of trope, in the Orthodox imagination should not be underestimated.

With Randall Poole's essay, "The Apophatic Bakhtin," we come full circle, back to Bakhtin's first writings, especially "Author and Hero." We turn as well to another link between Bakhtin and a vital strand of the Orthodox spiritual tradition: that of *apophasis,* approaching God by relinquishing all conceptual categories. Orthodoxy emphasizes belief in *theosis:* that the human person, made in the image and likeness of God, is ultimately called to deification, to a sharing in or union with the Divine life. Thus the person (*lichnost*) can also be approached apophatically because each person is made in the image of God. And Bakhtin's personalism, Poole shows, bears remarkable resemblances to Orthodox apophaticism.

In the early parts of his essay, Poole helpfully elucidates Bakhtin's indebtedness to—and departure from—the philosophy of Kant. Drawing from Kant, Bakhtin asserts that consciousness is irreducible to nature; a person is thus a subject. As Bakhtin emphasizes, I can never fully coincide with myself as pure object ("A&H" 109). But whereas for Kant this insight becomes the occasion for developing a transcendental idealism, and leads him to postulate the existence of God, Bakhtin insists that his focus is upon concrete lived life, the way a subject experiences his life phenomenologically. "Bakhtin brings Kant down to earth," and as part of his phenomenology Bakhtin explores my relationship with the other—and with the Other, God. In Poole's reading of Bakhtin, however, my "internal uniqueness of consciousness" does not necessitate metaphysical theism. As Poole writes, "If [Bakhtin] was a believer, it was, apparently, on other grounds."

But Bakhtin does insist upon "the unknowability of the self to itself (I-for-myself) and thus in the need for the seeing and knowing other—'deity becoming human,' becoming, that is, an embodied grace-bestowing other, Christ, Bakhtin's ideal image of the other." Here is where Poole locates the "apophatic moment" in Bakhtin. He links it to Timothy Ware's commentary on *theosis*—in which the particular identities of self and Other are preserved—and to the Cappadocian emphasis upon the particular personhood of each member of the Trinity, thus Bakhtin's imaging of Dostoevsky's worldview as "the church as a communion of unmerged souls" (*PDP* 26). My communion with the other opens up "the possibility of creation" and a recognition of my call to assist the other to "help fill in the apophatic gap of non-self-sufficiency that every self faces." For, what God is for me, "I must be for the other" ("A&H" 56).

As Philip Swoboda has written, "deification"—the culmination of which is *theosis* in which we shall know even as we are known—denotes a process, not a finished state: "The salvation of man comes about by his sharing, through sacrament and prayer, in the deified humanity of the Incarnate Logos."[43] Bakhtin draws on this patristic emphasis upon process. Poole aptly calls it a "process of self-discovery": God is unknown; but if he were known we would not grow in personhood, in our true form as the image and likeness of God. Thus process entails "grace, confession, penitence and prayer, and faith." And hope: for Bakhtin, apostle of the second chance, the self can always recall its loophole of non-self-coincidence. Furthermore, in confessional self-accounting, "the very fact of becoming conscious of myself in being, testifies in itself that I am not alone in my self-accounting, . . . that someone wants me to be good" ("A&H" 144).

Poole points out that "someone" is capitalized "Someone" in the notes that Bakhtin's friend and colleague L. V. Pumpiansky took on Bakhtin's lectures on Kant and religion in 1924–25. These lecture notes are included in this volume as an appendix, for which Poole's essay—and Vadim Liapunov's framing remarks—serve as a fine introduction. Bakhtin's lectures on Kant offer keen insights into the opening sections of the *Critique of Pure Reason* and contextualize the philosopher's achievements within a typology of philosophic systems. Central to these discussions, as N. I. Nikolaev points out in his introduction to the Pumpiansky notes, is the notion of responsibility or answerability, which Bakhtin recasts in personalist moral terms. Of most immediate interest to readers of this volume are Bakhtin's 1924 lecture, "The Problem of Grounded Peace," and his 1925 response to a paper by M. I. Tubiansky, whom Clark and Holquist describe as "a particularly contentious member of the [Leningrad] circle and a consistent opponent of Bakhtin."[44] In reading Bakhtin's response to Tubiansky, some may call to mind the encounter depicted in Eichenberg's woodcut from Dostoevsky's novel *The Brothers Karamazov* (cited hereafter in this introduction as *BK*; see note 45). The Grand Inquisitor fears authentic miracle and revelation, and fears the gift of personal relationship that Christ offers him: "[W]hy dost Thou look silently and searchingly at me with Thy mild eyes? Be angry. I don't want Thy love, for I love Thee not."[45] Christ's response—a silent kiss—glows in the Inquisitor's heart. Ivan Karamazov, of course, authors this encounter, and if, as his brother Alyosha discerns, the story reveals Ivan's own fears, the "hell" he carries in his heart and head (*BK* 243), it also suggests Ivan's hope, his recognition that "Someone needs me to be good," and that, with trust, he might accept the gift that Someone offers.

As Bakhtin tellingly suggests in Pumpiansky's notes, the gift of "grounded peace" is most starkly offered in the acknowledgment of sin and movement toward repentance:

> The true being of the spirit begins only when repentance begins, that is, essential and fundamental non-coinciding: everything that can be of value, *everything* exists outside of me; I am only a negative agency, only a receptacle of evil. . . . I am infinitely bad, but Someone needs me to be good. In repenting, I specifically establish the One in Whom I posit my sin. And it is this that constitutes grounded peace, which does not make up or fabricate anything. Tranquillity or peace of mind can be either the tranquillity of self-complacency or that of trust; what must free me from the tranquillity of self-complacency, that is, from the tranquillity of an

aesthetic mythologem, is precisely disquietude, which will develop, through repentance, into trust.

Ivan, in his anguish to discern his responsibility for his father's murder, lives the process Bakhtin sketches here. As Bakhtin says, "for religious consciousness there is a third one—a possible someone who evaluates"; Ivan raises his hand and declares to Smerdyakov: "'God sees . . . perhaps I too was guilty.'" Bakhtin writes that religious consciousness entails "conscience," the recognition that "no one in the entire world, besides myself, can accomplish what I myself must accomplish"; Ivan knows he *must* confess and give evidence at the trial the next day if his brother Mitya is to be saved (*BK* 598). But upon leaving Smerdyakov, his tranquillity and joy quickly disappear, for they are founded upon self-satisfaction, not trust in another. After Ivan assists the peasant he had earlier left for dead, he thinks, "'I am quite capable of watching myself'" (*BK* 600). Clutching a loophole, an alibi-of-Being, he puts off going to the prosecutor to tell what only he can tell, "and, strange to say, almost all his gladness and self-satisfaction passed in one instant" (*BK* 601). The "touch of ice on his heart," the devil that appears to him, embodies his anxiety, which begins to subside only with the arrival of Alyosha: "'You did drive [the devil] away: he disappeared when you arrived. I love your face, Alyosha. Did you know that I loved your face?'" (*BK* 619). The face-to-face encounter with Alyosha, an image of Christ, "the incarnated God," fosters Ivan's will to confess. In Bakhtin's words, he now "demand[s] . . . the cross for himself and happiness for others": "'Tomorrow the cross, but not the gallows,'" he assures Alyosha. And in his fractured confession the next day, Ivan comes as close as he ever does in the novel to accepting the cross and the kiss that Christ offers. Throughout this process, Ivan encounters what Bakhtin calls "the distinguishing feature of religion": "a personal relationship to a personal God," what he will later name "a feeling for faith" ("TRDB" 294).

Bakhtin's Feeling for Faith

Although the contributors to this volume present a variety of views on the religious dimension of Bakhtin's life and work, all see him as deeply immersed within the tradition of Christian thought. Sometimes this immersion is noted in terms of his appropriation of the biblical narrative—particularly of the Creation, Fall, and Incarnation. For others, the point of contact with the Christian tradition is a specific doctrine—the Chalcedonian formulation of Christ's divine and human nature, kenosis, or *apophasis*—which acts for Bakhtin as a structural principle or generative metaphor. Still others see in the Gospels an originary moment that is developed into the Bakhtinian notions of dialogue and the novel. The writers themselves explore in centrifugal patterns the richness of Bakhtin's indebtedness to the Christian tradition. Such diversity of approaches should not surprise us, for as Bakhtin notes,

> [A]ny concrete discourse (utterance) finds the object at which it was directed already as it were overlain with qualifications, open to dispute, charged with value, already enveloped in an obscuring mist—or, on the contrary, by the "light" of alien words that have already been spoken about it. It is entangled, shot through with shared thoughts, points of view, alien value judgments and accents. . . . The word, breaking through to its own meaning and its own expression across an environment full of alien words and variously evaluating accents, harmonizing with some of the elements in this environment and striking a dissonance with others, is able, in this dialogized process, to shape its own stylistic profile and tone. (*DI* 276–77)

As these essays find their "own stylistic profile and tone" within this harmonizing and dissonant environment, they nevertheless point to a central object (or rather subject)—the person of Christ. The Incarnation figures as a centripetal force in Bakhtin's writings and, consequently, in those of his interpreters. Why is this so? The answer is that the image of Christ—as Bakhtin believed Dostoevsky understood it, and as Bakhtin might well have understood it himself—embodies many of Bakhtin's major ideas, particularly that of the self-other distinction and the importance of outsideness.[46]

   In "Author and Hero," the most explicitly theological of his writings, Bakhtin articulates the central role of Christ as the analogy for the ideal author/self. The task of creating meaning in a novel or in the world demands that an author/self choose to enter into a hero/other, experience his life, but then return to himself and his own place in the world. From this position of outsideness, the author/self must then bestow a charitable gaze on the other, using his own "excess of vision" (what he can see that the other does not) to consummate the other and give him meaning; the goal of such interaction must be the creation of meaning, not solipsistic narcissism or domination. In other words, the author/self must become incarnated (but not identical), redemptive, and transformative.

   Such a process of entering, withdrawing, and looking is powerfully illustrated in Eichenberg's woodcut, for the ultimate author/self who creates meaning is Christ himself. In Bakhtin's words, in Christ we see "an *I-for-myself* that renders full justice to the other as such, disclosing and affirming the other's axiological distinctiveness in all its fullness" ("A&H" 56). That is, Christ bestows a redemptive gaze that both completes the other and acknowledges his or her individuality. Or, as Bakhtin notes in *Toward a Philosophy of the Act*, paraphrasing a Russian proverb: "In aesthetic seeing you love a human being not because he is good, but, rather, a human being is good because you love him" (*TPA* 62). Such aesthetic seeing—the charitable gaze—recalls the Gospel accounts in which Christ looks with compassion on the rich young man (Luke 10:21), the widow of Nain (Luke 7:13), or the crowds milling about like sheep without a shepherd (Mark 6:34). The charitable gaze is also imaged in Eichenberg's woodcut as Christ "look[s] gently" into the Grand Inquisitor's face (BK 243). In each instance, Christ, as the perfect self, offers to those upon whom he looks a transformed and completed vision of themselves and their world.

The incarnated Christ is, for Bakhtin, not only the analogue or model for the perfect self-other relationship, but also the enabler of such relationships. While the Incarnation has a horizontal dimension—Christ the man among other men—it also retains its vertical dimension—Christ as God descending to the earth. The meaningfulness of the world, and of all the dialogic relationships within that world, is predicated on the prior presence of a loving creator God:

> *I-for-myself* is the *other* for God. God is no longer defined essentially as the voice of my conscience, as purity of my relationship to myself . . . as the one into whose hands it is a fearful thing to fall. . . . God is now the heavenly father who is *over me* and can be merciful to me and justify me where I, from within myself cannot be merciful to myself and cannot justify myself in principle, as long as I remain pure before myself. ("A&H" 56)

God's love, enacted both as the creator "who is over me" and as the incarnated Christ, grounds and enables the charitable interchanges that guarantee the creation of meaning in "Author and Hero."

The Incarnation not only images for Bakhtin the self-other relationship, but also marks out the body and its outsideness as a center of value. Physical matter is good, first, because it is created by God and second, because Christ authenticates it, hallows it by himself becoming matter: "[E]ven God had to incarnate himself in order to bestow mercy, to suffer, and to *forgive*—had to descend, as it were, from the abstract standpoint of justice" ("A&H" 129). As Lock and others point out in this volume, the goodness of physical matter is central to both Bakhtin and the Christian tradition; gnosticism, while casting a persistent shadow on the history of the church, has been consistently denounced as heretical.

Although Bakhtin's references to the Christian tradition are most explicit in his early works, the dynamics of his entire *oeuvre* are intertwined with this religious framework. As Bakhtin notes near the end of "Author and Hero," the creation of meaning, by an author or by a self, "can be founded only upon a deep trust in the highest level of authority that blesses a culture—upon trust, that is, in the fact that there is another—the highest other—who answers for my own special answerability, and trust in the fact that I do not act in an axiological void. Outside this trust, only empty pretensions are possible" ("A&H" 206). And in the concluding lines of *Toward a Philosophy of the Act,* Bakhtin summarizes his ethical project in the following words:

> The concrete ought is an architectonic ought: the ought to actualize one's unique place in once-occurrent Being-as-event. And it is determined first and foremost as a contraposition of *I* and the *other.*
>
> This architectonic contraposition is accomplished by every moral act or deed, and it is understood by elementary moral consciousness. Yet theoretical ethics has no adequate form for its expression. . . . Whence it does not follow at all, of course, that the contraposition of *I* and the *other* has never been expressed and stated—this is, after all the sense of all Christian morality, and it is the starting point for altruistic morality. But this [three illegible words] principle of morality has still not found an adequate scientific expression, nor has it been thought through essentially and fully. (*TPA* 75)

Bakhtin thus articulates his own project as that of "[thinking] through essentially and fully" the tradition already expressed in Christian morality. Bakhtin's own late notes offer suggestive codicils to his more developed arguments:

> God can get along without man, but man cannot get along without Him. ("TRDB" 285)
>
> The word as something personal. Christ as truth. I ask him. A profound understanding of the personal nature of the word. . . . The unuttered truth in Dostoevsky (Christ's kiss). (*SpG* 148)

Mihailovic is certainly correct, therefore, when he claims that "Bakhtin's work is framed at the beginning and end of his career by telling references to the ancient teachings about the Johannine logos and its possible relation to metalinguistics and the philosophy of the word."[47]

The Incarnation, then, is the centripetal point to which both Bakhtin and the writers in this volume adhere. Bakhtin's turn toward the Incarnation at key points in the development of his thought helps us to understand his relationship to Christianity. Bakhtin is not a traditionalist, accepting passively a set of beliefs as the authoritative word. Rather, he engages the Christian tradition as a penetrated word or, to use Jaroslav Pelikan's terminology, as an icon, as that which "is what it represents" but that nevertheless "bids us look at it, but through it and beyond it, to that living reality of which it is an embodiment."[48]

Bakhtin's thought thus evinces "a feeling for faith," much in the way that he recognizes and comments upon such a feeling in Dostoevsky: it is "an integral attitude (by means of the whole person) toward a higher and ultimate value" ("TRDB" 294). As *Problems of Dostoevsky's Poetics* makes clear, this value takes a personal and authoritative form in Christ. Bakhtin writes, "Even 'truth in itself' [Dostoevsky] presents in the spirit of Christian ideology, as incarnated in Christ: that is, he presents it as a personality entering into relationships with other personalities" (*PDP* 31–32). But Bakhtin makes clear that

> [t]he image of the ideal human being or the image of Christ represents for [Dostoevsky] the resolution of ideological quests. This image or this highest voice must crown the world of voices, must organize and subdue it. . . . not fidelity to his own convictions and not fidelity to convictions themselves taken abstractly, but precisely a fidelity to the authoritative image of a human being. (*PDP* 97)

Jackson's helpful gloss on Dostoevsky's "feeling for faith" contrasts faith, a static fidelity to abstract convictions, with faithfulness to this authoritative image of Christ. One leans toward this image and stands "in a positive relation to it."[49] That stance, however, retains its open-endedness, its unfinalizability in the image of the "word become flesh" as a penetrated, internally persuasive rather than a totalitarian word. It is not "truth-as-formula" or "truth-as-proposition" that motivates Dostoevsky or Bakhtin, but "an orientation toward the other's voice, the other's word" (*PDP* 98). The Christic penetrated word makes its "persuasion through love" ("TRDB" 292).

It is possible to read Bakhtin's "feeling for faith" as merely a structural principle. Yet the movement in Bakhtin is always away from the abstract toward the personal, interactive, committed, responsible life—from faith, as an object that one possesses, to a feeling for faith, the engagement with a personal subject. As Bakhtin noted of Dostoevsky, "Dostoevsky understands worldview not as an abstract unity and sequence in a system of thoughts and positions, but as an ultimate position in the world in relation to higher values. Worldviews embodied in voices. A dialogue among such embodied worldviews, in which he himself participated" ("TRDB" 296). As Poole notes of Bakhtin, if self-consciousness is truly achieved "'a place for God is opened up,' because consciousness itself is not possible '[i]n an absolute axiological void'" ("A&H" 144).

Exploring Bakhtin's own openness to God and the Christian tradition has been the motivation behind this collection of essays. If they move us a little closer to a verdict on "the role of truth and faith in Bakhtin's thought," our hope is that they also enrich the conversation that is sure to continue. As Bakhtin reminds us, "Even *past* meanings, that is, those born in the dialogue of past centuries, can never be stable (finalized, ended once and for all)—they will always change (be renewed) in the process of subsequent, future development of the dialogue. . . . Nothing is absolutely dead: every meaning will have its homecoming festival" (*SpG* 170).

Christ Pantocrator, sixth-century icon (reproduced by permission of the Holy Monastery of Saint Catherine, Sinai, Egypt). Photograph by Gloria Ruff.

Notes

1. Katerina Clark and Michael Holquist, *Mikhail Bakhtin* (Cambridge: Harvard Univ. Press, 1984), 120.

2. See, for instance, "Dialogue: Conversation between Robert F. Barsky and Professor Michael Holquist. Hamden CT, Saturday–Sunday, August 18–19, 1990," *Discours social/ Social Discourse* 3 (1990): 12–13.

3. Caryl Emerson, *The First Hundred Years of Mikhail Bakhtin* (Princeton: Princeton Univ. Press, 1997), 72.

4. The earlier English translation of *chuvstvo very*, "a sense of faith," has been altered by the translator Caryl Emerson to "a feeling for faith" in order to capture the palpable and sensate tone of the original Russian and to parallel the previous phrase *chuvstvo teorii*, "a feeling for theory." "Feeling" is also the preferable translation in order to avoid confusion with *smysl*, which means "sense" rather than "meaning," as in a dictionary definition ("TRDB" 294).

5. Robert Louis Jackson, *Dialogues with Dostoevsky: The Overwhelming Questions* (Stanford: Stanford Univ. Press, 1993), 278.

6. Nicholas Rzhevsky, "Kozhinov on Bakhtin," *New Literary History* 25 (1994): 434.

7. Ibid.

8. V. V. Kozhinov, "Bakhtin i ego chitateli. Razmyshleniia i otchasti vospominaniia," *Dialog, Karnaval, Khronotop*, no. 2–3 (1993): 120–34. Translation by Leonid Livak.

9. Ibid.

10. Sergey Bocharov, "Conversations with Bakhtin," translated by Stephen Blackwell, introduction and translation edited by Vadim Liapunov, *PMLA* 109 (1994): 1019.

11. Ibid., 1012.

12. V. N. Turbin, "Iz neopublikovannogo o M. M. Bakhtine (I)," *Filosofskie nauki* 1 (1995): 235–43. Translation by Leonid Livak.

13. Here Bakhtin endorses the point of view of Zosima in Dostoevsky's *The Brothers Karamazov.*

14. Alexandar Mihailovic, *Corporeal Words: Mikhail Bakhtin's Theology of Discourse* (Evanston: Northwestern Univ. Press, 1997), 5.

15. Rzhevsky, "Kozhinov on Bakhtin," 440.

16. Kozhinov, "Bakhtin i ego chitateli."

17. Julia Kristeva, "The Ruin of a Poetics," in *Russian Formalism: A Collection of Articles and Texts in Translation*, ed. Stephen Bann and John E. Bowlt (Edinburgh: Scottish Academic Press, 1973), 106.

18. Anton Ugolnik, "Tradition as Freedom from the Past: Contemporary Eastern Orthodoxy and Ecumenism," *Institute for Ecumenical and Cultural Research,*

Occasional Papers, no. 17 (November 1982): 2; "An Orthodox Hermeneutic in the West," *St. Vladimir's Theological Quarterly* 27, no. 2 (1983): 93–118.

19. Caryl Emerson, "Russian Orthodoxy and the Early Bakhtin," *Religion and Literature* 22 (1990): 109–31.

20. Ibid., 118.

21. St. John of Damascus, *On the Divine Images: Three Apologies against Those Who Attack the Divine Images,* trans. David Anderson (Crestwood, N.Y.: St. Vladimir's Seminary Press, 1980), 61.

22. Charles Lock, "Carnival and Incarnation: Bakhtin and Orthodox Theology," *Journal of Literature and Theology* 5 (1991): 77.

23. Ibid., 80–81.

24. Mihailovic, *Corporeal Words,* 5.

25. Ibid., 15.

26. Ruth Coates, *Christianity in Bakhtin: God and the Exiled Author* (Cambridge: Cambridge Univ. Press, 1998).

27. Bocharov, "Conversations with Bakhtin," 1018.

28. See Konstantin G. Isupov, "The Death of the 'Other'," trans. and annotated by Craig Cravens, in *Critical Essays on Mikhail Bakhtin,* ed. Caryl Emerson, *Critical Essays on World Literature* (New York: G. K. Hall/Twayne, 1999), 153–67.

29. Mihailovic, *Corporeal Words,* 6.

30. Wayne C. Booth, *The Company We Keep: An Ethics of Fiction* (Berkeley and Los Angeles: Univ. of California Press, 1988), 173 n. 6.

31. Erich Auerbach, "Sermo Humilis," in *Literary Language and Its Public in Late Latin Antiquity and in the Middle Ages,* trans. Ralph Manheim (Princeton: Princeton Univ. Press, 1965), 51.

32. See, for instance, Ian Watt, *The Rise of the Novel: Studies in Defoe, Richardson, and Fielding* (London: Chatto and Windus, 1957), 13; Nancy Armstrong in *Desire and Domestic Fiction: A Political History of the Novel* (New York: Oxford Univ. Press, 1987); and others who have explored the influence of the many eighteenth-century novels by and for women and have complicated this understanding of the novel's development. Our thanks to Jana French for this observation.

33. "The Grand Inquisitor," woodcut by Fritz Eichenberg. Our gratitude to Nick Pellicciari and Mel Piehl for alerting us to Eichenberg's woodcut.

34. For a further discussion of such authoring, see Paul J. Contino, "Zosima, Mikhail, and Prosaic Confessional Dialogue in Dostoevsky's Brothers Karamazov," *Studies in the Novel* 27 (1995): 63–86.

35. Caryl Emerson, "The Tolstoy Connection in Bakhtin," in *Rethinking Bakhtin: Extensions and Challenges,* ed. Gary Saul Morson and Caryl Emerson (Evanston: Northwestern Univ. Press, 1989), 156–57.

36. Emerson, *The First Hundred Years,* 185; Michael André Bernstein, *Bitter Carnival: Ressentiment and the Abject Hero* (Princeton: Princeton Univ. Press, 1992).

37. Turbin, "Iz neopublikovannogo."

38. Caryl Emerson's observation on this point is germane: "Many Russians would concur with Natalia Reed's wary remark in response to Turbin's (obviously exultant) recollection of Bakhtin's insistence that the Gospels were carnival, too: 'Indeed they are. Up to and including the mob-lynching of Christ'" (*The First Hundred Years*, 175).

39. For discussions of Gregory's notion of *diastēma* see Hans Urs von Balthasar, *Presence and Thought: An Essay on the Religious Philosophy of Gregory of Nyssa*, trans. Mark Sebanc (San Francisco: Ignatius Press, 1995), 27–35; Paulos Mar Gregorios, *Cosmic Man: The Divine Presence* (New York: Paragon House, 1988), 67–69.

40. See John of Damascus, *On the Divine Images*, 84–87; Charles Lock, "Iconic Space and the Materiality of the Sign," *Religion and the Arts* 1, no. 4 (1997): 6–22.

41. The icon, housed in the Holy Monastery of St. Catherine, Sinai, Egypt, is known as Christ Pantocrator.

42. Emerson, *The First Hundred Years*, 239.

43. Philip Swoboda, "'Spiritual Life' versus Life in Christ: S. L. Frank and the Patristic Doctrine of Deification," in *Russian Religious Thought*, ed. Judith Deutsch Kornblatt and Richard F. Gustafson (Madison: Univ. of Wisconsin Press, 1996), 242.

44. Clark and Holquist, *Mikhail Bakhtin*, 102.

45. Fyodor Dostoevsky, *The Brothers Karamazov*, ed. Ralph E. Matlaw, the Constance Garnett translation revised by Matlaw (New York: Norton, 1976), 238.

46. Emerson suggests that "Bakhtin employs the image of Christ . . . as 'binder' for the human values and ethical concepts most precious to him" ("Russian Orthodoxy," 113).

47. Mihailovic, *Corporeal Words*, 234.

48. Jaroslav Pelikan, *The Vindication of Tradition* (New Haven and London: Yale Univ. Press, 1984), 55.

49. Jackson, *Dialogues with Dostoevsky*, 278.

Bakhtin and the Hermeneutics of Love

Alan Jacobs

It is not the purpose of love to generate interpretation, but vice versa.

[Dmitri] Likhachev [later a historian and activist] was arrested in 1928 for taking part in a students' literary group called the Cosmic Academy of Sciences. . . . For election as an "academician," Likhachev presented a humorous paper on the need to restore to the language the letter "yat." The Bolsheviks banned the letter as part of a campaign to "modernize" Russian after the revolution. Later, one of Likhachev's interrogators railed at him for daring to waste his time on such things.

"What do you mean by language reform?" the interrogator shouted. "Perhaps we won't even have any language at all under socialism!"

The Building of Charity

In section 36 of the first book of *On Christian Doctrine*, St. Augustine makes one of the more remarkable statements in the history of hermeneutics:

> Whoever . . . thinks that he understands the divine Scriptures or any part of them so that it [i.e., his interpretation] does not build the double love of God and of our neighbor does not understand [the Scriptures] at all. Whoever finds a lesson there useful to the building of charity, even though he has not said what the author may be shown to have intended in that place, has not been deceived, nor is he lying in any way.[1]

The "double love of God and of our neighbor" that Augustine mentions derives from a famous passage in Matthew's Gospel. When a scribe asks Jesus to name the greatest of the commandments, Jesus responds by citing two injunctions, one from Deuteronomy (6:5) and one from Leviticus (19:18):

> You shall love the Lord your God with all your heart, and with all your soul, and with all your mind. This is the great and first commandment. And a second is like it, You shall love your neighbor as yourself. (Matt. 22:37–39, *RSV*)

Jesus then goes on to make the greater and more startling claim that upon these commandments "depend all the law and the prophets." This, then, is what Christian theologians call the "summary of the law"; it is comprehensive and rigorous in its simplicity. No sphere of human life is excluded from it; every possible human activity is implicitly included within its scope.

Augustine contends that interpretation, too, must follow this charitable imperative. But what might this mean? What would interpretation governed by the law of love look like? Strangely, Augustine does not say. One must presume that he sought to meet the charitable imperative in his own exegetical work, but it is surely legitimate to ask what, specifically, makes Augustine's interpretations charitable, and how they might be distinguished from uncharitable interpretations.[2]

Moreover, Christian theology has neglected Augustine's provocative statement; there are, to my knowledge, no thorough accounts of loving interpretation. This failure is surprising, not only because so few Augustinian hints have remained untaken in the course of the centuries, but also because it seems so obvious, once Augustine points it out, that Christian interpreters—and I refer not just to interpreters of Scripture, but to interpreters of any and every kind of text—are just as obliged to conduct their work according to the principles of Christian charity as any other workers. An account of the hermeneutics of love is one of the great unwritten chapters in the history of Christian theology. This essay attempts to write a few paragraphs of that chapter.

Not that the *phrase* "charitable interpretation" has been completely overlooked: for instance, it has been exposited by no less unlikely a figure than the philosopher Donald Davidson.[3] But what Davidson means by charitable interpretation is very different from what Augustine means, and the distinction is, for the purposes of this essay, instructive. Davidson believes that we come to a conversation (reading being one form of conversation) with the assumption that our interlocutor speaks sensibly and intelligibly. Sometimes we end by abandoning that assumption, but we do so with the greatest reluctance and only after striving to find some way to reconcile our interlocutor's words with what we take to be intelligible utterance. Only when our hermeneutical resourcefulness is exhausted do we, regretfully, accept unintelligibility.

For Davidson this "principle of charity," as he calls it, is not something we choose, or pursue, or cultivate. It's just what we do. We only choose charitable interpretation insofar as we choose to converse with people; but once we do choose to converse with people, this "Davidsonian charity" is immediately consequent. (It is, barely, possible to imagine someone who always conversed with the assumption that her interlocutors made no sense, but this would require a titanic act of will that no one could sustain over time.) In this matter Davidson is concerned, like Gadamer, not with "what we do or what we ought to do, but what happens to us over and above our wanting and doing."[4]

But this is precisely what distinguishes Davidsonian charity from Augustinian charity. Various Christian thinkers might characterize *caritas* as the fruit of spiritual discipline, the achievement of moral labor, or the unearned gift of the Holy Spirit, but no one would say that the kind of love that Jesus commands and Augustine praises simply "happens to us": it is neither natural nor inevitable, while charity as described by Davidson is both. For Augustinian Christians, and I suspect for all Christians, charity flows from a properly oriented will, and is thus in the etymological sense voluntary, not just given. How, and by what force, the will may be redirected is a matter of theological dispute, but that it requires forcible redirection in order that we might meet Jesus' commandment is a given for Christian theology. It is clear, then, that Davidson and Augustine are talking about two wholly different spheres of action.

But if that is the case, how may an Augustinian charitable hermeneutics be elucidated? One of the few thinkers to approach this question is Mikhail Bakhtin, especially in his early, fragmentary manuscripts *Toward a Philosophy of the Act* and "Author and Hero in Aesthetic Activity" (though, as we shall see, similar concerns make a less overt reappearance late in his career). Indeed, whatever importance these works may be deemed to have within the Bakhtinian canon, and within the cultural and intellectual context of Eastern Orthodoxy, they are indispensable to anyone, from within whatever Christian tradition, who wishes to elaborate Augustine's gnomic and cryptic injunction to read lovingly. (This is so even though Bakhtin rarely mentions Augustine.) These early and incomplete works of Bakhtin sketch the outline of a charitable hermeneutics that theologians would do well to study and then develop.

Loving Attentiveness

For the early Bakhtin, the initial trait of charitable hermeneutics is *attentiveness*. Nothing can compensate for a failure to attend to what is being said. "The valued manifoldness of Being as human (as correlated with the human being) can present itself only to a loving contemplation. . . . Lovelessness, indifference, will never be able to generate sufficient power to slow down and *linger intently* over an object, to hold and sculpt every detail and particular in it, however minute" (*TPA* 64).[5] An indifferent reading, then, will neglect particulars, will be content to acquire a general or "schematized" overview of the work or the person. And the particulars it does happen to pick up will remain fragmented, disconnected from one another: "an indifferent or hostile reaction . . . always . . . impoverishes and decomposes its object" (*TPA* 64). Thus lovelessness fails to account either for plurality or unity, while loving attention always recognizes the "manifoldness," that is, the irreducibly complex wholeness of a work (or a person, or an event) that Bakhtin would much later in his career call its *"open unity"* or *"open totality"* (*SpG* 6, 7). "Loving contemplation," then, is best described through specifying what it does *not* do: it neither circumscribes a work within rigid boundaries, ignoring all elements of the work that cannot be assimilated to a presupposed theoretical schema, nor does it enumerate a mere chaos of details.[6] To use terms Bakhtin would favor in the 1930s, loving contemplation keeps centrifugal and centripetal forces in balance with one another (*DI* 272–73).

But what, specifically, makes this kind of attention a *loving* attention? Because Bakhtin does not explicitly answer this question, we must proceed by indirection, linking (and then contrasting) Bakhtin's notion of attentiveness with that of Simone Weil—who will stand, throughout this essay, as exemplary of certain potent Christian traditions regarding love and ethics that Bakhtin sometimes rejoins and sometimes rejects. In a lecture for schoolchildren on the spiritual value of academic work, Weil claims that the habit of attending to anything aids the cultivation of the discipline of prayer. Moreover, she continues, with her characteristic emphasis on those who suffer:

> Not only does the love of God have attention for its substance; the love of our neighbor, which we know [through Christ's answer to the scribe's question] to be the same love, is made of this same substance. Those who are unhappy have no need for anything in this world but people capable of giving them their attention. . . .
>
> The love of our neighbor in all its fullness simply means being able to say to him: "What are you going through?" It is a recognition that the sufferer exists, not only as a unit in a collection, or a specimen from the social category labeled "unfortunate," but as a man, exactly like us, who was one day stamped with a special mark by affliction. For this reason it is enough, but it is indispensable, to know how to look at him in a certain way.
>
> This way of looking is first of all attentive.[7]

Weil echoes Bakhtin's rejection of the schematic in her identification of the dangers of categories; moreover, her emphasis on attention as a way of *looking* at someone rejoins the relentlessly visual language of *Toward a Philosophy of the Act* and its companion text, "Author and Hero."[8] But, in some quite important respects, Bakhtin's view differs from Weil's and from this main current of Christian thought, and these differences are notably instructive if we wish to understand the potential theological significance of Bakhtin's charitable hermeneutic.

First of all, while Weil discounts certain schematic categories, she retains one: the notion of "man," or human being. We should see the other as a human being, "exactly like us." It is interesting how absent the notion of a common or universal humanity is from Bakhtin's work, early and late—not that he rejects it explicitly, but rather that he doesn't seem to think it does much useful work. One reason for his skepticism will be investigated later in this essay: to invoke a general category ("humanity") as a justification for an ethical action is to abstract oneself out of the particular, unique moment of ethical decision, and for Bakhtin this distancing abstraction is ethically disastrous. As Alexandar Mihailovic notes, for Bakhtin such "hackneyed abstractions . . . as 'humanity' or 'man' have little resonance for the incarnated consciousness; for such a person, the distinction between *I* and *Other* is far more important than such generalities."[9]

Bakhtin would hold to this position throughout his career, but his implicit critique of a generalized ethical humanism can best be understood through a passage in the revision of his Dostoevsky book. He refers to a passage in *The Brothers Karamazov* in which Alyosha, who has just tried without success to give two hundred rubles to Captain Snegiryov, tells Lise ("in a sort of rapture") that he is certain the Captain will take the money the next day. It is Lise's response that interests Bakhtin:

> Listen, Alexei Fyodorovich, isn't there something in all this reasoning of ours, I mean, of yours . . . no, better of ours . . . isn't there some contempt for him, for this wretched man . . . that we're examining his soul like this as if we were looking down on him? That we have decided so certainly, now, that he will accept the money?[10]

Bakhtin contends that Lise is right because such judgment is a sin against what Bakhtin called the "unfinalizability" of the person, even if the judgment proves correct: "The truth about a man in the mouths of others, not directed to him dialogically and therefore a *secondhand* truth, becomes a *lie* degrading and deadening him, if it touches upon his 'holy of holies,' that is, 'the man in man'"(*PDP* 59). Bakhtin implicitly but clearly attributes this viewpoint to Dostoevsky himself, as does Gary Saul Morson.[11] But it is not evident that Dostoevsky endorses Lise's judgment—if one calls it a judgment, since it takes the form of a question—given Alyosha's response, which is quoted by neither Bakhtin nor Morson:

> "No, Lise, there is no contempt in it," Alyosha answered firmly, as if he were already prepared for the question. "I thought it over myself, on the way here. Consider, what contempt can there be if we ourselves are just the same as he is, if everyone is just the same as he is? Because we are just the same, not better. And even if we were better, we would still be the same in his place . . . I don't know about you, Lise, but for myself I consider that my soul is petty in many ways. And his is not petty, on the contrary, it is very sensitive . . . No, Lise, there is no contempt for him!"

Dostoevsky, of course, does not explicitly endorse this claim, but he does doubly emphasize (through his narrator's introductory comment and Alyosha's own statement that he has already considered Lise's objection) that this is a thoughtful response by someone we already know to be an intelligent, humble, and above all nonjudgmental young man. The response, then, carries ethical weight, and even if ultimately rejected should not be ignored in the way that Bakhtin and Morson ignore it. Dostoevsky here presents an appeal precisely to the universal or common humanity that Weil appeals to and that has two sources in Christian thought, the doctrine of creation *in imago dei* ("Let us make man in our image" [Gen. 1:26, *RSV*]) and the doctrine of universal sinfulness ("[A]ll have sinned and fall short of the glory of God" [Rom. 3:23, *RSV*]).

If this way of thinking—that one can grow in love of one's neighbor by reminding oneself that the neighbor is another human being "exactly like us"—has such a fine pedigree, why is Bakhtin uncomfortable with it? Because even such a category can become dangerously schematic: it provides an analogical framework ("you are like me") which, like all analogies, can be applied rigidly; my own limitations, especially the limitations of my self-understanding, can build a Procrustean bed that I cut others to fit. For Bakhtin the "secondhandedness" of the knowledge of others generates this temptation because we see only what others do before us and hear only what they say to us. Even that kind of knowledge might be reliable were it not that "[a] man never coincides with himself. One cannot apply to him the formula of identity A = A" (*PDP* 59). What Bakhtin called the "unfinalizability" of persons means that any attempt to understand them in light of a prefabricated category—even one so broad as "humanity"—sets limits to their potential development. Better to remain immersed in the particulars of their case.[12]

Self-Love and Love for the Other

There is another way in which Bakhtin distances himself from some widely held views about Christian love—views for which I have chosen Weil as a characteristic representative. Underlying Weil's comments are a version of the Golden Rule: see others as you would be seen by them. (Or, to connect with the previous point, recognize their humanity as you would have your own humanity recognized.) Thus, love of one's neighbor, love of the Other, is comprehensible to us by virtue of our prior self-love. And in the Pauline-Augustinian tradition of Christianity, nothing about human beings is more certain and obvious, more *given*, than this *amour propre*. Augustine notes dryly, "there is no need for a precept that anyone should love himself,"[13] and confidently states that "this principle was never questioned by any sect."[14] Yet this "unquestionable" assertion is bluntly denied by Bakhtin: "I love another, but cannot love myself" (*TPA* 46). What can this mean?

Bakhtin does not explain his statement in *Toward a Philosophy of the Act,* but "Author and Hero in Aesthetic Activity"—which is a continuation of the project for which *Act* is a kind of prologue—offers a fuller exposition. Bakhtin raises the question of why it is so difficult "to visualize one's own outward image in imagination, to 'feel' oneself from outside" ("A&H" 29). He then goes on to contend that even when such an effort is partially successful, it fails to yield the satisfaction the visualizer is seeking:

> And when we succeed in doing this, we shall be struck by the peculiar *emptiness, ghostliness,* and an eerie, frightening *solitariness* of this outward image of ourselves. What accounts for this? It is explained by the fact that we lack any emotional and volitional approach to this outward image that could vivify it and include or incorporate it axiologically within the outward unity of the plastic-pictorial world. All of my emotional and volitional reactions that apprehend and axiologically structure another person's outward expressedness in being (admiration, love, tenderness, compassion, hostility, hatred, and the like) are directed ahead of myself out into the world and are not immediately applicable to myself as I experience myself from within. My own inner *I*—that wills, loves, feels, sees, and knows—I structure from within myself in terms of entirely different value-categories, and these are not directly applicable to the outward expressedness of myself. ("A&H" 30)

Now, Bakhtin believes that in the purely *intellectual* sphere we have "no difficulty at all" in abstracting ourselves from our concrete historical place in order to recognize ourselves as human beings among other human beings. In that sense, the general category of "human being" is both familiar and useful. But in the *aesthetic* and *ethical* spheres this self-abstraction is, for the reasons just noted, difficult and in the strict sense impossible. One can go through the motions, as it were, of some objectifying self-contemplation, seeing ourselves as though through the eyes of "a possible other," but the very attempt

> introduces a certain spurious element that is absolutely alien to the ethical event of being. For, inasmuch as it lacks any independent value of its own, what is engendered is not something productive and enriching, but a hollow fictitious product that clouds the optical purity of being. . . . [T]hrough the eyes of this fictitious other one cannot see one's true face, but only one's mask-face. ("A&H" 32)[15]

Therefore I cannot love myself because it is not possible for me to formulate or imagine a self, as object of love, distinct from the I who loves; whereas I *can* so understand the otherness of my neighbor so as to love her. Bakhtin thus summarizes his argument:

> I may be solicitous for myself and I may be equally solicitous for someone I love, but this does not justify the conclusion that my emotional-volitional relationship to myself and to the other is similar in kind—or, in other words, that I love myself the way I love the other. For the emotional-volitional tones that lead in both cases to the same actions of solicitude are radically dissimilar. I cannot love my fellow being as myself or, rather, I cannot *love* myself as a fellow being. ("A&H" 48)

Bakhtin throughout this discussion operates under the assumption that the boundaries between self and other are fixed. He has not yet reached the convictions that would animate so much of his later work, that boundaries between persons, while real, are both flexible and permeable, and that (consequently) each self consists largely of the recovered and redeployed voices of others—though at times, in "Author and Hero," he thinks his way toward that position:

> [O]ne can speak of a human being's absolute need for the other, for the other's seeing, remembering, gathering, and unifying self-activity—the only self-activity capable of producing his outwardly finished personality. This outward personality could not exist, if the other did not create it: aesthetic memory is *productive*—it gives birth, for the first time, to the *outward* human being on a new plane of being. ("A&H" 35–36)

Bakhtin's stress on "outward" here suggests that he still wants to maintain a distinction between an external or superficial self, whose shape and form are molded by others, and a core inner self that retains its integrity. But when Bakhtin returns to the impossibility of self-love in his notes "Toward a Reworking of the Dostoevsky Book" (1961), he abandons this distinction altogether in favor of an utter or complete dependence of the self upon the other, the constant interpenetration of what appear to be two different beings:

> I cannot manage without another, I cannot become myself without another; I must find myself in another by finding another in myself (in mutual reflection and mutual acceptance). Justification cannot be *self*-justification, recognition cannot be *self*-recognition. I receive my name from others, and it exists for others (self-nomination is imposture). Even love towards one's own self is impossible. (*PDP* 287–88)

By this point, Bakhtin has long held his key conviction that consciousness is always-already dialogical and heteroglot, built from and constantly dependent upon other voices. Early in his career, he was still under the strong influence of a Cartesian-Kantian (in short, modern) notion of selfhood with which he was struggling mightily, trying to find a vocabulary capable of expressing his instinctive dissent.

Given, then, that the early Bakhtin's notion of selfhood is still modern, and given that self-experience has an ineradicably different phenomenological character than other-experience—a difference that makes self-love impossible— what exactly is the nature of one's responsibility to oneself and others, in aesthetics and ethics? In *Toward a Philosophy of the Act*, the key phrase that expresses Bakhtin's imperative is "I-for-myself." By this Bakhtin does not mean "living for oneself" but rather "living from within oneself." It is tempting here to recall Sartre's famous categories of *en-soi* and *pour-soi*, but Bakhtin is talking about something different. "Living for oneself," as Bakhtin uses the phrase, means something very close to what it does in ordinary usage: it is selfishness, egotism; it involves treating others as objects and oneself as the only subject (I-it versus I-thou relations). The "I-for-myself," to the contrary, belongs to authentic living, and is for Bakhtin an *achievement*, as he indicates by his identification of it as one of the "emotional-volitional moments" that it is the task of moral philosophy to describe and the task of the moral life to achieve:

> These basic moments are I-for-myself, the other-for-me, and I-for-the-other. All the values of actual life and culture are arranged around the basic architectonic points of the actual world of the performed act or deed: scientific values, aesthetic values, political values (including both ethical and social values), and, finally, religious values. All spatial-temporal values and all sense-content values are drawn toward and concentrated around these central emotional-volitional moments: I, the other [for me], and I-for-the-other. (*TPA* 54)

The authentic answerable act (*postupok*) will take these three forms, and insofar as I am able fully to incarnate and comprehend all three forms of answerable action, I achieve "self-activity." As Mihailovic says,

> What is given in any life is the fact of existence, a state that requires no effort or work and which is simply *there*. . . . The true realization of the uniqueness of one's existence comes about through work or "activeness" (what Liapunov sometimes translates as "self-activity" [*aktivnost'*]); the fulfillment of the ethical imperative is assigned (*zadana*) rather than given.[16]

We can see here again that Bakhtin has not yet managed to deconstruct the Cartesian-Kantian self. He still understands the labor of achieving answerability as something one achieves from within oneself and, in a sense, for oneself: even the achievement of living as I-for-another is one's own achievement, not the other's. But what remains perfectly clear, and essential for our purposes, is the obligation to achieve, through "self-activity," a genuinely answerable "I-for-myself."

What means, though, suffice to distinguish the genuine "I-for-myself" from our ordinary quotidian egoism? Mihailovic offers a compelling answer to this question:

> Crucial here is the distinction that Bakhtin draws between incarnation and embodiment. The former is the fullest flowering of the act in all of its ramifications whereas the latter represents a partial realization of the act. When we incarnate rather than merely embody the act in our lives we put our signature on it (*podpisat'sia pod nim*), which is to say that it in a certain sense has the stamp of our individuality on it. . . . Embodiment (*voploshchenie*) refers only to the change that an individual undergoes when he or she becomes consciously aware of the fact that all human lives are different; the actual deed of ethically integrating with others follows after this awareness, and is described by Bakhtin as both a partaking . . . and an incarnation.[17]

And it is not only "all human lives" that are different: every moment of each life is different from all others, and makes a distinctive demand upon me. Bakhtin laments the "unfortunate misunderstanding" that leads people to think that "the truth of a situation is precisely that which is repeatable and constant in it" (*TPA* 37). The truly answerable deed, in his view, is one that focuses all its attention on the "unique context," the "unique moment" with its utterly particular demands. Some people live in generality, and their lives are "fortuitous and incapable of being rooted" (*TPA* 56); to recognize the fact of uniqueness is embodiment, and is a necessary but not sufficient step toward answerability; but true answerability is achieved only when I recognize that that "fact of uniqueness" imposes a responsibility upon me that I cannot avert. When I acknowledge my responsibility and act upon it—whether in a conversation with a friend or in reading a novel—I realize the authentic "I-for-myself" and "I-for-another." This is true love; this is the incarnated deed.

However, let it not be thought that the uniqueness of the moment and of the person deprives the ethical life of coherence and continuity. To the contrary, one of the reasons *this* moment is unique is that it succeeds *previous* moments in which I was also called to incarnational "self-activity"; and if I responded appropriately *then* by "undersigning" my deed I commit myself still more to a similar acknowledgment *now*:

It is not the content of an obligation that obligates me, but my signature below it—the fact that at one time I acknowledged or undersigned the given acknowledgment. . . . And in this performed act the content-aspect was also but a constituent moment, and what decided the matter was the acknowledgment or affirmation—the answerable deed—that had been actually performed at a previous time, etc. What we shall find everywhere is a constant unity of answerability. (*TPA* 38–39)

Here we see one of the first appearances of that characteristic Bakhtinian notion of an "open unity," that which coheres without being fixed, schematized, or finalized. And the term that Bakhtin uses to describe this open yet "constant unity of answerability" is simple, familiar, and quite beautiful: he calls it *faithfulness*.

Two Versions of Kenosis

I have explored Bakhtin's claim that self-love is impossible—along with a few of its manifold implications—in such detail because otherwise it might be tempting to assign a certain meaning to that claim which, though initially appealing, is ultimately unjustifiable. I refer to the idea that genuine love of others is *kenotic* in a particular sense of that word: genuine love of others requires an emptying out of one's own self and a consequent refilling of the emptied consciousness with attention to the Other. This notion derives from St. Paul's account of Christ's kenosis or "self-emptying," "self-divestiture":

Have this mind among yourselves, which is yours in Christ Jesus, who, though he was in the form of God, did not count equality with God a thing to be grasped, but emptied himself, taking the form of a servant, being born in the likeness of men. (Phil. 2:5–7, *RSV*)

Weil thinks a kenotic movement necessary for the love of others, as she explains in the continuation of the passage quoted earlier: "This way of looking is first of all attentive. The soul empties itself of all its own contents in order to receive into itself the being it is looking at, just as he is, in all his truth."[18] Here again—now in her claim that real attentiveness to, and hence love for, the other depends upon an evacuation of the ego—Weil is a representative rather than a unique figure. Karl F. Morrison has identified this kenotic tradition as one of the great streams of ethical thought in the Western world: it describes, in his view, a "hermeneutics of empathy" that finds its most focused expression in the phrase "I am you."[19] Here, too, we find an idea with a strong pedigree; yet the evidence suggests that Bakhtin directly rejects the particular Western kenotic tradition just described—though in another sense the kenosis passage from St. Paul is utterly essential to his (more Eastern and Orthodox) charitable hermeneutics.

Strong indications of Bakhtin's rejection may be found in the preceding section of this essay, in which we explored his emphasis on achieving an answerable "I-for-myself." To live "for oneself" in the answerable rather than the egotistical sense requires that one not engage in self-annihilation. One must place one's "signature" on the "emotional-volitional moment" of "I-for-myself" just as forcefully as one places it on the "I-for-another" moment; moreover, one's recognition of the *other's* answerable deed ("the other-for-me") requires a commitment to the richness and unfinalizability of *both* the other and oneself. The clear implication is that the three key "emotional-volitional moments" are mutually reinforcing: no one of them can be reached in isolation from the others.

But Bakhtin goes further in saying that the loss or abdication of selfhood, so prized by the interpretation of kenosis I have described and also by other forms of mysticism, leads also to the abdication of answerability and the refusal of self-activity—in short, it is to assume an "alibi for Being."

> Participation in the being-event of the world in its entirety does not co-incide, from our point of view, with irresponsible self-surrender to Being, with being-possessed by Being. What happens in the latter case is that the passive moment in my participation is moved to the fore, while my to-be-accomplished self-activity is reduced. The aspiration of Nietzsche's philosophy reduces to a considerable extent to this possessedness by Being (one-sided participation); its ultimate result is the absurdity of contemporary Dionysianism. (*TPA* 49)[20]

The evacuation of the self in favor of Being, *or* of the other, actually *prevents* a genuinely answerable and self-active "I-for-another." As Bakhtin writes in "Author and Hero," in the Christ of the Gospels there appears for the first time in human history "an infinitely deepened *I-for-myself*—not a cold *I-for-myself*, but one of boundless kindness toward the other; an *I-for-myself* that renders full justice to the other as such, disclosing and affirming the other's axiological distinctiveness in all its fullness" ("A&H" 56).

This is one of Bakhtin's most consistent themes. He would write much later in the notes "Toward a Reworking of the Dostoevsky Book" that what is required is "[n]ot merging with another, but preserving one's own position of *extralocality* and the *surplus* of vision and understanding connected with it" ("TRDB" 299). In notes made near the end of his life, Bakhtin would define "[u]nderstanding as the transformation of the other's into 'one's own/another's'"; the "principle of outsidedness" remains essential; neither the self nor the other is expendable, since self cannot be purely self nor other purely other (*SpG* 168). Perhaps the fullest and boldest exploration of this theme comes in "Discourse in the Novel," where Bakhtin explains that a "passive understanding of linguistic meaning"—or, it follows for Bakhtin, of personal actions more generally conceived—"is no understanding at all."

> [E]ven . . . an understanding of the speaker's intention insofar as that understanding remains purely passive, purely receptive contributes nothing new to the word under consideration, only mirroring it, seeking, at its most ambitious, merely the full reproduction of that which is already given in the word—even such an understanding never goes beyond the boundaries of the word's context and in no way enriches the word. (*DI* 281)

The failure to "enrich the word" is for Bakhtin an *ethical* failure: passive reconstruction "leaves the speaker in his own personal context, within his own boundaries." An "active understanding" is "precisely . . . that [which] the speaker counts on" (*DI* 282): to refuse it in the name of accurate reconstruction is to imprison one's interlocutor in a Cartesian fortress-self.[21]

But passive reconstruction damages the self of the interpreter as well as that of the speaker. One of the best accounts of this damage may be found in Solzhenitsyn's novel *The First Circle*, when State Counselor Innokenty Artemyevich Volodin reads forbidden books for the first time:

> It turned out that you have to know how to read. It is not just a matter of letting your eyes run down the pages. Since Innokenty, from youth on, had been shielded from erroneous or outcast books, and had read only the clearly established classics [of the Marxist-Leninist canon], he had grown used to believing every word he read, giving himself up completely to the author's will. Now, reading writers whose opinions contradicted one another, he was unable for a while to rebel, but could only submit to one author, then to another, then to a third.[22]

Solzhenitsyn here describes what Bakhtin would call a universal ethical failure: authors, teachers (including other mediators or transmitters of works), and readers alike engage in a simple hermeneutical system in which the word produced is authoritative and its reception purely passive. Innokenty's interpretive humility is a false humility: having abdicated "self-activity," having claimed an "alibi for Being"—in obedience to authorities who demand just that from him—Innokenty has rendered himself incapable of achieving the "emotional-volitional moments" that Bakhtin finds necessary to the truly answerable consciousness. At age thirty, he is beginning to learn for the first time what it might mean to be a responsible human being. And the first step, for him, is claiming the right to evaluate and respond to what he reads—to achieve an authentic "I-for-myself" that can then be the foundation for an authentic "I-for-another."[23]

So kenosis in the sense of self-evacuation or self-annihilation is forbidden by the Bakhtinian understanding of love. However, there is, Bakhtin suggests, a self-*renunciation* that is not only appropriate but necessary for proper answerability:

> If I actually lost myself in the other (instead of two participants there would be one—an impoverishment of Being), i.e., if I ceased to be unique, then this moment of my not-being could never become a moment of my consciousness; non-being cannot become a moment in the being of consciousness— it would simply not exist for me, i.e., being would not be accomplished through me at that moment. Passive empathizing, being-possessed, losing oneself—these have nothing in common with the *answerable* act/deed of self-abstracting or self-renunciation. In self-renunciation I actualize with utmost activeness and in full the uniqueness of my place in Being. The world in which I, from my own unique place, renounce myself does not become a world in which I do not exist, a world which is indifferent, in its meaning, to my existence: self-renunciation is a performance or accomplishment that encompasses Being-as-event. (*TPA* 16)

What Bakhtin counsels here is an ascetic self-discipline that does not eradicate the self but rather chastens it. It is very different than the kind of kenosis recommended by Weil and others in that tradition—but it owes its character to the passage from Philippians in which the term kenosis appears. Immediately succeeding the sentences just quoted is this comment: "A great symbol of self-activity, the descending [?] of Christ" (*TPA* 16).[24] Mihailovic seems to think that Bakhtin refers here to Christ's descent into hell,[25] but it is more likely and more fitting that Bakhtin has in mind the passage from Philippians: the descent of the eternal Word from heaven to earth, its enfleshment.

St. Paul's description of what happened in this kenosis is utterly germane to Bakhtin's description of genuine self-renunciation. Note that what Christ renounces in taking human form is an "equality with God" that is rightfully his: he does not shed false or prideful claims to superiority, but rather the "form of God" that (in traditional Christian theology) is appropriate to his divine nature, in order to "take the form of a servant." He does not cease to exist, he does not eradicate his "I," but rather achieves true "self-activity," assumes a genuine "I-for-myself," precisely by virtue of his perfect servitude, his thoroughgoing commitment to "I-for-another." Let us recall again Bakhtin's description, in "Author and Hero," of Christ's "infinitely deepened *I-for-myself*—not a cold *I-for-myself*, but one of boundless kindness toward the other; an *I-for-myself* that renders full justice to the other as such, disclosing and affirming the other's axiological distinctiveness in all its fullness" ("A&H" 56).

If this is, as already noted, quite unlike the kenosis-as-self-evacuation described by Weil, it bears a somewhat closer resemblance to what Clark and Holquist call the specifically "Russian kenotic tradition."[26] This tradition emphasizes the ethical necessity of humbling oneself, of depriving oneself of all luxuries and even of that which might rightfully be said to belong to one, in order to "gain Christ" or "attain God." (This is a constant theme in the *Philokalia*, especially in the theology of St. Theodosius and in the much earlier texts attributed to St. Theodorus the Great Ascetic.) Yet this tradition doesn't quite fit either. Bakhtin's ethics shares the emphasis on humility, servitude, and the voluntary assumption of poverty, but, perhaps because it is an ethics rather than a theology, it focuses on love for the other rather than on "gaining Christ":

> It should suffice to recall the inequality in principle between the *I* and the *other* with respect to value in Christian ethics: one must not love oneself, one must love the other; one must not be indulgent toward oneself, one must be indulgent toward the other; and in general, we must relieve the other of any burdens and take them upon ourselves. ("A&H" 38)

Of course, Christian theology has always asserted that love of God and love of the neighbor are complementary rather than opposed, but the exact relationship between the two can in practice be hard to understand, still harder to realize. One would not expect Bakhtin, in his early philosophical works, to explore this problem, but at one point in "Author and Hero" he seems to do just that. In the same passage in which he posits Christ's answerable or self-active "I-for-myself," he reemphasizes the altruistic character of Christian ethical demand: "in all of Christ's norms the *I* and the *other* are contraposed: for myself—absolute sacrifice, for the other—loving mercy" ("A&H" 56). But he then adds this crucial, even transformative, point:

> But *I-for-myself* is the *other* for God. . . . God is now the heavenly father who is *over me* and can be merciful to me and justify me where I, from within myself, cannot be merciful to myself and cannot justify myself in principle, as long as I remain pure before myself. What I must be for the other, God is for me.

This point is potentially transformative because it may explain how the demands of Bakhtin's ethics can be met. The suggestion here is first that God's "I-for-myself" and "I-for-the-other" finds its perfect expression in the kenosis of Christ: the Word become flesh (John 1:14) is God's signature, in Bakhtin's sense, upon his love for us. But second, that divine signature, once recognized by me, provides the ground for, or source of, my own determination to act answerably, to "undersign" and "incarnate" my love for the other. Bakhtin verges here on the Solovyovian insistence that three—not two, as Bakhtin would say in his later notes (*SpG* 170)—is the "dialogical minimum." Vladimir Solovyov claims that "I can only acknowledge the absolute significance of a given person, or believe in him (without which true love is impossible), by affirming him in God, and consequently by belief in God Himself, and in myself, as possessing in God the center and root of my own existence."[27] This is necessary because my fallen and sinful state deprives me of the power to acknowledge or believe in the other:

> Man can restore formatively the image of God in the living object of his love, only when at the same time he restores that image in himself. However, he does not possess the power for this in himself, for if he possessed it he would not stand in need of restoration; and as he does not possess it in himself, he is obliged to receive it from God.[28]

The comments about Christian ethics I have cited from Bakhtin are brief passages in long works that otherwise make little or no mention of these issues. Still, those comments' resemblance to Solovyov's claims—which are themselves characteristic of traditional Christian ethics—strongly suggests that the early Bakhtin understood at least theism and perhaps even Christian belief to be necessary for anyone who hopes to love the other in the ethical or aesthetic (hermeneutical) spheres. The kenosis of Christ establishes the pattern for our own answerable deeds: it is his "I-for-myself" and "I-for-another" that reveal to us the proper form of self-activity and empower us to pursue it persistently and faithfully. This may be a point at which the Bakhtinian ethics-aesthetics-hermeneutics ceases to be merely consistent with Christian theology and becomes an elaboration of that theology.

Conclusion

If the scholars are correct in their dating, Augustine wrote his reflections on charitable interpretation almost exactly sixteen hundred years ago. I believe that those reflections began to find a proper elaboration only seventy-five years ago, in the early and fragmentary work of Mikhail Bakhtin. Bakhtin counsels a course of hermeneutical action that may at times (as we saw in the previous section) derive directly from a specifically Christian theology, but which in any case remains perfectly consistent—more so, perhaps, than any other model of hermeneutics— with healthy Christian belief and practice. It is possible, of course, to extract a list of hermeneutical principles from Bakhtin's early work: we should, in our reading, be ceaselessly attentive to details without abandoning the quest for unity or making recourse to a reductive and totalizing schema—that is, we should seek "open unity" or "open totality"; we should pursue active, answerable understanding rather than passive reconstruction; we should renounce the tyranny of the magisterial self not by annihilating that self but by practicing a servant's asceticism, which is the highest and most Christlike way to "undersign" one's interpretation; and so on. And it may not be inappropriate to articulate such principles: Mihailovic makes the case that for the early Bakhtin, while "theoretism" is pernicious, "the theoretical *does* have its place in the subject's efforts to get its bearings in a bewildering and tumultuous world: it serves as a bridge linking the personal to the public that, however flimsy it may be, [the subject] has no choice but to cross."[29] But for Bakhtin, the failure to incarnate (in his distinctive sense of the word) that theoretical understanding would indicate that such "understanding" was illusory. Interpretation, like all other distinctly human activities, calls for the kind of "active love" preached by Father Zosima in *The Brothers Karamazov*. Theoretical accounting is sometimes necessary, but its sphere is finite. The labor of charitable interpretation, on the other hand, is always productive but nevertheless endless: "There is neither a first nor a last word and there are no limits to the dialogic context (it extends into the boundless past and the boundless future)" (*SpG* 170).

Notes

Epigraphs: The first epigraph is a quotation from Brian Stock, *Augustine the Reader* (Cambridge: Harvard Univ. Press, 1996), 185, summarizing Augustine's position. The second epigraph is an excerpt from David Remnick, *Lenin's Tomb: The Last Days of the Soviet Empire* (New York: Vintage, 1994), 104.

    1. St. Augustine, *On Christian Doctrine*, trans. D. W. Robertson Jr. (Indianapolis: Bobbs-Merrill, 1958), 30.

    2. Among the attempts to think through, perhaps in a preliminary way, what charitable interpretation may have been for Augustine, some of the more interesting are Donald G. Marshall, "Making Letters Speak: Interpreter as Orator in Augustine's *De Doctrina Christiana*," *Religion and Literature* 24, no. 2 (1992): 1–17; Margaret R. Miles, *Reading for Life: Beauty, Pluralism, and Responsibility* (New York: Continuum, 1997), esp. chap. 3; and Stock, *Augustine the Reader*, esp. part 2.

    3. See Donald Davidson, *Inquiries into Truth and Interpretation* (Oxford: Oxford Univ. Press, 1984).

    4. Hans-Georg Gadamer, *Truth and Method*, 2nd ed., translated and revised by Joel Weinsheimer and Donald G. Marshall (New York: Crossroad, 1992), xxviii.

    5. As is almost always the case with Bakhtin, his comments in *Toward a Philosophy of the Act* apply equally well to what is usually called "ethics" (involving relations among persons) and what is usually called "hermeneutics" but which

Bakhtin called "aesthetics" (involving persons' encounters with texts). For Bakhtin, and this is true at any stage of his career, acts of interpretation are always ethically fraught, while ethical questions always assume hermeneutical form. This is why Bakhtin can move so easily between literary criticism and moral philosophy—or rather, erase the boundaries between the two—and why Alexandar Mihailovic focuses on the importance of the concept of "discourse" (*slovo*) for Bakhtin: "discourse" is how we live as well as what we read. See Mihailovic, *Corporeal Words: Mikhail Bakhtin's Theology of Discourse* (Evanston: Northwestern Univ. Press, 1997), chap. 1.

6. Both positions exemplify what Gary Saul Morson and Caryl Emerson (*Mikhail Bakhtin: Creation of a Prosaics* [Palo Alto: Stanford Univ. Press, 1990], 28) call "semiotic totalitarianism" because both claim to be able to say all there is to say about the object of their attention: either there is a definitive code that explains all, or there is an utter absence of pattern that is equally definitive and therefore equally omnipotent in its explanatory power. "Art and life are not one," Bakhtin writes in the early essay "Art and Answerability": "Semiotic totalitarianism" is the attempt to impose from "outside" a false oneness. Conversely, to acquiesce in the entropic and fissiparous rupturing of art and life into a chaotic "weightlessness" is a failure of responsibility: "Art and life are not one, but they must become united in myself—in the unity of my answerability" ("A&A" 2). Through the assumption of the responsibility that is "assigned" to us, we ensure that words take on their proper weight: in the responsible or answerable consciousness, words have substantial heft but are mobile and usable (see Mihailovic, *Corporeal Words*, 74). My vocabulary here echoes that of Vaclav Havel: "Words that are not backed up by life lose their weight, which means that words can be silenced in two ways: either you ascribe to them such weight that no one dares to utter them aloud, or you take away any weight they might have, and they turn into air. The final effect in each case is silence: the silence of the half-mad man who is constantly writing appeals to world authorities while everyone ignores him; and the silence of the Orwellian citizen" (*Letters to Olga*, trans. Paul Wilson [New York: Holt, 1989], 306–7).

7. Simone Weil, *Waiting for God*, trans. Emma Craufurd (New York: G. P. Putnam, 1951), 114–15. For Weil, here and elsewhere in her work, human particularity is best grasped through personal suffering coupled with the recognition of suffering in others. She would surely agree with Tolstoy's famous opening line of *Anna Karenina*: "Happy families are all alike, but each unhappy family is unhappy in its own way." A liberal-ironist version of the same contention—that human solidarity is best based on a common suffering—turns up in the work of Richard Rorty (*Contingency, Irony, and Solidarity* [Cambridge: Cambridge Univ. Press, 1989], chap. 9). An interesting question is why St. Paul's injunction to "weep with those who weep" is received so enthusiastically by such a wide range of thinkers, while scarcely anyone acknowledges the other half of the saying: "rejoice with those who rejoice" (Rom. 12:15, *RSV*).

8. For important reflections on the "problematics of vision" in the early Bakhtin, see Caryl Emerson, "Keeping the Self Intact during the Culture Wars: A Centennial Essay for Mikhail Bakhtin," *New Literary History* 27 (1996): 110–11.

9. Mihailovic, *Corporeal Words*, 59–60.

10. Fyodor Dostoevsky, *The Brothers Karamazov*, trans. Richard Pevear and Larissa Volokhonsky (New York: Vintage, 1990), 217.

11. Gary Saul Morson, "Bakhtin and the Present Moment," *The American Scholar* 60 (1991): 215.

12. Bakhtin's concerns, then, are substantial, and his tendency to avoid the language of "human nature" and "common humanity" an understandable one. But we should not forget that Alyosha uses his belief in the common humanity that he shares with Captain Snegiryov not only to formulate judgments about the Captain, but also to formulate them about himself. Understanding himself to be in a definable analogical relationship with the Captain, Alyosha not only comes to believe that the Captain will take the money but also comes to see the "sensitivity" of the Captain's soul, the pettiness of his own, and the certainty that he, too, would take the money were he in the Captain's place. In other words, Alyosha puts his self-concept at risk in the very way that Bakhtin thinks essential to the understanding of persons as persons rather than as "cognized things": "The genuine life of the personality is made available only through a *dialogic* penetration of that personality, during which it freely and reciprocally reveals itself" (*PDP* 59). This is precisely what Alyosha does. The category "man" or "human being" can certainly serve as a reifying instrument, especially in the hands of the mechanistic modern psychology that Dostoevsky so deplored (see *PDP* 61), but in this case it serves to link Alyosha tightly with one from whom he might otherwise wish to distinguish himself. Therefore, despite the dangers that Bakhtin properly identifies, the analogical understanding of persons rooted in Christian doctrines of creation and sin *can be* a powerful tool in the growth of love for one's neighbor. So even Bakhtin himself can sometimes use, without disapproval or ironizing distance, the concept of man: he identifies Dostoevsky's repudiation of mechanistic, reifying psychology as part of "his struggle on behalf of man" (*PDP* 62). But the term "man" for Bakhtin can only be used in just such a context, when it has been stripped of its reifying and finalizing implications.

13. Augustine, *On Christian Doctrine*, 30.

14. Ibid., 20.

15. Bakhtin is so insistent that this abstracting and objectifying of the "I" is "absolutely alien to the ethical event of being" because of his insistence, noted briefly above but repeated throughout Bakhtin's early work, that ethics is properly understood only in relation to the "answerable act" (*postupok*), and that the truly answerable act is always historically concrete and particular (in this regard, see especially *TPA* 30). This is the sense in which Bakhtin's early work is most

thoroughly anti-Kantian: it understands the abstracting and universalizing of ethical decision-making inherent in Kant's categorical imperative as utterly inimical to true ethical—that is, answerable—action. See Mihailovic, *Corporeal Words*, 65ff.

16. Ibid., 74.

17. Ibid., 68–69.

18. Weil, *Waiting for God*, 115.

19. Karl F. Morrison, *I Am You: The Hermeneutics of Empathy in Western Literature, Theology, and Art* (Princeton: Princeton Univ. Press, 1988).

20. One finds a similar argument being made by Vladimir Solovyov, who has sometimes been put forth as an influence upon Bakhtin (see, for example, Mihailovic, *Corporeal Words*, 70). Solovyov says bluntly that "[t]he meaning of human love, speaking generally, is *the justification and salvation of individuality through the sacrifice of egoism*" (*The Meaning of Love*, revised translation by Thomas R. Beyer Jr. [Hudson, N.Y.: Lindisfarne, 1985], 42). Notice that the elimination of egoism is the salvation of individuality, which remains. Thus, Solovyov distrusts the mystical dissolution of the self, because "in mystical love the object of love comes in the long run to an absolute indistinction, which swallows up the human individuality. Here egoism is abrogated only in that very insufficient sense in which it is abrogated when a person falls into a state of very deep sleep" (47). Solovyov wants to preserve the integrity of both the lover and the loved one, but to have them joined together in what he calls a "living *syzygetic* relation" (113)—the term derived from the Greek word *syzygy*, meaning (says Solovyov) "close union." The whole picture resembles the early Bakhtin's notions of love in several ways. See also Caryl Emerson, "Solov'ev, the Late Tolstoi, and the Early Bakhtin on the Problem of Shame and Love," *Slavic Review* 50 (1991): 663–71.

21. Gerald Bruns, in a brilliant book to which I owe a great deal, describes Spinoza's interpretive attitude: "Call this Cartesian hermeneutics, or the allegory of suspicion, in which the text comes under the control of the reader as disengaged rational subject, unresponsive except to its own self-certitude. . . . The motive of Cartesian hermeneutics is to preserve alienation as a condition of freedom from the text" (*Hermeneutics Ancient and Modern* [New Haven: Yale Univ. Press, 1992], 149). A century and a half after Spinoza, Hegel would point out that the "demand for neutrality has generally no other meaning but that [the interpreter] is to act in expounding [the texts he interprets] as if he were dead" (quoted in Bruns, 150).

22. Aleksandr Solzhenitsyn, *The First Circle*, trans. Thomas P. Whitney (New York: Harper and Row, 1968), 344.

23. Another brilliant illustration of the consequences of this abdication comes in Dostoevsky's *Demons*, in the bone-chilling but utterly penetrating remark Peter Verkhovensky makes to Kirillov regarding the latter's belief—buttressed by what appears to Kirillov to be an ineluctable set of logical steps—that he must commit suicide in order to be truly free and thereby to become God: "I only know it was

not you who ate the idea, but the idea that ate you" (trans. Richard Pevear and Larissa Volokhonsky [New York: Vintage, 1994], 558).

24. The bracketed question mark indicates the editor's uncertainty about the word translated as "descending." The manuscript now titled *Toward a Philosophy of the Act* is not only fragmentary, but also damaged by decades of neglect after it was hidden away. The sentence about the "descending of Christ" is immediately fol-lowed by thirty-two indecipherable words—though some attempts at conjectural reconstruction of those words have been made (see note 54, *TPA* 90). The reading "descending" (which the editors were confident enough about to put in the text rather than recording it as indecipherable) is perfectly consistent with the theme of the passage. Here is an English translation of the reconstructed passage (provided to me by Caryl Emerson and Alexandar Mihailovic, to whom I am grateful): " . . . through communion, through the separation of his blood and flesh as he suffers a permanent death, alive and active in the world of events. It is through his non-immanence in the world that we are alive and commune with it, are attached to it."

25. Mihailovic, *Corporeal Words*, 75.

26. Katerina Clark and Michael Holquist, *Mikhail Bakhtin* (Cambridge: Har-vard Univ. Press, 1984), 84. In discussing this "Russian kenotic tradition," Clark and Holquist invoke George P. Fedotov's book *The Russian Religious Mind* (Cambridge: Harvard Univ. Press, 1946) as a key source. Another important contribution to this topic is Steven Cassedy's essay "P. A. Florensky and the Celebration of Matter," in *Russian Religious Thought*, ed. Judith Deutsch Kornblatt and Richard F. Gustafson (Madison: Univ. of Wisconsin Press, 1996), 95–111. Cassedy's work is particularly valuable in showing how Russian thinkers, including Dostoevsky, were influenced by Western understandings of kenosis as self-annihilation: "the term . . . was taken from nineteenth-century German Protestant theology and introduced into Russian theology in the 1890s" and "immediately filled a terminological need that had been there for many years" (95). The note appended to this passage refers the reader to "a history of the term *kenosis* in Russian theology" found in the unpublished Ph.D. dissertation of Paul Valliere on "M. M. Tereev" (Columbia University, 1974).

27. Solovyov, *The Meaning of Love*, 88.

28. Ibid., 85–86.

29. Mihailovic, *Corporeal Words*, 63.

Philosophy and Theology in "Aesthetic Activity"

Graham Pechey

Philosophy begins where contemporary life ends.

The novelist is drawn toward everything that is not yet completed.

The first of my epigraphs is a statement made by Bakhtin in an interview in the last year of his life; the second comes from his essay "Epic and Novel" written some thirty years earlier.[1] Since Bakhtin saw himself as a philosopher, and since he is a known champion of the novel genre, both propositions carry an implication and intonation that is positive. The first suggests that philosophy is a discourse that only gives "life" perspective insofar as it is distanced from contemporaneity; the novel's thriving precisely and especially in an element of contemporaneity is the clear import of the second. Do they therefore contradict each other? Did Bakhtin change his mind? The short answer to both of these questions is, "No"; the long answer would be an unfolding of the dialogical relations these utterances set up simply by being laid alongside each other. This essay is a version of that long answer.

To resolve the issue of how these two categories that are so strongly affirmed for opposite reasons relate to each other—to reach the space where their incompatibility emerges as merely apparent—we could do worse than look at the negotiations of two other categories in one of Bakhtin's earliest writings. Aesthetics is the sector of philosophy to which Bakhtin was increasingly drawn, and which he went on so thoroughly to historicize that he almost drove it out of philosophy altogether, turning it instead into a sociology of modern culture fronted methodologically by a "translinguistics" whose privileged object is novelistic prose. Theology is the premodern forerunner of philosophy from which Bakhtin's early aesthetics derives many of its terms. It seems that at this phase a theologically inflected aesthetics— or an aesthetically inflected theology—was for him the only sure means of access and fidelity to that fundamental ethical reality of answerability that is the ground and condition of our whole being-in-the-world. The book-length study entitled "Author and Hero in Aesthetic Activity" is the place where, uniquely, as never before or later, we see vividly at work this coinflection of dimensions. It is also, as we will see, the place where Bakhtin strikingly overturns some of our preconceptions about the timing of secular modernity.

Value Spheres: Aesthetics and
Theology in the Context of Modernity

I take this work of the early 1920s to be one among many such interventions in that period to make a virtue out of the lateness of Russia's social transformation. If the atheistic and socialist intelligentsia who came to dominate politically after the Revolution followed a strategy of aggressive modernization, breaking with the past, and catching up with or overtaking the West, there were other intellectuals— among them Bakhtin—for whom the realization elsewhere of possible futures for their country's developmentally belated polity and economy gave its culture a compensatory perspectival advantage over cultures whose polities and economies had modernized "on time." Bakhtin's work shows that the desire to fashion an appropriate modernity for Russia by critically activating its "outsideness" to the West was not simply the knee-jerk reflex of chauvinistic antisecularists but, at least in his case, a real wish to avoid the social and spiritual pathologies of rationalization and instrumentalization that the modern project had spawned in other places.[2]

In "Author and Hero," then, Bakhtin seeks to free aesthetics from its sub-ordination to epistemology in Western philosophy, drawing to its pole all those impulses of community and intersubjectivity that modern thought had effectively driven into the exile of theology and a specialized spiritual experience. In the aesthetic, Bakhtin finds a modern category that nonetheless welcomes the lost or sidelined modes and knowledges of other times. The reminder that the other is my lovingly consummating author and I am in turn his or hers—that I can never be "the hero of my own life" ("A&H" 112)—is a reproach to modernity's hubristic claim to self-grounding, its exciting though perverse fiction of the hero as self-authoring. When direct philosophizing became dangerous, Bakhtin turned from a modern category of thought to *the* literary genre of modernity, that is to say, the novel, and first of all the protomodernist "polyphonic" novel of Dostoevsky. On the face of it, this seems a turnabout: surely the quasi-authorial autonomy he claims for Dostoevsky's characters is just that fiction of self-authoring he had earlier implicitly denounced? But this is not the case: secularity denies or brackets out the Author, reserving Him for last instances and first beginnings, and finally doing away with Him altogether. Bakhtin's concept of novelistic discourse working at full stretch strongly posits the author and thinks of human freedom as nothing if not grounded in a potentially infinite dialogue with the latter. Pushing the freedom of the hero to its limit, we find ourselves back at the authority of the author: life is the difficult and endless passage of one into the other; any other (supposedly unauthored, uncreated) freedom is illusory.[3]

And so it is that we find Bakhtin later in the decade entering with gusto into the spirit of modern writing and finding there not faith canceled in doubt or spiraling relativism but faith eternally problematized. The obverse of the better-known Bakhtin who celebrates the novelization of the high genres and the carnivalization of the sacred is the Bakhtin who in effect sacralizes the novel, who makes of it a talisman we may wear against the idolatrous temptations of our late-modern world. The objects of modern irony and parody are not the holy or otherworldly as such but their worldly simulacra. Bakhtin wishes us to see that challenges to representation within representation do not threaten what is beyond representation. On the contrary, they reinforce its claim upon our attention; the grotesque in art does not work against the sublime any more than incarnation works against transcendence. It is in this sense that the novel is our gospel, and (like the Gospels themselves) it offers at every turn a direct route from the everyday into the most elevated. Every character, thanks to the orchestration of dialogism, can be a "personality," every voice (as he was to put it later) a "social language"; every element is potentially more than itself, everything exceeds its own bounds, speaks to a context that has no earthly limits. The novel is a holy writ of endlessly permutable content: modern writing as epitomized by the novel is perennially postmodern insofar as it turns any story into the means of breaking open the linear continuum of history and admitting the blazing light of the other.

This view of Bakhtin and the novel is not as bizarre as it may at first sound; it is there already in a bold claim that seems to underlie the careful phenomenological description of "Author and Hero." For if the Bakhtin of the middle years dates modernity's onset from the Renaissance, the early Bakhtin is not alone in implicitly mapping the story of modernity upon the much longer narrative of Christianity itself. As a classically trained philologist, Bakhtin would have been familiar with the etymology of the word "modern" as a derivative of *modernus*, the term by which fifth-century Christians in the Roman Empire distinguished themselves from pagan believers.[4] The Christians were, then, the first conscious moderns—the first community to make a defining characteristic out of their historically unprecedented otherness: long before the novel, there was the ancient novelty of the Gospel. Bakhtin's contemporary Erich Auerbach wrote an entire book in 1945 on the premise that the modernity of modern prose was inspired by the precedent of the Christian story, that behind its junking of the classical separation of styles and its discovery of the serious and the tragic in the everyday was a run-of-the-mill police action in Roman Judaea that had shaken the world.[5] If we also take in Auerbach's later work on the semantic revolution whereby Christianity transvalued key words from the classical languages,[6] and on the new faith's deep implication in the polyglossia of the Mediterranean basin, then it becomes possible to see that many of the motifs that Bakhtin was later to identify with modernity at its most positive and emancipatory find their prototype in an analogous cultural upheaval some fifteen hundred years earlier.

Let us return, however, to aesthetics and theology, and to a closer examination of some relevant episodes of the argument of "Author and Hero." Whatever their relationship in that essay, it is certain that theology and aesthetics have much in common. Both are cognitive discourses that thematize that which is other than, or at least not wholly, cognitive; and both are relatively logically ordered meta-languages whose object is either language incommensurably differently oriented and organized or beyond language altogether. It has then to be said that Russian Orthodox theology and the kind of neo-Kantian aesthetics practiced by Bakhtin have yet more in common, inasmuch as each allows that the value categories of its object discourse bear a greater existential authenticity than its own. Both, that is to say, strategically rationalize that which exceeds rationality. Russian Orthodox spirituality claims to know no absolute boundary between mysticism and theology, between what Vladimir Lossky calls "the realm of the common faith and that of personal experience." Theology is "an expression, for the profit of all, of that which can be experienced by everyone."[7] Such a distillation of situational uniqueness into the suprapersonal is exactly Bakhtin's notion of cognitive discourse. Aesthetics for Bakhtin should then stand to aesthetic activity as (Orthodox) "mystical theology" stands to religious experience. Of all the cognitive discourses, aesthetics is the one that carries the least threat of "theoreticism," and it is therefore the best placed to challenge epistemology on its own conceptual ground.

Being Outside: The Hero as a Whole in Space

Bakhtin begins from the simple truth that you cannot ever be where I am, or see yourself as I see you. I occupy a unique place in being, insofar as I am always (and wherever I might be) outside everyone else. It is on the ground of this ineluctable absolute of the noncommutability of my position with any other—of my outsideness to your experience of yourself and the world, and yours to mine—that Bakhtin builds the whole house of value. He begins with an absolute distinction between two value categories: that of the *I,* and that of the *other.* Cognition is indifferent to both; ethics is interested only in the *I.* Aesthetic activity differs from these other sectors of philosophy in that it alone embraces both the I and the other. Indeed, it is nothing less than that interaction of both that is instanced in all the manifold phenomenal forms of loving "consummation" offered as a gift by the other (or author) to the I (or hero). This dyad of author and hero operates in the two dimensions of space and time, the first addressing itself to the hero's body (where the consummation is "plastic-pictorial," mainly, though not exclusively, in the visual arts) and the second to the hero's soul (where the consummation is achieved by "rhythm," more or less confined to "verbal art"). To space and time Bakhtin adds a third dimension: "meaning." Aesthetic activity constitutes the hero not only as a whole in time and space, but also as a "whole of meaning." Aesthetic value is conferred upon "the hero's meaning-governed attitude in being—that interior place he occupies in the unitary and unique event of being" ("A&H" 138). "Author and Hero" takes its structure from these three dimensions, examining the hero under the aspect of each in turn.

The first thing to be said about this early delineation of the "aesthetic event" and its dependence upon a radical "outsideness" is that it deals in ideal types, that it is uncompromisingly wedded to pure taxonomic exemplifications. In the ideal-typical aesthetic event, the author's posture is one of being neither inside nor beside nor against the hero, but purely *over against* the latter. Where the author loses this stable position, various dilutions result, as (allegedly) in Dostoevsky and Kierkegaard who let the hero take "possession of the author" ("A&H" 17). The aesthetic event always "presupposes two noncoinciding consciousnesses" ("A&H" 22); anything in writing or reading that conflates or effaces these tends to syncretize the aesthetic, threatening to transform the event in the case of conflation into an ethical event and in that of effacement into an event of cognition. It is for this reason that the "religious event" is paradigmatic for aesthetic activity: structurally similar in the strict noncoincidence of constituent consciousnesses, prayer and ritual differ from the aesthetic event only in that the author is not any other (human) other but the (divine) Other of all of us. If the gulf between aesthetic activity and spirituality seems sometimes to narrow almost to the vanishing point, if each seems on occasion to be a mere figure for or subset of the other, it is perhaps truer to say that they stand in a relation of infinite asymptotic approximation that always stops short of coincidence. Bakhtin clearly sees that we are all heirs to a modern split in knowledge that has the character of a fatality, but that it would be far worse to deny or submit to a too-perfect (Hegelian) reconciliation. An aesthetics distinct from, yet friendly toward, theology would avert this threat, ensuring for Christian spirituality an appropriately modernized presence within the terrain of profane knowledge, while at the same time challenging the hegemony of those epistemological (subject-object) models on which almost all modern thinking is founded.

At its strongest, then, the argument of "Author and Hero" becomes a polemic against the shortcomings of "thought" itself. As we read, it becomes ever clearer that the author's surplus of "inner and outer seeing" is being offered as an alternative to that universal *aporia* of a typically disembodied and desituated modern subjectivity. The modern subject makes up for its inability vividly and roundedly to image its body in the world by recourse to a "thought" that relativizes the I and the other—renders them mutually convertible at the cost of their derealization. The thought that "has no difficulty at all in placing *me* on one and the same plane with all *other* human beings" ("A&H" 31) may be the thought that in going abroad from itself conquers nature and the object, proud of its strength. Its weakness lies in its failure to acknowledge in existential terms the real price to be paid for that fiction of thought's power and facility. My consciousness may, and can, encompass the world, but it can never image my outward appearance and my body's boundaries as encompassed *by* the world. I am not given as an outward body in myself but created as such by the other; I owe my freedom from the solipsism of an "absolute consciousness" ("A&H" 22) to my bringing-to-birth in the horizon of the other. Aesthetics for Bakhtin is a pragmatically oriented ontology of the kind that would later show itself in phenomenology of the Merleau-Pontian kind. His aesthetics is a means of escape from the hegemony of epistemology insofar as it begins from that absolute incommensurability of the I and the other that it shares with Christian ethics and that cognition programmatically denies. It is an aesthetics that might be said simultaneously to be doing two seemingly contrary things: transcendentalizing Christian ethics, reading its injunctions of other-valuing and self-negation back into our very conditions of possibility as beings in the world; while also forestalling any tendency toward a Kantian formal ethics by a strong stress upon "outward expressedness," upon the body presented along all of its outwardly adverted boundaries to and for the other's loving "overshadowing" ("A&H" 41). Bakhtin seeks to preserve the body as a value by positing on the analogy of the outer body an "inner body" as much in need of consummation from spatial outsideness as the former. Formal ethics attempts the impossible in extrapolating from my self-relation in the inner body to my relation-to-others in the outer body. Bakhtin splits the body in this way as a tactic for giving back to it its full value; only thus can he show for all to see the work of disincarnation secretly performed by a lawlike "morality."

We could sum all of this up by saying that aesthetics has for Bakhtin the task of tempting ethics away from "morality" and toward an ontology of the uniquely situated body. In pursuit of this aim, Bakhtin takes his argument into a sharp diachronic tangent and, first of all, back to our earliest childhood and the creativity of love in that phase of one's life. Complementing this is a more properly historical excursus into the currents that have shaped the body as a value in European modernity. The logic of Bakhtin's case here seems to be as follows: If the Law disincarnates the subject, then conversely an incarnating ethics will destabilize the Law. To use such an idiom is of course then to recall a better-known Incarnation, and to commit oneself to a rehearsal of the Christian transvaluation of the valued body. And this is precisely what Bakhtin does, suggesting thereby a fascinating analogy between his project of renewing an ethics of love under the complicated conditions of late modernity and the first launching of that absolute ethical novelty upon the world. Christianity breaks with both the classical emphasis upon the body and its Neoplatonic denial and does so by means of a complexly hybridized blend of positions—a heteroglot discourse on the body in which the leading and most deeply transformative voice is that of Jesus Himself:

> In Christ we find a synthesis of unique depth, the synthesis of *ethical solipsism* (man's infinite severity toward himself, i.e., an immaculately pure relationship to oneself) with *ethical-aesthetic kindness* toward the other. For the first time, there appeared an infinitely deepened *I-for-myself*—not a cold *I-for-myself*, but one of boundless kindness toward the other; an *I-for-myself* that renders full justice to the other as such, disclosing and affirming the other's axiological distinctiveness in all its fullness. All human beings divide for him into himself as the unique one—and all other human beings, into himself as the one bestowing loving mercy—and all others as receiving mercy, into himself as the savior—and all others as the saved, into himself as the one assuming the burden of sin and expiation—and all others as relieved of this burden and redeemed.
>
> Hence, in all of Christ's norms the *I* and the *other* are contraposed: for myself—absolute sacrifice, for the other—loving mercy. But *I-for-myself* is the *other* for God. God is no longer defined essentially as the voice of my conscience, as purity of my relationship to myself. . . . God is now the heavenly father who is *over me* and can be merciful to me and justify me where I, from within myself, cannot be merciful to myself and cannot justify myself in principle, as long as I remain pure before myself. What I must be for the other, God is for me. ("A&H" 56)

The terms in which Bakhtin has argued the essential relationship of author and hero are here traced to their spring in the words of the Gospels. It is as if all the intricate and nuanced phenomenological description of that relationship both before and after this passage had been distilled into a few maxims and had taken on the downright tone of Christian ethical affirmation.

Opening a window as Bakhtin here does onto the spiritual tradition to which his aesthetics is affiliated by no means closes his argument; rather it adds its own (German-philosophical) idiom to the intellectual heteroglossia of Christianity. That particular mingling of idioms would not anyway have been odd in Russia, where German idealist philosophy arrived in the company of German mysticism and was read together with the latter as its modern continuation. We are not surprised then to find that in telling the story of the later fortunes of the gospel ethic, Bakhtin distances himself from Neoplatonic elaborations and invokes against these the names of Bernard of Clairvaux and Francis of Assisi, those powerful figures of Western medieval spirituality to whom the Rhineland mystics owed so much, who feature in prominent episodes of Dante's *Paradiso*, and who (as it happens) forge a further link between Bakhtin himself and Auerbach.[8] Insofar as these otherwise so different representatives of the *imitatio Christi* stand not for the body's denial but rather for its justification here-and-now and its transfiguration in eternity, they might be seen as the saints who preside over Bakhtin's "strictly secular" ("A&H" 149) project in this essay. Creaturely images abound in the style of both mystics, functioning as figural enactments of an Incarnation that means what it says and is no mere disposable historicity, no mere metaphorical shell of physicality. Bakhtin's own style here uses something like the "low" sublime of both saints to earth and round out a neo-Kantian idiom that might otherwise etherealize the bodiliness of which it speaks. St. Bernard's talk of monks as "acrobats and jugglers"[9] to the world and the popular-grotesque motifs of St. Francis's *vita* not only connect with the "holy fool" of Orthodox tradition, but also place Bakhtin's later preoccupation with carnival in a new light. Bakhtin in any case leaves us in no doubt that by the time of the Enlightenment the ethical-aesthetic valuation of the body in the great mystics of the Middle Ages has long gone and that the body has degenerated "into an organism as the sum total of the needs of 'natural man'" ("A&H" 58). His alternative narrative of modernity will later turn on the figure of Rabelais, who articulates in writing an anonymous culture of the medieval folk. Though we might say his bearings at this earlier phase are in Dante, the situation is actually more complex than that. Dante is only the near (or modern) end of a potentially infinite regress-and-return of mediations, one that takes us through those two exemplary lives so lovingly contextualized in the *Paradiso* to the prototype of that self-negating and other-valued Body of Christ on which all of them model their lives.

Being Later: The Hero as a Whole in Time

We are not surprised to find that when Bakhtin turns to the problem of the hero as a whole in time, "Author and Hero" becomes less a general-aesthetic project than an aesthetic treatise focused on the verbal arts, a sort of ontologically inflected poetics that weaves (if anything) more freely than ever back and forth between art-as-such and everyday life. What holds the whole project together nonetheless is the analogy that Bakhtin maintains throughout between the spatial and the temporal whole and that licenses him to speak of outsideness in the dimension of time. The soul is the inner whole that is nothing apart from such "laterness" in the other. The soul is, then, the spirit as it "looks *from outside,* in the other" ("A&H" 100). The analogy is not between space as literal extension and time as literal duration, inasmuch as both of its terms have already undergone a certain figurative skewing from a "pure" conceptuality—a metaphorization by which their cognitive abstraction from value is undone and their unity restored. Just as space in verbal art is connoted rather than plastically or pictorially realized in the material, so time is as often as not a hypothetical rather than the real condition of being "after" the hero. In the hero as a temporal whole the soul is realized "on one and the same plane with the other's outer body," that is, in an aesthetic foreshadowing of the "moment of death" or (ultimately) of "resurrection in the flesh" ("A&H" 101). The soul can never be mine or spring from my effort within life-as-it-is-lived; it "descends upon me—like grace upon the sinner, like a gift that is unmerited and unexpected" ("A&H" 101). Pushing his analogical idiom to the limit, Bakhtin declares that the soul is that subtle body or "inner flesh" that is turned toward me by the other for the contemplation of my "inner eyes" ("A&H" 102).

The adventure of meaning to which Bakhtin here invites us is like nothing so much as a ladder by which we climb from the headier reaches of conceptuality up into the boldest metaphoricity, then up again into a space where even these distinctions cease to hold and allegory gives way to what the old hermeneutic of the four levels of meaning would have called *anagogy*. The formal analogy that he elaborates between spatial and temporal wholes yields oxymoronic metaphors like "temporal seeing" ("A&H" 103) and "inward outsideness" ("A&H" 101). Beyond these semantic liberties there beckon those epiphanic states in which such figures reach back toward referential truth, and are no longer metaphoric: the coincidence of body and soul at the moment of death; waking to bodily life forever at the end of all things. One strong implication of this most powerfully charged chapter of Bakhtin's essay says to us that aesthetic activity is an everyday ritual in which these sublime moments of individual and universal ending are proleptically played out. Another— a loophole for the determinedly secular perhaps—allows us to return from heaven to earth, reversing the semantic traffic of that last formulation and reading those moments of death or apocalypse as figures for ethical-aesthetic activity at work in *this* world.

The word that Bakhtin uses for this aesthetic consummation of an inner life in time is *rhythm*. Only in the rhythm of aesthetic activity is any lived experience in the other freed from the future of meaning "into the absolute past, into the *past of meaning*" ("A&H" 116). Rhythm installs meaning immanently within the lived experience; no longer drawn forward by the *ought* forever posited ahead of it as the possibility of another life, such a life is stilled from within, taking on inner flesh as "something contentedly present-on-hand" ("A&H" 115). Sin in Bakhtin's ethical-aesthetic sense is the absurd presumption that I can, as it were, "rhythmicize" my own life. Faith is the rightfully insane belief against all odds that I do not coincide with myself, the desperate refusal of the last word that spurs on my life-as-it-is-lived. The hero is born in the other's memory of her "formal" death, a rhythmic re-membering in which death itself is overcome.[10] Bakhtin brilliantly dramatizes the unearthly strangeness of aesthetic consummation by saying that rhythm is what we have when the "requiem tones at the end [are] already heard in the cradlesong at the beginning" ("A&H" 131). To use the postmodern philosophical terms of Jean-François Lyotard: the author and the hero belong to incommensurable phrasal universes; sin is the trespass of one upon the other; faith is the posture of the hero in hers; love that of the author in his. There is a benign rupture at the heart of being: my *Consummatum est* and your "I can change my life yet!" are neither translatable into each other's terms nor resolvable into a higher instance.

Extrapolating from these observations, we might say that Bakhtin's model of aesthetic activity acknowledges secular modernity's projection of regulative ideas into the future but warns it against the assumption that its favored phrasal universe of the hero is everything there is, or (worse still) that it can smuggle into that universe an idiom of self-consummation. This sinful hubris of modern reason produces in the twentieth century the terroristic heresies of its characteristic politics. Walter Benjamin was writing in the same vein at precisely the time of "Author and Hero":

> Only the Messiah himself consummates all history, in the sense that he alone redeems, completes, creates its relation to the Messianic. For this reason nothing historical can relate itself on its own account to anything Messianic. Therefore the Kingdom of God is not the *telos* of the historical dynamic; it cannot be set as a goal. From the standpoint of history it is not the goal, but the end. Therefore the order of the profane cannot be built up on the idea of the Divine Kingdom, and therefore theocracy has no political, but only a religious meaning. To have repudiated with utmost vehemence the political significance of theocracy is the cardinal merit of Bloch's *Spirit of Utopia*.
>
> The order of the profane should be erected on the idea of happiness. The relation of this order to the Messianic is one of the essential teachings of the philosophy of history. It is a precondition of a mystical conception of history, containing a problem that can be represented figuratively. If one arrow points to the goal towards which the profane dynamic acts, and another marks the direction of Messianic intensity, then certainly the quest of free humanity for happiness runs counter to the Messianic direction; but just as a force can, through acting, increase another that is acting in the opposite direction, so the order of the profane assists, through being profane, the coming of the Messianic Kingdom. The profane, therefore, although not itself a category of this Kingdom, is a decisive category of its quietest approach.[11]

The lesson that modernity needs to learn is that "theocracy has no political, but only a religious meaning"; and that the "profane dynamic" of history that leads a "free humanity" to seek happiness will only help to bring about the Kingdom of God on condition that it keeps to a course exactly opposed to that of an incommensurable "Messianic intensity" of suffering. This Benjaminian fragment helps us to understand how Bakhtin's (also fragmentary, though much longer) intervention speaks to a historical context in which a peculiarly totalizing and triumphalist version of modernity's profane dynamic acknowledged no legitimating narrative other than its own. The pathos of modernity is a pathos of the hero not in itself reprehensible; its pathology is the hero who forgets that there is no history except in the other and that "consummation" is not the goal toward which history tends but the grace of an ending that comes down upon it.

There is, it is true, nothing quite as vivid in Bakhtin as Benjamin's well-known Angel of History who is propelled into the future by the storm of progress and yet stares resolutely backward, counting the cost of that upheaval in the light of the past.[12] What the two contemporaries nonetheless share is an ability—summed up in that brilliant image—to make us see modernity from outside, to help us think outside its premises. Perhaps the point of their nearest approach is when Bakhtin complements his account of the soul's formation in rhythm with a description of the soul's "surrounding world" ("A&H" 132). The world-for-me is the "horizon" of my "act-performing (forward-looking) consciousness"; the world-as-a-given that is fused with and consecrated by the soul-as-a-given is that soul's "environment" ("A&H" 134). The world that already exists has the hopeless finality of a word already uttered and it remains mired in mere unjustified factuality until I introduce into it the other, who is its hero, who does not exist outside it, and around whom it arranges itself as a positively valued ambience regardless of meaning. Premodern mythical thought and late-modern "aestheticizing intuitive philosophy" concur with each other and with art in thus seeing the world as the world of "man-as-the-other": "All characterizations and determination of present-on-hand being that set [the world] into dramatic motion blaze with the borrowed axiological light of *otherness*" ("A&H" 134). Being as the environment of the hero is one universal epiphany, the permanent possibility of apocalypse, irradiated by the concentrated essence of potential or actual stories—of all beginnings and middles and endings. When Bakhtin tells us that being conceived as the world's body lives only as the sensitively resonating environment of the soul of the other, and that it dies insofar as it lies within the horizon of spirit, we are in the presence of an aesthetics whose ontological pretensions are at last fully open to view.

Also manifest at this point are the gender bearings of Bakhtin's essay, inasmuch as being in his aesthetic ontology is explicitly gendered as feminine. Clearly he is writing here in a tradition of Orthodox spirituality that has a pedigree stretching back to Plato and the figure of Wisdom (Sophia) in Proverbs 8 and that had been revived by some of his compatriots at the end of the nineteenth century. On this view, Western spirituality had banished cosmology and left the world bereft by its elevation and abstraction of God; Western secularity had meanwhile deified man. The world forsaken by a God-centered Christianity had made good its loss by the demonic faith of secular humanism. This tradition of Russian spirituality sees these opposites as bedfellows, offering to define itself against both by positing as the substratum of the Trinity a fourth (and feminine) principle known as Sophia, the wisdom of God: Godhead in its aspect of created oneness, God's body, mediatrix between heaven and earth. Bakhtin echoes in his aesthetics the cosmological theory of Vladimir Solovyov, the chief Russian theorist of "sophiology," for whom everything issues everlastingly from the union of an active Logos and a passive Sophia.[13] Nowhere is this gendering of being more explicit than in his brief phenomenological account of dancing. In the dance, Bakhtin finds the paradox of "passive activity," a transcendental androgyny in which yet other epiphanic wonders are played out:

> In dancing, my exterior, visible only to others and existing only for others, coalesces with my inner, self-feeling, organic activity. In dancing, everything inward in me strives to come to the outside, strives to coincide with my exterior. In dancing, I become "bodied" in being to the highest degree; I come to participate in the being of others. What dances in me is my *present-on-hand* being (that has been affirmed from outside)—my *sophianic* being dances in me, the *other* dances in me. . . . Dancing represents the ultimate limit of my passive self-activity, but the latter occurs everywhere in life. I am passively active whenever my action is not conditioned by the purely meaning-directed activity of my *I-for-myself*, but rather is justified from present-on-hand being itself, from nature; that is, whenever this present-on-hand being is elementally active in me rather than the spirit. . . . Passive self-activity . . . does not enrich being with what is in principle unattainable; it does not alter the meaning-governed countenance of being. ("A&H" 137)

Dance does not reconcile body and soul because, for Bakhtin and the spiritual tradition he represents, body and soul are on the same plane in terms of value and never in conflict anyway. What it undoubtedly does is to figure on earth the union of heaven and earth at the end of history; or alternatively: heaven is that ideal coincidence of inner and outer in me that their optimal coincidence in dance encourages us to imagine. Dance, in short, replays the Incarnation in reverse; it is very properly, then, sophianic insofar as Sophia in her godly-creaturely ambiguity is the guarantee that this *theosis* of "man" is anything but a loss of "body."

The importance of this discussion of the dance (and a related discussion of joy) is its liminal status where the aesthetic is concerned: its placing at that border where art and the holy and the everyday meet, or at least give promise of each other; its very removal from "art" in any parochially European or modern sense. Bakhtin thereby ensures not only that we remain decisively in a space beyond the subject-object model, and are therefore never in danger of losing that defamiliarizing gaze upon modernity that he is akin to Benjamin in so valuably offering us, but also that we have access to the positive side of that critical optic, namely, a posing of the question of being, so notoriously forgotten in modern philosophy and in those theologies that have yielded crucial territory to its secularized reason. For what Heidegger calls the "forgetting of being" is what Bakhtin might have called our forgetting of the other—that other in whom alone I rejoice and who alone dances in me when I dance. The modernity that we see from outside is reminded of those androgynous experiential encounters with being, those experiences of at once encompassing and being encompassed, that it has for so long exiled beyond its purview in favor of the masculine movement of knowing. The paradox of "passive activity" in such states directs us to the outsideness of outsideness itself, taking us back into the ungrounded ground that is presupposed both in the world of tasks and risks and in the movement of (aesthetic) love by which the heroes of that world are consummated.

Transforming Forms: The Hero as a Whole of "Meaning"

Coming at last to the hero as a "whole of meaning," we can return to that seeming contradiction of propositions with which I began. If the focus here on forms of speech and writing is a foretaste of the turn Bakhtin would soon take from the act to the word, it is all the more remarkable that the novel has no place among those forms. Thus, it is that we begin with "confessional self-accounting" and end with the saint's life, while the properly modern forms (here represented by biography and autobiography) have to find a place for themselves within this frame. By the same token, the premodern forms are viewed from their limits—limits that are in no sense seen as negative, but are valued as the very source of their peculiar powers and effects. And so it should be: aesthetics is for Bakhtin the most welcoming of discourses, treating those cultural texts that elude or antedate the whole category of "art" not as the historically superseded but simply as the differently oriented whose difference from the strictly aesthetic is exactly its value. In examining from the standpoint of aesthetics forms that date from before the enlightened modernity that invented the category of the aesthetic, Bakhtin reconceives the forms of modernity as belonging not to any linear progression from the premodern but rather to a continuum of mutual illumination and animation, a dimension he will later call "great time." By showing as he does that the secular forms are transformations of the founding forms of Christian belief, he effects at a stroke the archaization of secularity and the modernization of spirituality. For example, he suggests very strongly the transhistorical power of confessional self-accounting when he claims that the characteristic forms of modern writing are merely confession diverted or perverted: irony and cynicism can be traced to confession that has a theomachic or anthropomachic cast, fighting against the judgment of God or man or both. Confession's worst perversion is invective, which utters in tones of malice all that the other might utter penitentially about herself, marking her as the one who *has no other.* The forms of despair relate inwardly to those of faith: just as the aesthetic whole of a Dostoevsky novel embraces the rhythmless confessions of its heroes, so the ethical-aesthetic perspective opened up here returns even the perversions of grace to the acts that they negate.[14]

Autobiography in Bakhtin's generic schema is marked off as decisively modern by the fact that in it I internalize a "possible other" ("A&H" 152), anticipating others' memories of myself, partially assimilating myself to the world of heroes. Measured by ideal-typical criteria of the aesthetic that absolutely distinguish author from hero and that for Bakhtin are classically epitomized in the lyric, it is a hybrid form. Its author is no more the pure artist "consummating" from without an episode of life-as-it-is-lived than its hero is the purely ethical agent immersed in that life. Writing a modern "life" for myself, I as author forever strive and equally forever fail to place myself in the shoes of that characteristically modern "superaddressee" called posterity. If autobiography is then "highly insecure or precarious" and if it "points beyond its own bounds" ("A&H" 165), then that ethical-aesthetic hybridity is just what will later for Bakhtin give the whole field of novelistic discourse— of modern narrative—its power to intervene in our late modernity. Miming the project of self-grounding that is modernity's great conceptual and experiential innovation, the syncretic and problematic aesthetic activity of modern storytelling nonetheless so re-imagines that project as to neutralize the pathologies to which it has led historically. Dostoevsky matters so much for Bakhtin because his writing keeps faith with modernity's promise of freedom while resisting its will to totality. The polyphonic novel is a space in which cynical and ironic voices are given full weight and free play, where heroes sound like (but are not) authors and the author sounds like (but is not) just one hero among others, and where relativism and dogmatism are no longer locked in binary opposition. Modern writing takes on the aspect of a *felix culpa*, a fortunate fall: grace—the reality of absolute understanding, truth telling, and forgiveness—is expelled beyond the space of the text not in order for cynicism to triumph but to preserve both (human) cynicism and (divine) grace in their creative separateness. Or, to vary the metaphor: in modern writing we have the principle of the minimum dose, a homeopathic cure for the ills of modernity.

To conclude, then: In the classical forms Bakhtin posits an archaic source for modern secularity; in the Christian forms he encodes, conversely, an archaic source for a spirituality no less perennially modern; modernity's true novelties are those problematic forms that invent what he calls "biographical value," and that subsist on the boundary between the "produced work" and the "*act* performed" ("A&H" 165). It is in this space that he would soon place the novel, leaving behind ideal-typical analysis and staking all upon this upstart aesthetic hybrid and its fortunes in history. Philosophy expands to take into its long view this form of contemporaneity; the novel for its part, in all its aesthetic hybridity, keeps philosophy focused on that aesthetic-ethical boundary where culture engages most directly with the world of answerable deeds in which we all live.

Notes

A version of this essay was first published in *Dialogism* 1 (1998): 57–73; it is reprinted by permission of the editors.

1. Sergey Bocharov, "Conversations with Bakhtin," translated by Stephen Blackwell, introduction and translation edited by Vadim Liapunov, *PMLA* 109 (1994): 1019 (the interview in question took place on 29 October 1974); M. M. Bakhtin, "Epic and Novel," in *DI* 27.

2. In this paragraph and the two following I have borrowed formulations and lines of argument from my "The Post-Apartheid Sublime: Rediscovering the Extraordinary," in *Writing South Africa: Literature, Apartheid, and Democracy, 1970–1995*, ed. Derek Attridge and Rosemary Jolly (Cambridge: Cambridge Univ. Press, 1997), 57–74. See also n. 13.

3. For Bakhtin's recorded reflections on "spiritual freedom" as "true freedom," see Nicholas Rzhevsky, "Kozhinov on Bakhtin," *New Literary History* 25 (1994): 429–44. This article, among others, is also the source of the assertion in my first paragraph that Bakhtin thought of himself as a philosopher (see 435).

4. This observation is made by Jürgen Habermas; see his "Modernity—An Incomplete Project," in *Postmodern Culture*, ed. Hal Foster (London: Pluto Press, 1985), 3.

5. See the epilogue to Erich Auerbach, *Mimesis: The Representation of Reality in Western Literature*, trans. Willard R. Trask (Princeton: Princeton Univ. Press, 1953), 555. For an early-twentieth-century Russian view of the relationship of Christianity and Western modernity from an intellectual with whom the early Bakhtin may have identified, see Mikhail Bulgakov, *A Bulgakov Anthology*, ed. James Pain and Nicholas Zernov (London: SPCK, 1976). The following observation might be taken as representative: "The new Europe has been spiritually nurtured and educated by the Christian Church, and modern European culture with its science and learning is Christian in origin, although it is beginning to forget this" (62).

6. See especially Erich Auerbach, "Sermo Humilis," in *Literary Language and Its Public in Late Latin Antiquity and in the Middle Ages*, trans. Ralph Manheim (Princeton: Princeton Univ. Press, 1965), 27–66.

7. Vladimir Lossky, *The Mystical Theology of the Eastern Church* (Cambridge and London: James Clarke, 1957), 14, 9.

8. See editorial notes nos. 80 and 81 to M. M. Bakhtin, "A&H" (243); M. M. Bakhtin, *RAHW* 56–57 and 78; and Erich Auerbach, "St. Francis of Assisi

in Dante's *Commedia*," in *Scenes from the Drama of European Literature*, trans. Catherine Garvin (Manchester: Manchester Univ. Press, 1984), 79–98.

9. Rowan Williams, *The Wound of Knowledge: Christian Spirituality from the New Testament to St. John of the Cross* (London: Darton, Longman and Todd, 1979), 108.

10. The feminization of the hero, while not Bakhtin's explicit formulation, is consonant with his aesthetic ontology.

11. Walter Benjamin, "Theologico-Political Fragment," in *One-Way Street, and Other Writings*, trans. Edmund Jephcott and Kingsley Shorter (London and New York: Verso, 1979), 155–56.

12. Walter Benjamin, "Theses on the Philosophy of History," in *Illuminations: Essays and Reflections*, trans. Harry Zohn (London: Jonathan Cape, 1970), 259–60.

13. In the preparation of this brief excursus on sophiology I have drawn on the following: Caitlin Matthews, *Sophia Goddess of Wisdom: The Divine Feminine from Black Goddess to World-Soul* (London: Mandala, 1991); and Samuel David Cioran, *Vladimir Solov'ev and the Knighthood of the Divine Sophia* (Waterloo, Ont.: Wilfrid Laurier Univ. Press, 1977).

14. In this paragraph and the one following I have once again borrowed from my "The Post-Apartheid Sublime" (see note 2).

The First and the Second Adam in Bakhtin's Early Thought

Ruth Coates

One of the consistent features of Bakhtin's thought is a predilection for mutually hostile, dynamic binary oppositions, one pole of which is morally elevated above the other. For example, "monologism" is set up against "polyphony," the "centripetal" forces of language do battle with their "centrifugal" enemies, and "official" culture is constantly under threat from the guerrilla warfare of "unofficial" cultural forms. These oppositions can be traced back to Bakhtin's earliest essays, *Toward a Philosophy of the Act* and "Author and Hero in Aesthetic Activity" (circa 1920–23), an analysis of which, I believe, reveals their point of departure to be the Christian concept of the struggle between good and evil. According to Christian theology, evil enters the human domain, with death in tow, at the moment when Adam and Eve disobey God by sampling the fruit from the Tree of Knowledge of Good and Evil, that is, with the Fall. Thereafter God's law of life fights a hopeless battle with sin's law of death until the second Adam is sent, in the Incarnation, to redeem humankind by his own, sacrificial, death. My contention is that Bakhtin creatively mobilizes the motifs of fall and incarnation to articulate his worldview, one of the most unshakeable premises of which is that the world is being fought over by two implacably opposed forces and that its survival depends on the continuing resilience (if not the outright victory) of the "good" one.[1] This conviction survived the transition from philosophy to literary theory that Bakhtin made when he wrote *Problems of Dostoevsky's Art* (1929), but not without significant internal modification. The second purpose of this essay is to bring out the modulations in Bakhtin's treatment of the two motifs I have identified, modulations that reflect critical developments in Bakhtin's worldview as a whole.

The Pathos of the Fall

Toward a Philosophy of the Act is suffused with the pathos of the Fall. The essay elaborates a view of the world[2] as fundamentally split, and split in such a way as to impoverish life and endanger culture. It is polemically addressed to trends in philosophy and the other sciences that were dominant at the time Bakhtin was writing and that, in his view, were failing to engage with the world as a complex and vital "event" in a continual process of development.[3] Bakhtin maintains that this failure led to a "schism" (*raskol*) being opened up between the actual products of intellectual activity and the living cultural processes that give rise to them:

> And as a result, two worlds confront each other, two worlds that have absolutely no communication with each other and are mutually impervious: the world of culture and the world of life, the only world in which we create, cognize, contemplate, live our lives, and die for—the world in which the acts of our activity are objectified and the world in which these acts actually proceed and are actually accomplished once and only once. (*TPA* 2)

In his analysis, the "world of culture" is negatively evaluated as "given," that is, finalized and closed, whereas the "world of life" receives a positive evaluation as "posited," or open and incomplete.

The "dualism of cognition and life" (*TPA* 7) is first and foremost lamentable because, once detached from the "world of life," the "world of culture" becomes morally unaccountable: there is no longer any "way out" of the abstract-cognitive into the concrete-ethical realm. As a result, both realms are impoverished, the former losing its vitality, and the latter its meaning. Worse, thought detached from life can take a dangerous autonomous path: Bakhtin likens it to "the world of technology: it knows its own immanent law, and it submits to that law in its impetuous and unrestrained development, in spite of the fact that it has long evaded the task of understanding the cultural purpose of that development, and may serve evil rather than good" (*TPA* 7). This situation amounts to nothing less than a crisis of culture. *Toward a Philosophy of the Act* is Bakhtin's attempt to analyze the symptoms and propose a cure.

There is perhaps nothing particularly original about the general thrust of Bakhtin's arguments. In the early decades of the twentieth century, representatives of the phenomenological movement in western Europe were all concerned about the direction the sciences were taking, and were developing projects to restore the relevance and credibility of philosophy. However, Bakhtin's account is striking for its recourse to the Christian worldview both in the way it describes the problem and in its formulation of the proposed solution. I have suggested that *Toward a Philosophy of the Act* is suffused with the Christian pathos of fallenness. This is expressed in particular through the Russian prefixes *ot-* (denoting movement "off," "from," and "away") and *samo-* (meaning "self"), which occur with astonishing frequency throughout the essay. *Ot-* attaches to a whole matrix of expressions used by Bakhtin to describe the initiation or the perpetuation of the "schism" between cultural product and human action, theory and practice, and connotes the biblical sense of man's cutting himself off, or falling away, from God.[4] *Samo-* is used in the context of a consistently negative evaluation of autonomy, be this the dangerous autonomy of culture once divorced from life, or the false autonomy of human beings who abrogate responsibility for their actions by claiming to have nothing to do with the world: The latter are derided as *samozvantsy*, impostors or pretenders, literally, "those who name themselves." The verb *pretendovat'* (to "claim falsely" or "pretend") is itself employed in this context. Such usages strongly connote the bid of Adam and Eve for autonomy from God as they eat the fruit of the Tree of Knowledge of Good and Evil in the Garden of Eden. Frequently the two prefixes are brought together in one sentence, for example, "[t]he detached [*otorvannyi*: literally, 'torn off'] content of the cognitional act comes to be governed by its own immanent laws, according to which it then develops as if it had a will of its own [*samoproizvól'no*]" (*TPA* 7). And just as in the biblical account of fallen humanity, the essay's concept of a falsely conceived autonomy is bound up with the notion of pride, the sin of which all "impostors" are found guilty by Bakhtin (*TPA* 52).

The fall motif of *Toward a Philosophy of the Act* is greatly reinforced in "Author and Hero," which was originally conceived as an illustration of the "primary philosophy" being outlined in *Toward a Philosophy of the Act*: Bakhtin felt that, of all the branches of culture, art most nearly approximated life in its basic structures and could provide a convenient model for the purposes of philosophical investigation. Hence the "aesthetic activity" of the author of literary art is merely one form of the human act that has been isolated for further investigation. Indeed, the philosophical framework of the two essays is essentially the same: in particular, both rest on the same distinction between givenness and positedness, openness and closure. At the same time, "Author and Hero" introduces a completely new dimension to this framework, since Bakhtin's aesthetics is in the first instance *relational*. Whereas in *Toward a Philosophy of the Act* the authoring subject is faced with the "event of being," in "Author and Hero" he or she is faced with another human person, the "other," the object of aesthetic activity. This complicates the earlier essay's presentation of givenness and positedness, since we find a new and fundamental evaluative distinction being made between I (the author) and the other (the hero) with respect to these modes of existence: semantic and axiological closure is appropriate to the hero but pernicious in the author. Or, to be perhaps more precise, one's existence on what Bakhtin calls the cognitive and ethical plane of being (the plane that is the subject of *Toward a Philosophy of the Act*) is essentially posited and open, but one's existence on the aesthetic plane of being is by its nature given and closed. The term "hero" is applied to the self as the object of the aesthetic act. In effect, a person who is being subjected to aesthetic contemplation exists simultaneously on two levels, the ethical and the aesthetic, and is thus at the same time (ethical) subject and (aesthetic) object. The author/contemplator, on the other hand, is pure subject.

The picture of a divided world that stands in need of reintegration, painted in *Toward a Philosophy of the Act*, is in "Author and Hero" extended to the human condition. Bakhtin argues that we, as selves, are fragmented, incomplete, and as a consequence profoundly insecure: "In the dimension of time . . . I find only my own dispersed directedness, my unrealized desire and striving—the *membra disiecta* of my potential wholeness" ("A&H" 123). Consequently, we have an absolute aesthetic need for the other person, who can use his or her position outside of us to give us an integral form, and thereby can lift us out of the eternally unresolved ethical plane of existence onto the beautiful, harmonious, and complete aesthetic plane. The bestowal of form that constitutes the aesthetic act is a gift from author to hero, which the hero, as a subject (self) cannot and, crucially, may not (does not have the right to) bestow on himself or herself.

The fall motif makes itself particularly explicit in "Author and Hero" at those points in the narrative when Bakhtin condemns what he calls prideful attempts of the self to pursue his or her own form. Such attempts presume a claim to autonomy, to closure, which Bakhtin, as we have seen, believes to be both unnatural and morally wrong. The following passage provides an excellent illustration of this:

> Now, if my interior being *detached itself* from [*otryvaetsia ot*] the yet-to-be meaning confronting it . . . and if it opposes itself to that meaning as an independent value (becomes *self-sufficient* and *self-contented* in the face of meaning), then, in so doing, my interior being *falls into* [*vpadaet v*] a profound contradiction with itself, into a negation of itself [*samootritsanie*]. That is, it negates the content of its own being through the being of its factual givenness: it becomes a falsehood [*lozh'iu*: "lie"]—the being of falsehood and the falsehood of being. We could say that this constitutes a *fall* (a lapse into sin) [*grekhopadenie*] that is immanent to being and is experienced from within being: it is inherent in the tendency of being to become sufficient unto itself [*k samodostatochnosti*]; it is an inner *self-contradiction* of being—insofar as being pretends [*pretenduet*] here to self-contented abiding, in its presently given makeup, in the face of meaning; it is a *self-consolidated self-affirmation* on the part of being in defiance of the meaning that engendered it (a breaking off from the source); it is a movement that has suddenly come to a stop and is discontinued without justification—a movement that has turned its back on the goal that had brought it into being. . . . It is an incongruous and perplexed completedness that feels ashamed of its own form. ("A&H" 124, my emphasis)

The terminology of this passage is identical to that of *Toward a Philosophy of the Act*. There are no fewer than nine uses of the prefix "self" (the translator is faithful to all but two of them, which I have provided in square brackets, above). There is the verb *pretendovat'*, which, as I have noted above, means "to lay false claim to," in addition to its rendition here as "to pretend." There is the verb *otryvat'sia*, translated above as "detach from," but meaning literally "to tear itself away from." Finally, there are two references to falling (the root verb in Russian is *padat'*), including the Russian term for the Fall itself, *grekhopadenie*.

What the passage adds to the fall motif as it is manifested in *Toward a Philosophy of the Act* is precisely the concept of sin (*grekh*), which the *Concise Oxford Dictionary* defines as "the breaking of divine or moral law, especially by a conscious act" and which is the function of a *relationship*, constituting a willful act of disobedience to a more authoritative power. Indeed, it is easy and compelling to read this passage as a paraphrase of Genesis 3: I inhabit the world in an unsullied relationship of absolute dependency on the semantic future as Adam and Eve dwelled in Eden before the face of God. The relationship is severed on my own initiative by my defiant and unjustified bid for semantic autonomy, as Adam and Eve defied God by eating the fruit of the Tree of Knowledge of Good and Evil, because they believed that this would make them "like God" (Gen. 3:5, *RSV*) and thus no longer dependent on Him. As a result I fall into a warped state of self-contradiction and self-negation: like Adam and Eve, I become aware of my nakedness and experience the shame of my (unwarranted, premature, and self-imposed) form.

Some elucidation of this element of authority may be helpful here. It has been pointed out, most eloquently perhaps by Ann Jefferson,[5] that the author-hero relationship is an unequal one. The inequality is built into the conditions of the aesthetic relation: the author has an advantage over the hero insofar as he or she enjoys an external vantage point affording exclusive information on the hero, and therefore power over him or her. For example, the author may withhold the gift of form. In this the aesthetic act is like any other act of engagement in the world, the necessity of which Bakhtin argues in *Toward a Philosophy of the Act*. In the passage quoted above, the concepts of "meaning" (*smysl*), "source" (*istochnik*), and "goal" (*tsel'*) fulfill the function of the author, and this also perhaps requires some comment. For Bakhtin, the authorial role is ultimately modeled on a metaphysical category (he insists it is not located in time) which he refers to in various ways according to the object of discussion: for example, as the "absolute semantic future" (*smyslovoe absoliutnoe budushchee*), as the "Author," as a "higher authority" (*vysshaia instantsiia*), and as God.[6] What others can do for us aesthetically is imperfect: absolute meaning comes from beyond, from a completely different realm.

An interesting feature of the passage quoted above is the way it shifts from an analysis of the self to an analysis of being. Though the bulk of "Author and Hero" is devoted to human aesthetic need, Bakhtin does not lose sight of the plight of the world, his description of which recalls the lament of the apostle Paul that "the creation [has been] subjected to futility" and is in "bondage to decay" (Rom. 8:20–21, *RSV*):

What is already present-on-hand in all of being or the *countenance* of being *that has already determined itself* in respect to its content (i.e., the *'thisness'* of being) needs a justification outside the realm of meaning. For in relation to the yet-to-be-attained [*zadannoi*, or "posited"] fullness of meaning of the *event* of being, the "thisness" of being is only *factual* (obstinately present-on-hand). . . . Everything that *already exists* exists without justification: it has dared, as it were, to become already determinate and to abide (obstinately) in this determinateness within a world, the whole of which is *yet-to-be* in respect of its meaning and justification. ("A&H" 132–33)

In this passage, the world is presented as dual-aspected along the same lines as in *Toward a Philosophy of the Act*: it has both a given (closed, "present-on-hand") and a posited (open, indeterminate) aspect, of which the former is deemed improper and shameful by Bakhtin. The new ingredient here is the sense of the accountability of being as a whole to a metaphysical source of ultimate meaning, as a result of which there is a subtle sense of sin, conveyed in the concepts of justification (the world has no right to determine itself) and obstinacy (the world is being willfully disobedient).

Kenotic Incarnation

Taken together, then, we may say that *Toward a Philosophy of the Act* and "Author and Hero" present a picture of the world and of human experience as broken and internally divided, with a proneness to retreating into an illusion of autonomy that is at the same time the symptom of this division and its cause. Moving on from this, I believe it to be the case that both essays also seek to articulate a project of healing and reconciliation in response to their analysis, central to which is the figure of incarnation. Perhaps the most economical approach to this subject is through an analysis of Bakhtin's treatment of the figure of Christ. Taking this path, one is struck at the outset by the anthropocentrism of Bakhtin's "theology." While in both essays Christ is presented as a unique and revolutionary historical paradigm for human behavior, one that for the first time makes the redemption of existence possible, the redemption itself is carried out by human beings. Related to this is a second distinguishing "theological" feature: redemption in Bakhtin is always conceived as a process rather than an accomplished act, as a consequence of which the redemptive project is always in jeopardy.[7]

In *Toward a Philosophy of the Act* Bakhtin argues that the key to reconciling the worlds of theory and life is the voluntary participation of human individuals in the world through responsible action. Christ is introduced in this context as "[a] great symbol of self-activity, the descending [*niskhozhdenie*] of Christ. The world from which Christ has departed will no longer be the world in which he had never existed; it is, in its very principle, a different world" (*TPA* 16). All the central features of Bakhtin's theory of the act derive from Christ's example. First, and most importantly, there is its "kenotic" bias. "Kenosis" is a theological term that denotes the voluntary self-humiliation of Christ in the Incarnation, best articulated in Paul's Letter to the Philippians: "Have this mind among yourselves, which is yours in Christ Jesus, who, though he was in the form of God, did not count equality with God a thing to be grasped, but *emptied himself*, taking the form of a servant, being born in the likeness of men. And being found in human form he *humbled himself* and became obedient unto death, even death on a cross" (Phil. 2:5–8, *RSV,* my emphasis). This passage implicitly contrasts the humility and obedience of Christ—who subjects his divine status, which is rightfully his, to humiliation for the sake of the world—with the pride and disobedience of Adam and Eve. Bakhtin insists that truly responsible and redemptive human activity is also always rooted in sacrifice and conducted in a spirit of humility, and is not, as one might be tempted to argue, an egotistical act of self-projection: "One has to develop humility to the point of [*smirit'sia do*] participating in person and being answerable in person" (*TPA* 52). He further states, "One should remember that to live from within myself [*iz sebia*], from my own unique place in Being, does not yet mean at all that I live only for my own sake. For it is only from my own unique place that *self-sacrifice* [*zhertvovat'*] is possible, that is, the answerable centrality of myself can be a *self-sacrificing* centrality" (*TPA* 48). The concept of living *iz sebia*, literally "out of oneself," is linked to the kenotic motif: the self-emptying act of Christ is also expressed as a movement, as a descent (*niskhozhdenie*). Bakhtin describes each human act similarly, as a self-denying yet also self-transcending movement outward (the move is horizontal rather than vertical) into the world: "I *come upon* this world, inasmuch as I *come forth* or issue from within myself [*iskhozhu iz sebia*] in my performed act or deed of seeing, of thinking, of practical doing" (*TPA* 57). It is by risking this departure from myself that I am able to effect the reconciliation of the split between abstract meaning and concrete experience by embodying the one in the other.

Second, only when Christ becomes a flesh-and-blood human being is he able to interact with, and thus make an impact upon, the world, in particular, by making the final sacrifice of voluntary death.[8] Likewise, the spatial and temporal limits of human existence, human embodiment or incarnation, are for Bakhtin what make individual acts possible, necessary, and meaningful. Their possibility is, of course, contingent upon the borders that embodied existence establishes between any human self and the rest of the world: without borders there can be no individuation and, consequently, no discrete acts. Their meaningfulness derives from the fact that the interaction of an embodied subject with the world requires self-transcendence and therefore implies choice, at least in Bakhtin's view. As we have seen, in *Toward a*

Philosophy of the Act life's impostors are those who freely renounce self-transcendental interaction with the world in a solipsistic bid for autonomy. The choice to "go out of oneself" is morally freighted because of the uniqueness of each subject that also follows from the principle of embodiment. For Bakhtin, the most important aspect of human uniqueness from a phenomenological point of view is our unique *situatedness:* "I occupy a place in once-occurrent Being that is unique and never-repeatable, a place that cannot be taken by anyone else and is impenetrable for anyone else" (*TPA* 40). The moral necessity, even imperative, to act follows from this. Indeed, "[a]s *disembodied* [*razvoploshchennyi*] spirit, I lose my compellent, ought-to-be relationship to the world, I lose the actuality of the world. Man-in-general does not exist; *I* exist and a particular *concrete* other exists—my intimate [*blizhnii:* 'neighbor' in the biblical sense], my contemporary" (*TPA* 47, my emphasis). When one chooses not to interact with the world, with others, kenotically, one denies one's uniqueness and lives a "non-incarnated [*neinkarnirovannaia*] fortuitous life as an empty possibility" (*TPA* 43).

This choice is so crucial to Bakhtin because, as I have indicated above, the fate of being rests on human shoulders. For it is the action of embodied individuals that reconciles the empty world of theory with the concrete event of being, and it does this by concretizing abstract principles and truths, by investing theoretical time and space with "flesh and blood" (*TPA* 59), in short, by a process of *incarnation:* "an answerable deed . . . must not oppose itself to theory and thought, but must incorporate them into itself as necessary moments that are wholly answerable" (*TPA* 56). Thus the incarnational principle has a double manifestation in *Toward a Philosophy of the Act:* redemption is conditional upon the existence of embodied subjects, and it also consists in the embodiment of abstract concepts, just as Christ embodied the abstract concept of God.

Turning to "Author and Hero," we see the same centrality of the embodied subject, in this essay the aesthetic subject, or author, whose aesthetic activity is contingent upon his or her unique situatedness in time and space. From this unique position separate from and external to the hero/other (Bakhtin calls this *vnenakhodimost'*, "outsideness"), the author/self exploits his or her "surplus of vision" (*izbytok videniia*) to bestow the gift of form. Here the same moral imperative applies. Interpreting and applying the sphere of aesthetics very broadly, Bakhtin insists that we all experience aesthetic need, the need for form, and that only the other is, literally, in a position to rescue us from the excruciating formlessness of our lives as we experience them from the eternally unresolved ethical plane of being. Thus, the aesthetic act, freely performed for others, is a gracious act of *love*. Finally, there is the same kenotic impulse, the same self-renunciation, described as "the author's loving removal of himself [*ustranenie sebia*] from the field of the hero's life, his clearing of the whole field of life for the hero and his existence" ("A&H" 15).

It is therefore unsurprising to find that Christ is presented in this essay, as in *Toward a Philosophy of the Act,* as the perfect model of human activity:

> In Christ we find a synthesis of unique depth, the synthesis of *ethical solipsism* (man's infinite severity toward himself, i.e., an immaculately pure relationship to oneself) with *ethical-aesthetic kindness* toward the other. . . . All human beings divide for him into himself as the unique one—and all other human beings, into himself as the one bestowing loving mercy—and all others as receiving mercy, into himself as the savior—and all others as the saved, into himself as the one assuming the burden of sin and expiation—and all others as relieved of this burden and redeemed. ("A&H" 56)

It is notable that in this extract Bakhtin explicitly merges the categories of the ethical and the aesthetic ("ethical-aesthetic kindness toward the other"): the act of redemption can for him be described in terms of both, and ultimately the two are indistinguishable. The passage also gives strong expression to the motifs of self-denial and the moral obligations of uniqueness that I have been exploring.

Apart from incarnation as a precondition for redemptive action, "Author and Hero" also, of course, shares with *Toward a Philosophy of the Act* the equally central concept of incarnation as a form of salvation in itself. The gift of aesthetic form is nothing other than an embodiment of the object of aesthetic contemplation, whether in memory or in a material art form, such as a painting, a sculpture, or a novel. Such embodiment "saves" the fragmented self by removing him or her onto another plane of existence where life is eternal; thus the author wins for the hero an "aesthetic victory over death": "The deeper and more perfect the embodiment [*voploshchenie*], the more distinctly do we hear in it the definitive completion of death and at the same time the aesthetic victory over death—the contention of memory against death" ("A&H" 131). Here we can note the following fascinating distinction between the incarnational processes in *Toward a Philosophy of the Act* and "Author and Hero." Whereas in *Toward a Philosophy of the Act* incarnation rescues a closed world by drawing it into an open one, in "Author and Hero" the hero is rescued from an open world by being removed into a closed one. Both movements, however, involve the healing of a wound, the bridging of a divide.

Incarnation as the Penetrative Word

Approximately five years divide the "completion"[9] of the philosophical essays from the publication of Bakhtin's first monograph, *Problems of Dostoevsky's Art* (1929),[10] which, as its title suggests, is on a literary and literary-theoretical subject. Despite this, however, all the ideas expressed in it flow from the philosophical premises that Bakhtin had earlier worked out in *Toward a Philosophy of the Act* and "Author and Hero." One senses this intuitively when reading the book, which seems to transcend its immediate subject matter and to make a broad statement about the most fundamental structures of human experience. Moreover, certain sections of the work give quite explicit expression to its philosophical foundations, and in these sections the strong bond of the book with the earlier essays is absolutely plain.

The opening section of chapter 3, "The Idea in Dostoevsky," in which Bakhtin grounds his definition of the "monologic" author within a wider description of modern culture, is the most explicit of all in this respect. It is this section more than any other that persuades one of a direct link between the "abstract theoreticism," the "world of theory" of *Toward a Philosophy of the Act*, and the concept of "monologism." Having identified the indissoluble bond between the idea and the personality in Dostoevsky's representation of character, in which self-consciousness is said to dominate, Bakhtin embarks on a highly critical analysis of the role of the idea in non-Dostoevskian, "monologic" works, the principal feature of which, he argues, is the detachment of the idea from the personality: "Such an idea, in itself, belongs to *no one*. The hero is merely the carrier of an independently valid idea; as a true signifying idea it gravitates toward some impersonal, systemically monologic context; in other words, it gravitates toward the systemically monologic worldview of the author himself" (*PDP* 79). Already at this point we can note the consistency of Bakhtin's denigration of abstract, systemic, impersonal truths with *Toward a Philosophy of the Act*. He goes on to claim that the principles of monologism in literature "go far beyond the boundaries of artistic creativity alone; they are the principles behind the entire ideological culture of recent times" (*PDP* 80). Despite a disingenuous disclaimer, so characteristic of *Problems of Dostoevsky's Art*, to the effect that philosophy is not relevant to his discussion, the analysis of "ideological monologism" that follows is directed largely at philosophical idealism, in which "[t]he monistic principle, that is, the affirmation of the unity of *existence* [*bytiia*], is, in idealism, transformed into the unity of the *consciousness*" (*PDP* 80), in practice always the unity of a single consciousness:

> Alongside this unified and inevitably *single* consciousness can be found a multitude of empirical human consciousnesses. From the point of view of "consciousness in general" this plurality of consciousnesses is accidental and, so to speak, superfluous. Everything in them that is essential and true is incorporated into the unified context of "consciousness in general" and deprived of its individuality. That which is individual, that which distinguishes one consciousness from another and from others, is cognitively not essential and belongs to the realm of an individual human being's psychical organization and limitations. . . . True judgements are not attached to a personality, but correspond to some unified, systemically monologic context. (*PDP* 81)

This passage is entirely consistent with Bakhtin's attack on "abstract theoreticism" in *Toward a Philosophy of the Act,* directed at the (neo-Kantian) idealistic philosophical reductionism of his day, which he felt, as we have seen, had lost touch with the "event of being," thereby creating a crying cultural need to reintegrate truth, science, into life. Individuality can only be meaningful—that is, more than mere biological and psychic separateness—when it incorporates truth and gives it roots in reality. Bakhtin felt that Dostoevsky was swimming against the cultural tide with his vision of truth embodied in personality.

The "polyphony" of the Dostoevskian novel may therefore be read as an artistic model for Bakhtin's ideal pluralistic and vital world, in which the only unity is the antireductionist unity of existence. The ultimate safeguard against degeneration into monologic tyranny in this world, as in Dostoevsky's novels, is embodiment, or incarnation. Once again, Christ is introduced as a model in this regard, and though this time the analogy is ascribed to Dostoevsky's worldview, the parallels with Bakhtin's early essays are so strong that we need not hesitate to dismiss this as a device to placate the censors. Christ first receives mention, in fact, in connection with the very status of the idea that I have been discussing:

> For Dostoevsky there are no ideas, no thoughts, no positions which belong to no one, which exist "in themselves." Even "truth in itself" he presents in the spirit of Christian ideology, as incarnated in Christ; that is, he presents it as a personality entering into relationships with other personalities. (*PDP* 31–32)

This passage is highly reminiscent of Bakhtin's own stated view, in "Author and Hero," that "[a]ny valuation is an act of assuming an individual position in being; even God had to incarnate himself in order to bestow mercy, to suffer, and to *forgive*—had to descend, as it were, from the abstract standpoint of justice" ("A&H" 129). The incarnational principle is opposed to abstraction of any kind, at any level. Further, when applying it on a large scale, to human communities, Bakhtin appeals to the image of a church, the body of Christ (again, not omitting the required disclaimer):

> Dostoevsky's world is profoundly *pluralistic.* If we were to seek an image toward which this whole world gravitates, an image in the spirit of Dostoevsky's own worldview, then it would be the church as a communion of unmerged souls, where sinners and righteous men come together; or perhaps it would be the image of Dante's world, where multi-leveledness is extended into eternity, where there are the penitent and the unrepentant, the damned and the saved. (*PDP* 26–27)

In *Problems of Dostoevsky's Art* Bakhtin in fact addresses the problem of community for the first time (in *Toward a Philosophy of the Act* the subject stands against an undifferentiated "event of being," while the argument of "Author and Hero" is based on the I-Thou dyad). These two images, the image of Christ and the image of the church, succinctly convey the central requisite features of an embodied community: coexistence (the "communion of unmerged souls") and interaction ("a personality entering into relationships with other personalities"), the first constituting the guarantee of alterity, and thus semantic plurality, the second providing the wherewithal for unity, and thus a higher, integral meaning.[11]

The incarnational principle, then, protects the world against that of "fall" in *Problems of Dostoevsky's Art* as it does in the philosophical essays. However, when it comes to the aesthetic relation of author and hero, the picture in *Problems of Dostoevsky's Art* is somewhat more complex. For the first time in this book, it appears, Bakhtin begins to take full account of the implications of human fallenness for the role of author. For in "Author and Hero," while the author/self is as fragmented and needy as the heroes/others with whom he or she is confronted, the possibility that the author might abuse the authorial role, might act irresponsibly, is largely rejected, even though in *Toward a Philosophy of the Act* this potential is clearly articulated in general terms. In "Author and Hero," all authors are benign, since the aesthetic act must of necessity be motivated by love.[12] The introduction of the monologic author, with its consequent bifurcation of the authorial role into two types, clearly represents a shift from this position. It also constitutes a refinement of the concept of irresponsible action as worked out in *Toward a Philosophy of the Act*. Now, the false and prideful claim to autonomy of the early essay is shown to consist not so much in passivity, in a refusal to act (though a certain laziness on the part of the monologic author is, in fact, implied), as in an active exploitation of one's transgredient authorial perspective for one's own egotistical ends. The monologic author exploits art, like a thing, to project his or her own worldview at the expense of others' worldviews.

One, perhaps unintended, consequence of this is that a shadow is cast over the authorial position in general, undermining the role even of the favored polyphonic author. Again, apparently for the first time, in *Problems of Dostoevsky's Art*, Bakhtin takes full cognizance of the fact that, from the hero's point of view, an author is as abstract a concept, and as materially absent, as the transcendent God is for real human beings. In *Problems of Dostoevsky's Art* he struggles to get around this, positing the polyphonic author as an equal participant in dialogue with his heroes, who are "capable of standing *alongside* their creator, capable of not agreeing with him and even of rebelling against him" (*PDP* 6). The polyphonic author is said to be in a different league from his monologic counterpart: Dostoevsky does not abuse his "outsidedness"; the self-sacrifice (kenosis) inherent in the aesthetic act is expressed as a radical and humble self-restraint, as absolute respect for the self-consciousness of his heroes, as a refusal to use his authorial privilege to finalize his characters in any way. But ultimately, of course, the transgredient position of the author has to remain intact if the object of Bakhtin's own discourse—the poetics of a particular novelist, Dostoevsky—is not to disappear. This poses a dilemma for Bakhtin that he was to wrestle with for the rest of his life, and that eventually led him to theorize the silencing, if not the death, of the author.[13] This step is not taken, however, in *Problems of Dostoevsky's Art*, which remains torn between the old model of loving transgredience and a new and impossible utopia of authorial-heroic equality.

Does incarnation, then, have nothing to offer in response to the tyrannical potential of authorial transgredience, this "new" manifestation of fall, so disastrous for culture? At first glance it would seem not. One entire strain of the incarnation motif as it is articulated in "Author and Hero" is jettisoned once and for all in *Problems of Dostoevsky's Art*: the "gift of form" no longer saves but enslaves; it has been recast as reification, as an act of violence that violates the sacred freedom of the heroic soul. No author who sought Bakhtin's respect would dare to represent others in this way. The hero has the right to his or her fragmentariness and "inner striving," to seek meaning, however vainly, without having it imposed from without.

However, this notwithstanding, I would like to argue that *Problems of Dostoevsky's Art* also manifests an intensification of interest in incarnation, not only as an antidote to abstract, tyrannical truth, as explored above but also, I suggest, as a potentially new model of "authorship." In the fourth chapter, "Discourse in Dostoevsky," Bakhtin lays out for the reader a whole typology of forms of discourse. He goes on to present Dostoevsky as a master of "double-voiced discourse," defined by him as "discourse with an orientation toward someone else's discourse" (*PDP* 199). His survey of the development of double-voiced discourse in Dostoevsky's works proceeds chronologically, culminating in an examination of the great novels, *Crime and Punishment, The Idiot, The Devils,* and *The Brothers Karamazov.* Discussing the early works, Bakhtin pays most attention to heroic monologues and to narrative discourse. Among other things, Bakhtin notes how the narrator's speech becomes less prominent, and certainly less parodic, in the later period (*PDP* 227). Instead, what interests him about the novels is first and foremost Dostoevsky's handling of dialogue between characters (*PDP* 237), and it is significant, I think, that he focuses on a highly limited number of examples of such dialogue, all of which center on the notion of the "penetrative word."

The penetrative word is defined twice by Bakhtin, the first time as "a word capable of actively and confidently interfering in the interior dialogue of the other person, helping that person to find his own voice" (*PDP* 242), and later on as "a firmly monologic, undivided discourse, a word without a sideward glance, without a loophole, without internal polemic" (*PDP* 249). Prince Myshkin is the first character to whom Bakhtin ascribes this dialogic technique, which in his case arises out of "his deep and fundamental horror at speaking a decisive and ultimate word about another person" (*PDP* 242). He and others like him (in specific relation to the penetrative word Bakhtin also mentions Tikhon of *The Devils* and Alyosha Karamazov) use their "outsideness," their position as an embodied other, to love and affirm their partners in dialogue, without, crucially, imposing a definition on them that would be a violation of their own position on themselves. Thus, Myshkin encourages and affirms that side of Nastasya Filippovna's own consciousness that justifies and forgives her for her depraved sexual past; Tikhon persuades Stavrogin to acknowledge that better side of himself that repents of his actions; and Alyosha Karamazov teases out Ivan's unacknowledged sense of guilt at his father's murder and absolves him of it: "Alyosha, as 'other,' carries tones of love and reconciliation, which are of course impossible on Ivan's lips in relationship to himself" (*PDP* 256). In other words, these characters offer a model for responsible, embodied authoring in which, as before, their "otherness" is absolutely necessary to the "hero," and yet who kenotically assist the latter to approach a finalized image of themselves (their own "monologic, undivided discourse"), rather than doing the finalizing for them.

It cannot be a coincidence, either, that the major representatives of penetrative discourse are either Christlike figures themselves (Myshkin), or have found a stable understanding of themselves under the profound influence of Christianity (Tikhon, Alyosha). One is reminded here of Bakhtin's reading of Dostoevsky's attitude to truth:

> [W]hat unfolds before Dostoevsky is not a world of objects, illuminated and ordered by his monologic thought, but a world of consciousnesses mutually illuminating one another, a world of yoked-together semantic human orientations. Among them Dostoevsky seeks the highest and most authoritative orientation, and he perceives it not as his own true thought, but as another authentic human being and his discourse. The image of the ideal human being or the image of Christ represents for him the resolution of ideological quests. This image or this highest voice must crown the world of voices, must organize and subdue it. (*PDP* 97)

Dostoevsky's polyphonic world and Bakhtin's "event of being" are pluralistic, but not relativistic. There is no single all-consuming abstract truth, but there are incarnated truths, some of which are more authoritative than others. Individuals may never, in such a world, be forced to acknowledge an alien truth, but they may, if they wish, make a compelling one their own. This is what Bakhtin, many years later, in his notes toward the revision of his Dostoevsky book, was to call "persuasion through love" ("TRDB" 292).

I have tried to draw out the significance to Bakhtin, in his first decade as an author, of the dynamic tension in Christian theology between the first and the second Adam, the Fall and the Incarnation, particularly the movement from the one to the other. The figure of the two Adams is especially appropriate to Bakhtin since, as we have seen, in his work redemption is delivered by human beings, and Christ is valued precisely for his human, flesh-and-blood dimension. In Bakhtin the proud (arrogant) and selfish (autonomous) behavior of those who would perpetuate the split between word and deed, culture and life, or, worse, exploit it for their own ends is countered by the self-sacrificing action of others whose main concern is the integrity of the world and of other human beings. At the same time, Bakhtin's understanding of "fall" develops from a basically passive concept (the refusal to act of *Toward a Philosophy of the Act*) to a vigorously active one (the reifying activity of the monologic author). In response to this, the aesthetic function of incarnation, the embodying activity of human "authors," is brought into question, and by 1929 has yielded to an intensified notion of embodiment as the precondition for a vital, plural world, one feature of which is a new kind of healing and saving aesthetic activity that may be termed "dialogic."

Notes

1. As Caryl Emerson says in her afterword, my formulation here may seem to point to a Manichean side to Bakhtin. While the Orthodox bias in his work which this book so clearly establishes makes one hesitant to proclaim Bakhtin a dualist, it is nevertheless striking that he never offers us a vision of the triumph of good (his negative response to Pinsky's question as to the possibility of this may not have been as rhetorical as Lock supposes). I believe it is also true to say that, for all Bakhtin's devotion, it is not the Byzantine "harrowing of hell" which inspires him in Christ, but the more quintessentially Russian kenotic self-humiliation and self-giving love (see also Jacobs). As I argue, the redemption of the world is always in process (and in jeopardy) for Bakhtin: he never once mentions the Crucifixion as the defeat of death once and for all.

2. In both *Toward a Philosophy of the Act* and "Author and Hero" Bakhtin employs the term *bytie*, literally, "being," to denote the concept of "everything that exists." I have used the English terms "world" and "existence" variously to convey the sense of *bytie*, in addition to the clumsier and less accessible "being."

3. For a lucid exposition of the philosophical context of *Toward a Philosophy of the Act* and "Author and Hero in Aesthetic Activity," see Randall Poole's essay in this volume.

4. Some examples include: *otpavshaia* (fallen away): "A life that has fallen away from answerability cannot have a philosophy" (*TPA* 56); *otpustivshii* (having released): "the performed act itself, having released theory from itself, begins to deteriorate" (*TPA* 55); and *otdaetsia* (gives itself over): "The whole wealth of culture

is placed in the service of [literally, gives itself over to] the biological act" (*TPA* 55). There are many others. The very word for "abstract" (*otvlechennyi*) contains the prefix, as does the verb "to reject, refuse" (*otkazat'sia*).

5. Ann Jefferson, "Bodymatters: Self and Other in Bakhtin, Sartre and Barthes," in *Bakhtin and Cultural Theory*, ed. Ken Hirschkop and David Shepherd (Manchester: Manchester Univ. Press, 1989), 152–77.

6. See, for example, *TPA* 122 (*Smyslovoe absoliutnoe budushchee*: Liapunov translates this as "this absolute future, the future of meaning"); 79 ("Author"); and 206 ("highest authority": Liapunov translates this as "the highest level of authority").

7. On the dualistic implications of this, see note 1 above.

8. See "Author and Hero" 129: "Any valuation is an act of assuming an individual position in being; even God had to incarnate himself in order to bestow mercy, to suffer, and to *forgive*—had to descend, as it were, from the abstract standpoint of justice."

9. Neither essay was in fact ever formally completed, nor were they prepared for publication.

10. *Problemy tvorchestva Dostoevskogo* (Leningrad: Priboi, 1929). The text of this work has not been published as a separate English translation. As is well known, Bakhtin later revised and expanded the book for publication in 1963 as *Problemy poetiki Dostoevskogo* (Moscow: Sovetskii Pisatel', 1963). The later version exists in translation as *Problems of Dostoevsky's Poetics*, edited and translated by Caryl Emerson (Minneapolis: Univ. of Minnesota Press, 1984). In this article I refer by name only to the earlier work, but quotations are taken from Caryl Emerson's translation of the later one, which is abbreviated *PDP* with page numbers cited in the text, since all the passages quoted were incorporated without change into the second book.

11. Alexandar Mihailovic, in his essay for this volume, and more fully in his book *Corporeal Words: Mikhail Bakhtin's Theology of Discourse* (Evanston: Northwestern Univ. Press, 1997), persuasively traces Bakhtin's models of unity in diversity to early Christian formulations of the coexistence of divine and human natures in Christ (the Chalcedonian definition "without confusion or separation") and of the three Persons of the Trinity (the patristic concept of *perichoresis*, or interpenetration) (*Corporeal Words* 167–77).

12. Alan Jacobs's article for this volume explores this contention of Bakhtin's in depth.

13. For an elaboration of this idea, and generally for a more extensive treatment of the influence of Christianity on Bakhtin's writings, see my *Christianity in Bakhtin: God and the Exiled Author* (Cambridge: Cambridge Univ. Press, 1998).

Bakhtin, Laughter, and Christian Culture

Sergei Averintsev

This article poses the question of whether it is possible to combine Bakhtin's theory of the "culture of laughter" and its subordinate internal categories—"carnivalization" and the "menippea"—with Christian culture and, in particular, with that old tradition according to which Christ never laughed. To this end, I will analyze some theoretical and historical aspects of the philosophy of laughter and argue that Bakhtin's life experience is more pivotal to the theory of the "culture of laughter" than his theoretical and historical constructs.

This is not an article on Bakhtin. This is an extended note on the margins of Bakhtin's book on Rabelais.[1]

Did not Bakhtin, the thinker who tirelessly repeated that not a single human word could be either final or complete, invite us to continue speaking "on the subject of" and to keep thinking "tangentially," unwinding in one way or another the uninterrupted thread of our conversation? As our common teacher, he did not let anyone be his "follower" in the trivial sense of the word. "Bakhtinianism," if one can speak of such a thing at all, contradicts the most profound intention of Bakhtin's thought. One cannot lose Bakhtin by diverging from his point of view, but it is possible to lose him by leaving the dialogical situation.

Neither the bonds of a scientific or even philosophical tradition nor the continuity of a "school," but something lighter, something more resilient yet more durable, unites us with Bakhtin—namely, the aforementioned thread of our conversation whose coherence is maintained at each turn.

There is one "theological" (paratheological, as it were) question that has not been posed in Bakhtin's book, *Rabelais and His World*, although if we were to extend almost all of the book's logical trains of thought beyond what is actually said, they would lead us to this question and intersect in it. We have been reminded of this question recently: it was dramatized in a fourteenth-century stage setting, and not without connection with improvisations on Bakhtinian themes as well, in Umberto Eco's novel, *The Name of the Rose*, on the occasion of the very first agon of its protagonists. But mental games do not interest us. We are interested in the question itself, and that question requires from us a certain degree of naïveté. Otherwise, any discussion of spiritual and worldly topics runs the risk of turning into an intellectual parade.

Thus, after all that Bakhtin has said about the "culture of laughter" and its subordinate internal categories—"carnivalization" and the "menippea,"[2]—the following question arises: what constitutes the rightness, the truth of the old tradition, according to which *Christ never laughed;* what truth can be found in it?

Perhaps there is no such truth, no meaning to be grasped here, but only a bare historical fact that needs to be exposed: namely, the so-called "medieval serious-ness," which we may abandon without the slightest reservation to its fate of being torn apart under the onslaught of the commonplace sociological phraseology[3] of the 1930s.[4] But if the tradition does contain some truth, does the condemnation of laughter derive logically from it?

Let us try to find an answer. To begin with, laughter is a highly dynamic event—simultaneously a movement of one's mind, one's nerves and muscles. It is an impulse, as impetuous as an outburst. The common metaphor of "bursts of laughter" is not accidental—laughter captures and carries away our spiritual and physical sides simultaneously. It is not a state but a transition whose entire charm—and significance—are derived from its instantaneousness. The very idea of a drawn-out act of laughter is unbearable not merely because interminable paroxysms and heavings soon turn into a torment for the tired body, but simply according to a certain *a priori* judgment of reason. Any "culture of laughter," in order to be a culture, has to take this into account; the common people, with their inherent common sense, have never forgotten this.[5] The transition runs the risk of losing its meaning if it loses its tempo, for with the loss of its tempo it will also lose the living sense of its own temporality.

Thus, laughter is a transition—but from what to what? Following Bakhtin, let us say that it is from a certain unfreedom to a certain freedom. It goes without saying that an axiom like this characterizes at this point not so much the phenomenon of laughter as our interests in dealing with laughter. As a point of departure, this axiom will do. However, one must immediately make two remarks in connection with it.

First, a transition to freedom is, by definition, not the same as freedom, as being "in" freedom. Laughter is not freedom but liberation, a very important difference. But then even empirical evidence does not prompt us at all to conjoin laughter and freedom too closely. The concrete experience of laughter makes us live through special moments of unfreedom which are specific to laughter. Among them, first of all, are traits of mechanical behavior that have been pointed out by such a classical philosopher of laughter as Bergson not only in the structure of the comic but also in the structure of laughter itself.[6] Warding off the mechanical behavior of the object of ridicule, we, through this very laughter, are drawn in and become involved in a process subject to mechanical laws. This is laughter as an automatic reaction of nerves and muscles that can be manipulated, as is done publicly in any comic presentation; laughter as an effect that can be purposely provoked, as if by pressing an invisible button. All this is surely rather far from the triumph of the personal principle. Given a sufficiently strong burst of laughter, we laugh "uncontrollably." The laughter that corresponds best of all to the concept of laughter is "involuntary" or "spontaneous," that is, the laughter that temporarily suspends the action of our personal will. Personal will is not consulted at all; it is irrelevant here. Laughter belongs to the class of states that in the language of Greek philosophical anthropology are called *pathe*—not what I do, but what is done to me.[7] Therefore, the transition from unfreedom to freedom introduces an element of a new unfreedom.[8] But there is a far more important issue: this transition, by definition, presupposes unfreedom as its point of departure and its precondition. A free person does not need to be liberated; only he who is *not yet free* can be liberated. It is always harder to make a wise man laugh than a simpleton because the wise man, in regard to a greater number of particular cases of inner unfreedom, has already crossed the line of liberation, the line of laughter, and is already beyond the threshold.

And now is the very time for us to return to our "paratheological" question. If we imagine a man, who from the very beginning and in every moment of his existence possesses the fullest freedom, then this would be the God-Man Jesus Christ, as he has always been conceived and represented by the Christian tradition. He is free absolutely, and not free from the moment of a certain liberation, an "awakening," like Buddha (literally—"the Awakened One"), but before the beginning of his earthly life, before the creation of the world, from the very depths of his "timelessness" (*predvechnost'*). In his Incarnation, Christ voluntarily limits his freedom but he does not expand it, for there is nowhere to expand. That is why the tradition according to which Christ never laughed is rather logical and convincing from the point of view of the philosophy of laughter. *At the point of absolute freedom, laughter is impossible for it is superfluous.*

Humor is a different matter. If laughing ecstasy corresponds to liberation, then humor corresponds to the sovereign use of freedom.

Second, it is not out of pedantry that we have called laughter a transition not just from unfreedom to freedom, but from "a certain" unfreedom to "a certain" freedom. The words "a certain" divest the words "freedom" and "unfreedom" of their valorizing tone,[9] obliging us to specify—freedom from what? As is well known from European historical experience, one can liberate oneself, among other things, even from freedom.[10] Excuse the truism: the positive or negative value of any liberation is inversely proportional to the negative or positive value of that (whether it is outside or inside ourselves) from which we liberate ourselves. Bakhtin's constructs take into account only that case when one needs to free oneself from a social mask imposed upon the frightened human being by "official culture," that is, in plain Russian, by the *nachal'stvo* [the "authorities"]. It goes without saying that this is a vital problem for any era and for any culture, and this problem was lived through at the cost of great suffering by that circle of people to which Bakhtin himself belonged—by the witnesses of a time when, according to the immortal expression of Iurii Zhivago from Pasternak's novel, reality itself was so intimidated that it went into hiding and, perhaps, it does not exist any longer.

Nevertheless, it would be clearly unreasonable to reduce the whole diversity of liberation by laughter to this particular case. For example, from time immemorial human beings have laughed at physical disabilities in order to overcome them in themselves. Laughter is a binding spell cast upon a disability to which a human being forbids himself to yield, and it is, simultaneously, an explosive release of intolerable tension. Even Christian martyrs laugh at torture in order to put to shame, discredit, and annihilate the power of fear, which is Satan's weapon. Folk culture knows still another type of laughing at human weakness, namely when chastity as self-control ridicules lust as loss of self-control. This "cold virginal laughter," which is far more ancient than Christian morality and which already resounded in the time of Artemis and her nymphs, is undoubtedly a spontaneous and sincere laughter that may be at most guilty of cruelty or heedlessness but in no way of sanctimoniousness. Liberation is, in this case, an evading, a triumphant escaping from an externally imposed passion but also from one's own weakness. That is, once again, an exorcism of disability. (It seems that one could indeed describe Rabelais without ever mentioning anything of this sort, but the real problem is that Bakhtin treats Rabelais not as an individual author of a given period but as a universal philosophical-anthropological paradigm.)

Thus, at one extreme pole we have the human being laughing at himself; the hero laughing at the coward within himself; the saint laughing at the World, the Flesh, and Hell; the laughter of honor at dishonor and that of self-possession at inner chaos; a human being's laughter at revolting behavior, of which he is perfectly capable, but in which he forbids himself to engage, and along with that, his laughter at the pride which insinuates that his "virtue" would not suffer any loss even if he did something revolting. . . . In the act of laughing at oneself, the one and the same person divides, as it were, into himself as the laughing self and himself as the self at whom he laughs, and the logical structure of this act is quite comparable to the classical New Testament prayer: "I believe; help my unbelief" (Mark 9:24, *RSV*), in which the person praying divides into a believer who prays and a nonbeliever who, by definition, cannot pray but for whose sake the prayer is said. Indeed, if there exists a laughter that could be recognized as Christian *cachasmos*[11] then it is laughter at oneself, self-ridicule, that annihilates one's attachment to oneself. In the poem "The Ballad of the White Horse" by the Catholic writer G. K. Chesterton, such laughter is presented as an initiation that truly introduces a Christian king to his rights, as a mystery of grace, incomprehensible for the earthly world of nature and fairy tale:

> And the beasts of the earth and the birds looked down,
> In a wild solemnity,
> On a stranger sight than a sylph or elf,
> On one man laughing at himself
> Under the greenwood tree—[12]

The noblest form of laughter at another could also be interpreted to some extent as laughter at oneself: in laughing at a tyrant the lover of freedom is laughing, first and foremost, at his own fear of the tyrant. And in general, someone weaker laughing at someone stronger is, first and foremost, laughing at his or her own weakness, just as laughter at a false authority is laughter at one's own susceptibility to being conned, and so forth.

Laughter involving a liberation from conventions, which belong in terms of ancient or Thomistic-Alphonsian casuistry to the domain of what is morally indifferent, has to be recognized in those same terms as laughter that makes no difference.[13] And to free ourselves from the truisms that admit only the tone of an "agelast,"[14] let us quickly pass over the middle of the spectrum and identify its opposite extreme, namely cynical laughter, insolently churlish laughter in the act of which the one who laughs divests himself of shame, of pity, and of conscience.

The problem of judging laughter spiritually, however, can in no way be reduced to simple copybook maxims, to wit, that liberation from evil is a good, that freeing oneself of something indifferent is a matter of indifference, and that liberation from something good is an evil. But that is why laughter is what it is— something elemental, something playful and crafty, so that in its operation it could be capable of intermingling heterogeneous motivations or even substituting one motivation for an entirely different one. In starting to laugh we lift anchor, as it were, and let the waves carry us in a direction that cannot be predicted in advance. What exactly we laugh at, and why we laugh, reveals itself to us and turns us this way or that in the very process of laughing, and what is always possible in this process is the interplay of semantic transitions and interpenetrations; indeed, laughter draws its life from this interplay. This can be felt by anyone who, on the one hand, is not completely deprived of a taste for laughing and of the experience of laughing, or, on the other, is not overly inhibited by spiritual caution, that is, of something akin to what in asceticism is called the gift of distinguishing spirits. We know from experience how many times our conscience has caught us in the act of imperceptibly substituting the wrong object of laughter for the right one, in the act of inner apostasies and instantaneous dislocations of our spiritual position, which were made possible precisely by laughter. Any of the substitutions are already made easier solely by the one defining circumstance in the phenomenology of laughter as a whole, namely, that the neuromuscular reaction aroused by a thought picks up the impetus of that thought and then immediately seizes the initiative from it—just a moment ago we were laughing *because* we found the thought to be funny, and then, before we know it, we find another thought to be funny *because* we go on laughing. In laughter, consciousness and the unconscious provoke each other incessantly, as quickly as a ball is passed in a game from one player to another. As far as spiritual caution is concerned, that is, of course, not a popular matter. At the risk of incurring the displeasure of my readers, let me state that it does not resemble in the least the disapproving and pompous self-importance of "agelasts," and if such caution is necessary, then it is not because laughter is of the Devil, as Jorge of Burgos thinks in Eco's novel, but simply because laughter is something elemental. The thirst to "surrender oneself" to something elemental is a well-attested dream of civilized humanity. Those who have truly known only the elements that live inside human beings, including the element of laughter, as did Aleksandr Blok, usually hold a different opinion.[15]

Bakhtin did not pose such questions because the worldview that found expression in his book on Rabelais posits laughter itself as the criterion for judging the spiritual goodness of laughter—of course, not laughter as an empirical, concrete, palpable given, but as the hypostatized and highly idealized essence of laughter, or, as he puts it himself, "the truth of laughter." This "truth" was for Bakhtin an object of unconditional philosophical belief that prompted him to make statements such as the following (contextually it refers to the Middle Ages, but it also has a broader significance):

> One understood that there is no violence lurking behind laughter; that laughter does not build fires to burn people at the stake; that hypocrisy and deception never laugh but rather put on a mask of seriousness; that laughter does not create dogmas and cannot become authoritarian; [. . .] That is why one spontaneously distrusted any seriousness and put one's trust in festive laughter."[16]

What is highly characteristic in this passage is the syntactic construction of this phrase with an indefinite subject (in German it would start with *man*, and in French with *on*). It elevates the utterance to such heights of abstract universality that raising the question of verification becomes, of itself, impossible. "One understood," "one distrusted"—who was it exactly? The so-called "common people"? People "in general"? "Medieval man"—that was a personage about whom one could easily discourse in the nineteenth century; in the twenty-first century, the level of our knowledge about the Middle Ages makes it virtually impossible to do so. But even earlier one could ask, for example, about Joan of Arc: since she certainly belongs to the common people of the Middle Ages, does it follow therefore that she intuitively "distrusted any seriousness" (the seriousness of what? of her Voices? of the unction in Reims?), or that she would lapse into seriousness, the way one lapses into feeble-mindedness, because she was weak and intimidated?[17] And what about the participants in popular religious movements, whether heretical or not: did they or did they not "trust" their own "seriousness" (which was anything but "official")? One could go on asking questions of this kind endlessly.

Let us instead turn our attention to the actual characterization of laughter (in the passage quoted), a characterization set forth, as they say, apophatically, by way of nothing but negations: "there was no violence," "did not create dogmas," and so on. Among the constituents of this symbol of faith, uttered in a tone of incontestable authority, one assertion is a truism: laughter "does not create dogmas." It would seem that laughter does not create anything at all outside the bounds of its own playing field. Yes, it is true that creating dogmas is not a function of laughter. And yet laughter does have a highly characteristic capability which is vigorously exploited by every kind of authoritarianism: it has the power to forcibly *impose* opinions and judgments, ideas and evaluations that are not and cannot be fully understood, that are not and cannot be fully expressed, that is to say,"dogmas," by terrorizing those who waver with what the French call *peur du ridicule* (the fear of appearing laughable). By means of laughter one can make someone shut up as if laughter were a gag thrust in his mouth. Again and again the illusion is produced that unresolved questions have been appropriately resolved long ago, and anyone who has not yet understood that is a backward bungler—for who would want, after all, to identify himself with some character in a farce or in a caricature? The terrorism of laughter is not only an effective substitute for repressive measures where, for some reason, they cannot be used but is equally effective in cooperating with repressive terror where the latter can be used. "Laughter does not build fires to burn people at the stake"—is there anything we can say concerning this claim? Fires are built as such by people, not by personified abstract notions; personifications can act independently only in the world of metaphors, in rhetoric and poetry. But then, once a real fire is built, laughter is heard beside it often enough, and this laughter is part of the inquisitors' design: fool's caps on the heads of the victims, as well as other comic accessories, are indispensable parts of the *auto-da-fé.*

"There is no violence lurking behind laughter"—how odd that Bakhtin could make so categorical a statement! All of history, literally, cries out in protest against it. There are so many contrary examples that one feels almost helpless about choosing the most striking ones. In Athens, the noblest city of classical antiquity, the great Aristophanes was in unanimous agreement with his audience when he treated the motif of torturing a slave as a witness at a trial (in *The Frogs*) as highly amusing. The Roman comedies of Plautus continuously resound with ringing laughter about the beatings and floggings inflicted on slaves as punishment, about the purple *violence* [margin annotation]

Phoenician patterns that rods cut into human skin, and even about the possibility of a slave starting to "dance" on a cross (*crucisaltus*) and thus dying valiantly on it. Violence does not "lurk" behind such laughter, far from it: violence declares itself in such laughter loudly and confidently, it plays with violence, and renders violence diverting.

The scene in the Gospels where Christ is mocked throws us back, as it were, to the very sources of the folk culture of laughter, back to the ambivalent procedure of crowning-discrowning that is as old as the world itself, and yet it is this procedure that throws into relief the bitter seriousness of the agony of the innocent victim who will be taken, upon completion of the mock ritual, to his execution. As concerns the Archaic period, when the ritual of crowning-discrowning was not an improvisation, as it was for the Roman soldiers in first-century Palestine, but a regularly repeated ceremony—we should not forget that then as well the outcome was the same—the chosen victim was put to death; so that what we find at the very origin of any sort of "carnivalization" is—blood. It goes without saying, of course, that genesis does not predetermine the judgment of value, for all sorts of components that become part of culture may be genetically connected with the bloody rituals of Archaic times. But neither does a genesis of this sort dispose us to believe in the natural innocence of the tradition of laughter, in its, as it were, immaculate conception and the incompatibility of its very nature with violence . . .

Personally, Bakhtin's hero François Rabelais found confessional bloodshed distasteful, but he did so not because he was an incarnation of folk laughter but rather because he was a humanist with the mind-set of a humanist. The historical period, however, in which Rabelais lived, knew countless Protestant caricatures of the pope and Catholic caricatures of prominent Reformers; it knew countless farcical tricks played by the opponents on each other, and these tricks were often quite ingenious and invariably designed to produce repercussions in the "marketplace," among the masses. *And the question is*—can we really expel all these *bagatelles pour un massacre* [piano pieces for a massacre] from the folk culture of laughter?

Now consider Russian history: if one can discern in the midst of it the monumental figure of a "carnivalizer," then it could be no one else, of course, but Tsar Ivan the Terrible, who was a real expert in all varieties of "ambivalence." He was the one who could expertly stage a ritual of crowning and discrowning his victims; he was the one who in his letters exhibited expert mastery in manipulating the most extreme registers of irony and ambiguity, but also of deliberate coarseness [*grobianizm*];[18] and finally, he was the one who devised the unique system of mock-monastic rituals for his *oprichniki*.[19] And there is no denying that the Russian folktale accepted the bloodiest of Russian autocrats precisely as a frightening yet great jester or wag, who was capable of imparting a certain amplitude even to a farce about people changing their status by changing their clothes, as in the following passage from a folktale: "Listen, boyar! Take off your splendid clothes and your boots! And you, potter, take your caftan off and get your bast-shoes off your feet![20] And now you, boyar, put on his bast-shoes, and you, potter, put his clothes on."

It is well known that Ivan the Terrible was an exemplary figure for Stalin; and, as a matter of fact, Stalin's regime would not have been able to function without a "carnival" of its own—without playing games with the ambivalent figures of popular imagination, without the deliberately coarse and provocative tone of the press, without all the deliberately calculated psychological effects produced by the constant and unpredictable turns of the wheel of fortune, the constant and unpredictable crownings and discrownings, ascents and downfalls, so that everyone lived under the threat of harsh punishment yet at the same time everyone had a wild chance of surviving, as in "The Lottery in Babylon" by Jorge Luis Borges.[21] But even earlier, in the 1920s, was it not an instance of carnival, when God was put on trial at Komsomol meetings?[22] How much laughter there was—youthful, ruddy-cheeked, athletic laughter testing its strong teeth on the values of "the Old World"! From the top of a village belfry (during the campaign against religion in the late 1920s) one could subject a religious procession to the same act that was performed by the hero of *Gargantua* upon Parisians (book 1, chapter 17).[23] If anything was in plentiful supply at that time, then it was "carnival atmosphere"!

There are more than enough examples of a direct connection between laughter and violence, carnival and authoritarianism. I would like to single out two particular cases. During the French Revolution, the celebrated *philosophe* and mathematician Marquis de Condorcet devised a "means for producing laughter"—a method of exerting influence upon those nuns who refused to recognize the so-called Constitutional Clergy. These nuns would be sought and captured in the street, their bottoms would be publicly exposed and whipped with birch rods. This chastisement was meant to be perceived, moreover, as no more than an innocuous incident in the nursery, almost like an incident in the spirit of the pictures of Greuze, as a chastisement of disobedient overgrown children who are simply not mature enough to be treated as adults. (To be sure, contemporaries do mention cases where the Parisian crowd, carried away in its use of this "means for producing laughter," would go too far and would whip the victim to death.) The second case is closer to our time and everybody still remembers it: the use of castor oil in the treatment of dissidents in Mussolini's Italy. It goes without saying that I do not mean to equate Condorcet, who has his place in the history of European thought, with banal Blackshirts.[24]

It is even more important for me to avoid any misunderstanding on another point. I have absolutely no doubts about the irreproachable purity of Bakhtin's philosophical intentions, especially in view of the fact that all his efforts were devoted totally and without remainder to defending the freedom of the spirit at a time in history when such an undertaking appeared to be hopeless. Perhaps

Why this claim?.

only those who were both Mikhail Mikhailovich's compatriots and contemporaries could understand the full meaning of the position he held as a human being. The gratitude we owe him must never fail. But the kingdom of thought (as a man of the nineteenth century might put it) is governed by other laws, laws not easily compatible with a sense of reverence. In order to attain a clear idea of the possibilities inherent in a particular thought as thought, we must examine it without any deference by turning it this way and that and placing it in the strangest combinations. And that is why we would like to pose the following question: can one really fail to notice how smoothly both forms of outrage committed upon the dissidents (both the "means for producing laughter" and the castor oil) fit into the system of categories that Bakhtin elaborated for describing "the truth of laughter" in his Rabelais book? For everything really does fit and tally without a hitch! One can really find everything in both cases—not only the "lowering" or "humbling" produced by laughter and the playing with the *topoi* of the domain concerned with "the lower part of the material body" ("a powerful motion downward," as Bakhtin puts it in another passage), but also—and this has a more fundamental and essential significance—ambivalence and the invigorating prospect of an open future. It is indeed the case that the image of execution, brutal punishment, moral annihilation is ambivalently placed on a par with the archetype of rejuvenation in the first case, and with the archetype of recovering one's health in the second case, and with that of renewal in both cases. The nuns, in terms of what their torturers intended, were given something like a chance to return to their childhood and from there to start their life from the beginning, a chance to get up after the whipping as good and law-abiding girls who thank their instructors for teaching them a useful lesson. The one whose thoughts were not in tune with the Italian Fascist regime was given the possibility of fully realizing that his dissident thoughts were like constipating accumulations of excrement that poisoned his body (an instance of the "materialization of metaphor," highly typical of the carnival), and as a result he needed to undergo the action of a laxative, he had to undergo a "laughable" humiliation that destroyed the seriousness of his entire previous life, so that he would feel (once again as in the case of the flogged nuns) like a little boy soiling his pants. To feel that you are simultaneously a corpse and a child—in what way is this not an instance of "the ambivalence of birth-giving death"?

With all the means at his disposal, Bakhtin emphasized the unfinished, nonclosed nature of everything that is alive, and in doing so, he sought any chance to fight against those who wanted to be in command of life and who wanted to close up history. The trouble is that totalitarianism, in its own peculiar way, fully appreciates the value of what is unfinished, nonclosed, pliable; it has its own special interest in exaggerating these aspects of being, of abnormally enlarging their significance, by surrounding them with an emotional aura of laughter and ruthless cheerfulness that is peculiar to them. The only thing it considers to be

What the hell is "The people"?

complete and consummated is itself, or, to be exact, the attribute of incontestable, unquestionable authority which is inherent in every expression of "the Leader's" will; the actual content of these expressions of will is a matter of improvisation. Reality has to be pliable so that it can be taken hold of and reshaped. People must be unfinished, underage, in process of becoming, so that one can educate and reeducate them, "re-forge" them; there is no need to take them into consideration, to take them seriously, but at the same time they must not become dejected, because their whole life is still ahead of them—just as in the case of children. In the language of Stalin's time, career advancement was called "growing"—a human being had the obligation of continuing to "grow" until ripe old age. What is highly characteristic are the myths that Stalinism in its late phase introduced into the biological sciences: life is continually engendered from lifeless matter; the cells form spontaneously out of a formless but living mass; a stalk of wheat produces as many ears of wheat as one requires it to produce; acquired traits are immediately inherited; biological species are unstable. As a result, the entire biological universe presents itself indeed as Bakhtin's "grotesque body," bursting from incessant pregnancy yet alien to any form, order, or Logos.

And yet Bakhtin was right, profoundly right, when he placed his hope in the fact that as long as the people *are* the people, the last word has not yet been spoken. There is no other earthly hope besides the one that people will not allow themselves to be programmed. Bakhtin had the right to connect this hope primarily with a "soberly mocking" attitude, for in a time of recurrent ideological mass hysteria such a bias is perfectly understandable. He said with a force that is immortal:

> The people never fully share the lofty feelings inspired by the ruling truth. If the nation is threatened, the people carry out their duty and save the nation. But they never take seriously the patriotic slogans of a class society, their heroism retains their soberly mocking attitude towards all the lofty rhetoric of the ruling power and the ruling truth. That is why a class ideologue, with all his lofty feelings and his seriousness, will never be able to penetrate to the core of the people's soul. In this core he comes up against a barrier that is insurmountable for his seriousness, the barrier of a mocking and cynical (humbling) merriment; he comes up against that carnival spark (a little fire) of cheerful abuse which melts any narrow-minded seriousness.[25]

But does the secret freedom of a man of the people have to express itself solely in laughter?—that is the question. Joan of Arc was burned to death at the stake, and it appears as if that's the end of it, it's finished, the last word belongs to the executioners. But then all of a sudden an English soldier (who just a moment ago had implemented, along with all the others, his culture of laughter at the expense of the victim) falls down in a faint, and when his comrades manage to carry him to

X sounds like an excuse

the nearest tavern and to bring him back to consciousness, he hastens immediately, without delay, to express contrition for his sin. In this case that same unattainable "core of the people's soul" is protected against the outside not by laughter, but by entirely different powers: this time liberation coincides not with laughter but with the cessation of laughter, with the regaining or recovery of sobriety following laughter. Bakhtin absolutized laughter in the same way as the existentialists, his contemporaries, absolutized the *acte gratuit* and for the same reasons: when the defense of freedom is conducted at the point of no return, one is confronted with the temptation of gripping some talisman (laughter, *acte gratuit*), of holding on to it the way a man drowning clutches even a straw (according to the Russian proverb), and of believing that as long as you feel the talisman in your hand, freedom has not been lost. This behavior is quite understandable. But the question of freedom is much more complex and at the same time much simpler.

The motif of "cheerful abuse" that appeared in passing in the quotation above is particularly important for Bakhtin in a peculiarly personal way. About obscene expressions using the word "mother," he writes that "It would be absurd and hypocritical, however, to deny that they continue to retain a certain degree of magical power or charm (and they do so, moreover, without any relation to eroticism)."[26] This is *surely* something like a personal admission or confession. What I mean to say is that when we are discussing in an academic manner the problems of the late Middle Ages, then it is not particularly difficult to offer objections to Bakhtin's arguments. Why, for example, is the use of foul language by the French kings (apparently legitimized for their rank by unwritten law, like the custom of taking mistresses)[27]—why is this supposed to be a piece of the folk culture of laughter, whereas the plebeian piety of Joan of Arc, which prompted her to combat the knights' habit of cursing (by improperly invoking the name of a sacred being), is supposed to be an expression of what Bakhtin calls "official culture"? Let me note in passing that the term "official culture" does not really fit, it seems to me, the conditions of the Middle Ages and is really appropriate only to the conditions of mature absolutism. The very phenomenon of Joan of Arc alone (it is amazing how quickly this phenomenon became incomprehensible in the following centuries) attests in itself that there was no boundary separating the "official" and the "unofficial" in the later sense of these terms.

But the academic approach is hardly adequate to Bakhtin. The moment we think of other matters (such as the years Bakhtin spent in exile, when he worked in a consumers' cooperative and heard more than enough of the real and undoubtedly "unprintable" speech of the Kustanai collective farmers), we immediately find ourselves following a truer course. One can argue with theories, but one cannot argue with a soul's accumulated experience. The fact that the thinker, in a time of personal hardship, saw and came to love the common people the way they were in reality (with all their faults and imperfections rather than ideally nice and virtuous) and managed to preserve so faithfully and to express so forcefully the warmth of his feelings toward that core of the people's soul which is impervious to all the ruling truths—that fact alone is an inalienable part of the history of Russian culture. Except that this fact must be perceived in its real, not its fabricated, context. The courageous fortitude with which Bakhtin dealt with his personal fate not only forms the basis of his theoretical constructions; it is far more unassailable than they are.

Notes

Notes marked with an asterisk are by Vadim Liapunov.

1. The Russian original of this essay is "Bakhtin, smekh, khristianskaia kul'tura," in *M. M. Bakhtin kak filosof* (Moscow: Nauka, 1992), 7–19. The essay was first published in the almanac *Rossiia // Russia*, vol. 6 (Marsilio: Editory S.p.A. in Venesia, 1988). It was translated from the Russian by Leonid Livak and revised by Alexandar Mihailovic, and has been extensively revised by Vadim Liapunov.

2. We would like to remind the reader that Bakhtin found a high concentration of the quality he called "Menippean" in the New Testament and in early Christian literature in general.

3. That is, the vulgar sociological approach of the 1930s.*

4. "Unlike medieval laughter, seriousness was permeated with elements of fear, weakness, meekness, resignation, lying, hypocrisy or, to the contrary— with some elements of violence, intimidation, threat, prohibition. In the hands of the authorities, seriousness intimidated, demanded and prohibited; in those of subordinates, it trembled, subdued itself, praised, eulogized. That is why people were wary of medieval seriousness. It was official discourse and they treated it like everything official. Seriousness suppressed, frightened, fettered; it was false and hypocritical; it was stingy and lenten." M. M. Bakhtin, *Tvorchestvo Fransua Rable i narodnaia kul'tura Srednevekov'ia i Renessansa* (Moscow: Khudozhestvennaia literatura, 1965), 105. All translations of the Rabelais book are from the original Russian. Cross-references are given to Hélène Iswolsky's English translation from the French edition, *Rabelais and His World* (Cambridge: MIT Press, 1968), 94.

As someone who knew Mikhail Mikhailovich personally, I have to say that he himself recalled such passages in his book on Rabelais with regret. In our conversations he cited them as a proof that he, Bakhtin, was no better than the time in which he lived. I hope that such an ability to give a strict and sober judgment of his own text does not detract from, but rather enhances, our image of Bakhtin.

5. The commonsensical judgment of the people in regard to laughter, as expressed in numerous proverbs, is not in contradiction with the tendency to

parade excessive laughter, a tendency peculiar to certain types of "belly-laugh" plebeian humor. Similar to the flaunting of gluttony, heavy drinking, or sexual excess, this tendency is based precisely on the notion that prolonged laughter is onerous for the body: physical stamina proves itself precisely in playing with hardships and, moreover, with hardships that are unnecessary (otherwise it would not be a game). In this respect, laughter's essentially temporary character remains in force. However, it is completely different when some strictly intellectual, "neo-pagan" imagination, raised on Romanticism and Decadence, seriously dreams about "eternal" laughter. One could recall the last line of Hermann Hesse's poem "Eternity": "Cool and star-bright is our everlasting laughter" ("*Kühl und sternhell unser ewges Lachen*"). The common-sense tradition of Christian peoples can find a place for eternal laughter perhaps only in hell, whereas unceasing laughter would be located immediately next to hell, for instance, in the place where a creature from hell forces a human being to laugh to death. It is evident that the Hesse of the *Steppenwolf* period (from which the poem is quoted) denied the distinction between heaven and hell as a matter of principle. But even he can speak of "eternal laughter" only by means of an insufficiently comprehended metaphor in which laughter is identified with something like Mozart's music, i.e., when it is unacceptably understood as "beautiful." Laughter is not music, and music is not laughter.

6. Henri Bergson, *Le Rire: Essai sur la Signification du Comique* (Paris, 1900).

7. Cf., for instance, the list of such *pathe* in Iamblichus (*De vita Pythagorica*, ed. U. Klein [Leipzig: Teubner, 1937]).

8. The dialectics of the unity between the "unfettering" of flesh and the enslavement of the personal principle of that flesh (Tsvetaeva speaks of "vicious convicts of the flesh") unites, of course, laughter with orgasm, but we will not elaborate on this subject.

9. We cannot help quoting Bakhtin: "Words that acquire special weight under particular conditions of sociopolitical life become expressive exclamatory utterances: 'Peace!' 'Freedom!' and so forth. (These constitute a special sociopolitical speech genre)" (*SpG* 85).

10. Let us recall that, as a real, if very imperfect, phenomenon, European freedom was established by the "Puritans" in their struggle with the licentiousness of the "Cavaliers." Totalitarianism opposes democracy not only with the threat of terror, but also with the temptation of lifting prohibitions—a false liberation of sorts; it would be a big mistake to see only its repressive side. In his biblical novella *The Tables of the Law*, Thomas Mann emphasizes, in relation to German National Socialism, precisely that orgiastic mood that is an "abomination to the Lord": in a stylized prophecy, Hitler is spoken of as the one who seduces with false freedom (from the law). Totalitarianism knows its own "carnivalization," but that is a separate topic.

11. Fundamental doubts about this point have been expressed from time to time. On the whole, Eastern Orthodox spirituality is more distrustful toward

laughter than Western spirituality, while Russian Orthodox spirituality specifically is particularly distrustful toward it. Apparently, this is asceticism's reaction to certain features in the Russian national character denoted by such words as *bezuderzhnost'* (reckless unrestraint), *razymchivost'* (susceptibility to being carried away), and so on. Gogol, who did not know how to combine within himself a comic genius and a pious man, constitutes a very Russian example. The word *shut* (jester, joker) is a common Russian euphemism for the devil, and in the traditional language of the people this meaning of the word casts a compromising light on such words as *poshutit'* (to jest, to make a joke), *shutka* (a jest, a joke), etc. It is telling that while an ancient testimony informs us how the strictest ascetic, Anthony the Great, in the beginning years of monasticism, softened his behavior toward laymen with humor, a highly respected nineteenth-century spiritual writer ventured to reinterpret this passage, despite the clarity of the Greek text, in order to dispel at all cost from his readers' minds the idea that humor was admissible for an ascetic.

12. G. K. Chesterton, *The Collected Poems of G. K. Chesterton* (London: Methuen, 1943), 266 [translator's note].

13. Thomistic-Alphonsian casuistry: "In [Catholic] theology casuistry signifies that part of moral theology, or that method, that treats of the application of moral principles to singular cases. . . . Casuistry allows one to bridge the gap between the concrete action and the abstract norms. . . ." St. Thomas Aquinas (1225–74) comments upon the need for casuistry given human imperfection and tendency toward sin: "'Anyone who perfectly knew the principles according to all their virtualities would not need any conclusions proposed to him separately. But, because those who know principles do not know them so as to consider everything that is found virtually contained in them, it is necessary for them that, in the sciences, the conclusions be deduced from principles'" [*Summa Theologiae* 2a2ae, 44.2]. (E. Hamel in the *New Catholic Encyclopedia*, vol. 1. Washington, D.C.: Catholic Univ. of America, 1967, 195). St. Alphonsus Liguori (1696–1787) greatly contributed to Catholic moral theology. In his moral theology, Alphonsus drew from St. Thomas, among many others. "In Alphonsian moral theory the study of the concrete circumstances of action rules out the mechanical application of a system, however sound it may be." Alphonsus is the patron of confessors and moralists. (L. Vereecke in the *New Catholic Encyclopedia*, vol. 3. Washington, D.C.: Catholic Univ. of America, 1967, 340) [editors' note].

14. "Agelast," one who never laughs—as used by Rabelais. The term denotes someone who is devoid of any sense of humor. It is derived from the Greek verbal adjective *agelastos*, "never laughing."*

15. As a randomly selected example, see Blok's diary entry (the night of June 1, 1909) in which he speaks about "hysterical laughter" as a threat to a poet's personality; the entire entry is very eloquent in this regard. Aleksandr Blok, *Zapisnye knizhki* (Moscow, 1965), 145.

16. Translation from the original, 107; cf. *RAHW* 95.

17. Translation from the original: "As long as there was room for fear, since the medieval human being was still too weak in the face of natural and social forces, the *seriousness of fear and suffering* in its religious, social, political, and ideological forms could not fail to be appealing. The individual consciousness of a particular human being could seldom free itself from the seriousness of fear and weakness" (emphasis added by the author), 106; cf. *RAHW* 94–95.

18. Averintsev uses here an unusual term, *grobianizm* (which he later also uses to describe the journalism under Stalin). He borrows the term from the German *Grobianismus* (a neologism for the Latin term *rusticus*, "crude, uncultivated," created by adding to the German word *grob*, "crude, coarse," the ending *-ian* as an ironic analogy to saints' names). *Grobianismus* refers in the history of German literature to the coarse, obscene modes of behavior denounced in the *grobianische* literature of the fifteenth and sixteenth centuries. In Sebastian Brant's *Narrenschiff* ("Ship of Fools," 1494), "St. Grobianus" is exalted as the patron saint of *Grobianismus*. The most important work of this type of literature was *Grobianus*, a Latin poem by F. Dedekind (published in 1549) in which he ridiculed vulgar and coarse behavior by ironically praising the advantages of boorishness.*

19. The *oprichniki* were members of the lower gentry who served in the household troops of Tsar Ivan IV the Terrible within a peculiar institution the tsar created for himself (1565), the *oprichnina* ("separate estate"), a private court that administered those Russian lands which had been separated from the rest of the realm and placed under the tsar's direct control. These "separated" lands were created by forcibly removing the boyars (the upper nobility) from the lands they owned, and executing or relocating them. The term *oprichnina* is often used to refer to the reign of terror which the tsar conducted by means of his *oprichniki* to break the resistance of the upper nobility and the church against his policies. The *oprichniki* were clad in black and presented themselves as a kind of religious order (with pseudomonastic rules and rituals). See also Geoffrey Hosking, *Russia: People and Empire, 1552–1917* (Cambridge: Harvard Univ. Press, 1997), 53–56.*

20. The caftan and the bast-shoes are typical apparel for a poor peasant. A caftan is a long outer garment with long sleeves; bast-shoes are woven from the strong inner fibrous bark of various trees, especially the birch.

21. Here is a story that is highly characteristic of the Stalinist period, regardless of whether it is true in fact. During the campaign against "Cosmopolitanism," an important official responsible for overseeing the arts made a wrong move, attacking a stage actor of Jewish descent who, as it turned out, was a favorite of Stalin's. At a reception in the Kremlin, Stalin asks the official: "Who is the man you wrote about?" The official tells him the actor's name. "Rubbish! You wrote about the People's Artist so-and-so," says Stalin, enumerating the actor's various titles (and decorations). "And who are you?" The official thinks that Stalin wants him to respond in an official

tone and enumerates his various positions and titles. "Nonsense!" says Stalin, "You are nothing but so-and-so." And that response of Stalin's meant that right there and then the official had been instantaneously stripped of all his ranks and titles. This is practically identical to what happens in the folktale about Ivan the Terrible: the boyar is stripped and the potter is dressed up.

The oft-mentioned phone calls that Stalin made to various writers are also part of his peculiar "carnival." Take, for example, the case of M. A. Bulgakov, who was caught totally by surprise when he heard "This is Stalin speaking," and suspected a hoax, and then heard the Leader's voice ask him directly: "You must be really sick of us by now, aren't you?" (*Novyi mir,* no. 8 [1987]: 198). There is no way Woland [in Bulgakov's novel *The Master and Margarita*] could have matched that!

22. Komsomol (KOMmunisticheskii SOyuz MOLodezhi, or Communist Union of Young People) was the official youth organization during the Soviet period [editors' note].

23. Cf. Bakhtin's analysis of this episode: *RAHW* 190–92; on the symbolism of urine in particular, cf. *RAHW* 335.

24. Although in speaking about Condorcet, it is worth reminding the reader that only one step separates not just the sublime from the ridiculous, but also the sublime from the ignoble. . . . Condorcet perished when Robespierre was in power; during that same period the culture of laughter found itself constrained to a considerable extent, and nuns were simply decapitated, as in the case of the Compiègne Carmelites who were guillotined on June 17, 1794.

25. M. M. Bakhtin, *Literaturno-kriticheskie stat'i* (Moscow, 1986), 513–14. The form of brief observations or remarks is more appropriate for such thoughts than the form of a dissertation or treatise which fate forced upon the Rabelais book.

26. Translation from the original, 320; cf. *RAHW* 28.

27. *RAHW* 189–90.

Bakhtin and the Tropes of Orthodoxy

Charles Lock

Much has been made in recent years of the discrepancy between Russian and Western views of Bakhtin. In Russia a virtually hagiographic discourse has enshrined the memory of a man at whose feet, apparently, a younger man was not ashamed to fall and plead, "Mikhail Mikhailovich, tell us how to live so that we can become like you."[1] It is easy to mock the event as risible, or the account as implausible: easy, and, in the cynical West, almost obligatory. Yet I find this episode neither implausible nor discreditable. It would account for the strategies of self-deprecation of which Bakhtin was a master. Clark and Holquist told in 1984 the story of Bakhtin, as he was nearing death, asking to have read out "his favorite story, the tale in the *Decameron* ['How Ser Ciapelletto Became Saint Ciapelletto'] where miracles are performed at the tomb of a man regarded as a saint, but who had in fact been a dreadful rogue."[2] Presumably the person asked by Bakhtin to read that story was one of those who might have prostrated before him, or at the least, treated him as a wise man, a *starets*. To the Shakespeare scholar Leonid Pinsky, who had asked in 1974 "whether or not good would eventually triumph," Bakhtin gave the sharp response: "No, of course not."[3] Such pessimism is strictly rhetorical, a refusal of the question precisely and exclusively in terms of the one to whom it had been, all and only hopefully, addressed.

Yet one must insist on the value of ambivalence and unease, for it should be no surprise that Bakhtin was admired as a person. With the opening of official files, and with the intense scrutiny to which Bakhtin's life has been exposed, nobody has been able to charge him with political compromise or collusion. That he falsified his educational record, that much of what appears to be his own writing is the translation of large chunks of German scholarship, are accusations of intellectual and academic impropriety that have often been made in the past, and can no longer be ignored or simply denied.[4] But not even those scholars who have argued that Bakhtin's theory of carnival is a justification of Stalinism (notably Boris Groys)[5] have attempted to claim that Bakhtin collaborated with the regime. This is remarkable. Before we dismiss the hagiographic approach, we should wonder at the integrity of a man who was reprieved by the state, was in official employment for over thirty years, and compromised himself by no more than the occasional tribute to Marxist-Leninism. His "sorrowful" confession to Sergei Averintsev, "*Ya byl ne luchshe svoego vremeni"* ("I was no better than my time"), strikes no note of shame, but reaches down to a fine dignity. In the present climate, it is too easily forgotten how few individuals endured the Soviet regime so untainted: in that context it is no wonder at all that younger scholars might have wanted to learn "how to live so that we might become like you."

The anecdotal and the circumstantial are appropriate modes with which to inquire into the "spiritual life"—which is also, and emphatically for Bakhtin, the bodily, the embodied life. A person's faith or belief ought never to be the object of investigation; it must belong to that intimacy which eludes and exceeds the very condition of knowing, that Bakhtin names *vnenakhodimost'*, or "outsideness." "Hence," said Bakhtin in an early lecture, the record of which is translated in this volume, "it is clear how hopeless is the attempt to understand ritual, prayer, etc., *morally.*" "Morally" might be glossed as "spiritually," "inwardly." The very contiguity in Bakhtin's argument of the words "prayer" and "ritual" makes his case: we can understand prayer only through the *outsideness* of ritual, and through paradigms, the "outward shows" of faith and thought. As other contributors to this volume have demonstrated, notably Alexandar Mihailovic and the editors, the central paradigm of Bakhtin's thinking is the Incarnation as understood in patristic and Orthodox theology. The formula affirmed at the Council of Chalcedon in 451, that the person of Christ is a hypostasis of two natures, divine and human—"without confusion, without change, without division, without separation"—serves Bakhtin as a paradigm for the dialogical: two voices in the hypostasis of one word.[6]

The task of demonstrating, at the level of the text, the significance of Orthodoxy for the understanding of Bakhtin has fallen to Western scholars, in the past for good reasons, today for no better reason than that that relevance is so taken for granted in Russia as to stand in no need of demonstration: "speculation on the connection between Bakhtin's ideas and Christian faith is now routine in Russia. . . . [I]n the mid-1990s, a counterwave against the excessive theologizing of his thought was already being felt."[7] In her recent study, Caryl Emerson has paid due attention to the significance of Lunacharsky's review of Bakhtin's 1929 monograph on Dostoevsky.[8] Bakhtin's "rehabilitation" in the 1960s and his survival, both bodily and textual, may also owe something to efforts made on his behalf by the daughter of Yuri Andropov (then head of the KGB), who was a student of Bakhtin's. It is therefore hardly surprising that those readers in the Soviet Union who may have seen elements in Bakhtin hardly reconcilable with party doctrine would have chosen to keep silent. Yet there is a significant prehistory to the now "routine" affirmation of Bakhtin as an Orthodox thinker, and it is to be found in the Russian emigration.

Georges Florovsky (1893–1979), one of the most distinguished and influential Orthodox theologians of modern times, wrote in 1931, in Paris, an essay on "Religious Themes in Dostoevsky" in which Bakhtin's book is cited. In his magnum opus, *Ways of Russian Theology* (1937), Florovsky makes a reference to that essay, and an amplification:

> See my article "Religioznyia temy Dostoevskago," *Rossia i Slavianstvo* 117 (February 21, 1931). Many valuable observations are also to be found in the book by M. M. Bakhtin, *Problemy tvorchestva Dostoevskago* (1929). See the idea (pp. 41–42) that Dostoevsky's world was profoundly pluralistic. If one is to seek the image of unity to which all these worlds gravitate, then it would be the Church as "a community of undiffused souls." This can be compared to Dante.[9]

Here Florovsky paraphrases that now-celebrated passage of Bakhtin in which, as we shall see, Mihailovic hears Chalcedonian resonances. Elsewhere in his great study of Russian thought, Florovsky displays knowledge of P. N. Medvedev's three monographs of 1922, 1926, and 1928 on Aleksandr Blok.[10] We should not assume too impermeable a partition between the USSR and the Russian emigration; more research is needed on reviews in the emigration not only of Bakhtin but of the works by Medvedev, Voloshinov, and other members of what is now known as the Bakhtin circle.[11]

The first account in English of Bakhtin's affinity to Orthodoxy, from 1983, is to be found within the ambit of Florovsky's influence in Orthodox circles in North America. In "An Orthodox Hermeneutic in the West,"[12] an essay deeply indebted to Florovsky, Anthony Ugolnik introduces Bakhtin as "a Soviet academic who used a Marxist idiom to express ideas in harmony with his Orthodoxy." In a most suggestive footnote, Ugolnik writes, "Though critical discussion of Bakhtin has been centered on issues related to Marxism, Orthodox sensitive to the theological dimensions of materiality will recognize Bakhtin's grounding in our tradition."

That footnote was both an invitation and a provocation to the present writer, for Ugolnik had omitted any mention of Bakhtin's work on Rabelais. It was the Rabelais book and the theme of carnival that had been seized on by Marxist critics as a radical assertion not only of materiality as such, or of dialectical materialism, but of "revolutionary materialism"—of the revolutionary potential in matter. Yet it was precisely the theological dimensions of materiality—Christ's Incarnation as the most revolutionary moment in the history of matter—that seemed to be of the greatest relevance to Orthodoxy. The essay that I wrote, partly in response to Ugolnik's footnote, asserted a set of connections in its title, "Carnival and Incarnation: Bakhtin and Orthodox Theology."[13] My aim was not to demonstrate the Orthodoxy of Bakhtin's thinking, nor to identify Bakhtin as an "Orthodox believer."

In pointing to the homologous paradigms of thinking about matter in Rabelais, Marx, and Orthodoxy, I was concerned to show how easy it is to misunderstand matter and its valuation when reading from within a Protestant culture. I was tempted to speculate that Marxism found such fertile soil in Russia precisely on the ground of that misunderstanding. One could follow the number of scholars who have pointed out the "double articulation" of Bakhtin's term "dialogic"— on a literary axis opposed to the monologic, on a philosophical axis opposed to the dialectic—and describe Bakhtin's larger project as the development of a "dialogical materialism." To note that "dialogical materialism" is a precise gloss of "the Word became flesh" is not to insinuate a creedal affirmation but to suggest that paradigm shifts may be less interesting than "paradigm continuities." Instances at which philosophical premises can be ascribed to theological paradigms remain rare moments of illumination. We are perhaps only now learning to treat theology not as passé and irrelevant but as the repressed, the shadow side of philosophy.

"Religion" or "theology" are terms that within a Protestant paradigm—to speak historically and conceptually, rather than of essences—invoke the categories of ethics (behavior) and belief (intellectual conviction). Within an Orthodox paradigm, the immediate associations would be neither creedal nor ethical but liturgical (bodily presence) and sacramental (the holiness of matter). When Bakhtin's commentators address the religious question, they look to the early work, to "Art and Answerability" and "Author and Hero," for it is in these essays that the ethical is articulated as a theme. This is entirely consistent with Bakhtin's philosophical schooling in a Petersburg (and Nevel) recension of Marburg neo-Kantianism.

Bakhtin's development from the essays of about 1920 to the book on Rabelais marks a progressive emancipation from the institutionally approved discourse of Russian academic philosophy, modeled on Western patterns. The nonacceptance of Bakhtin's writings after 1929, either for publication or, in the case of the dissertation on Rabelais, for an academic degree, has something to do with the mode of their writing—the circular, repetitive, assertive movement that ends abruptly where it might have begun. We should pay less attention to what Soviet ideologues and censors might have found objectionable in Bakhtin's writings and consider instead how deviant these writings are from the discourses available to the Western liberal academy. They do not conform to the dialectical mode of argumentation, and they largely eschew the conventions of reference and evidence.

My essay concluded with a question in which I speculated that Bakhtin's thinking owed much to the theological notion of the double-natured hypostasis, that which holds together the two natures, divine and human, of Christ in the incarnate Jesus. That question finds a response in Alexandar Mihailovic's monograph, *Corporeal Words: Mikhail Bakhtin's Theology of Discourse*, especially in its fourth chapter, "'Without Confusion or Separation': Bakhtin and the Chalcedonian Ideal of the Divided Union." Mihailovic usefully shows the frequency with which the Chalcedonian formula *adiairetos achoristos*, "distinct yet undivided/indivisible," in Russian *nesliianno i nerazdel'no*, is invoked in Russian writing of the "Silver Age" (circa 1900–20).[14] And Bakhtin's book on Dostoevsky is, according to Mihailovic, "full of Chalcedonian reverberations, the most conspicuous being his famous statement that the archetypical image of Dostoevsky's world is that of a church, a single meeting-place for . . . disparate and unmerged souls (*kak obshchenie nesliiannykh dush*)."[15]

Mihailovic's argument is curiously phrased: "Bakhtin's theological metaphor curiously coexists with other and completely nontheological tropes (most significantly those drawn from biology and sociology). . . . If Bakhtin was a believing Christian, how could he juxtapose images taken from his own faith with ones drawn from the presumably rationalist and reductive natural sciences?"[16] This is a good instance of the globalization of Protestant paradigms and anxieties. Orthodoxy never underwent a Reformation, nor any sort of conflict between faith and reason. To the embarrassment of the Party, one of the most distinguished scientists and engineers in the Soviet Union was a priest, Pavel Florensky (who has often been compared to Bakhtin).[17] One could mention the delightful story about the great scientist Pavlov being challenged by Lenin: How could such an eminent scientist be a churchgoer? "Ah, Vladimir Ilyich, one learns much from science about the force of habit, instincts, reflexes."[18] A sacramental theology finds nothing reductive in the cosmos, and celebrates reason as part of creation, as that which links divine and human natures. In the act of celebrating the Eucharist, the priest characterizes the liturgy as "this reasonable and bloodless worship," *slovechnio siie i beskrovniie sluzhbi.*[19]

The conflict between science and religion, or between reason and faith, is one that exists within Orthodoxy only as an import: the Marxist postulate of such a conflict met little resistance in Russia because there was no tradition of dialectical debate and encounter between faith and reason.

There is a homologous, or isomorphic, relationship between the absence of conflict between faith and reason and the absence in Orthodox theology of mind-body dualism. In Orthodoxy, a religion which is constituted (whether in Byzantium or Russia) as a public condition—as a condition of participation in the public sphere—words and thoughts are necessarily incarnated. Mihailovic attempts to set Bakhtin in opposition to official Orthodox dogma by invoking the theologian M. M. Tareev (1866–1934), who "argued for what he called 'inner [*vnutrennee*] Christianity,' a conception that depended absolutely on the autonomy of the individual consciousness."[20] Yet Tareev is a striking instance of what Florovsky terms the "western captivity" of Orthodoxy, "the most extreme representative of moralism in Russian theology" and a virtual gnostic in his refusal of the Chalcedonian understanding of the Incarnation: "The Christ of the Gospels is . . . a heavenly man, a soul filled with a single religious idea . . . who has practically no contact with the earth, almost no stain of historical life, not the slightest earthly dust."[21]

Tareev followed Protestant pietistic models in setting up an opposition between "spiritual learning" and "logically compelling judgments" until he doubted the "Greco-Eastern conception of Christianity": "We need to be freed from the Byzantine yoke."[22] It would be precisely the task of Florovsky, Vladimir Lossky, and others to salvage Orthodox theology from this sort of confusion by calling explicitly for a return to Byzantine theology, to the formulations of the Councils of Nicaea and Chalcedon, and by aspiring to what Florovsky termed a "neo-patristic synthesis."[23] These theologians, Florovsky most explicitly, were motivated by a desire to cleanse Russian theology of the influence of German Protestant pietism; the relationship between that pietism and the neo-Kantianism of the Marburg school is hardly elusive. A strong reading of the work of the Bakhtin circle in Nevel might urge that Orthodoxy is invoked as a challenge to neo-Kantianism and to its popular influence as pietistic dualism.[24]

Rather than taking Tareev as representative of Orthodoxy, and Bakhtin as an isolated exception, it would be more instructive to see Bakhtin in the context of those of his contemporaries, such as Florovsky, engaged in similar projects of resistance to dualistic models of thinking and being. For an early instance, we could mention a contemporary of Tareev, Viktor I. Nesmelov (1863–1920), who in 1886 wrote a pioneering study of St. Gregory of Nyssa.[25] The rediscovery of this particular patristic thinker has been instrumental in the development of a contemporary Orthodox anthropology, that is to say, of a model of culture and thought that is distinct from and resistant to the hegemony of the West, and that is not dependent—as is the Western model—on creedal, intellectual assent.[26] Nesmelov reckoned with Feuerbach's "*Der Mensch ist, was er isst*" (man is what he eats) and turned Feuerbach's atheism (in a Protestant context) into an Orthodox affirmation that the human is conditioned by the body, that the body is not in conflict with the mind but is its necessary and constitutive other. Incarnation is the model of a monistic or integral understanding of the human person.

Without arguing that Bakhtin had any particular acquaintance with St. Gregory of Nyssa, but assuming the renewed interest of the Russian intelligentsia in patristic thought,[27] it is worth considering Gregory's revolutionary notion of *diastēma*. According to Gregory, Christ's two natures are to be understood in terms of the distinction between Creator and creation. The paradox formulated at Chalcedon—"without confusion or separation"—would for Gregory be possible only because of the asymmetry pertaining between Creator and creation. *Diastēma* is an attribute of creation but not an attribute of the Creator. In the paraphrase of the Indian (Syriac) theologian Paulos Mar Gregorios, "the whole creation is *diastēma* or extendedness in time and space. This creation is open to the knowledge of man."[28]

The human, being created in *diastēma*, has knowledge of all that which is constituted by *diastēma*. There is no *diastēma* in the Creator, that is, in the Trinity, nor between the persons of the Trinity. But the concept becomes complicated: the foundational *diastēma* is between that which knows no *diastēma* and that which is (already) constituted and created by *diastēma*. *Diastēma* is the possibility of mutability, and therefore of space and time; Gregory's particular innovation is to ascribe mutability not only to the sensible world (as in Stoicism), but also to the intelligible world. Thus, Gregory legitimates an externalization and a historicization of consciousness, that inscription of consciousness in time and space that has been most vigorously resisted by the entire tradition of Western philosophy that would secure consciousness in the realm of ideas and treat even time and space as merely contingent to the intelligence. Gregory's objection to the Stoics is that if there were no mutability in the intelligible realm, then intelligibility would belong to the Creator, not to creation. And as intelligence and intelligibility both belong to the created order, so they must both be subject to change.

Yet from Plato to Kantianism, the distinction between the sensible and the intelligible has been maintained, a distinction that emerges in modernity as the dualistic split between the sensible body and the intelligible mind.

Kant's move to reconcile the sensible and the intelligible, by approximating knowledge to representation, grounds the intelligible in that which cannot be represented, the *a priori* forms of space and time. As *a priori* forms, space and time are immutable. A number of commentators have observed that Bakhtin's notion of the chronotope is developed in opposition to the Kantian forms of time and space. I would contend that such an opposition is effected by recourse to the *diastēma* of Gregory of Nyssa and to the theological argument that time and space and intelligibility all belong to creation—God is the creator of "time and space, with all their consequences"[29]—and must therefore all be subject to change and variation. The *diastēma* is that which separates the Creator from creation, but asymmetrically:

> To apply the term *diastēma* also to this gap between Creator and creation is thus slightly misleading, for it is not the distance between two points—one at the boundary of creation and the other at the boundary of God. For God is infinite, has no boundary. The creation is finite and has a boundary. The creation cannot exist but in God, but God is not spatial, and therefore the *diastēma* between the Creator and the creation cannot itself be conceived in any spatial terms. It is a *diastēma* between the undiastatic Creator and the diastatic or extended creation. We can conceive no mental image of such a gap, but it is our experience.[30]

Paulos Mar Gregorios's last sentence cleverly rehearses and modifies Kant's point about *a priori* forms: they cannot be made apparent, but we all experience them as the very condition of appearances: "Time is the formal condition *a priori* of all appearances whatsoever. Space, as the pure form of external intuition, is limited as a condition *a priori* to external appearances alone."[31] Kant then determines to remove time and space from the ravages of motion and change:

Motion, for example, presupposes the perception of something movable. But space considered in itself contains nothing movable; consequently motion must be something which is found in space only through experience. . . . In like manner, Transcendental Aesthetic cannot number the concept of change among its data *a priori*; for time itself does not change, but only something which is in time.[32]

The chronotope is that which subjects time and space to mutability, as part of the created order. As neo-Kantianism insisted on the purely subjective nature of space and time, so the transcendental subject could be established as immutable, immune from the created physical sensible order. And Bakhtin's chronotope is nothing other than the conceptual device which subjects time and space to mutability, which insists on the containment of time and space within the created order.[33]

Gregory's concept of *diastēma* challenges the law of identity, for it insists that as all knowledge takes place in creation, in the condition of *diastēma*, all knowledge must be based on spatial and temporal difference. This is articulated by Gregory in a series of dialogues with his sister, St. Macrina:

"Don't say 'same,'" my teacher [Macrina] said. "This is another impious argument. Say that the one is *like* the other. . . . For it would not be an image if it were the same as its original in all respects."[34]

Thus knowledge, within the created order, is founded on difference, the spatial differentiation of displacement and the temporal differentiation of deferral; something rather *like* that nonconcept that Derrida summons by the name of *différance*. The principle of difference, that which holds distinct the two parts of the Saussurean sign, *signifiant* and *signifié*, "without confusion or separation," has been in recent thinking promoted as noncontingent, nonreducible to the principle of identity. From the *Parmenides* to the Hegelian dialectic, Western thought has figured difference in terms of contingency and has constructed models by which the many should be reduced to the One, the different to the identical, the other to the same. And yet, as Derrida remarks apropos of Heidegger, we cannot attack metaphysics except in language saturated with its own presuppositions. How can we speak of the noncontingency of difference without supposing its determined necessity, that is, without invoking the law of identity? Here, we can see not only how the recent thinking of difference and the other is in the process of liberating some of the suppressed traditions of Western thought: we can also see the particular importance of the idea of asymmetry. Gregory of Nyssa points to the asymmetrical relation between the Creator and Creation—so that while creation occurs within and is bounded by *diastēma*, that *diastēma* that limits creation cannot be said to limit the Creator, nor to separate the Creator. On this basis, Florovsky formulated what he termed "an asymmetrical Christology."[35] And asymmetry has become an insistent element in Levinas's thinking on the face, as also in Derrida's thinking about hospitality.

And Derrida's earlier move toward writing and textuality is, among much else, another attempt to break down the barrier between the intelligible and the sensible, to include the intelligible within the mutable, the tropic. This is the force of grammatology. Derrida's move has been hardly less scandalous than was Gregory's: both subvert the claim of reason and intelligence to a privileged, transcendent position. There is no inner "insensible" origin or mental intention outside the conditioning of the sensible text and the (dis)figuring reach of tropes. What is deconstruction? What is Derrida's anxious-playful fixation on figures and tropes but a refusal of language as timeless and a refusal of intention as immune from the decrepitudes of time-turned discourse? If we think in language— if there is no prelinguistic consciousness—then our very intelligence is subject to mutability. And of course Gregory's word that is translated as change or mutability is *tropē*: "Thus," writes Paulos Mar Gregorios, "*diastēma* and *tropē* are inseparable as characteristics of created existence."[36]

When the Word became flesh, He revealed Himself as a trope. For all these speculations about creation and the Creator circle around the event of the Incarnation. With the thinking of Gregory of Nyssa and others to help them, those present at the Council of Chalcedon were able to conceptualize the Incarnation in terms of a hypostasis in which two natures—human and divine—were joined together, without confusion, without separation. What is not addressed at Chalcedon or in subsequent theology is the consequences of this hypostasis for words, for language. The Incarnation of the Logos had remarkably little effect on linguistic theory. In what follows, I take my cue from Bakhtin's reported words in the lectures delivered in 1924–25: "the Incarnation in itself has destroyed the unity of the Kantian person."[37]

Here we need to investigate further the term *vnenakhodimost'*, "outsideness," about which Caryl Emerson is the only scholar to have provided a substantial account in English. As she shows, this term runs through Bakhtin's thinking from the 1920s to the 1970s. The key to this concept—as to any concept—is to be located in the difference that marks it out from what it replaces. And the replaced concepts are essence and transcendence. In neo-Kantian thought, my knowledge of another depends on my access to the transcendental subject. Thus, one can participate in the very essence of an other; and a philosophical and aesthetic discourse develops around the ideas of sympathy and, in Bakhtin's contemporary, Wilhelm Worringer, of *Einfühlung*, empathy, the sharing of inwardness.[38]

Transcendence allows for reciprocal and symmetrical relations between subjects. Transcendence may be said to enable such relations, or to depend on those relations. Both democracy and imperialism may be ascribed to the transcendence of the subject: I know how you feel, and I know what's good for you. To know how you feel is to posit a common essence, a respect towards the other as towards oneself; knowing what's good for you goes beyond the respectfulness of democracy, and legitimates the interference of imperialism. This must be the fundamental ethical objection to the concept of the transcendental subject: it provides no safeguard for one's privacy, one's inwardness, one's right to silence and nondisclosure.

This predicament may be resolved by resisting, or sacrificing, those attractive concepts, symmetry and reciprocity. Without either reciprocity or symmetry we can recognize and accept the limitations on our knowledge of an other. I can not know an other in any way adequate to the other's self-knowing. Kant had endeavored to place human relations outside the conventional paradigms of the sensible and the intelligible, outside and inside. Rather, by marking the intelligible as the very essence of the human, Kant was able to figure human relations in terms of inwardness. The opponents of Kant and the neo-Kantians, Bakhtin among them, insisted that the human could not be so privileged. Knowing oneself may be an inward knowledge, but how one knows an other is necessarily outward. Here language becomes the issue: for the Kantians, language is a pure and unrefracted representation of thought, mind, inwardness; for the opponents, there is no ground for equating language with thought, and language must be considered to belong to the outside, the world of appearances.[39]

If language belongs to outsideness, then one knows another through outsideness, even (or especially) in language. Insofar as one's knowledge of oneself, as inward knowledge, is incommunicable except as language, or through other signs, it is a useless sort of knowledge. To know oneself from the outside is to know oneself as an other, and this is not a knowledge easily achieved. One's inner knowledge of self is, according to Bakhtin, less valid than another's knowledge of oneself. That is why Bakhtin can say that the self, the very idea of selfhood and subjectivity, is a gift from the other. Outsideness is the proper site and space of knowledge.

In that condition of *vnenakhodimost'* there is no space for the binary division of self and other. Greek mythology may hold in the stories of Echo and Narcissus a prolepsis for the path that Western philosophy would take, from Plato to the neo-Kantians. It is a philosophical tradition dependent on the separation and opposition between self and other, subject and object. Confronted by one's own self as image or shadow or reflection, one is categorically bound to err: for that image is neither self nor other, but oneself known from the outside, in a knowledge that is not inferior for being outside. All our knowledge of the other has, in Western philosophy, been predicated on sympathy and, early in the twentieth century, on empathy, and on the superiority of inward to outward knowledge, of depth over surface, profundity over superficiality, essence over appearance. One's knowledge of oneself is uniquely endowed with inwardness and depth, and that knowledge has therefore been set as the standard to which all other forms of knowing should aspire. Entire conceptual and academic disciplines have set as their task the knowledge of the mind, the inwardness, the intention of others. In German those disciplines are well-labeled *Geisteswissenschaften.* If language can give us no access, no unmediated representation of *der Geist,* the inwardness of mind, then such disciplines are vain.

Bakhtin's *vnenakhodimost'* is, like Gregory's *diastēma,* a concept determined by an asymmetrical, nonreciprocal boundary. Emerson has placed particular emphasis on Bakhtin's use of the word *granitsa* (boundary): "What is the primary work of the boundary? To divide, define, protect, defend, wall off, or connect? . . . Bakhtin believed that separation and connection happen simultaneously."[40] Phrased otherwise, separation and connection are not, in the space of outsideness, mutually exclusive. For the space of outsideness is not open space but borderland, the space of the threshold, the line which—as any line must—both divides and connects. Yet the clue always to be recalled is that the space created by a threshold is not symmetrical. What is on the other side cannot be understood reciprocally as a symmetrical form of what is on this side. The threshold establishes the division between inside and outside, but gives only the access of outsideness to the other side. The threshold is the very condition of contiguity and metonymy, of naming by adjacency and proximity, of naming and knowing by displacement. Philosophy has always been loyal to the literal transparency of language, to a straightforwardness around which meaning and intention may be symmetrically disposed. The two major tropes, of metaphor and metonymy, have always been resisted by philosophers, and by other literalists of the imagination, because they force us to acknowledge the imprecision of language, the slippage between intention and representation: above all, they allow for no symmetry.[41] Tropes are asymmetrical, and nonreciprocal. They are an inconvenience (a scandal) in a cosmos of spatial and temporal continuities, and within a logic of identities. By contrast, in the asymmetrical creation of, and through, the *diastēma,* tropes make sense.

In making Himself, through the Incarnation, circumscribable, God—inaccessible, essential, transcendent—rendered Himself as an outside, took on outsideness. Bakhtin's concept of *vnenakhodimost'* is, in Emerson's words, "part of the larger and prior 'battle against interiority' that dominated debates during Bakhtin's [Nevel] and Leningrad years."[42] This battle against interiority was being waged not only, as we have seen, by various thinkers reacting against the Marburg school, but also by Orthodox theologians among Bakhtin's contemporaries—Georges Florovsky, Vladimir Lossky—against those pietistic notions exemplified by Tareev's "inner Christianity." The connection between Kantianism and pietistic Protestantism need hardly be stressed; a sacramental and iconic religion, such as Orthodoxy, has a vocabulary and a conceptual apparatus of considerable value and endurance in the battle against interiority.

ethical ⟷ aesthetic

Vnenakhodimost' is a concept that can dispense entirely with notions of essence and interiority as positive terms, objects of knowledge. Bakhtin can hold together, through this concept, both the ethical and the aesthetic: the nonintrusive, disinterested aesthetic view (entirely indebted to Kant) is itself the ethical view. The Kantian distinction between the ethical and the aesthetic—the great "either/or" of Kierkegaard's anguished Protestantism—is shown to be redundant. One can behave ethically (or unethically) only to that which has a form, an outline, an appearance; in Levinas's terms, it is the face of the other which initiates the ethical. Furthermore, the essential, positivist self can be displaced, to be replaced by that adjacent differential self that is given by the other—for it is the other that sees my own outsideness much more clearly than I do, or than I can. Bakhtin even denies that I can have any autonomous knowledge of myself: "it is precisely our own selves that we cannot know, since the human psyche is set up to work 'from the outside in'—that is, to encounter and come to know truths from others."[43]

Outsideness works with the tropes of metonymy, through contiguity, proximity, thresholds, openings, limits, boundaries. Essence, by contrast, depends on the logic of identity. We recall St. Macrina's injunction to her brother: "Don't say 'same.' . . . Say that the one is *like* the other." Macrina's resistance to the logic of identity is remarkably forceful: "For it would not be an image if it were the same as its original in all respects." I may say of a photograph on what might be called my identity papers, or *carte d'identité*, "That's me," and I would be appealing to the logic of identity which treats as merely contingent such "superficial" differences as that between flesh and card. The work of identity is carried out by the essence that both the card and my body represent. Macrina's objection is that no one thing can be identical with another thing because the two cannot share the materiality of their representation. Their outsideness is of more importance, of decisive and divisive importance, than their "essence." Contiguous surfaces (metonymies) can be like or unlike one another. They can be metaphorically related, but they cannot be inscribed in the law of identity.

Outsideness is the trope of incarnation and of iconography. "The unity of the Kantian person" is the unity of a subject within a body, of a necessary, essential inner and a contingent outer. The Incarnation transposes value from the inward to the outward, from the "reality" to the "appearance," from the intention to the deed, from the mind to the body. Augustine would agonize over Genesis 1:27, that "God created man in his own image," and never be able decisively to relinquish the Manichean view that this likeness could have nothing to do with the body or "externals." Augustine's recourse to John 4:24—"God is a Spirit"—meant that the image of God in man was no sort of likeness but the inward principle of reason.[44] That capitulation of Western Christianity to Plato and Plotinus is one that was recognized and resisted in the Eastern Church from the earliest days. The vocabulary of "anti-Platonic" resistance that developed within Orthodox theology would be drawn on in various ways by Russian thinkers in the twentieth century, sometimes to "materialist" ends.

We find a good example in V. N. Voloshinov's explication of Saussure:

> [U]nderstanding is a response to a sign with signs. . . . [N]owhere is there a break in the chain, nowhere does the chain plunge into inner being, nonmaterial in nature and unembodied in signs. . . . The individual consciousness is a social-ideological fact. . . . It is precisely the problem of consciousness that has created the major difficulties and generated the formidable confusions. . . . By and large, consciousness has become the *asylum ignorantiae* for all philosophical constructs.[45]

What is the outsideness of language? Or, rather, what is it to conceive of language as having no inside? "The unity of the Kantian person" is predicated on the inwardness of speech, consciousness, and intentionality. What event in language corresponds to or has been consequent upon the Incarnation? The outsideness of language is writing (one is tempted by parenthetic apposition: scripture). (And grammatology.)

Emerson draws our attention to some elliptical phrases in Bakhtin's early essay "The Problem of Content, Material, and Form in Verbal Art" (1924): "In the novel . . . the phoneme yields almost completely its auxiliary functions (to designate signification, to elicit movement, to be the basis for intonation) to the grapheme."[46] Intonation issues from inwardness, as does inner form. As early as 1924 Bakhtin is evaluating the novel above the lyric on this axis: "The significance of the creating inner organism is not the same in all kinds of poetry. It is maximal in lyric. . . . The involvement of the inner organism in form is minimal in the novel" ("PCMFVA" 314). We find already here the outline of the argument of "Epic and Novel," that the novel is the only form of verbal art that is entirely dependent on the grapheme: "Of all the major genres only the novel is younger than writing and the book: it alone is organically receptive to new forms of mute perception" (*DI* 3).

It is the absence of both the phonetic and the acoustic that liberates novelistic discourse from the interiority of what Derrida names the (phono)logocentric. In the novel, language is without intonation, without phonetic indication of an originating voice or intending mind. Rather, in a novel the word loses its unbounded capacity for representation and is instead framed, contained, limited as an object of representation: "Under conditions of the novel every direct word . . . is to a greater or lesser degree made into an object, the word itself becomes a bounded [*ograničennij*] image, one that quite often appears ridiculous in this framed condition" (*DI* 49–50). The outsidedness of the word and the boundedness of the image are concepts theologically inflected; indeed, neither concept is thinkable without the Incarnation.

Outsidedness and boundedness would not alone explain the power and originality of novelistic discourse. In "dialogism," Bakhtin names a concept by analogy to the Chalcedonian concept of "duophysitism," the two natures of the incarnate Christ. Something of this is suggested by the physical, geological, and chemical metaphors by which Bakhtin describes the work of dialogism:

> The development of the novel is a function of the deepening of dialogic essence, its increased scope and greater precision. Fewer and fewer neutral, hard elements ("rock bottom truths") remain that are not drawn into dialogue. Dialogue moves into the deepest molecular and, ultimately, subatomic levels. (*DI* 300)

The development of "free indirect discourse" has been traced both as a fictional device, going back to the late-eighteenth-century novel, and as an analytical concept developed by some of the students of Karl Vossler. All classical and traditional grammars and rhetorics have derived writing from voice, and, in analysis, reduced writing to speaking. For well over a century, linguists and grammarians either ignored the linguistic evidence of "prose fiction" or labored to explain how every clause and phrase could be ascribed to an individual, unitary voice. So steeped in "logocentrism" had literary and philological scholarship been that there was apparently no possibility of recognizing the textual phenomenon of discourse not reducible or assimilable to the individual voice.

For the first time, round about 1910 (when Virginia Woolf declared human nature to have changed—but in the orbit of Marburg rather than of Bloomsbury), Gertrud Lauch, Etienne Lorch, and Charles Bally came almost simultaneously to the recognition of the phenomenon of *erlebte Rede*, or *uneigentliche Rede*, or *style indirect libre*. The terms *libre* and *uneigentliche* refer to the undecidability of ascription.[47] For the first time, writing was seen to have an effect not reducible to speech. There are words in a novel that belong to no single voice. Remarkably, it does not follow that there are words that belong to no voice at all; only that there are words which belong to more than one voice.

What is striking is that it took even these scholars some years to realize that the device could be found long before Flaubert, even in the eighteenth-century novel. At first it was assumed that the phenomenon was a stylistic device, deliberately cultivated by such conscious artists as Flaubert. As it was realized that even Flaubert had never spoken explicitly about it and that the female novelists of the late eighteenth century, in whose works the phenomenon can be found, would have lacked the terms and concepts to explain what was happening in their writings, it began to be understood that free indirect discourse came about through no writer's conscious effort: it is simply a given of what Bakhtin, seeking to distinguish the novel from the traditional concept of "prose," called "novelistic discourse." At first, of course, Bakhtin thought it especially prevalent in Dostoevsky; it certainly explains, for example, the common complaint by stylistic purists that Dostoevsky's language is often indistinguishable from that of vulgar journalism. By the mid-1930s it was not a particular Russian novelist but "novelistic discourse" itself that Bakhtin would celebrate. What is not possible in speech is possible in writing: a Chalcedonian, two-voiced, double-natured discourse.

The traditional and "classical" arguments against the novel—that it is vulgar and "unartistic"[48]—are similar to the iconoclastic arguments against the representation of the incarnate God. God is uncircumscribable, and therefore should not be contained in a bounded image. The classical genres, open-ended in their intentionality and endless replication of vocalization, frame and contain language in a merely contingent way. Their challenge is merely the creation of a bounded image of a person, a speaker. The novel's task is more extensive, for it fixes language in the text, insists, we might venture, on the incarnation of language, and therefore on its representability, even at the expense of often appearing ridiculous:

> Characteristic for the novel as a genre is not the image of a man in his own right, but precisely the *image of a language*. . . . [T]he central problem for a stylistics of the novel may be formulated as the problem of *artistically representing language, the problem of representing the image of a language.* (DI 336)

Bakhtin's dialogism is fundamentally a characteristic of text, an event of writing. Derrida's opposition to logocentrism can here again be shown to be accordant with Bakhtin's dialogism: both are opposed to the singleness of voice, the ownership of voice, and at the political level, to voice's constitution of the idea of the subject as possessive individual.[49] Indeed, the condition of the dialogical is that the external image of the person is exploded: "The epic wholeness of an individual disintegrates in a novel" (DI 37).

We must, in this phrase, hear an echo of Bakhtin's earlier saying: "The Incarnation in itself has destroyed the unity of the Kantian person." Epic is the presentation of the pure exterior, the diegesis of narrative and description, lyric of the interior voice. The novel breaks down the Aristotelian distinction between dialogue and diegesis, as it ignores all distinctions of genre. Another form of writing had already made a mockery of classical rhetoric and poetics, as Augustine had been by no means the first to notice:

> [The Scriptures] seemed to me unworthy in comparison with the dignity of Cicero. My conceit was repelled by their simplicity, and my gaze did not penetrate its interior [*et acies mea non penetrabat interiora eius*].[50]

As Tertullian had already observed, the low style, the *sermo humilis*, was entirely appropriate both to give an account of, and to account for, the Incarnation.[51] Whereas Augustine finds lofty and sublime meanings "hidden" in the "interior" of the scriptural text—behind the humble and rustic facade—Bakhtin will concentrate instead on the facade itself. The argument that novelistic discourse found its origins in Scripture, and specifically in the Gospels, was one that Bakhtin was hardly free to advance explicitly. But that very argument is the core of Erich Auerbach's *Mimesis:* "It was the story of Christ, with its ruthless mixture of everyday reality and the highest and most sublime tragedy, which had conquered the classical rule of styles."[52] Where Auerbach had explored that mixture of styles already observed by the early Christian Fathers, and traced its consequences through the Middle Ages and into modernity, Bakhtin would ignore the problem of style and look instead at the mixture of voices.

Where there is more than one voice to which words can be ascribed, there can be no one voice nor voices heard. What we "hear" may metaphorically be named "polyphony," but there is only the silence of the text, the silence of potential voicings. Free indirect discourse, reconceptualized by Bakhtin as dialogism, makes and holds the connection between outsideness and silence. Voice speaks from within, opens up an interior space, dissolves the boundaries of the body. Silence, by contrast, affirms the body and insists in the body. Silent prayer is considered in the monastic traditions of both East and West to be a "higher" or more advanced form than articulated prayer, but with an important difference. In the West, and in pietistic circles in Orthodoxy, silent prayer is taken as a sign of inwardness, of contempt or indifference for the outer world. By contrast, in that tradition of Orthodox prayer known as hesychasm (from the Greek word for "silence"), associated especially with St. Gregory Palamas—the fourteenth-century Byzantine theologian whose rediscovery and scholarly editing proved to be of incalculable consequence for Orthodox theology in the twentieth century[53]—silence is a condition of the body, a state of exteriority. And the aim of hesychastic theory was to conceive of silence as something other than an absence of discourse; silence is not merely an unrealized or unfulfilled sound, a suppressed or latent voicing. John Meyendorff's editorial heading for a set of passages from Palamas's *Triads* is eloquent: "The Hesychast method of prayer, and the transformation of the body."[54]

Because of the identification of the voice with the intelligible (as in the Greek *logos*), silence could, conversely, be considered as "sensible" or corporeal: a bodily practice. St. John Climacus, as early as the fifth century, speaks of the practitioner of silent prayer as "he who tries to circumscribe the incorporeal in his body."[55] "Circumscription" is a term often used in the debate about icons, with reference to the circumscription of the divine nature in the human person of Christ.

Palamas accused his opponents of trying to turn Christianity "into a religion of disincarnation."[56] Writing in 1959, Meyendorff summarized Palamas's theology as "Christian materialism." The silence of hesychastic prayer intensifies awareness of the body and celebrates that awareness; for the body, the flesh, is that of Christ's Incarnation. The hesychast St. Gregory the Sinaite (circa 1265–1346) glossed the Incarnation as the Word "thickening," as the strokes of a letter might thicken out, and thus become an image.[57]

Hesychasm has a theory of discourse whose significance has long defied understanding. In explicating it here, I make no claim for any connection between Kostenecki and Bakhtin: the likenesses between two theories of silence, graphism and embodiment, should be quietly evident.

One of Palamas's most notable disciples was the hesychast bishop Eftimy, patriarch of Turnovo from 1375 to 1393; he argued that Slavonic letters are themselves icons, and therefore should be fixed in their formation. Eftimy's follower, Constantine Kostenecki, then edited Eftimy's writings and compiled (circa 1420) a *Treatise on the Letters* in which the form of the shaping of Slavonic characters is established: a letter must be inscribed in the prescribed form. In a different form it may still be readable, recognizable as the sign of a particular sound, but it will not, as a letter, be an icon. Worse, it will be an idol. In this seemingly abstruse debate of the fifteenth century, we see a fascinating but misguided attempt to establish writing itself as a practice of silence.[58] St. Gregory the Sinaite was so devoted to silence that even the "still small voice" of 1 Kings 19:12 was too disruptive and had to be reconfigured as "a slight breath of light."[59] Today we can look back on Kostenecki's *Treatise* as an attempt, at the moment of Gutenberg, at the very inception of Florentine humanism and Neoplatonism, to assert that which the West was about to suppress for half a millennium, to reaffirm Orthodoxy's opposition to the privileging of voice in Hellenistic thought—in the name of (let us write) grammatology.

Letters, when spoken, lose their outsideness, and their thickenings. Dialogic discourse—"unspeakable sentences" in Ann Banfield's precise title[60]—resists voicing and makes outsideness an absolute state, not one merely provisional and contingent on the voice. If we are to understand Kostenecki's extreme position, we should conceive of outsideness as being like—but not the same as—iconicity. The obvious way to silence writing is to see it as an icon, as calligraphy; as such, however, it loses its status as writing. What hesychasm seeks is a writing that cannot be read aloud but that can, still, be read. We should recall that only in the past two hundred years, and only in the West, has "reading" ceased to imply "reading aloud." Gregory the Sinaite refuses all figures of hearing, even of hearing the Word of God. Even when the hesychast has advanced beyond the need of a text, the text still supplies the appropriate figure:

He looks on God and receives from Him divine ideas. Instead of a book he has the spirit; . . . instead of ink, the Light. So dipping his mind in the Light, and himself becoming light, he inscribes words.[61]

It is from within this theological context and tradition—in which vast claims have been made for textuality and calligraphy—that Bakhtin can develop his concept of outsideness, from the tentative mention of "grapheme" in 1924 to the celebration of the pure exteriority of Rabelais's text:

> [T]here is not a single instance in the entire expanse of Rabelais' huge novel where we are shown what a character is thinking, what he is experiencing, his internal dialogue. In this sense there is in Rabelais' novel no world of interiority. All that a man is finds expression in actions and in dialogue. (DI 239–40)[62]

Bakhtin's formulation of the dialogic resolves the arguments about inner and outer speech that preoccupied the German Romantics, notably Lessing, on Homer, and Schiller on *Naive and Sentimental Poetry.* Epic is made of dialogue and diegesis, the clearly distinguished and attributed voices of characters and narrator; the novel consists of neither. Novelistic discourse is the first to answer Kostenecki's demand that a text be readable without being readable aloud. Dialogism is the discourse whose trope is outsideness and whose moment is Incarnation. Bakhtin writes that the novel is the only genre to have originated since the invention of writing. Writing may stand here for the incarnation of the word: novelistic discourse is the linguistic consequence of the Incarnation. Bakhtin, deploying the tropes of Orthodoxy as well as Marxism, can well be described as a dialogical materialist.

Throughout Bakhtin's work, dialogics stands as the alternative to dialectics, an alternative that grounds itself in bodies in their outsideness, and refuses the easy resort to inwardness and transcendence, that slick move of the dialectic that destroys as it sublates. The West today dreams itself to be at the end, the summit, the triumph of its own dialectic: the finishing touches are called globalization. Yet for those who insist on the value of outsideness—of the particularity and singularity of signs, on the split, the difference, the *diastēma,* the irreducible doubleness incarnate in every concept and every body—the dialectic ("Hegelian spirit") has been a distraction and an irrelevance for more than two millennia.

At the close of his impassioned meditation on the fate of Orthodoxy, *Ways of Russian Theology,* Georges Florovsky, attentive like Bakhtin to the wonders of otherness and the horror of its dialectical negation, wrote in 1937 about the task and responsibility of the theologian: "learning in general is not and must not be a dia-lectical, but rather a dia-logical moment."[63] If this is not an allusion to Bakhtin, it must at least point to a superficial (and therefore significant) likeness, in the

Chalcedonian trope of the Logos incarnate: the double-nature and double-voice of word play.

Notes

1. Cited in Caryl Emerson, *The First Hundred Years of Mikhail Bakhtin* (Princeton: Princeton Univ. Press, 1997), 50.

2. Katerina Clark and Michael Holquist, *Mikhail Bakhtin* (Cambridge: Harvard Univ. Press, 1984), 347 (also 4–5).

3. Emerson, *The First Hundred Years*, 52.

4. See Brian Poole, "Bakhtin and Cassirer: The Philosophical Origins of Bakhtin's Carnival Messianism," *South Atlantic Quarterly* 97 (1998): 537–78; and a response, Charles Lock, "The Bakhtin Scandal/L'affaire Bakhtine," *Literary Research/ Recherche Littéraire* 31 (1999): 13–19.

5. See Emerson, *The First Hundred Years*, 171.

6. See Jaroslav Pelikan, *The Christian Tradition: A History of the Development of Doctrine*, vol. 1, *The Emergence of the Catholic Tradition (100–600)* (Chicago and London: Univ. of Chicago Press, 1971), 263–66.

7. Emerson, *The First Hundred Years*, 175.

8. Ibid., 75–78.

9. Georges Florovsky, *Ways of Russian Theology*, pt. 2, trans. Robert L. Nichols (Vaduz, Lichtenstein: Büchervertriebsanstalt, 1987), 336 n. 219 (translation amended).

10. Ibid., 375 n. 30.

11. Oleg Osovsky has provided documentation of émigré reviews of Bakhtin in "Kniga M. M. Bakhtina o Dostoevskom v otsenkakh literaturovedeniia russkogo zarubezh'ya," in *Bakhtinskii sbornik II: Bakhtin mezhdu Rossiei i zapadom* (Moscow: Kollektiv avtorov, 1991), 379–85. Vitaly Makhlin has edited and reprinted some of these reviews; for details, see Emerson, *The First Hundred Years*, 82–83, nn. 12–14. The Florovsky reference has not hitherto been noticed; it may well be that through Florovsky other theologians and Orthodox colleagues at Institut St.-Serge, the Orthodox Theological Institute in Paris, were alerted to the significance of Bakhtin. Also ignored in the emigration is the thirty-page chapter devoted to Bakhtin in Vladimir Seduro's *Dostoevsky in Russian Literary Criticism, 1846–1956* (New York: Columbia Univ. Press, 1957). One needs also to weigh the influence of Seduro's article, "Dostoevski kak sozdatel' polifonicheskogo romana," *Novyi Zhurnal*, bk. 52 (March 1958): 71–93.

12. *St. Vladimir's Theological Quarterly* 27, no. 2 (1983): 93–118. Bakhtin is mentioned on pp. 108–9 and in n. 29. Ugolnik has written more extensively on

Bakhtin in *The Illuminating Icon* (Grand Rapids: Eerdmans, 1989), 158–73. (Ugolnik's theological writings are cited by Clark and Holquist, *Mikhail Bakhtin*, 85.)

13. Charles Lock, "Carnival and Incarnation: Bakhtin and Orthodox Theology," *Literature and Theology* 5, no. 1 (1991): 68–82. Reprinted in *Critical Essays on Mikhail Bakhtin*, ed. Caryl Emerson, *Critical Essays on World Literature* (New York: G. K. Hall/Twayne, 1999), 285–99.

14. Alexandar Mihailovic, *Corporeal Words: Mikhail Bakhtin's Theology of Discourse* (Evanston: Northwestern Univ. Press, 1997), 126.

15. Ibid., 131. See *PDP* 26–27. This passage was, according to Bocharov, the occasion of much subsequent anxiety for Bakhtin, who regretted that, having invoked the church, he felt compelled to dispose of it together with "Hegelian spirit": "both 'Hegelian spirit' and 'church' distract equally from this immediate task" (Sergey Bocharov, "Conversations with Bakhtin," *PMLA* 109 [1994]: 1012–13).

16. Mihailovic, *Corporeal Words*, 146.

17. See Randall Poole's discussion in the present volume.

18. This joke may have an anecdotal source; positive authentication would be welcomed.

19. *Liturgy of St. John Chrysostom*, Anaphora. The word "reasonable" [*slovechnaia*] occurs also in the Anaphora of the *Liturgy of St. Basil*: "every creature of reason and understanding worships Thee." *Slovechne* in Slavonic has a similar semantic range to the Greek *logos*.

20. Mihailovic, *Corporeal Words*, 99.

21. Cited by Florovsky, *Ways*, 216.

22. Ibid., 219.

23. See George H. Williams, "The Neo-Patristic Synthesis of Georges Florovsky," in *Georges Florovsky: Russian Intellectual, Orthodox Churchman*, ed. Andrew Blane (Crestwood, N.Y.: St. Vladimir's Seminary Press, 1993), 287–340.

24. See the appendix to the present volume. This tension, between patristic Orthodoxy and Russian pietism, is exemplified in the story told by Sergei Averintsev in the present volume, in which the humor displayed by St. Anthony the Great had to be explained away by "a highly respected nineteenth-century spiritual writer."

25. See Florovsky, *Ways*, 221.

26. For the best modern accounts of Orthodox anthropology or, even, of Orthodoxy as anthropology, see Paulos Mar Gregorios, *Cosmic Man—The Divine Presence: The Theology of St. Gregory of Nyssa* (c. 330–395 A.D.) (New Delhi: Sophia, 1980); Christos Yannaras, *The Freedom of [from] Morality*, trans. E. Briere (Crestwood, N.Y.: St. Vladimir's Seminary Press, 1984); and John D. Zizioulas, *Being as Communion: Studies in Personhood and the Church* (Crestwood, N.Y.: St. Vladimir's Seminary Press, 1985).

27. For example, Gregory of Nyssa's role in Russian Symbolism, and even his affinity with Mandelshtam, is argued by Irina Paperno in "On the Nature of the

Word: Theological Sources of Mandelshtam's Dialogue with the Symbolists," in *Christianity and the Eastern Slavs*, vol. 2 of *Russian Culture in Modern Times*, ed. Robert P. Hughes and Irina Paperno (Berkeley and Los Angeles: Univ. of California Press, 1994), 287–310.

28. Gregorios, *Cosmic Man*, 83.

29. Gregory of Nyssa, cited in Jaroslav Pelikan, *Christianity and Classical Culture: The Metamorphosis of Natural Theology in the Christian Encounter with Hellenism* (New Haven and London: Yale Univ. Press, 1993), 117.

30. Gregorios, *Cosmic Man*, 95. For concise and lucid terminological distinctions between *diastēma, diaphora, diairesis, diastole,* and *diastasis,* see Lars Thunberg, *Microcosm and Mediator: The Theological Anthropology of Maximus the Confessor,* 2nd ed. (Chicago: Open Court, 1995), 51–61.

31. Immanuel Kant, "Transcendental Doctrine of Elements," in *Critique of Pure Reason*, 1, §7 c.

32. Ibid., 1, §8.

33. Bakhtin's "chronotope" can be traced back to the Nevel years, specifically to the fourth lecture (October 25, 1924); see the appendix to this volume. The earliest challenge, from a neo-Kantian, to Kant's notions of space and time may be that of F. A. Trendelenburg, whose *On a Gap in Kant's Proof of the Exclusively Subjective Nature of Space and Time* appeared in 1867. See Klaus Christian Köhnke, *The Rise of Neo-Kantianism: German Academic Philosophy between Idealism and Positivism,* trans. R. J. Hollingdale (Cambridge: Cambridge Univ. Press, 1991), 11–35, 170.

34. St. Gregory of Nyssa, *The Soul and the Resurrection,* trans. C. Roth (Crestwood, N.Y.: St. Vladimir's Seminary Press, 1993), 45.

35. See Williams, "The Neo-Patristic Synthesis," 300, and n. 34. Meyendorff points to the lack of symmetry in the Chalcedonian doctrine of the Incarnation, and notes that it was "precisely a 'symmetrical' Christology which was rejected" as the Nestorian heresy at the Council of Ephesus in 431. John Meyendorff, *Byzantine Theology: Historical Trends and Doctrinal Themes,* 2nd ed. (New York: Fordham Univ. Press, 1979), 154.

36. Gregorios, *Cosmic Man*, 84.

37. See appendix; see also Emerson, *The First Hundred Years,* 235.

38. The art historian Wilhelm Worringer published his thesis *Abstraktion und Einfühlung* in 1908. The word "empathy" entered English (from Greek via German *Einfühlung*) in 1909. See also Alan Jacobs's essay in this volume.

39. Bakhtin's place in this argument should be evident. We should recall that among the other opponents of neo-Kantianism, the other thinkers who reacted strongly against the Marburg school were Heidegger and Buber. In the terms "phenomenology" and "existentialism" are indicated the rejection of their antonyms: the idea that we might have access to the noumenal or the essential. Martin Buber's *Ich und Du* (1923)—a book much admired by Bakhtin—insists on

asymmetry as an ontological condition, and initiates that tradition of asymmetrical ethics that we can trace to Emmanuel Levinas and the recent work of Derrida. In this volume, see the third section of Alan Jacobs's essay.

40. Emerson, *The First Hundred Years*, 239.

41. On Bakhtin's contemporaries, Roman Jakobson, the Russian Formalists, and the poets of the Silver Age, see Charles Lock, "Debts and Displacements: On Metaphor and Metonymy," *Acta linguistica hafniensis* (Roman Jakobson Centennial Symposium) 29 (1997): 321–37.

42. Emerson, *The First Hundred Years*, 211.

43. Ibid., 212. Emerson here paraphrases N. Bonetskaia, "M.M. Bakhtin i traditsii russkoi filosofii," *Voprosy filosofii*, no. 1 (1993), who goes on to distinguish Bakhtin's "outside-in" anthropology from "the mainstream teachings of Russian Orthodox philosophers (Soloviev, Lossky, Frank, Florensky)." This is problematic: Solovyov is by no reckoning "mainstream," nor is his follower Florensky. S. L. Frank and N. O. Lossky were academic philosophers who identified with Orthodoxy. If one looks at the theologians of the "neo-patristic synthesis," Florovsky, V. N. Lossky, A. Schmemann, and especially at those (often inspired by Florensky) concerned with the revival of iconography as a theological and incarnational discourse (even, among our contemporaries, B. A. Uspensky, *The Semiotics of the Russian Icon* [Lisse: Peter de Ridder, 1976]), we find a view of the value of exteriority not far from Bakhtin's.

44. See, for example, Augustine, *Confessions*, III, iv (10)–III, vii (12).

45. V. N. Voloshinov, *Marxism and the Philosophy of Language*, trans. L. Matejka and I. Titunik (Cambridge: Harvard Univ. Press, 1986), 11–13 (translation slightly adjusted).

46. Emerson, *The First Hundred Years*, 247, citing "PCMFVA" 313. "Grapheme" sounds (or looks) suspiciously like a later interpolation; we await detailed editorial work on Bakhtin's manuscripts.

47. The very verb "ascribe" manifests the link between writing and individuation, that every written word should issue from and represent a particular voice.

48. See the section of Bakhtin's "Discourse in the Novel" entitled "Modern Stylistics and the Novel" (*DI* 260–75).

49. See Robert Cunliffe, "Bakhtin and Derrida: Drama and the Phoneyness of the Phonè," in *Face to Face: Bakhtin in Russia and the West*, ed. Carol Adlam et al. (Sheffield: Sheffield Academic Press, 1997), 347–65.

50. Augustine, *Confessions*, III, v (9).

51. See Erich Auerbach's classic essay, "Sermo Humilis," in *Literary Language and Its Public in Late Latin Antiquity and in the Early Middle Ages*, trans. R. Manheim (Princeton: Princeton Univ. Press, 1965), 25–66; see especially 51–52. The editors of this volume have drawn attention to some of the similarities between Auerbach and Bakhtin in their introduction.

52. Erich Auerbach, *Mimesis: The Representation of Reality in Western Literature* (1946), trans. W. Trask (Princeton: Princeton Univ. Press, 1953), 555.

53. See John Meyendorff, *Introduction à l'étude de Grégoire Palamas* (Paris: Seuil, 1959); and *A Study of Gregory Palamas*, trans. G. Lawrence (Crestwood, N.Y.: St. Vladimir's Seminary Press, 1964).

54. Gregory Palamas, *The Triads*, ed. J. Meyendorff (New York: Paulist Press, 1983), 41.

55. Cited in Meyendorff, *A Study*, 146.

56. Ibid., 156.

57. St. Gregory the Sinaite, *Discourse on the Transfiguration*, ed. David Balfour (Athens: Theologia, 1982), 44–45. The Greek word is παχυνθεισ.

58. See Harvey Goldblatt, *Orthography and Orthodoxy: Constantine Kostenecki's Treatise on the Letters* (Florence: Studia historica et philologica, 1987).

59. See St. Gregory the Sinaite, *Discourse on the Transfiguration*, 17.

60. Ann Banfield, *Unspeakable Sentences: Narration and Representation in the Language of Fiction* (London: Routledge, 1982).

61. St. Gregory the Sinaite, *Discourse on the Transfiguration*, 155.

62. The similarity of this passage to that of Voloshinov cited above (see note 45) is plain.

63. Florovsky, *Ways*, 306–7.

Bakhtin's Dialogue with Russian Orthodoxy and Critique of Linguistic Universalism

Alexandar Mihailovic

I ask the reader to relate to God as to an actual person, a neighbor, and to express that knowledge according to the very same categories that such an individual would use in expressing relations with a brother or a friend.
                    —from Maria Yudina's notes on Orthodox doctrine

My love for variations and for a diversity of terms for a single phenomenon. The multiplicity of focuses.
                    —from Bakhtin's notes written in 1970–71

Introduction: Bakhtin's Love of Diversity

Why should a "feeling for faith" be more important than faith itself? The epigraph to the present volume is as illuminating as it is deceptively transparent. In grappling with this statement, we should bear in mind that it is a workshop product, one of the many seemingly disconnected assertions from Bakhtin's notes on Dostoevsky published posthumously as "Toward a Reworking of the Dostoevsky Book." Bakhtin's equation of Eastern Orthodoxy with political shibboleths such as man, progress, and revolution (which he follows with a withering "etc.") eloquently speaks not just to his assertion in the interviews with Viktor Duvakin that he was always apolitical, but also to his awareness of the ideological or politicized component of Russian Orthodoxy itself.[1] A feeling for faith, Bakhtin declares, is "an integral attitude (by means of the whole person) toward a higher and ultimate value [*tsennost'*]" ("TRDB" 294).[2] The particular object of that faith is not important, only the sense of dialogue that takes place between the self and Other.

We would all do well to heed the editor Liudmila Gogotishvili's warning that many statements in Bakhtin's sketchbooks and notes represent virtual quotations and paraphrases of other authors' and commentators' work, some of which are cast in only the slightest of polemical dies.[3] While many of Bakhtin's reformulations of others' conclusions are themselves profoundly dialogic in relation to their sources, the task of teasing him from his entanglements with opponents is often difficult indeed. Nonetheless, the framing of the statement above in the form of an exclusionary qualification tugs at the skein of the apparently makeshift and random statements in Bakhtin's preliminary notes for the second edition of his Dostoevsky book, pointing in the direction of the critic's own idiosyncratic conceptualization. We begin to remember similar locutions, also situated as primary clauses, in the same set of notes: "[n]ot theory (transient content), but a 'feeling for theory' [*chuvstvo teorii*]"; "[n]ot types of peoples and fates finalized in an objective way, but *types of worldviews*"; "[n]ot merging [*sliianie*] with another, but preserving one's own position of *extralocality* [*vnenakhodimost'*] and the *surplus* of vision and understanding connected with it" ("TRDB" 294, 296, 299).[4] These clearly parallel formulations enable us to establish links between, on the one hand, faith (in the sense of an adherence to a particular belief system), theory, reductive objectifications of human life, and the absorption or merging of identity; and, on the other, the sense of theory, types of worldviews, and productive outsidedness or transgredience. The overall opposition that Bakhtin establishes is between the self-sufficiency of ideas as frozen, codified truths and our actual engagement with them; it represents the tension between the abstraction of the letter of the law and the human agent's interaction with (and eventual skewing of) it, between the tendencies of monologic and dialogic discourse.

But in specific terms, what form does this tension take in regard to Bakhtin's own dialogic relation with Orthodoxy, which he draws attention to in his statement about the primacy of a sense of, or feeling for, faith over faith itself? As I demonstrate in my book *Corporeal Words: Mikhail Bakhtin's Theology of Discourse*,[5] the influence of Eastern Orthodox religious thought on Bakhtin's work is abundantly evident if viewed from the twin perspectives of Russian intellectual history and textological issues in Bakhtin's work. Bakhtin's adaptation of the Johannine logology with its incarnational model and the Chalcedonian and Trinitarian paradigms of unity within diversity are especially evident in his concepts of novelistic discourse and polyphony. In this regard, one turn of phrase in particular from the series of qualifying statements quoted above points to Bakhtin's sense of religious faith in Eastern Orthodoxy: "not merging [*ne sliianie*]." Indeed, we then realize that the inventory of statements above can be augmented with another, more involuted one from an earlier point in these notes: "Unity not as an innate one-and-only, but as a dialogic *concordance* [*soglasie*] of unmerged [*nesliianykh*] twos or multiples" ("TRDB" 289).[6] Framed in this particular set of Russian terms, the image of a nonconvergent yet contiguous interaction between entities numbering two or more has a distinct theological provenance: the formula of the human and divine natures of Christ coexisting "without confusion or separation" (Russian *"nesliianno i nerazdel'no"*) drafted at the Fourth Ecumenical Council at Chalcedon in 451.

In coming to terms with Bakhtin's surprisingly explicit references to the Chalcedonian notion of the bisected unity of the human and the divine—which he often recasts into either the tense interrelation of high and low in carnival or the participants in a dialogue—we must bear in mind that he regards that particular doctrine as inextricably linked to other theologically grounded thematics. Two other notions in his criticism claim a particular kinship to the Chalcedonian subtext in his work. To the extent that these concepts predate the Fourth Ecumenical Council and achieve a kind of synthesis with it, I will briefly outline them in their relations to Bakhtin's criticism before discussing their recapitulation in the Chalcedonian notion of coinherence.[7]

The first of these concepts is grounded in a specific passage from the Gospels. In a series of sketchy yet revealing notes written from 1970 to 1971, Bakhtin explicitly connects both theoretical and applied linguistics to the Johannine philosophy of the word: "Metaphysics and the philosophy of the word. Ancient teachings about logos. John [*Ioann*]. Language, speech, speech communication, utterance [*vyskazyvanie*]. The specific nature of speech communication" (*SpG* 152).[8] Discussing Bakhtin's roots in turn-of-the-century Russian religious thought, Natalia Bonetskaia draws special attention to the systemic consistency and unity of Bakhtin's ideas throughout his work, particularly in regard to the theological and philosophical ramifications of language.[9] In their pathbreaking 1984 biography of the critic, Clark and Holquist link Bakhtin's concept of the word with enfleshment or embodiment (*voploshchenie*)—the word becoming real and substantial when people engage in dialogic interaction with one another—without venturing the possibility of an indebtedness in his work to the famous Logos of John 1:1 and 1:14: "In the beginning was the Word [Greek *logos;* Russian *slovo*], and the Word was with God, and the Word was God. . . . And the Word became flesh [Russian *plotiiu*], and dwelt among us" (*RSV*).[10] Bakhtin often uses the ambiguous Russian term *slovo* to designate both discourse and the individual word or utterance, emphasizing the links between these different levels of language and culture by rapidly shifting the focus from one to another of these meanings of the term, even within the same essay. His now-classic study "Discourse in the Novel" is an especially salient example of the contrapuntal relation between the primary and secondary meanings in his terminology. Certainly the concept of the word's stages of gestation and generation plays a key role in almost all of Bakhtin's writing, particularly in his dissertation on Rabelais, where the notion of the enfleshment of the word takes on a distinctly organic, and sometimes even carnal, character.

The second theological notion crucial to Bakhtin's work is the Greek patristic concept of *perichoresis* or interpenetration (Latin *circumincessio, permeatio;* Russian *vzaimopronikovenie, vzaimopronikovennost'*) used to describe the coinherence of the Trinity's hypostases, which, in some ways, anticipated the Chalcedonian notion of separation tempered by unity. Although the term's Latin equivalent was used by Augustine in his treatise on the Trinity, *perichoresis* has traditionally played a greater role in Orthodox Christology than in Western Christianity. The church fathers adapted this term from the Stoicist legacy (where it was used to describe the passing through, coextension, or interpenetration of physical bodies at all points of each other) in order to elaborate upon and clarify the consubstantiality of the Father and Son in their unimpeded interaction yet fundamental separateness.[11]

Over the past 160 years, many commentators have seen in *perichoresis* the cornerstone of Orthodoxy both as a belief system and a cultural tradition. During the 1840s, the Slavophile Aleksei Khomiakov formulated the most famous philosophical variation of hypostatic interdwelling or interpenetration in his notion of *sobornost'*, a term that denotes the kind of social all-oneness, communality, or conciliarism that he considered a hallmark of Eastern Orthodoxy as opposed to the overweening individualism and social atomism that he believed stemmed from the Western religious tradition. Fifty years later, the philosopher Vladimir Solovyov jettisoned Khomiakov's term—which to this day remains a highly charged and vigorously debated concept—for a more complex vision of individuality and egoism sacrificed at the moment of the self's close interaction with the Other.[12] With an eye to this polemic, the modern-day Orthodox theologian Kallistos Ware asserts that "there is in God something analogous to 'society'" in the sense that "He is not a single person, loving himself alone, not a self-contained monad or 'The One.'" As Ware explains, God is rather a "triunity: three equal persons, each one dwelling in the other two by virtue of an unceasing movement of mutual love," and "[t]he final end of the spiritual Way is that we humans should become a part of this Trinitarian coinherence or *perichoresis*, being wholly taken up into the circle of love that exists within God."[13]

The Russian translation of *perichoresis* (*vzaimoproniknovenie*) occurs in many instances throughout Bakhtin's writing as a term and an idea, sometimes through related words such as *pronikat'* (to penetrate, permeate) and *[vzaimo]proniknovennost'* ([inter]penetrability). Particularly significant from the Bakhtinian perspective is the assertion here of the miraculous paradox of one human generation being spatially coterminous and temporally coincident with another, to the point where they are unified within a single person or hypostasis. The divine Word is unitary, but has within it a multiplicity of interlocking essences.[14] Particularly revealing in this regard is a passage from Bakhtin's second Dostoevsky book in which Bakhtin describes how the voices of other characters find their way into Raskolnikov's consciousness, resonating in one consciousness and becoming mutually penetrable (*vzaimopronitsamymi*) to each other, intersecting (*peresekaiut*) each other.[15] Nonetheless, it is important to note that the term *sobornost'* never occurs in Bakhtin's work, and it is most revealing of nativist readings of Bakhtin that some scholars in Russia who attempt to discuss the philosophical roots of Bakhtin's terminology of interrelation have unfortunately adverted to this ideologically saturated concept. Given the effective coopting of the theological concept by Khomiakov and others, I would go so far as to say that Bakhtin is in fact polemicizing against the Slavophile notion of "all-oneness" by discussing *perichoresis* in a way that underscores a *limited* union between Self and Other, one that is completely incompatible with any vision of unimpeded collectivism.[16] While no less cognizant of this dilemma than Bakhtin himself, other Russian thinkers were far more hesitant and therefore less successful in liberating Russian notions of communality from compromising elements of nationalist ideology and *realpolitik*.[17]

Bakhtin attempts to return to the original substance of the Chalcedonian notion of the interrelation between the human and the divine, only in a way that is more thoroughgoing than any formulation of it that we find in Solovyov and other Russian religious philosophers. At the Chalcedonian Council, simultaneity and interrelation was asserted, the shuffling and intermixing of human and divine essences going against the grain of their presumed hierarchical ordering and reaching an apogee of paradox. The council was notable in affirming not only the consubtstantiality (Greek *homoousia;* Russian *edinosushchie*) of Father and Son, but also the two natures (Russian *estestvá*) of Christ as human and divine. The classic statement of the Fourth Council was that the two natures of Christ exist "without confusion [Russian *nesliianno* or *neslitno*], without change, without separation [*nerazdel'no*]."[18] The council's pathbreaking formulations set the stage for a much closer interaction among various theological notions. Thus, as underscored in one nineteenth-century Russian commentary, Chalcedonian doctrine reinforces the Johannine concept of the bodied-forth Logos insofar as it dictates that the human and divine natures of Christ coexist in one hypostasis, united in the Word of God (*Boga Slova*).[19] Furthermore, beginning with Maximus the Confessor, some church fathers and theologians also applied the Chalcedonian paradox to the description of circumincession or *perichoresis*, the interrelation among the three parts of the Trinity, fusing the two ecclesiologically distinct doctrines. By characterizing dialogue as an interaction of "twos *or* multiples [emphasis added]," Bakhtin deftly adverts to this syncretic and shifting theological legacy. He underscores this dynamic of dialogue as an ever-unfolding multiplicity (as opposed to a rigid dyad of speakers locked in a single discussion) when he states elsewhere in the same set of notes that Dostoevsky was hostile to worldviews which "see the final goal in a merging [*v sliianii*], in a dissolution of consciousnesses in one consciousness. No Nirvana is possible for a *single* consciousness. A single consciousness is *contradictio in adjecto*. Consciousness is in essence multiple. *Pluralia tantum.*"[20]

Nonetheless, from his study on Rabelais to the second edition of the Dostoevsky book, the theological metaphors in Bakhtin's work operate more as structural paradigms than as philosophical or piously hortatory precepts. Thus, Bakhtin stresses the genre-based ambiguity of carnival, casting its utterly synchronic blend of praise and blame into the Chalcedonian mold of the coexisting yet separate twin natures of Christ. This particular structural dynamic is irreconcilable with the rigid separation of the rhetorical genres of panegyric and obloquy that was widely observed in Soviet novels, poems, and political speeches during the 1930s.[21] Such references in Bakhtin's criticism to theological concepts manifest a profound indebtedness toward Christology as conceptual matrix but paint what seems to be an ambivalent picture of actual belief. In a certain very real sense, the antipathy toward political orthodoxy that Bakhtin expresses so pointedly in the Duvakin interviews is paralleled by his idiosyncratic and nontraditional attitude toward confessional adherence or "correct" belief.

Interpreted cumulatively, however, Bakhtin's protracted and meticulously orchestrated use of these *topoi* signal a return to their axiological content and even theological context. As we have seen, three theological notions form the cornerstones of Bakhtin's theology of discourse: the Johannine Logos, Trinitarian interpenetration or *perichoresis*, and the Chalcedonian image of the divided union of the human and the divine in the person of Christ. The fact that the theological motifs in his work emerge as a triadic configuration only serves to reinforce and call attention to their theological provenance and Bakhtin's acute awareness of it. Moreover, Bakhtin shrewdly plays these three ideas off each other, emphasizing the extent to which they themselves are interrelated and therefore operate *vis-à-vis* each other according to the same ontological principle of "connectedness" that is variously espoused by each of them separately. In this context, Bakhtin's unpublished notes on aspects of the Renaissance novel are especially suggestive. There, he characterizes the role of the novelistic image in terms that recall both the dualism of the Chalcedonian paradox and the notion of hypostatic coinherence: "The image [*obraz*] as the emblem of the double-faced [*dvulikogo*] contradiction of life as a whole [*tselogo*]. . . . The presence of the whole [*tselogo*] in every image and detail."[22] The Chalcedonian subtext of interdwelling hypostases becomes clearer once we juxtapose this statement about double-sidedness with similar ones in *Toward a Philosophy of the Act*, Bakhtin's unpublished dissertation, and *Rabelais and His World*.[23] Bakhtin's professed apoliticism complements a kind of practical agnosticism that recognizes the gap between our explanations of (or terms for) the divine and the ontology of the godhead itself: all too often, what claims to be real belief is really more self-referential and esoteric and less a direct expression of a spiritually lived reality. To coin a phrase from *Problems of Dostoevsky's Poetics* itself, the idea of any comprehensive belief system or cosmology is no less alien to Bakhtin's own work than the image of "a unified spirit" is to Dostoevsky (*PDP* 26).

We see additional evidence of Bakhtin's feeling for faith—his interest not so much in the content or religious credo of Orthodoxy, as in its structural paradigm of interrelation that many commentators see as a crucial emphasis in Eastern Christianity, particularly in its Russian manifestation—in his views on linguistics as well. Given the politically charged discussions about language and its class content and the acrimonious discussions that raged almost from the very beginning of Soviet linguistics, one would think that the field would provide particularly infertile soil for the cultivation of theologically-informed references. And yet, of all places, we find here that Bakhtin brings theological motifs to bear upon his concept of dialogue in a pointedly political way, polemicizing with Stalin's famous late articles on linguistics by adverting to the Chalcedonian ideal of plurality within interrelation. The so-called Marr controversy of the early 1950s—what one commentator calls the "melancholy spectacle" of Stalin's criticizing an influential school of Soviet linguistics that he himself allowed to flourish for many years[24]—sheds an unexpectedly revealing light on Bakhtin and throws into sharp relief the open-ended theological model of connectedness that partly informs his concept of dialogue. The idea of linguistic unity—actually advanced by *both* Stalin and the Soviet linguist Marr—was one that Bakhtin was particularly eager to attack from this perspective.

Nikolai Marr and the Bakhtin Circle

The story of Nikolai Yakovlevich Marr (1864–1934) and the highly influential school of Soviet linguistics he created is no less strange than its sudden fall from favor in 1950 as a result of the campaign that Stalin himself mounted against it. The upheaval in the field of linguistics caused by the congealing of Marr's strange notions into inflexible dogma somewhat influenced the course of Bakhtin's writing on language from the 1930s through the early 1950s.

Born to a Scottish father and a Georgian mother in the Georgian countryside, Marr grew up in comfortable if not lavish surroundings. His university-educated father was the director of an agricultural school. When not reading from his voluminous library on horticulture and the natural sciences, Yakov Marr cultivated a large garden in his free time. His mother occupied herself in the traditional role of a homemaker, having had at best a modest domestic education.[25] As Marr recalls in an autobiographical sketch, his parents did not have a mutual language in which to speak to one another; they communicated through a series of mutually understood gestures that seemed to the boy to take the form of his mother obeying his father's orders. When Marr turned eight years old, his father passed away and he quickly fell out with his mother. Judging from the wistfulness of his recollected family life and the subsequent discord brought on by his father's death, there is much in Marr's account suggesting that he viewed his childhood as Edenic and his parents' marriage as ideal.[26] The image of an apparently effortless cross-cultural communication structured along the lines of a clear-cut hierarchy would forever remain for Marr a touchstone of a paradise lost but potentially regainable.

Marr's preoccupation with religious literature was evident from the very beginning of his scholarly career and was still evident in his research during the early Soviet period. In 1901 he submitted as his dissertation a translation of the third-century church father Ippolitus's commentary on the "Song of Songs," a text that was presumed lost until Marr discovered a Georgian version of it in a Tbilisi library. The discovery caused a sensation, and Marr was awarded a professorship at the University of St. Petersburg on the basis of his research.[27] After the Revolution, Marr developed his own concept of language evolution, which he referred to as the theory of linguistic "stadialism" (i.e., stages) and ultimately christened the Japhetic theory, after Japheth, the third son of Noah.[28] In the biblical account of Genesis 9–10, Noah's sons Shem and Ham are described as the ancestors of the Semitic and Hamitic peoples. Marr appropriated the figure of Noah's third son, Japheth, as an emblem for his theory apparently in the belief that the languages of the remaining peoples and nations shared certain properties. Evidently, Marr's attraction to theological literature extended to its symbols and paradigms, and was not merely motivated by the textological challenges it represented. Even in his student days before the Revolution, however, he quickly abandoned this trichotomy as too restrictive by claiming to have discovered during an expedition to Egypt and Palestine startling parallels and phonetic links among Georgian, Armenian, and Hebrew.[29] In claiming connections among these languages, Marr opposed one of the most central tenets of contemporary comparative linguistics: that the Caucasian, Indo-European, and Semitic language groups are entirely separate and unrelated in their genealogy. No less iconoclastic was Marr's contention that language does not have a life or history of its own that is separate or distinct from the historical dialectic; like any other superstructural growth over the economic base, it is entirely secondary, a delayed epiphenomenon of the inevitable historical process.

Marr was especially contemptuous of comparative linguistics, which he regarded as yet another manifestation of cultural imperialism peddled by bourgeois Western scholars. The very concept of an Indo-European protolanguage and culture, Marr argued, is misleading, if not altogether false.[30] All similarities between purportedly related language groups such as (for example) Slavic and Baltic can be explained by two facts that do not presume the existence of a separate protolanguage such as Indo-European: (1) such correspondences are actually later borrowings from one language into another, and (2) all structural and seemingly more profound similarities between such languages are, in the final analysis, nothing more than permutations of four phonemes: *sal, ber, yon,* and *rosh.*[31] Operating on the assumption that these phonemes were the direct and inevitable product of the physiology of the speech-producing organs, Marr concluded that they were linguistic universals whose particular manifestation might differ here or there but whose significance as primordial paradigms was indisputable.

From this series of assumptions it follows that the seemingly genetic similarities between certain languages and their classification into groups are, more often than not, optical illusions. But far more curious than Marr's rejection of traditional Indo-European comparative studies was his notion of linguistic convergence (*skreshchivanie; sliianie*). Marr asserted that languages would have a common end;

with the ineluctable march of history toward world communism, all languages would simplify and merge into one world language, the ultimate synthesis of the dialectical process. It is easy to see how someone brought up in a home of linguistically noncommunicating parents would think that all languages shall— or perhaps ought to—coalesce into one all-embracing *lingua franca*, and in his autobiographical essay Marr actually uses the term "convergence [*skreshchivanie*] of languages" to describe his own bilingual upbringing in Russian and Georgian. In the Marrist concept of stadialism, perhaps the only thing more significant than a well-defined beginning and end of the collective development of language is the fact that they are curiously similar to one another; for Marr, utopian visions of universal communication historically frame the evolution of language. By 1929, Marr's Japhetic theory had gained considerable ascendancy in Soviet and Russian linguistics, appreciating in scholarly currency well into the 1930s and 1940s.[32]

Marr's gradualist concept of language development is well represented in one of his earlier and most comprehensive works, the series of lectures he gave at the Azerbaijan University in Baku in 1927 that was published as a textbook the following year under the characteristically immodest title *The Japhetic Theory: A General Course of Study about Language.* Marr's contention that all languages move toward convergence and unification is sketched out here in close association with the assumption that language in general is a superstructural phenomenon springing from the economic base. The Japhetic theory, Marr explains, teaches us that language is not a gift from nature but rather humanity's attempt to adapt to and eventually subdue it. The theory clarifies the ways in which language evolves through the constant mutation of the sounds that people produce in accordance with their developing material needs. Language is an instrument, a technological tool for bending material reality to the requirements of a new world order. Insofar as progress is defined by all of humanity's attaining socialism, all languages will inevitably become one, forming a new world language out of a crucible of merging (*sliianie*) the material bases of various cultures.[33]

That Marr actually believed in the previous existence of a worldwide, morphologically consistent form of primitive speech (distinct from comparative linguistics' notion of protolanguages) is asserted several times throughout his writings. In his 1929 article, "Language and Writing," he explains that the ritualistic nature of the primitive word more or less passes away in the subsequent stages of a society's (and its attendant language's) development. Elaborating on tentative conclusions he made in another article from two years before, Marr stresses that the first linguistic sound uttered by humanity (which he calls with poetic obfuscation the "symbol of sound [*zvukovoi simvol*]") is not a gift from nature, but the artifactual product of a thaumaturgical act; it is an instrument or tool (*orudie*) that represents a new, dialectically advanced way of responding to the ever-changing material base, transcending the initial attempts at communication through hand gestures.

This primordial symbol of sound is the carrier of a magical power (*magisheskoi sily*): it is the special tool for securing the interaction (*vozdeistvie*) and consolidation (*uviazka*) of both the internal and external worlds of human existence. For Marr, the fact that language is a tool that is produced directly by the human body gives it a special significance as something that symbolically links consciousness with material reality.[34] The article, like so many in Marr's work, is a curious mixture of disparate approaches and attitudes, and even seems to betray a Jungian tendency in its delineation of a collective unconscious in the form of a mythic beginning of language. Thus, on the one hand, he firmly believes in the dialectical progress of history and in the ancillary and superstructural position of language; on the other, he also expresses something of a nostalgic concept of language. His Marxist historicism notwithstanding, Marr invests the primordial word with a prelapsarian quality that reflects an idealization of primitive society and culture. In this respect, Stalin's later accusation that Marr was guilty of idealism is undoubtedly justified.[35] Marr's belief in the existence of a single mother-tongue and the essentially tragic fragmentation that followed it lacks only an explicit reference to the Tower of Babel in being scripturally literalist as far as matters of history are concerned.

To be sure, various elements of Marr's notions were hardly original during even the 1920s. Members of the Russian avant-garde movements such as Futurism consistently emphasized the need to create a new language corresponding to the new social order of the Soviet Union. Many details of Marr's ideas echo these programs and even the poetic works of these writers. In their piece "The Word as Such," Aleksei Kruchenykh and Velimir Khlebnikov half-jokingly assert that the literary work reflecting the present moment can consist of as little as a single word, if that word is explored with enough skill and awareness of expressive possibilities.[36] Thus, in his famous borderline-nonsense poem "Incantation by Laughter," Khlebnikov concocts a long list of improbable variations of the Russian word for laughter (*smekh*). Khlebnikov emphasizes the mystical quality of the beginnings of language to an even greater extent in his 1922 dramatic poem *Zangezi*, where—in a series of striking parallels to Marr—he describes a primordial world dominated by the four sounds of *Er, Ka, El',* and *Ge* and the prophet Zangezi's prediction of a future where a new and universal world language would be born from the "Great Gods of Sound."[37] But the impetus to create an international language was also felt in linguistic circles outside the Soviet Union. Writing very much in the shadow of the human catastrophe of the World War I, prominent linguists such as Jespersen and Sapir seriously discussed the need for such a language and the features that it would have to possess. By 1932, Basic English was formulated by C. K. Ogden precisely in response to such agitation while working for the International Auxiliary Language Association.[38] Such similarities notwithstanding, there is no evidence of mutual influence between Marr and any of these other figures, and all of these conceptual parallels can be explained as common responses to contemporary social and political pressures.

Even from this brief outline of Marr's theories, we see that the linguist's emphasis on the absorption and merging of different languages and styles in the formation of a new *koine* could not be farther from Bakhtin's reverence for the individual utterance. Nevertheless, Marr's work provoked scholarly debate among members of the so-called Bakhtin circle (which existed in Leningrad during the 1920s). Valentin Voloshinov and Bakhtin themselves reacted in a highly specific manner to the baneful influence of Marrism on the Soviet study of language, which in the case of Slavic linguistics resulted in a wholesale purging and decimation of the field from the late 1920s through the 1940s, a period coinciding with Bakhtin's arrest and exile.[39] As we shall see, Marr's firm belief in the actual historical existence of a single Ur-language indeed corresponds to a blind faith in a quasi-religious notion as opposed to a sense or feeling (*chuvstvo*) for the actual process of cultural development.

Members of Bakhtin's circle in the 1920s knew Marr's writing before it became fully canonical and had on occasion crossed paths with his followers. In her unpublished memoirs, Maria Yudina, a well-known pianist and Bakhtin's close friend from those years, mentions that she then knew well from the university both Mikhail and a philologist named Vsevolod Bakhtin.[40] According to a separate, official document issued by a Petrograd historical institute, this latter Bakhtin (no relation to the critic) served with Marr on the Petrograd public library's commission for the study of manuscripts and paleography.[41] In 1928 Mikhail Bakhtin, along with his friends Aleksandr Meier, Lev Pumpiansky, and Yudina were arrested together with Vsevolod Bakhtin and many others for participation in the "Voskresenie" religious group in Leningrad. With the exception of Yudina, the five-volume KGB file pertaining to this group arrest contains extensive handwritten depositions from all of these individuals. We learn from Vsevolod Bakhtin's personal history page that he was still serving on the same public library commission during the time of his arrest and that he attended at least one of the "Voskresenie" society's meetings with Mikhail Bakhtin, who made a point of inviting him to future gatherings.[42] More tangible intersections with Marrism are evident in Voloshinov's 1929 study *Marxism and the Philosophy of Language*, where several seemingly favorable references are made to Marr's work. Although several scholars still believe that Bakhtin may have ghostwritten this book, one telling piece of archival evidence in the Manuscript Division of the St. Petersburg National Library suggests that its author may indeed be Voloshinov.[43] Leaving aside the vexed question of the book's authorship, the predominance of Bakhtin's ideas in *Marxism and the Philosophy of Language* is quite clear. A brief discussion of this text is useful in considering the general orientation of Bakhtin and his like-minded friends toward Marr's theories.

Voloshinov notes with particular approval Marr's assertions that prerevolutionary and contemporary non-Soviet linguistics have neglected the social factor in the genesis and development of language. Certainly Marr's characteristic criticism of "formalism"—particularly his identification of the formal method with historical linguistics and his antipathy to both—are consistent with Voloshinov's arguments.[44] In chapter 2, he also cites Marr in support of the general argument that contemporary linguistics—of which Indo-European studies form an important part and which bear the brunt of Marr's critique—has been handicapped by the classificatory rigidity of traditional philology in its preoccupation with the isolated word and the determination of frozen, dictionary-precise meanings of words.[45] In light of the exigencies and compromises of publishing in the former Soviet Union both then and in more recent times, it should go without saying that adulatory references to politically motivated scholarship such as Marr's does not necessarily amount to an endorsement or wholehearted agreement. In neither of these citations does Voloshinov make any mention of the more characteristic and notorious specifics of Marr's ideas or give them any positive support; he merely notes with approval the linguist's bracingly skeptical comments about preexisting scholarship.

The actual disparity between Voloshinov's and Marr's points of view is evident from their differing concepts about the origins of language. For Marr, the explosive concentration of meaning in the primordial single word (*odno slovo*) or "symbol of sound" has irrevocably passed, quickly giving way to the Babel of diversified and transitional speech by which culture—that epiphenomenal superstructure over the economic base—makes itself understood. Voloshinov, on the other hand, believes that language is a continuous unfolding or inscription of meaning, that the beginning is, in fact, ever-present. But the author of *Marxism and the Philosophy of Language* does more than merely hint at this disagreement: in his encoded critique, he implies that Marr's primordial single word is improbable or unreal. Voloshinov's insistence that such a word would have virtually no meaning or lacks stable meanings gives the lie to the all-signifying nature that Marr attributes to it. Marr's primordial all-signifying word is, for Voloshinov, more of a useful theoretical construct and myth than the historical reality that Marr in fact believes it to be.[46] Marr understands the "symbol of sound" absolutely literally and historically, as a phenomenon that predates the development of culture. For Voloshinov and Bakhtin, however, the inherently dialogic nature of language renders impossible the single word as a self-containing and essentialist entity. They assert that every isolated or single word realizes its true nature by expanding beyond its boundary toward other words or concatenations of words. In the end, we realize that Voloshinov in fact adduces Marr's concept of the word as an instance of pseudohistoricism or quasi-diachronicity in linguistics. It serves as a negative example in his argument that the manifold nature of the utterance occurs at *every* stage of a language's growth, and not just during those that follow upon its beginnings. Although clearly influenced by and drawn to the idea of a talismanic and age-old yet life-giving word or sound (for which, his Marxism notwithstanding, Marr retains a certain nostalgia), Voloshinov ultimately rejects the notion while retaining the term "word" in the sense of discourse or the Greek *logos* (Russian *slovo*) as a point of reference.

The affinities between Voloshinov's concept of the word and Bakhtin's become more evident when juxtaposed with Marr's. Nothing could be further from Marr's postlapsarian view of language than Bakhtin's valorization of dialogue, his characterization of it as a transfigurative and life-giving event. Like Voloshinov, Bakhtin in "Discourse in the Novel" insists on the perpetual latency and renewability of the synchronic word.[47] As he asserts in that lengthy essay (written during the height of Marrism in 1934–35): "The word [*slovo*] is born in a dialogue as a living rejoinder within it; the word is shaped in dialogic interaction [*vzaimodeistvii*] with an alien word that is already in the object. A word forms a concept of its own object in a dialogic way" (*DI* 279).[48] For Marr, such a word occurs only at the very beginning of human history. In contrast, Bakhtin's understanding of discourse (*slovo*) is more multifaceted than Marr's, denoting a full-fledged moment of communicative exchange. Voloshinov and Bakhtin do not adhere to a rigidly chronological understanding of the concept of "beginning." The issue of language's historical beginnings is hardly touched upon at all in their writings and evidently does not interest them. The differences between the Bakhtin circle's views of language development and Marr's are shown most revealing by hypothetically applying them to John 1:1, "In the beginning was the Word." In the hermeneutic light of the famous biblical verse, Marr's concept of the newly born Word emerges as dogmatically theological, whereas Voloshinov's and Bakhtin's are exegetically versatile, seeing in the Johannine word not so much an actual account of the genesis of language (as strict belief would have it) as an expressive metaphor for its actual operation and dynamics. It is no wonder that Marr adapted a biblical figure for the name of his linguistic theory: his ideas are completely saturated with notions of lapsarian and diluvian history in a way that suggests a distinctly religious view of anthropology.

But perhaps it is Marr's notion of the eventual merging (*sliianie*) of languages that provides the most useful point of contrast between him and Bakhtin. Here we would do well to recall Bakhtin's statement from his notes on Dostoevsky written almost thirty years later, one in which he echoes the Chalcedonian formula of the human and divine natures of Christ as coexisting "without confusion [*nesliianno*] or separation." It is "not merging [*ne sliianie*] with another" that is important, Bakhtin writes, "but preserving one's own position of *extralocality* and the *surplus* of vision and understanding connected with it" ("TRDB" 299).

In his dissertation on Rabelais, first submitted in 1940 but defended only in 1946 (in part because of the war), Bakhtin makes statements that seem to echo Marr while also diverging from him in key respects. In a passage from chapter 1 that remained largely intact in the 1965 *Rabelais and His World*, Bakhtin writes that primitive grotesque images "move within the biocosmic circle of cyclic changes," eventually moving away from that level and the cyclical sense of time being superseded by an historical one. In a statement not included in the later published book version of the study, Bakhtin also states that the cyclical sense of time is characterized by crisis (*krizis*).[49] Bakhtin's emphasis on the traumatic break between primitive and modern cultures—more pronounced in the dissertation and written during a time when Marrism was most widespread and pernicious in Soviet scholarship—indicates a residual influence of the Georgian linguist's theories about cultural stadialism. This affinity prompted one reader to underline this passage in red pencil and to write "Marr" on the facing, blank page of the thesis.[50] Yet even in his dissertation, Bakhtin's emphasis on the ambivalence or thematic ambiguity of the culture of laughter renders the grotesque irreconcilable with Marr's rigidly dialectical scheme. Using a distinctly Marrist turn of phrase, Bakhtin goes on to state in the same passage that even at the highest stage (*stadiia*) of its development the grotesque is unfinished, open-ended, and internally contrary, a notion that is completely incompatible with Marr's belief in the superstructural stadialism of cultural development. As foregrounded by works such as "Discourse in the Novel" and his dissertation on Rabelais, Bakhtin in his writing of the 1930s consistently attempts to counterbalance the notion of linguistic merging with the idea that speech is always internally stratified, preventing the complete absorption of one sort of speech into another. In his dissertation, Bakhtin highlights key terms that delineate a fusion tempered by separation of voices; thus, he characterizes the rhetorical dynamics of carnival praise and blame as "divided [*raz"edineny*] among *private* voices, *but in the voice of the whole they are fused* [*slity*] *into an ambivalent unity.*" The Chalcedonian reference is unmistakable in the paradoxical yoking of *divided/fused* (*raz"edineny/slity*).[51] Moreover, his assertion that the praise/blame dichotomy relates "to *all* of the present and *each* of its parts"—and that the past and future, young and old are thoroughly "*merged* [*slity*]" in it—indicate that Bakhtin's concept of the confluence of elements within a particular culture is completely different from Marr's. Bakhtin's theological subtext effectively points up his specific points of disagreement with then-regnant notions of linguistic anthropology. Needless to say, the idea that a merging of voices occurs only at the end of a kind of end-time (as Marr asserts in his quasi-religious way) is completely at odds with Bakhtin's work.

"A Janus-Faced Coin": Stalin versus Marrism and Bakhtin's Response

The crusade that Stalin launched against the methodology of Marr and his followers is one of the most curious episodes in the history of Soviet linguistics. The first shot in this fusillade was an article written by the Soviet leader himself titled "Concerning Marxism in Linguistics," which he wrote in consultation with the Georgian linguist Arnold Chikobava, and which appeared in a 1950 issue of *Pravda*.[52] For the next three years leading up to Stalin's death, a raft of articles and books appeared written by Soviet scholars in which Marr's ideas were excoriated, always with loving references to Stalin's article. The anti-Marrist campaign was, of course, hardly an isolated incident. Along with the Lysenko scandal in Soviet biology and Zhdanov's jeremiads against contemporary artistic figures such as Anna Akhmatova and the composer Aram Khachaturian, the campaign was part and parcel of Stalin's renewed effort in the late 1940s and early 1950s to purge the arts and sciences of ideas perceived to be inimical to socialism. As a few commentators have insightfully noted, these efforts have more to do with Stalin's sense of isolation and hostile encirclement at the beginning of the Cold War than they have to do with the Marxian notion of class struggle, which in any case Stalin largely jettisoned during the course of the 1930s.[53] The gravitation of late Stalinist ideology toward the notion of state centralization through a single language and culture played an especially prominent role in the debate around the Marrist legacy.

The repercussions of Stalin's anti-Marr crusade were felt throughout the world of Russian scholarship, affecting even a marginal critic such as Bakhtin. According to Michael Holquist and Katerina Clark, Bakhtin wrote "The Problem of Speech Genres" in the hope that he could finally get something published, even if it would be in the disreputable wake of Stalin's article. The draft of the essay originally submitted by Bakhtin included a preamble with quotations from Stalin. In spite of his efforts at accommodation to the contemporary status quo, the essay was not approved for publication. To this day, in strict observation of Bakhtin's specific request, the piece is published without the preamble containing the critic's favorable references to Stalin's writing on linguistics.[54] Nonetheless, in the first published volume of Bakhtin's collected works, several notes and drafts for the essay are published for the first time, all of which, together with Gogotishvili's magisterial annotation and description of the political circumstances surrounding the piece, give us a very clear idea of Bakhtin's struggle with the ideological status quo. Bakhtin describes his references to Stalin as carrying an "unsavory taint," and in a 1962 letter to Kozhinov states, "Before sending off [the essay] I quickly read through it and found myself absolutely horrified. Around 1950, I added to it according to the 'recommendations' of VAK's commission of experts, and brought into it a great deal of revolting vulgarity in the spirit of that time." Bakhtin goes on to say that he was able only to "paste"—to insert crudely and obviously— these politically expedient references to Stalin's personality cult into his work.[55] A close look at Bakhtin's extant essay and its recently published draft notes in the context of the Marr controversy reveals that "The Problem of Speech Genres" is a conflicted work, containing positive references to Stalin's ideas that are clearly contradicted and opposed by Bakhtin elsewhere in the same work. In the final analysis, Bakhtin associates Stalin's linguistic ideas with the ideology of the Soviet leader's cult of personality, a connection that many have speculated about but which few have cogently explained. In the following discussion, I will elucidate that connection and explain the way in which Bakhtin uses the theological motif of the

Chalcedonian-tempered interrelation to critique Stalin, enabling us to separate the methodological wheat from the Stalinist chaff in "The Problem of Speech Genres."

Although Marr is not mentioned in the published article, a criticism of his approach is implicit. For Bakhtin, every style is inextricably linked to speech genres,[56] a category that reflects the history of a certain kind of speech at the various stages of its development. Marr's rigidly dialectic concept of the genesis of language—a methodology that assumes the supersession of each stage of a language's development—is clearly inimical to such an approach. Bakhtin's concept of the primacy of speech genres underscores a coexistence and a conditional merging of opposites that would be unthinkable to Marr. This conflation of synchronicity and diachronicity goes deeply against the grain of Marrist linguistics. Bakhtin is largely in agreement with Stalin's assertions in the anti-Marr articles that language belongs neither to the base nor the superstructure.

As in many other of his writings, in "The Problem of Speech Genres," Bakhtin characterizes discourse as having a tripartite structure. Like "Art and Answerability" from over thirty years before, this article begins with a trichotomy. Bakhtin describes the three moments that mark the unfolding of the utterance and their relation to speech genres: the thematic content, style, and compositional construction, which are all inextricably tied together within the *whole* [*tselom* (Bakhtin's emphasis)] entity of the utterance and are defined by the specifics of the given sphere of social interaction. "Each separate utterance is individual, of course, but each sphere in which language is used develops its *own relatively stable types* of these utterances," which can be called *"speech genres"* (*SpG* 60). Speech genres are diachronic as well as synchronic; they contain recognizable moments and stages and yet may also be thought of as finished or complete. The epistemological paradoxes of Bakhtin's concept of discourse (*slovo*) are fully manifest in his delineation and definition of speech genres.

In this essay Bakhtin attempts to determine the analyzable units or limits of language. As it turns out, these irreducible categories consist of "speech genres," which are not genres in the narrowly literary sense but rather are different kinds of speech acts. The sentence and the individual word, for example, are precisely such units and are analogous to one another: "The sentence, like the word, is a signifying [*znachashchaia*] unit of language."[57] Both types of speech are different manifestations of the utterance. In comparing these two speech genres, Bakhtin effectively exposes the internal dynamics of the utterance:

The sentence, like the word, has a finality [*zakonchennost'*] of meaning and a finality of *grammatical* form, but this finality [*zavershennost'*] of meaning is abstract by nature and this is precisely why it is so clear-cut: this is the finality of an element, but not of the whole. The sentence as a unit of language, like the word, has no author. Like the word, it belongs to *nobody*, and only as functioning as a whole utterance does it become an expression of the position of someone speaking individually in a concrete situation of speech communication. This leads us to a new, third feature of the utterance—the relation of the utterance to the *speaker himself* (the author of the utterance) and to *other* participants in speech communication.

Any utterance is a link in the chain of speech communication. (*SpG* 83–84)[58]

Here, any ostensible similarity between Marr and Bakhtin in their insistence on the importance of a community of speakers is completely superficial. Bakhtin believes in the one-on-one relation of a speaker to other speakers. Although he obviously will have no truck with the supremacy or valorization of the isolated individual, it is equally clear that he sets store in the existence and viability of the individual as a category, given its engagement in an exchange with other individuals. Marr, however, champions the dissolution of the individual within a larger whole. In his scholarly work, the beginning and end of a language's development are curiously alike: both are characterized by an erasing or resolution of boundaries into a kind of simplified all-purpose speech, be it that of the primordial word or of a streamlined new world *koine*. In further contrast to Marr, Bakhtin locates the significant boundaries of communicative completedness or finalization not at some later stage of a language's development but around the individual utterance. In the passage above, speaker and addressee, utterance and sentence, do not cancel each other out or have a teleological drift as in Marr. Each utterance not only constitutes an entire moment or instance of dialogic exchange, but also engages in conversation with other utterances both past and present.

But how can a particular utterance be separate, complete, and at the same time influenced by and inextricably tied to those of another interlocutor? In his unfinished essay "The Problem of the Text in Linguistics, Philology and the Human Sciences" (1959–61), Bakhtin clarifies this paradox by emphasizing that no finalization in speech is truly complete or uttered. In this essay, Bakhtin explains that every utterance and act represents a separate entity or "text" whose internal makeup is affected during dialogic contact with other utterances while the essential outlines of its identity remain intact. That every utterance is dialogically linked to other utterances is a relation that traditional linguistics is incapable of describing.[59] Dialogue is the convergence between past and present: it represents the conduit for the fluid and uninterrupted continuation of history, rather than merely the rendezvous point that allows for the mechanical succession and supersession of one distinct historical stage by another. Bakhtin and Voloshinov are in fact more finely attuned than Marr to the historical nature of a language's development. In comparison with their vision of language as a constantly evolving entity, Marr's stadial theory of language takes on the character of a cut-and-paste documentation of change that relies on artificial chronological boundaries.

Bakhtin's statement that a sentence must always be viewed in the context of the entire utterance to which it belongs—which is what brings us to the realization that it, like the word, "belongs to *nobody*" and is an inextricable link in the continuum of human communication—is especially revealing of the structure underlying his thoughts about language. Since Bakhtin believes that to partake of language in a dialogic way is not to lose one's identity as either an individual or a member of a particular social group, there can be no question of the emergence of a new world language in which all such differences are erased. Although Marr is not mentioned by name, his passion for paleography and the graphic sign is precisely the kind of desiccated approach of linguistics to culture that Bakhtin criticizes in the passage above, an approach that views the elements of language in their mutual isolation.[60]

Under the dispensation of the newly critical attitude in the early 1950s toward the Marrist legacy, Bakhtin was able to make more explicit the points that Voloshinov hinted at twenty-three years before in *Marxism and the Philosophy of Language*. Both in that book and in "The Problem of Speech Genres," the Marrist position is taken to task for what might be called a literalist interpretation of the Johannine word, one in which the inception of language in primitive society is portrayed in effect as an occult mystery, an inexplicable creation *ex nihilo*. Bakhtin takes language more on its own terms, without lingering on its graphic manifestation or surrounding it with a cabalistic haze of latent essences. In fact, much of the strangeness and irrationality of Marr's theory disappears with the realization that his theory of linguistic evolution is strongly religious in its drift. Thus, the primordial word represents an Edenic state that is quickly forfeited by humanity, which subsequently measures out its dreary postlapsarian existence in stages until it attains a millennium in which all of its people become united into an undifferentiated whole. If one defines a linguist in a broad sense as a student of language, Bakhtin is a genuine adept in comparison to whom Marr is an obscurantist seminarian. What emerges with startling clarity from all of this is the fact that Bakhtin regarded the Johannine theology of the incarnated word as a metaphor *above all*, a useful theoretical construct but not a description of a real historical moment. As he notes in "Discourse in the Novel," languages and subcultures throughout history have been pushed out and enslaved in the name of the "true word" (*istinnoe slovo*).[61] In the person of Marr, the concrete manifestations of such divinely inspired colonialism were quite real.

As we have seen, Bakhtin's concept of speech genres fundamentally contradicts Marr's belief in the strictly stadial course that a language runs after its initial divine spark of a beginning. Thus, it would seem, Bakhtin's agreement with Stalin's criticism of Marr is genuine. But to say that Bakhtin actually adopts Stalin's own linguistic concepts does not follow from the fact that both he and the Soviet leader are opposed to the Marrist position. In his article, Stalin himself adheres to a highly teleological concept of language that does for various kinds of speech what Marr does for the world's languages: he attempts to neutralize their uniqueness in the creation of a linguistic standard or norm. Thus, he insists that even in its more exotic manifestations, language is created for society as a whole—for all classes—and not for the enjoyment of any particular class.[62] For Stalin, different forms or levels of speech coexist peacefully side by side and are ultimately attenuated or subdued by their allegiance to a larger entity known as the unitary language (*edinyi iazyk*), a term that is also invoked by Marr and that in many respects corresponds to the Saussurian *langue* that Voloshinov and Bakhtin inveigh against. Stalin stresses that language is not a superstructure but a largely neutral medium for communication (*obshchenie*) and a tool (*orudie*) that people use in order to engage in an exchange of thoughts (*obmen mysli*). In the Soviet leader's own words, such an exchange represents "a constant and vital necessity, for without it, it is impossible to coordinate the joint actions of people in the struggle against the forces of nature, in the struggle to produce the necessary material values," a statement that parallels Marr's own insistence on the necessity of linguistic confluence for the subjugation of nature.[63] In the final analysis, it is only a slight exaggeration to say that Stalin's concept of language development is distinguished from Marr's solely by the absence of a Marxian superstructure in it. Stalin's jettisoning of this key concept has prompted at least one historian to see in the anti-Marrist campaign a genuine innovation and turning point in Soviet dialectical materialism.[64] Certainly in all other respects, the affinities between Stalin and Marr about language are startling indeed. Both regard language as an inert form or matrix for the conveyance of thought, and Marr himself went so far as to state that the inevitable merging of world languages would result in the communication of pure thought (*myshlenie*) over utterance, a process that he saw as analogous to the withering away of the state. For Bakhtin, the Marrist and Stalinist positions are flip sides of the same double-faced coin in their frozen ideological visions of the liquidation of all discourses into a single language.

Bakhtin pointedly does not view language as a utilitarian transaction or a neutral backdrop, and in this regard one notices that Stalin's view of language actually has a great deal in common with Marr, who also believed that utterances had artifactual values and therefore could be regarded as instruments or tools. Furthermore, in "The Problem of Speech Genres," Bakhtin registers an implied disagreement with Stalin in the form of a negative reference to a book written by the Soviet linguist A. N. Gvozdev. Not only does Gvozdev refer lovingly to Stalin's anti-Marr article, he also uses Stalin's classificatory system of class or group speeches in his description of how different stylistic levels operate.[65] In a highly critical footnote referring to pages in Gvozdev's book in which such group categories are outlined, it is precisely this classification that Bakhtin faults for lacking clarity and foundation.[66] In the final analysis, Bakhtin's references to Stalin are extremely perfunctory and cannot hide his deeper disagreement with both Marr and the Soviet leader. It is no surprise that the essay was published only twenty years later, during the Brezhnev era. In "The Problem of Speech Genres," Bakhtin transcends the formulations of both the Marrists and the linguists who attacked Marr under Stalin's banner. His concepts of dialogue and polyphony, with their theological subtext of interdwelling tempered by separation, provide the way out of the impasse of a contemporary scholarly polemic.

Conclusion: Bakhtin's Feeling for Faith

Pagan principles hold sway over us everywhere in our country. I believe according to the Orthodox way, for example, because I was born here, in Russia. The dominant factor in the choice of faith is dictated by the faith of ancestors.
—Aleksandr Meier, during a meeting of the St. Petersburg
Religious-Philosophical Society, March 1, 1922
(St. Petersburg National Library, Fund 601, Item 1586; pp. 64–65)

Needless to say, any full-fledged ambiguity or simultaneity of multiple discourses—where the centripetal gravitation toward linguistic merging is counterbalanced by the centrifugal one of separation and liminalization—is utterly impossible in both Marr's and Stalin's theories of language. The Bakhtinian ideal of "preserving one's own position of *extralocality* [*vnenakhodimost'*] and the *surplus* of vision and understanding connected with it" is clearly impossible in concepts of language development that see speakers as consensus-oriented agents or as passive receptacles for the mechanical barter of ideas. The Stalinist characterization of communication as an "exchange of thoughts" occurs in Bakhtin's "The Problems of Speech Genres," and clearly documents Bakhtin's unsuccessful attempt to square his ideas with Stalin's concept of language: "Every utterance (even the most monologic, isolated, and self-sufficient) participates in a social *exchange of thoughts*, representing a unit of such an exchange."[67] Earlier in the same notes, we sense the awkwardness of Bakhtin's attempts to reconcile Stalin's instrumentalization of language as a form of barter of content-values when he writes about the "reflection even in the monologic forms of the dialogic exchange of thoughts, the account taken of the active listener." But Bakhtin goes on to say that "[e]very utterance, piece of dialogue, and monologue are full of echoes of other utterances."[68] In his anti-Marr articles, Stalin sees such exchange very much in the mold of an almost contractually agreed-upon act of reciprocated services, stemming naturally from the fact that "language is directly connected with man's productive activity."[69] Bakhtin's notion of dialogic interaction as interpenetration or mutual saturation of discourses does not sit well at all with Stalin's rigid sequentiality of rhetorical modes that cancel each other out. It is no wonder that he jettisoned the references to Stalin's notions of language as exchange in the final draft.

Perhaps sensing the impossibility of reconciling such rigidly diachronic and binary notions of communication with his concept of dialogue as interchange (rather than exchange), several pages later in these notes Bakhtin asserts that "[w]hat is important is the dialogic interconnection [*vzaimosviaz'*] among styles, each of which functions in relation to others as dialogizing backdrops. The praise/blame dynamic of styles."[70] We realize the almost classically Chalcedonian structure of this interconnection by comparing it with statements in Bakhtin's thesis in which he echoes the theological formula of Christ's twin natures as separated yet fused, casting praise and blame as a single interpenetrative entity. Thus, the positive and derisive poles of humor are fused [*slity*] into an indissoluble unity in Gothic laughter: praise and blame are two sides of the same Janus-faced coin; words tend toward *"double-faced* and *ambivalent fullness"* wherever "conditions of *absolute* and *full* human relations are established."* The obscene or "unpublishable" forms of speech used by Rabelais and contemporary writers such as James Joyce "merge into one [*slivaiut vo-edino*]" elements of daily life that are customarily kept separate.[71] In contrast, the only place where we find any kind of double-voiced discourse in Stalin's anti-Marr essays is in the considerable affinities his statist and centripetal views about language have with those of his Georgian compatriot.

In my book *Corporeal Words*, I discuss the ways in which Bakhtin constructs his ethical criticism of Stalinism on the basis of the syncretic legacy of politicized theology in Russian letters that flourished from 1913 through the 1920s, the most rigorous example of which is the work of his friend Aleksandr Meier.[72] In his response to Stalin's anti-Marr campaign, we see that Bakhtin extends the same carefully coded criticism of the Stalinist purges of the late 1930s to the Soviet leader's linguistic theories, which he regards as being utterly of one piece with notions of centralized state socialism. Certainly the paradigm of language as exchange in the sense of a strict sequentiality of opposed rhetorical modes—based on a conception of history as an alternation between growth and purification or purging—was, as Bakhtin intuited, an ideological centerpiece of Stalinism.[73] For Bakhtin, theological terms and categories are galvanized by an awareness of their possibilities as expressions of political idealism and tools of social criticism. The ideal of dialogue as a divided yet separate—and therefore distinctly Chalcedonian—union never left his work. As his friend Maria Yudina understood in her notes about Orthodox doctrine, it was this spirit of dialogue—of relating to divinity as one would to an equal—that informed Bakhtin's own dialogue with Russian Orthodoxy in its doctrinal roots and later manifestations, extensions, and borderline revisions by twentieth-century Russian thinkers. Bakhtin's apparent equanimity and ease in appropriating such highly marked terms, his application of them to a wide range of patently nontheological subject matters, and his ultimate underscoring of their spiritual provenance and content by using them as tools of political criticism, all point to an unconstrained and highly personal, yet ethically mindful, interaction with a distinct cultural tradition. It was this kind of interaction that Bakhtin probably had in mind when he wrote late in his career of "a certain *internal* open-endedness of many of my ideas" and of the difficulty in sometimes "separat[ing] one open-endedness from another" (*SpG* 155). Unlike Marr, who developed his concept of language convergence as a kind of subconscious extension of his upbringing in a mixed language, Bakhtin worked to transcend a mere autobiographical fact (of being born into the Orthodox faith) into an awareness of what it could mean in "the vulgar prose of life." His dialogue with Russian Orthodoxy was indeed a matter not of faith itself, but a feeling for it as an example of open-endedness.

Notes

The first epigraph is from Maria Yudina's notes held in the M. V. Yudina Archive [Russian State Library, Moscow], Fund 527, Box 7, Item 8; p. 12. Here Yudina seems to be quoting an unnamed sermonist or religious philosopher, male in gender. Archival research for this article was supported in part by a grant from the International Research and Exchanges Board, with funds provided by the U.S. Department of State (Title VIII) and the National Endowment for the Humanities.

The second epigraph is from Bakhtin's notes in *SpG* 155.

1. Viktor Duvakin (1909–82) taped eighteen hours of interviews with Bakhtin in February and March 1973. Selections were published in the journal *Chelovek* between 1993 and 1995; the full transcription was published as *Besedy V. D. Duvakina s M. M. Bakhtinym*, ed. V. B. Kuznetsova, M. V. Radzishevskaia, and V. F. Teider (Moscow: Progress, 1996). These interviews, translated into English, are forthcoming from University of Texas Press.

2. M. M. Bakhtin, *Estetika slovesnogo tvorchestva* (Moscow: Iskusstvo, 1987), 338.

3. Although Gogotishvili makes this statement in specific reference to "The Problem of Speech Genres," she also indicates that it is true as a general characteristic of Bakhtin's extant notebooks: *Sobranie sochinenii* tom. 5 (Moscow: Russkie slovari, 1996), 541.

4. M. M. Bakhtin, *Problemy poetiki Dostoevskogo* (Moscow: Sovetskii Pisatel', 1963), 238, 340, 343.

5. Alexandar Mihailovic, *Corporeal Words: Mikhail Bakhtin's Theology of Discourse* (Evanston: Northwestern Univ. Press, 1997).

6. Bakhtin, *Problemy poetiki Dostoevskogo*, 332.

7. Some formulations of the following discussion about the Johannine Logos, *perichoresis*, and Chalcedonian coinherence are drawn from my book *Corporeal*

Words and "Mikhail Bakhtin's Conception of Interpenetration: The Theological Sources," in *Critical Essays on Mikhail Bakhtin*, ed. Caryl Emerson (New York: G. K. Hall, 1999), 300–18.

8. "Iz zapisei 1970–71 godov," in *Estetika slovesnogo tvorchestva*, 377.

9. N. K. Bonetskaia, "M. Bakhtin v 1920-ye gody," *Dialog karnaval khronotop* no. 1 (1994): 53–54 and passim.

10. Katerina Clark and Michael Holquist, *Mikhail Bakhtin* (Cambridge: Harvard Univ. Press, 1984), 86–87, 304, 306.

11. See Harry Austryn Wolfson, *The Philosophy of the Church Fathers: Faith, Trinity, Incarnation*, vol. 1 (Cambridge: Harvard Univ. Press, 1970), 418–21, 423–25; and Leporskii, "Troitsa," in *Entsiklopedicheskii slovar'* tom. 66 (St. Petersburg, 1901), 872.

12. Aleksei Khomiakov, "Opyt katikhizicheskogo izlozheniia ucheniia o Tserkvi," in *Izbrannye sochineniia*, ed. N. S. Arsen'ev (New York: Izd. imeni Chekhova, 1955), 210. "Conciliarism" is Andrzej Walicki's translation of the term, from his *A History of Russian Thought from the Enlightenment to Marxism*, trans. Hilda Andrews-Rusiecka (Stanford: Stanford Univ. Press, 1979), 102–4. See especially Vladimir Solovyov's highly influential essay "The Meaning of Love" ["Smysl liubvi"], in *Izbrannoe* (Moscow: Sovetskaia Rossiia, 1990), 156–57.

13. Kallistos Ware, *The Orthodox Way* (Crestwood, N.Y.: St. Vladimir's Seminary Press, 1986), 33–34.

14. For a summary of these views as espoused by the church fathers, see John Dillon, "Logos and Trinity: Patterns of Platonist Influence on Early Christianity," in *The Philosophy in Christianity*, ed. Godfrey Vesey (Cambridge: Cambridge Univ. Press, 1989), 11–13.

15. Bakhtin, *Problemy poetiki Dostoevskogo*, 78.

16. Thus, in a recent article, I. A. Esaulov discusses Bakhtin's polyphony in relation to *sobornost'* ("Polifoniia i sobornost': M. M. Bakhtin i Viach. Ivanov," in *Bakhtinskii tezaurus: materialy i issledovaniia* [Moscow, 1997], 133–40); and S. S. Khoruzhii stresses the links between Bakhtin's famous statement about the plurality of Dostoevsky's world—in which saints and sinners coexist in a church of "unmerged souls" (*PDP* 26)—and the nineteenth-century Russian version of the philosophical notion of "all-oneness" ("Ideia vseedinstva ot Geraklita do Bakhtina," in Khoruzhii's *Posle pereryva: puti russkoj filosofii* [Moscow: Aleteiia, 1994]). Strikingly, neither Esaulov nor Khoruzhii even mentions the conspicuous presence of Chalcedonian terminology in the examples they discuss.

That the nineteenth-century Slavophile notion of *sobornost'* was sublimated into Soviet notions of collectivism and state socialism has long been a truism, if not a cliché. In his burlesque *Slavs!* the American playwright Tony Kushner amusingly parodies the crypto-pantheistic religiosity of Soviet ideology in an over-the-top soliloquy by a Soviet apparatchik named Ippolite Ippopolitovich Popolitipov:

The Party dispenses miracles. The Party drove away the Czar, immortalized Lenin, withstood France and Britain and the United States, made Communism in one country, electrified Russia, milled steel, built railways, abolished distance, defeated Germany, suspended time, became eternal, dispersed the body of each and every member, molecule by molecule, across an inconceivably vast starry matrix encompassing the infinite: so that, within the Party, everything is; so that everything human, even Marx—was shown as limited and the Party, Illimitable; and through the illimitable Party the human is exalted, becomes Divine, occupant of the great chiming spaciousness that is not distance but time, time which never moves nor passes, light which does not travel and yet is light: And love, pure love, even in a degraded, corrupt and loveless world; love can finally be born. (*Little pause, more vodka*) (Tony Kushner, *Thinking about the Longstanding Problems of Virtue and Happiness: Essays, A Play, Two Poems and a Prayer* [New York: Theatre Communications Group, 1995], 134)

17. As pointed out by one twentieth-century commentator on Russian religiosity (Elizaveta Kuzmina-Karavaeva, an émigré writer known as "Mother Mary" by Russians who considered her to be a religious figure in her own right), Solovyov was heavily indebted to Khomiakov's concept of intersubjective confessionalism, notwithstanding his attempts to rebut it (E. Iu. Kuzmina-Karavaeva, "Mirosozertsanie V. Solov'eva," *Izbrannoe* [Moscow: Sovetskaia Rossiia, 1991], 302–3). On balance, it is fair to say that Solovyov at the very least attempted to revivify already stale discussions of *sobornost'* or conciliarism by re-grounding the term in the doctrine of *perichoresis* as expressed in the writings of the church fathers. In this regard, the American Slavist Richard Gustafson has argued convincingly that Solovyov's particular version of human connnectedness is inspired by Maximus the Confessor's understanding of *perichoresis* (Richard Gustafson, "Soloviev's [*sic*] Doctrine of Salvation," in *Russian Religious Thought*, ed. J. Kornblatt and R. Gustafson [Madison: Univ. of Wisconsin Press, 1996], 45–46).

18. English translation by Jaroslav Pelikan, "Divinity Made Human: Aesthetic Implications of the Incarnation," in *Imago Dei: The Byzantine Apologia for Icons* (Princeton: Princeton Univ. Press, 1990), 73–74; Russian translation from "Khalkiedonskii sobor," in *Entsiklopedicheskii slovar'* tom. 73 (St. Petersburg, 1903), 21.

19. "Khalkiedonskii sobor," 21.

20. Bakhtin, *Estetika slovesnogo tvorchestva*, 331.

21. See my discussion in *Corporeal Words*, 199–204, and the legal scholar Arkady Vaksberg's account of the public prosecutor Vyshinsky's speech at the 1938 trial of the Bloc of Rightists and Trotskyites and the propagandistic poetry that followed it: *Tsaritsa dokazatel'stv: Vyshinskii i ego zhertvy* (Moscow: Kniga i biznes, 1992), 96–97, 134–36; English translation, *Stalin's Prosecutor: The Life of Andrei Vyshinsky*, trans. Jan Butler (New York: Grove Weidenfeld, 1991).

22. M. M. Bakhtin, "Materialy dokladov po problemam iazyka i osobennostei romana epokhi Vozrozhdenia i o zhanre romana voobshche (1930-e gody): Pervyi doklad" (M. V. Yudina Archive [Russian State Library, Moscow], Fund 527, Box 24, Item 26; p. 3). For a discussion of the Chalcedonian subtext of Bakhtin's notion of double-sidedness, see my *Corporeal Words*, 114, 202, and 204.

23. Mihailovic, *Corporeal Words*, 202, 204.

24. Lawrence L. Thomas, *The Linguistic Theories of N. Ja. Marr* (Berkeley and Los Angeles: Univ. of California Press, 1957), 146.

25. N. Ia. Marr, "Avtobiografiia N. Ia. Marra," *Izbrannye raboty* tom. 1(Leningrad: Izd. GAIMK, 1933), 6; and Thomas, *Linguistic Theories*, 1.

26. Marr, "Avtobiografiia N. Ia. Marra," 6–7. Marr himself sees considerable significance in his undergoing an idiosyncratic bilingual upbringing of Russian and Georgian that transformed him into a virtual speaker of patois.

27. Vera Tolz, *Russian Academicians and the Revolution: Combining Professionalism and Politics* (London: Macmillan, 1997), 90.

28. Thomas, *Linguistic Theories*, 149.

29. Ibid., 1–6. Thomas implies that Marr's initial use of this term was heuristic and not guided by the explicit historical and theoretical criteria that he made mention of in subsequent years. Also see Milorad Pupovac, *Lingvistika i Ideologija* (Novi Sad [Yugoslavia]: Knjizevna Zajednica, 1986), 97.

30. An ardent Georgian nationalist during his youth, Marr anticipated by several decades the arguments of Martin Bernal's *Black Athena* by regarding Indo-European philology as steeped in Eurocentric and racist attitudes toward non-European cultures (see Pupovac, *Lingvistika*, 95–98). Furthermore, his theory of the shared lineage of all world languages back to a single ur-tongue clearly influenced the Russian linguists in the 1970s who adhered to the so-called Nostratic theory, which asserted developmental links between seemingly unrelated language groups such as Finno-Ugric, Sino-Tibetan, and Indo-European.

31. Thomas, *Linguistic Theories*, 62–63.

32. Marr served as a mentor even for the brilliant Ol'ga Freidenberg, some of whose work bears distinct marks of his influence; see Nina Perlina, "Ol'ga Freidenberg on Myth, Folklore and Literature," *Slavic Review* 50, no. 2 (1991): 375–77. Judging from the international participation in a 1938 Festschrift devoted to him (*Pamiati Akademika N. Ia. Marra* [Moscow: AN SSSR, 1938]), he was also not without followers abroad.

33. Elsewhere, Marr refers to this evolutionary trend toward linguistic unification as monistic in character, constituting the resolution (or perhaps dissolution) of the many systems of speech into one; see Marr's 1931 pamphlet "Language and Thought" ["Iazyk i myshlenie"], *Izbrannye raboty* tom. 2 (Leningrad: Gosudarstvennoe sotsial'no-ekonomicheskoe izdatel'stvo, 1934), 118.

34. Ibid., 366.

35. Joseph Stalin, *Marksizm i voprosy iazykoznaniia* (Moscow: Gospolitizdat, 1950), 39.

36. Vladimir Markov, ed., *Manifesty I programmy russkikh futuristov* (Munich: Wilhelm Fink, 1967), 59.

37. Velimir Khlebnikov, *Tvoreniia*, ed. M. Ia. Poliakova (Moscow: Sovetskii pisatel', 1986), 479, 496.

38. Herbert N. Shenton, Edward Sapir, and Otto Jespersen, *International Communication: A Symposium on the Language Problem* (London: Kegan, Paul, 1931). See C. K. Ogden's preface (7–10), Sapir's "The Function of an International Auxiliary Language" (65–84), and Jespersen's "Interlinguistics" (95–120). In the last chapter of his *Mankind, Nation and Individual: From a Linguistic Point of View* (London: George Allen and Unwin, 1946), Jespersen makes several comments pertaining to the same subject (216–20).

39. For a detailed account of the devastation of Slavistics brought about by Marrism in the Soviet Union, see F. D. Ashnin and V. M. Alpatov, *"Delo slavistov" 30-e gody* (Moscow: Nasledie, 1994), 25, 27–28, 156–58.

40. M. V. Yudina Archive [Russian State Library, Moscow], Fund 527, Box 4, Item 1; p. 110. Yudina discusses both Vsevolod and Mikhail Bakhtin on the same page of these memoirs, which she apparently wrote during the early 1960s. In recalling her early years in St. Petersburg, she writes that she knew both men from the university and clearly states that the two are not related. As if to underscore that fact, Yudina offers up contrasting details of their lives, including the first name and patronymic of Vsevolod's wife.

41. Collection of the Research Institute of Book Studies (NIIK) [St. Petersburg National Library], Fund 316, Item 360. On the cover page of this particular file, Marr is listed as a full member (*deistvitel'nyi chlen*) of the commission and Vsevolod Bakhtin as a researcher (*nauchnyi sotrudnik*). Vsevolod Bakhtin's professional autobiography appears in the same collection of papers (p. 10) and, tallying with Yudina's general chronology of the period when she knew him, is dated 1926.

42. Russian State Security Archive (St. Petersburg), Inquest No. 108 (1928–29): vol. 1, 160, 176.

43. P. N. Medvedev collection [St. Petersburg National Library], Fund 474, Item 13. A torn-out title page of a copy of Voloshinov's *Marxism and the Philosophy of Language* with the inscription "To Pavel [Medvedev], not just 'amicably' [*druzheski*], but with love. Valentin," is dated January 23, 1929. If Voloshinov indeed had not written the book—and if, as many have suggested, everybody in the Bakhtin circle in Leningrad knew this fact—it seems highly unlikely that he would have penned such a personal inscription to Medvedev. While this document certainly does not offer definitive proof of the book's authorship, it is nonetheless powerfully suggestive.

44. Although Marr's Japhetic theory solidified into dogma only during the

early 1930s, his work was already gaining in attention and widespread respect during the second half of the 1920s, the period of Voloshinov's key work. Marr's meteoric rise to respectability and authority reached something of an apogee during the early 1930s with a spate of publications, including several approving commentaries on his work. His *Selected Works* (*Izbrannye raboty*, 1933–37) was the collection and culmination of several earlier and separate editions, some of them pamphlets. Among the many contemporary treatments of his work are: T. Artsybasheva, *Kratkii ocherk materialisticheskoi lingvistiki* (Krasnodar, 1931); S. N. Bykovskii, *N. Ia. Marr i ego teoriia: K sorokopiatiletiiu nauchnoi deiatel'nosti* (Moscow-Leningrad, 1933); B. V. Aptekar', *N. Ia. Marr i novoe uchenie o iazyke* (Moscow, 1934); A. M. Deborin, *Novoe uchenie o iazyke i dialekticheskii materilaizm* (Moscow, 1935); *XLV: Akademiku N. Ia. Marru* (Moscow-Leningrad, 1935). In his history of Soviet linguistics, *Lingvistika i Ideologija*, Milorad Pupovac gives one of the fuller accounts of the Stalin-Marr controversy (95–137).

45. V. N. Voloshinov, *Marxism and the Philosophy of Language*, trans. L. Matejka and I. R. Titunik (Cambridge: Harvard Univ. Press, 1986), 72, 76; *Marksizm i filosofiia iazyka* (Leningrad: Priboi, 1929), 73, 77.

46. In chapter 4 of part 2 of his book, Voloshinov subtly registers a disagreement with Marr. By essentially reducing Marr's primordial language to a manifestation or type of utterance (*vyskazyvanie*), Voloshinov transposes the all-signifying word into a context that Marr himself would doubtless have disagreed with. Consistent with his theory of the stadial nature of language's development, Marr insists on the uniqueness of the all-signifying word, its status as a highly specific and unique historical phenomenon at the beginning of humanity's cultural development. Voloshinov, however, suggests that this word does not fundamentally differ from utterances that one finds in modern languages. See page references for preceding note and *Marxism and the Philosophy of Language*, 101; Russian text, 103.

47. As I discuss in my book *Corporeal Words* (24–27), Bakhtin was influenced by the mystical esthetic of the Word as propounded by poets such as Bely, Maksimilian Voloshin, and Mandelshtam but reacted against their implicit valorization of poetic language.

48. M. M. Bakhtin, *Voprosy literatury i estetiki* (Moscow: Khudozhestvennaia literatura, 1975), 93.

49. M. M. Bakhtin, *Fransua Rable v istorii realizma* (Dissertation, Institute of World Literature, 1940), Institute of World Literature Archives, Moscow, Fund 427, Inventory 1, Item 19, 22; *Tvorchestvo Fransua Rable i narodnaia kul'tura srednevekov'ia i renessansa* (Moscow: Khudozhestvennaia literatura, 1990), 32; *RAHW* 24–25.

50. It is possible that this person was Boris Gornung, a member of Bakhtin's thesis defense committee who, in the transcript of the defense, makes statements about the grotesque's ancient origins in magical cults that bear a strong trace of Marr's ideas about culture in preliterate antiquity: "Stenogramma zasedaniia

Uchenogo soveta Instituta mirovoi literatury im. A. M. Gor'kogo. Zashchita M. M. Bakhtinym dissertatsii Rable v istorii realizma," *Dialog karnaval khronotop* 2–3 (1993): 91. In a recent article about Bakhtin's dissertation defense, Nikolai Pan'kov shrewdly notes parallels between Gornung's views (and, to a much lesser extent, Bakhtin's own) with the concepts of primitive culture formulated by Marr's talented student Ol'ga Freidenberg: "M. M. Bakhtin: Ranniaia versiia kontseptsii karnavala," *Voprosy literatury* 5 (September/October 1997): 116.

51. Bakhtin, *Fransua Rable v istorii realizma*, 568–69. Bakhtin kept this passage in his reworked version for book publication: *Tvorchestvo Fransua Rable i narodnaia kul'tura srednevekov'ia i renessansa*, 459; *RAHW* 415–16. In the manuscript of his thesis, Bakhtin underlines key words and phrases for special emphasis. We know that these underlinings represent Bakhtin's own highlighting of terms because they are made in the same blue ink he uses to insert words and corrections, which are written in what is very recognizably his own handwriting. Not only is the handwriting absolutely identical to the script of his numerous notes and letters (which are kept in various state libraries in Russia), but it seems that he used the same pen to write postcards to his friend Maria Yudina. In a particularly telling instance from his unpublished thesis, an insertion of an entire handwritten sentence contains a phrase that is underlined in the same ink, an emphasis that reappears in the book edition twenty-five years later: "The common human fund of familiar and abusive gesticulations is also based on these sharply defined images" (Dissertation, 416; *Tvorchestvo Fransua Rable i narodnaia kul'tura srednevekov'ia i renessansa*, 354; *RAHW* 318). Here, as in many other parts of her translation, Iswolsky ignores Bakhtin's highlighting, which I have restored in my quotation.

52. Kirill O. Rossianov points out Chikobava's collaborative role in Stalin's writing on linguistics in his article "Stalin as Lysenko's Editor: Reshaping Political Discourse in Soviet Science," *Configurations* 1, no. 3 (1993): 454.

53. Rossianov, "Stalin as Lysenko's Editor," 451, 453; Pupovac, *Lingvistika*, 120–23.

54. Clark and Holquist, *Mikhail Bakhtin*, 328.

55. L. Gogotishvili, commentary to "The Problem of Speech Genres," *Sobranie sochinenii* tom. 5 (Moscow: Russkie slovari, 1996), 536.

56. Bakhtin, *Estetika slovesnogo tvorchestva*, 253.

57. Ibid., 276.

58. Ibid., 277–78.

59. Ibid., 302–3. See also 298–89, 309–10, 324.

60. In his study of Rabelais, Bakhtin levels a similar criticism at Veselovsky, whose discussion of the figure of the clown in the Middle Ages is wrong-headed because it attempts to determine an unofficial truth as "objectively abstract," viewing it in isolation "from all the mighty culture of medieval humor" (*RAHW* 93).

61. Bakhtin, *Voprosy literatury i estetiki*, 84.

62. Stalin, *Marksizm i voprosy iazykoznaniia*, 7.

63. Ibid., 22–23; English translation, *Marxism and the Problems of Linguistics* (Peking: Foreign Languages Press, 1972), 21.

64. Gustav Wetter, *Dialectical Materialism: A Historical and Systematic Survey of Philosophy in the Soviet Union*, trans. Peter Heath (New York: Frederick A. Praeger, 1958), 199–201.

65. A. N. Gvozdev, *Ocherki po stilistike russkogo iazyka* (Moscow: Uchpedgiz, 1955), 10–15.

66. Bakhtin, *Estetika slovesnogo tvorchestva*, 255.

67. M. M. Bakhtin, "Iz arkhivnykh zapisei k rabote 'Problemy rechevykh zhanrov': Dialog II," *Sobranie sochinenii* tom. 5 (Moscow: Russkie slovari, 1996), 230.

68. Ibid., 223–24.

69. Stalin, *Marksizm i voprosy iazykoznaniia*, 24; *Marxism and the Problems of Linguistics*, 23.

70. Bakhtin, "Iz arkhivnykh zapisei," 237.

71. Bakhtin, *Fransua Rable v istorii realizma*, 37, 180–81, 577–78. The discussion of Gothic laughter and Bakhtin's mention of Joyce were not used in the 1965 book edition.

72. Mihailovic, *Corporeal Words*, 108–10, 132–34, 137–40.

73. Ibid., 200–7.

The Apophatic Bakhtin
Randall A. Poole

Apophatic, or negative, theology emphasizes the unknowability of God, the inadequacy of human conceptual categories to the divine. The transcendence of God means that theology must proceed by way of negation (the *via negativa*); God can be approached only by knowing what he is not. Conceptualization and theorization impoverish divine reality. Apophaticism is, "above all, an attitude of mind which refuses to form concepts about God. Such an attitude utterly excludes all abstract and purely intellectual theology which would adapt the mysteries of the wisdom of God to human ways of thoughts,"[sic] writes Vladimir Lossky in his classic treatise, *The Mystical Theology of the Eastern Church* (cited hereafter in this essay as *MTEC*). The apophatic approach is an aspiration toward an ever-greater plenitude, "straining always to conceive a greater fullness and to pass beyond the conceptual limitations which determine the divine being in terms proper to human reason."[1]

Man, created in the "image and likeness" of God, is called to participate in divine reality. In theistic anthropology, it is man's divine vocation that makes a human being a person; the image and likeness of God are what constitute personhood.[2] "Our ideas of human personality, of that *personal* quality which makes every human being unique, to be expressed only in terms of itself: this idea of *person* comes to us from Christian theology," Lossky affirms. Because the image of God in man is unknowable, personhood is a mystery. "The human person cannot be expressed in concepts," Lossky continues. "It eludes all rational definitions, indeed all description" (*MTEC* 53). Apophaticism thus encompasses human as well as divine nature. The mystical culmination of personhood is *theosis*, transcendent salvation in immortality and deification, "becoming" or union with God. This theistic doctrine of man, which closely links *apophasis* and *theosis*, is especially distinctive of Orthodox theology.[3]

Mikhail Bakhtin's philosophy of consciousness is both a powerful immanent analysis of the self and a defense of the intrinsic value of personhood (*lichnost'*). His concept of the person, although it is not grounded in a theistic ontology, bears striking similarity to the apophatic tradition in Orthodox theology, a tradition on which Bakhtin very likely drew in developing his ideas.[4]

Theism, Kant, and Bakhtin

Theism is metaphysical. It maintains that being is not exhausted by or reducible to nature, that being transcends the natural universe in space and time, and that this transcendent ontological reality is God. The spiritual is at some level ontologically real, not merely epiphenomenal. Naturalism, or atheism, is the opposite view: nature is all of being, and the "spiritual" is a metaphor for higher mental activity that is ultimately reducible to naturalistic processes. Relying on this dichotomy— is there, in the end, a third alternative?—philosophical theists often point to the nature of consciousness in support of their beliefs.[5] The issue, for them, is whether consciousness can be shown to be irreducible to nature, and, if so, whether that entails theism. Kant's *Critique of Pure Reason* is a classic example of a philosophical argument (transcendental idealism) for the irreducibility of consciousness to nature. Bakhtin, who has become perhaps best known as a philosopher of consciousness, drew heavily on Kant. This, when coupled with the claim that Bakhtin was a religious man, might easily lead one to associate him with philosophical theism. Is this association as straightforward as it seems? Bakhtin's use of Kantian categories (see below) ought not to obscure the differences between the two thinkers. Let us first consider Kant. Consciousness cannot be wholly explained by the facts of the natural, empirical world, Kant argues, because empirical experience itself depends on the transcendental functions of consciousness. Without these transcendental conditions, neither experience nor the self would be possible. They enable the self to be a self, that is, to have a world—a reality different from self, an outside capable of being experienced, otherness or alterity, objects. This startling capacity for objectivity, for differentiation between self and other, for the possibility of experience, is what Kant means by the term "transcendental."[6] His transformation in the concept of the nature of experience is transcendental idealism, his Copernican revolution. Among its main contentions is that the self cannot be reduced to the empirical, natural world because it is its very condition.

Kant's refutation of naturalistic reductions of consciousness turns on his striking insight that experience is necessarily objective since it is experience of something "other" than the self doing the experiencing. The subject of experience is the background against which there can be objects; it is a focus radically set apart from literally everything, for everything (even an object of thought) is an object for "it." This "it" is the self for which there can be a world or universe, the totality of things not-self. Experience thus presupposes pure self-consciousness as the capacity to confer objectivity. The capacity for objectivity is so central to experience, including thought (inner experience), that it cannot be done away with. The scare quotes around "it" are necessary because even in thinking about this capacity for objectification, for experience, we must objectify the self that has or is this capacity. But this original self, the very capacity for objectification, cannot be identical to the self (or aspect of the self) that is objectified or experienced in introspection, since it (the introspected self) thereby becomes an object of thought, and this presupposes a thought-background or original self that experiences or thinks the psychological self of introspection. Kant thus deduces a transcendental or pure self (the transcendental unity of pure apperception), or simply the *I think*, which can never be an object for "itself" because "it" is the very capacity for experience, including thought and introspection.[7]

Transcendental idealism refutes naturalism by seeking to show that nature does not stand on its own but is transcendentally conditioned. But does it entail theism? Although it cannot be proven that the *transcendental* conditions of experience strictly entail a *transcendent* level of being, it is difficult to think that the only alternative to naturalism is solipsism, a free-floating self anchored neither in this world nor another. Certainly Kant did not think so.[8] He believed that the irreducibility of the self leads to the "postulate" of a "noumenal" realm of being transcendent to space and time and inaccessible to theoretical knowledge.[9] The American philosopher Errol E. Harris goes a little further: transcendental idealism "leads unfailingly to theism."[10]

Where does Bakhtin stand? In his essay from the early 1920s, "Author and Hero in Aesthetic Activity," Bakhtin brings Kant down to earth, as it were, by focusing on actual lived experience, not the transcendental conditions of experience. Bakhtin is interested in subject and object not as abstract epistemological categories, but as embodied, concrete human beings, each occupying its own unique place in the world. True, Bakhtin's idea of subjectivity clearly owes very much to Kant.[11] In self-experience, I cannot perceive or know all of myself, Bakhtin argues, because I am unable to make all of myself an object for myself. In the act of self-objectification, an essential part of me always remains behind. I can never coincide with myself: *"I-for-myself* shall continue to be in the *act* of this self-objectification, and not in its product, that is, in the *act* of seeing, feeling, thinking, and not in the *object* seen or felt. I am incapable of fitting all of myself into an object, for I exceed any object as the active *subiectum* of it" ("A&H" 38). Self-knowledge will always be far from complete; it is the nature of subjectivity. (This is, to anticipate, the core of the apophatic Bakhtin.) The other, by contrast, is entirely an object for me, as I cannot be for myself. "The other, *all* of him, is laid out before me in the exhaustive completeness as a thing among other things *in* the world external to me" ("A&H" 36).[12] My position outside another person enables me to see him in a way he cannot see himself; it gives me an excess or surplus of seeing and knowing, which can help balance his own inevitable deficit of self-knowledge. And vice versa. In all this, Bakhtin repeatedly stresses that his concern is "concrete lived experience," and not, for example, the transcendental capacity for differentiation of subject and object.[13]

My condition of subjectivity produces the impression of idealism. "[W]hat makes idealism intuitively convincing is the experience I have of myself," Bakhtin writes. Solipsism, for the same reason, is likewise intuitively convincing, "or at any rate understandable" ("A&H" 39). However, what is intuitively convincing does not necessarily have extra-intuitive validity. Realism and materialism are also intuitively convincing, if I proceed not from self-experience but from experience of others, not from the inner world but from the external world ("A&H" 39–40). Bakhtin maintains that we cannot decide between idealism and materialism on the basis of experience alone; cognition may help but that, he insists, is not his concern. What matters to him is immanent, phenomenological description of "concrete lived experience"; theoretical abstraction from that experience is misleading. Bakhtin's approach is, in short, phenomenological, not transcendental. His earliest sustained work, *Toward a Philosophy of the Act*, indeed recommends phenomenology as a first philosophy (*TPA* 31–32).[14] Thus, while Bakhtin clearly valued Kant's account of subjectivity and objectivity as basic categories of experience, he does not endorse Kant at the level of theory. Idealism and naturalism are phenomenological descriptions of experience of self and other, not metaphysical conclusions.[15]

In one place in "Author and Hero," Bakhtin certainly seems to echo Kant on the irreducibility of consciousness to nature:

> I am not—for myself—*entirely* connatural with the outside world, for there is always something essential in me that I can set over against that world, namely, my inner self-activity, my subjectivity, which confronts the outside world as object, and which is incapable of being contained in it. This inner self-activity of mine exceeds both nature and the world: I always have an outlet along the line of my experience of myself . . . I always have a loophole, as it were, through which I can save myself from being no more than a natural given. ("A&H" 40)

The key phrase here is "for myself," at the beginning of the passage. Because my inescapable condition is subjectivity, it is not within my ability to conceive of being a natural object: only in this sense am I irreducible to nature (a subject just cannot do it). This brings out the essential difference between Kant and Bakhtin. Kantian transcendental idealism claims that the very possibility of nature depends on the transcendental capacity for objectivity, for differentiation between self and other. Reducing consciousness to nature is therefore something like reducing consciousness to itself. Bakhtinian phenomenology, by contrast, describes the situation of being a subject in the world. Bakhtin proceeds from ordinary assumptions that the subject is a human being already in the world; there is no metaphysical mystery.[16]

Another way of putting the difference is that for Bakhtin being a subject means having major real-life inadequacies (which is why I need the help of others), whereas for Kant it means the metaphysics of experience. The "loophole" by which

I can save myself from being no more than a natural given arises from one such inadequacy, that as a subject I can never coincide with myself. If I could, then I might know that I really am no more than a natural given (science can tell me that but I cannot really believe it as a subject). Bakhtin makes the most of this inadequacy: my intuitive idealism gives me a loophole that permits me to act on the assumption of freedom (unfinalizability). This says much, I believe, about Bakhtin's approach. He accepts the situation we are in as human beings in the world and tries to make the most of it through phenomenological disclosure of the ways we are persons (I-for-myself, I-for-another, another-for-me) and of how we can exploit these ways to help each other and enrich human interaction. What phenomenology reveals has its own value for Bakhtin: since, *for myself*, I am free and act according to my sense of "ought" ("A&H" 120), freedom and ethical responsibility are intrinsic values in no need of metaphysical sanction. It is enough that they are present in my lived experience of myself.

From all this, it is clear that Bakhtin was interested in religion in its immanent meaning for human consciousness, as one of the categories through which the self is constructed. His concern was man in the world, not God in metaphysics. Theism offered Bakhtin a powerful image of self-other relations, where the other is the idea of God. Susan Felch is certainly right in claiming that "Bakhtin rejects methodological naturalism in favor of methodological theism,"[17] since the first approach naturalizes or objectifies the human being while the second treats him as a person who has the potential for deification. Alexandar Mihailovic's idea of a Bakhtinian "human theology" is similarly apt.[18] But Bakhtin did not think the "internal uniqueness of consciousness" entailed the irreducibility of the self to nature, let alone metaphysical theism.[19] If he was a believer, it was, apparently, on other grounds.

Bakhtin wanted to stress that his philosophy of consciousness did not hold metaphysical implications one way or the other (theism or naturalism). He thought metaphysics implied a type of guarantee, while what consciousness needed was *faith* (see the final section of this essay, "Toward God as Other in Bakhtin's Dialogic Philosophy of Consciousness"). This helps explain Bakhtin's efforts to demystify, from a philosophical point of view, the "internal uniqueness of consciousness." His approach, depending on the actual extent of his theistic belief, may not be without contradiction. In any event, the apophatic framework fits Bakhtin very well because it rests on the conviction that the human person cannot be, and ought not to be, theoretically determined or finalized. This conviction, no matter what else it may have been, was at least an ethical one for Bakhtin. Meanwhile, those who think that the authentic freedom, unfinalizability, and ethics of personhood are good philosophical arguments against naturalism and for theism are not only still able to think that, but can point to Bakhtin's powerful immanent analysis of what it means to be a self as evidence in support of their beliefs.

Apophasis and Theosis in Orthodox Theology

In 1917, Sergei N. Bulgakov (1871–1944), one of Russia's most important religious philosophers,[20] published a major work, *Svet nevechernii* (*The Unfading Light*), which includes a chapter entitled "Negative (Apophatic) Theology."[21] Bakhtin would surely have known this work (which is cited hereafter in this essay as *SN*). The ideas that Bulgakov highlights in the apophatic tradition of Orthodox theology bear striking relevance to Bakhtin's thought.[22] The central conviction of negative theology is the transcendence of divine reality. Theology must be apophatic, Bulgakov argues, because "the basic content of *religious* experience—contact with the transcendent, divine world—clearly contains a contradiction for rational thought." This contradiction, immanent contact with or experience of the transcendent, amounts in fact to a fundamental antinomy: "that which is immanent cannot at the same time be transcendent and to that extent is not transcendent; that which is transcendent cannot be immanent to consciousness and remains beyond its limits" (*SN* 88). Divine reality, in its simultaneous transcendence and immanence, is the basic fact of *religious* consciousness and experience, but it cannot be understood in rational terms.

The antinomy of transcendence and immanence is most obvious in theology where the "object" of thought is the transcendent God. All thought, however, must face the inevitability of the transcendence of its object (any object) and the inexplicability of how a transcendent "object" can be an object of thought at all, that is, how it can be immanent to consciousness. In this connection Bulgakov turns to Kant, directly following another major Russian religious philosopher and contemporary of Bakhtin, Pavel A. Florensky (1882–1937),[23] whose work likewise displays impressive similarities to that of Bakhtin.[24] Kant's great service in theoretical philosophy, Bulgakov writes, was to have demonstrated that reason becomes entangled in antinomies because it is inadequate to its object. Reason (German *Verstand*, Russian *rassudok*) cannot make being fully immanent to itself; the inevitable result is a discrepancy between being and the laws of thought, a discrepancy expressed in antinomies. This clearly testifies to a certain transcendence of the object of thought and thus to the untenability of rationalistic, epistemological immanentism. "Antinomic thought seizes its object, makes it immanent to itself only in part, only to a certain extent, which comes out in an antinomy," Bulgakov explains. "The full transcendence of an object to thought would make it completely impossible as an object of thought, or ultimately inconceivable; its total adequacy to thought, on the other hand, would testify to its full immanence: in divine reason [German *Vernunft*, Russian *razum*], in which thought and being coincide in one act, there are and can be no antinomies . . . which make up a natural property of human reason" (*SN* 89).

Bulgakov emphasizes (as does Florensky) that antinomies reveal the impossibility of the full coincidence of subject and object, the inadequacy of the subject of thought to its object. These ideas soon took on great importance for Bakhtin. They form the basis of his critique of "theoreticism," first advanced in *Toward a Philosophy of the Act*. The theoretical world is the immanent world of abstract cognition, self-regulating and logical. Within its own bounds, its autonomy is fully justified. "But the world as object of theoretical cognition seeks to pass itself off as the whole world" (*TPA* 8). This is theoreticism: the attempt to immanentize the whole world, to reduce all being to theoretical consciousness. It is, among other things, to counter theoreticist tendencies in philosophy (in epistemology, first of all) that Bakhtin defines being as an "event."[25] Being, the world, remains irreducible and is always more than an immanent object of thought. Subject and object can never fully coincide. Self-sufficiency, a subject that is its own object, is a divine reality, not a human one. "Immanentism," or what Bakhtin calls "theoreticism" and also (in the Dostoevsky book) "monologism," is a pretension to a self-reliance that is God's, not ours.

Bulgakov thought Kant important enough for understanding negative theology that he devoted a separate section to him.[26] The main apophatic idea in Kant is the unknowable thing-in-itself, or noumenon. This affirmation of transcendence helps distinguish Kant from what Bulgakov calls the "whole pathos of immanentism" characteristic of post-Kantian German philosophy. Bulgakov's specific target is neo-Kantianism: "The pretension of the neo-Kantians to the total generation by thought of the object of thought (*reiner Ursprung*) is self-deception" (*SN* 90). Bakhtin, too, thought the neo-Kantians were especially to blame. Referring to the history of idealism, he wrote, "It becomes purely monologic only in a neo-Kantian interpretation" (*PDP* 100, note). In this, Bakhtin likely drew not only on Bulgakov but also on another Russian religious philosopher, Sergei A. Askoldov (1870–1945), whose work (at least on Dostoevsky) Bakhtin definitely knew and valued (*PDP* 11–14).[27] In 1914, Askoldov wrote that the first thesis of German neo-Kantianism,

> which can be called the *"position of immanence,"* consists in the assertion that any knowable object is always something given to consciousness or thought in one way or another, or even generated by thought, and that generally there is nothing in the sphere of being beyond the limits of consciousness and thought, that is, nothing transcendent to them. This thesis is newest in relation to Kant, who affirmed only the unknowability of the transcendent, but did not clearly and categorically reject its existence.[28]

Like Bulgakov and Askoldov, Bakhtin appreciated the main difference between Kant and the neo-Kantians: that Kant pursued the apophatic aim of hemming in the theoretical world, while the neo-Kantians wanted to extend it endlessly. The point of access to being (to the noumenal thing-in-itself) is not theoretical reason but practical reason, in moral consciousness of "ought." This conviction (which is, in fact, distinctively Kantian) was Bakhtin's point of departure in his essay on ethics, *Toward a Philosophy of the Act*.[29]

The preservation of the transcendence of the divine, against all-encompassing immanentism or theoreticism, is the main tenet of negative theology. In Bulgakov's formulation, "the transcendent God is forever an unknown, inaccessible, unfathomable, inexpressible Mystery, for which there is no approximation" (*SN* 90–91). The Mystery is that God transcends any distinction between subject and object, categories within which all thought, as such, takes place. For this reason, it cannot even be said that God is the "object" of theology. Here it begins to become clear that apophatic theology is mystical theology, that "knowledge" of God would actually be union with him, that *apophasis* is the way toward transcendent salvation in *theosis*. In *The Mystical Theology of the Eastern Church*, Vladimir Lossky writes that the apophatic way must culminate in freedom "from the subject as well as from the object of perception. God no longer presents Himself as object, for it is no more a question of knowledge but of union. Negative theology is thus a way towards mystical union with God, whose nature remains incomprehensible to us" (*MTEC* 28).

The Eastern tradition of apophatic or mystical theology, in conscious service of *theosis*, has its origins with Clement of Alexandria (d. 215) and Origen (d. 254). It achieved prominence with Gregory of Nyssa (d. 395) and became a major doctrinal force with the appearance (around the year 500) of the writings of Pseudo-Dionysius the Areopagite. It was then further developed in the important distinction Gregory Palamas (1296–1359) drew between God's essence (utterly inaccessible) and his energies (that enable human participation in divine reality), a distinction Palamas used to defend the hesychast method of prayer.[30] For the great Byzantine theologian Maximus the Confessor (d. 662), the intricate connection between the apophatic way and the goal of deification was the essence of "theological anthropology."[31] Bulgakov highlights the importance St. Maximus attached to the categories of subject and object. All thought presupposes multiplicity or, more precisely, duality: the thinker and the object of thought. "In God, however, there is no place for this dichotomy." God is absolute unity, "in Him the subject and object of thought coincide" (*SN* 110). The inevitability of subject and object in human thought therefore makes knowledge of God impossible and requires that theology be apophatic.[32] It also entails the interesting conclusion that to "know" God is to already be him (or at least to have transcended subjectivity and objectivity in a unity that is to us utterly inconceivable). Precisely this is the nexus between *apophasis* and *theosis*. In Lossky's words, "the way of the knowledge of God is necessarily the way of deification" (*MTEC* 39). Overcoming the distinction between subject and object—true self-sufficiency, self-coincidence, or self-reliance—would be an utter transformation in the human condition.

A corollary of the unknowability of God is the unknowability of man. If man cannot know God, neither can he know himself, created as he is in the image and likeness of God.[33] The impossibility of identity of subject and object that precludes knowledge of God also rules out complete self-knowledge. And in the same way, knowledge of God and perfect self-knowledge would equally be *theosis* (deification or union with God), since both entail an otherworldly unity of subject and object. But in this world, consciousness is not self-sufficient, subject and object do not coincide. This is one of Bakhtin's main ideas, and it must have been informed by his broad cultural knowledge of religious history and theology. For example, in discussing the Christian contribution to the history of the "idea of man," Bakhtin refers to "[t]he idea of the deity becoming human (Zielinski) and man becoming divine (Harnack)."[34] The apophatic moment in Bakhtin certainly consists, however, not in the mystical negation of subject and object that culminates in *theosis*, which is prototypical in the deification of the humanity of Christ, "man becoming divine"— but in the unknowability of the self to itself (I-for-myself), and thus in the need for the seeing and knowing other—for "deity becoming human," becoming, that is, an embodied, grace-bestowing other, Christ, which is Bakhtin's ideal image of the other.

The mystical union of self and other in God is not an idea congenial to Bakhtin's thought. The Orthodox doctrine of *theosis* does, however, include ideas that are, and that, in fact, form a large part of the religious imagery Bakhtin employs in depicting self-other relations (see "Toward God as Other in Bakhtin's Dialogic Philosophy of Consciousness"). The main compatibility is that *theosis* preserves the personal identity of the participants. "The mystical union between God and humans is a true union, yet in this union Creator and creature do not become fused into a single being," in Timothy Ware's formulation. "Orthodox mystical theology has always insisted that we humans, however closely linked to God, retain our full personal integrity. The human person, when deified, remains distinct (though not separate) from God."[35] Deification is *participation* in divine being, a "dwelling in" but not identity with the divine nature. The biblical basis is 2 Peter 1:4, which calls human beings to "become partakers of the divine nature" (*RSV*). It may not be going too far to see a reflection of this idea in Bakhtin when he refers to "the image of many unmerged personalities joined together in the unity of some spiritual event" (*PDP* 13). Bakhtin, in fact, left no doubt about what he most valued in religion: "a personal relationship to a personal God," as he remarked in 1925. "The personal nature [*personal'nost'*] of God and the personal nature of all believers are the constituent traits of religion."[36]

Concrete personhood, unity in diversity, gives the mystery of the Trinity a special place in the Orthodox tradition. To preserve the distinctiveness of the three persons (hypostases) of the Trinity, Byzantine theology, especially as expounded by the fourth-century Cappadocian Fathers (Gregory of Nazianzus,

Basil the Great, and Gregory of Nyssa), locates the principle of the unity of the godhead in the person of the Father, not in the divine essence that the three persons share (*homoousios*). Vladimir Lossky's prominence in twentieth-century Orthodox theology rests in part on his defense of Trinitarianism, specifically of the view that only the "monarchy" of the Father guarantees the concrete personhood of the three hypostases in the Trinity. "If one speaks of God it is always, for the Eastern Church, in the concrete," Lossky writes. "When, on the contrary, the common nature assumes the first place in our conception of trinitarian dogma, the religious reality of God in Trinity is inevitably obscured in some measure and gives place to a certain philosophy of essence"(*MTEC* 64). For Bakhtin as well, no philosophy of essence could usurp concrete personhood.

Fear of depersonalization helps explain the Orthodox rejection of the *Filioque*, the Roman Catholic doctrine—the unilateral adoption of which (and insertion into the Nicene Creed) contributed to the great schism between the Latin West and Greek East, customarily dated at 1054—that the Holy Spirit proceeds from both the Father and the Son ("double procession"), not from the Father alone. For the Orthodox, the *Filioque* is a subordination of the Holy Spirit to the other two hypostases and a diminishment of its own role in salvation.[37] The work of the Holy Spirit is sanctification of human persons. This is integral to and inseparable from the work of Christ, redemption of the common nature of humanity. "Within the Church the Holy Spirit imparts to human hypostases the fullness of deity after a manner which is unique, 'personal,' appropriate to every man as a person created in the image of God," according to Lossky. "The work of Christ unifies; the work of the Holy Spirit diversifies"(*MTEC* 166–67).

Bakhtin might well have seen a literary expression of Trinitarian personalism in Dostoevsky. In one of his better known observations, Bakhtin wrote, "Dostoevsky's world is profoundly *pluralistic*. If we were to seek an image toward which this whole world gravitates, an image in the spirit of Dostoevsky's own worldview, then it would be the church as a communion of unmerged souls, where sinners and righteous men come together" (*PDP* 26–27). And Bakhtin's own profoundly pluralistic world of unmerged souls surely owes something to P. A. Florensky's explicitly Trinitarian concept of personhood, advanced in *The Pillar and Foundation of Truth* (1914).[38] At any rate, the striking formal similarity between Bakhtin's dialogic philosophy of consciousness and Orthodox Trinitarianism could not be better captured than in Ware's characterization: "Deification is not a solitary but a 'social' process. . . . Humans, made in the image of the Trinity, can only realize the divine likeness if they live a common life such as the Blessed Trinity lives: as the three persons of the Godhead 'dwell' in one another, so we must 'dwell' in our fellow humans, living not for ourselves alone, but in and for others. . . . Such is the true nature of *theosis*."[39]

The Possibility of Creation

The broad significance of apophatic theology is that theory impoverishes divine reality, a reality that is God but includes man (by vocation). One of Bakhtin's fundamental ideas, and one that spans his entire career, is that theory is impoverishing. In "Author and Hero in Aesthetic Activity," Bakhtin writes that theories are typically impoverishing, "because they seek to explain the creatively productive event by reducing its full amplitude. . . . [T]he event is transposed in all its constituents to the unitary plane of a single consciousness, and it is within the unity of this single consciousness that the event is to be understood and deduced in all its constituents" ("A&H" 87). Theory, then, is impoverishing when it is a reduction to one consciousness. But what, specifically, is impoverishing about a single consciousness? Here as well, Bakhtin is clear. One consciousness cannot create.

> There are events which are in principle incapable of unfolding on the plane of one and the same consciousness and which presuppose *two* consciousnesses that never merge. Or, in other words, what is *constitutive* for such events is the relationship of one consciousness to *another* consciousness precisely as an *other*. Events of this kind include all of the *creatively* productive events—the once-occurrent and inconvertible events that bring forth something new. ("A&H" 86–87)

One consciousness cannot be creative because within it there is no outside from which another can give me something I lack. It does not provide the possibility of "formal enrichment," which Bakhtin describes as basic to cultural creation but which involves the idea of creativity as such. Let the other remain outside of me, "for in that position he can see and know what I myself do not see and do not know from my own place, and he can essentially enrich the event of my own life" ("A&H" 87). In my deficit of knowing and seeing, I am in an "apophatic" situation, and it is precisely this that gives the other a creative opportunity (and vice versa). If everything is reduced, or made immanent, to a single consciousness, then I already know and have everything. Nothing can be introduced from outside. I cannot, in principle, be enriched and therefore remain eternally impoverished.

Creation, in other words, needs transcendence, an outside from which something new can descend as a gift. Creation is not an "emanation" of one consciousness but something altogether new. In the value he placed on a multiplicity of consciousnesses that can therefore be outside each other, Bakhtin surely drew on the Christian mystery of creation *ex nihilo*. True, it is difficult to know what "outside" God means. "Yet creation *ex nihilo* does mean just such an act producing something which is 'outside of God'—the production of an entirely new subject," as Lossky tries to express the idea. "We might say that by creation *ex nihilo* God 'makes room' for something which is wholly outside of Himself; that, indeed, He sets up the 'outside' or nothingness alongside of His plenitude. The result is a subject which is entirely 'other'" (*MTEC* 92). The Christian dogma of creation *ex nihilo* took shape in part against Neoplatonic cosmogony, in which the world is "emanated," not genuinely created. In *The Unfading Light*, S. N. Bulgakov sharply contrasts Neoplatonism and Christianity on this point. In Neoplatonism, Bulgakov writes, "nothing happens or occurs in the world, for it does not lie *outside* the absolute, but is the absolute itself, only in a certain state of deprivation" (*SN* 139). Here there is a striking parallel with Bakhtin, probably a case of direct influence, for Bakhtin himself points to the example of Neoplatonism: in it, "the distinctiveness of the category of the *other* fails to gain a foothold. The emanationist theory prevails. . . . All events are concentrated in the unitary *I-for-myself*, without introducing the new value of the *other*." Everything—"the universe, God, other people"—is reduced to pure self-experience ("A&H" 55). In another context Bakhtin refers to the deep distrust of outsideness, writing that, "in religion this is associated with the 'immanentization' of God" ("A&H" 203).

From Neoplatonic roots, theoretical reductionism within a single, all-encompassing consciousness has grown to become a "profound structural characteristic" of modern times (*PDP* 82).[40] Bakhtin sees this development in, for example, the "epistemologism" pervading nineteenth- and twentieth-century philosophy. "Epistemological consciousness, the consciousness of science, is a unitary and unique consciousness, or, to be exact—a single consciousness" ("A&H" 88). We have seen that Bakhtin first advances his critique of "theoreticism" in *Toward a Philosophy of the Act*, where he also uses the term "rationalism" to describe the phenomenon (29–30). He returns to and develops this theme in *Problems of Dostoevsky's Poetics*, now also under the general rubric of "monologism," the culmination of European rationalism, "with its cult of a unified and exclusive reason." The highest form of ideological monologism is, in turn, monistic absolute idealism (Fichte, Schelling, Hegel). Bakhtin also singles out another expression of monologism: European utopianism, including socialism (*PDP* 80–82).[41]

For Bakhtin the most important consequence of monologism is that, within the single consciousness of absolute idealism, human consciousnesses can only be "empirical" or "accidental." Monologism is fundamentally debilitating. "In an environment of philosophical monologism the genuine interaction of consciousnesses is impossible" (*PDP* 81). And it is the genuine, dialogic interaction of consciousnesses that enables personhood. "I am conscious of myself and become myself only while revealing myself for another, through another, and with the help of another. The most important acts constituting self-consciousness are determined by a relationship toward another consciousness (toward a *thou*)." For these reasons, "consciousness is in essence multiple" ("TRDB" 287, 288). The multiplicity of consciousnesses is what is creative about each of them, for the "I-for-myself" needs the surplus of vision and knowing of the "other-for-me." This move, diametrically opposed to the omniscience of the monologic absolute consciousness, is the creative force behind the apophatic Bakhtin.

Toward God as Other in Bakhtin's Dialogic Philosophy of Consciousness

Dialogic interaction of self and other is the highest level in Bakhtin's conception of personhood, a level that presupposes prior enabling stages. The most basic of these, as specified in *Toward a Philosophy of the Act*, are ethical and, to an extent, ontological. Bakhtin advances three core ideas: being-as-event, non-alibi in being, and "ought." Bakhtin is not altogether clear on what he means by "being-as-event"; it is a basic and irreducible category. Bakhtin exploits the etymology of the Russian word for event (*sobytie*) to emphasize that being happens, or is an event, between or among interacting consciousnesses.[42] Being, at the moment it is an event, is also a constituent moment of consciousness. It enables consciousnesses to continue their interaction at higher levels, where they become fully creative of each other in personhood-bestowing dialogue. Being-as-event requires participation; once participation ends, it is no longer an event. Or, as Bakhtin also says, it requires actual communion.[43] Being is an event only in an act or deed. As an event, it cannot be transcribed in theoretical terms. Concrete uniqueness and singularity characterize an event. Theory, by contrast, deals with the general and recurrent. In this connection, Bakhtin relates being-as-event to an important distinction between truth as *pravda* and truth as *istina*. "It is an unfortunate misunderstanding (a legacy of rationalism) to think that truth [*pravda*] can only be the truth [*istina*] that is composed of universal moments; that the truth of a situation is precisely that which is repeatable and constant in it" (*TPA* 37). Throughout, Bakhtin's stress is the link among being-as-event, personal participation, and personhood-in-process. Thus, referring to his formulation of *pravda* as unitary and unique truth, Bakhtin writes, "It is precisely this truth that requires me to realize in full my unique participation in Being from my own unique place. The unity of the whole conditions the unique and utterly unrepeatable roles of all the participants. Being, as something determinate, finished, and petrified in respect to its content, would destroy countless uniquely valuable personal worlds" (*TPA* 45–46).[44]

Bakhtin draws important implications from the unique and irreplaceable position each participant occupies in being-as-event. First he stresses the utter uniqueness of that position. "I occupy a place in once-occurrent Being that is unique and never-repeatable, a place that cannot be taken by anyone else and is impenetrable for anyone else. . . . That which can be done by me can never be done by anyone else. The uniqueness or singularity of present-on-hand Being is compellently obligatory" (*TPA* 40). By "compellently obligatory," Bakhtin means that I am obligated to acknowledge my unique place in being-as-event, to acknowledge, that is, my "non-alibi in being." Theoreticism seeks to diminish this responsibility by universalizing it, by displacing it to everyone and so to no one in particular. Theoreticism proposes an alibi in being when in fact I don't have one.[45] It is only through affirming and living up to my non-alibi "that I do not sever myself from the ontological roots of actual Being" (*TPA* 44). Bakhtin is, however, far more concerned with ethics than with ontology. Acknowledging my "non-alibi in being" is a moral obligation; it is what I *ought* to do. My unique position in being produces a "concrete ought" to live up to it. "Ought" is a category of consciousness (*TPA* 6, 25); it, too, is basic and irreducible, the nexus between person and being. I perform an "answerable" deed when I act from or according to my non-alibi in being, that is, as I ought to. "This fact of *my non-alibi in Being,* which underlies the concrete and once-occurrent ought of the answerably performed act, *is not something I come to know of and to cognize* but is something I acknowledge and affirm in a unique or once-occurrent manner" (*TPA* 40, my italics). Bakhtin's approach to it is, in other words, apophatic.

Of all the deeds I *ought* to accomplish from my own unique place in being, the most valuable is what I *can* do for another. "That I, from my unique place in Being, simply see and know another, that I do not forget him . . . is something only I can do for him at the given moment in all of Being: that is the deed which makes his being more complete, the deed . . . which is possible only for me" (*TPA* 42). This type of deed, in which I help another to be more complete, comprises the highest level of Bakhtin's moral philosophy, where ethics becomes dialogic philosophy of consciousness. What I can and ought to do for another is help fill in the apophatic gap of non-self-sufficiency that every self faces. This realization that I am in the position to help complete another comes about through facing my own lack of self-sufficiency, through recognizing that, as Bakhtin strikingly puts it, "what God is for me, I must be for another" ("A&H" 56). And it is remarkable that Bakhtin invests his description of this process of self-discovery so heavily with the religious imagery of *apophasis* and *theosis:* grace, confession, penitence and prayer, and faith.

In "Author and Hero," Bakhtin considers some of Christianity's contributions to the history of the "idea of man." Among them is grace, the idea of bestowal, from outside, of loving mercy, justification, and restoration ("A&H" 57). Grace is a quintessentially apophatic image. It is not surprising that Bakhtin would use it to convey the idea of self-insufficiency. With Christ, Bakhtin writes, "God is no longer defined essentially as the voice of my conscience, as purity of my relationship to myself. . . . God is now the heavenly father who is *over me* and can be merciful to me and justify me where I, from within myself, cannot be merciful to myself and cannot justify myself in principle" ("A&H" 56). The grace of justification and fulfillment can descend only from outside; its source is transcendent. This idea of grace relates to the important distinction Bakhtin draws between spirit and soul. On my own (I-for-myself), I am unfinalized, incomplete spirit, not a soul (as I am for another). "My self-reflection, insofar as it is mine, is incapable of engendering a soul. . . . The soul descends upon me—like grace upon the sinner, like a gift that is unmerited and unexpected" ("A&H" 101). The implications go beyond Bakhtin's main context of aesthetics, since another's image of me can help my spirit ascend to ever higher levels. The soul may be a gift bestowed upon me, but it is always transcended by my open, unfinalizable spirit. And, likewise, "[t]he soul is a gift that my spirit bestows upon the *other*" ("A&H" 132), whose spirit then transcends it.[46]

Confession is the act in which I realize that I am not adequate to myself, that I cannot complete myself.[47] Confessional self-accounting strives for complete purity of self-relationship, for immanence and the exclusion of all moments "transgredient" to self-consciousness. As a result, it cannot in itself be consummating. It is a transitional moment in which I pass beyond myself and turn to God. "The negation of any justification in *this* world is transformed into a need for *religious* justification . . . for a mercy and grace that are totally otherworldly in respect to their value. Such justification is not immanent to self-accounting, but lies beyond its bounds" ("A&H" 143). A confession is made, Bakhtin repeatedly says, in penitent tones ("A&H" 57, 128, 141ff.). With this, he introduces the key apophatic image of repentance. In Vladimir Lossky's words, "the apophatic way of Eastern theology is the repentance of the human person before the face of the living God" (*MTEC* 238). On this point there is indeed a striking similarity between Lossky and Bakhtin. Of repentance, Lossky writes, "it is the opposite state of the soul to self-sufficiency." Like the way of ascent toward God, it can have no end (*MTEC* 204). In this context, Lossky refers to the prayer of the publican (*MTEC* 206), and writes that "the beginning of prayer is petition—'the prayer of supplication'" (*MTEC* 207). Bakhtin, too, singles out the prayer of the publican (a "pure and profound" example of confessional self-accounting); stresses that such penitential prayers do not end and, from within themselves, are incapable of being consummated ("repetition of prayers" represents movement as such, he says);[48] and makes the comparison to petition and supplication ("A&H" 145, 143).

Bakhtin's next link is perhaps his most profound: self-consciousness in faith. Within the inner world of I-for-myself, I always live for the future as someone who is yet to be achieved, someone who in the most essential respects does not exist yet. I never live up to my potential, but rather by the hope and faith that more of me always lies ahead, even that the essential me lies ahead. "The real center of gravity of my own self-determination is located solely in the future." No matter how much I achieve, "the center of gravity of my self-determination will continue

becoming

to shift forward, into the future, and I shall rely for support on myself as someone yet-to-be" ("A&H" 127). More than that, self-consciousness depends on the self not coinciding, not coinciding in principle with its factually given, present-on-hand existence. Living (as I inevitably do) by the hope and faith of such noncoincidence is, as Bakhtin puts it, a rightful folly or insanity, because "there are no guarantees of the ought-to-be" ("A&H" 128). It is the nature of the self to not coincide with itself; we know that this is one of Bakhtin's foundational ideas (and that it is essentially Kantian). One of the several basic implications Bakhtin draws from this idea is that consciousness is always forward-looking (or inherently progressive).

In striving forward toward "what ought-to-be," I try to exclude all external axiological forces of justification that could tempt me to be quiescent, to stop short in my passing-beyond-myself, and think that I do coincide with myself. This solitary "restlessness" is the first constituent moment of confessional self-accounting, which Bakhtin defines succinctly as an attempt to determine oneself in light of the ought-to-be ("A&H" 141). The goal is to overcome the "axiological self-contentment of present-on-hand being" and to appreciate that I "absolutely" do not coincide with myself. At this point, if I am successful, "a place for God is opened up," because consciousness itself is not possible "[i]n an absolute axiological void" ("A&H" 144). This is the second constituent moment of confessional self-accounting (the specifically confessional moment). Pure self-consciousness, as such, is impossible; the self does not coincide with and is inaccessible to itself. Therefore, consciousness requires a bearing in something "other" than self, first in "what ought to be," then, with the increasing clarity of self-accounting, in God. Self-consciousness, Bakhtin writes, is impossible "outside God, outside the bounds of trust in absolute otherness." Confessional self-accounting, striving to be absolutely solitary, ends up revealing the need for absolute otherness. The deeper the solitude and the deeper the repentance, "the clearer and more essential is one's referredness to God." Bakhtin's (analytic and compact) argument is that "what ought to be," toward which I strive and with which I never coincide, must be transcendent to consciousness, since were it only an immanent moment of my consciousness, that is, were it only a moment of present-on-hand being, it could not be that by virtue of which I am self-conscious. In other words, "the very fact of becoming conscious of myself in being, testifies in itself that I am not alone in my self-accounting, that someone[49] . . . wants me to be good" ("A&H" 144).[50]

The transcendent "moment of otherness" (what ought to be, ultimately God) is, Bakhtin stresses, not guaranteed.

> [F]or a *guarantee* would reduce it to the level of present-on-hand being (at best, aestheticized being, as in metaphysics). One can live and gain consciousness of oneself . . . only *in faith*. Life (and consciousness), from within itself, is nothing else but the actualization of faith; the process of life's gaining

self-consciousness is a process of gaining consciousness of faith (that is, of need and hope, of non-self-contentment and of possibility). ("A&H" 144)[51]

[handwritten: unknowability of God + becoming]

Bakhtin's point is not only the quite apophatic one that God cannot be known, but that were he known, human beings could not grow in self-consciousness and personhood. As present-on-hand being, he would no longer be the *ideal* toward which we aspire and by virtue of which we are self-conscious. Or, in the language of *theosis*, were God known, we could only serve him, not become him.

Notes

1. Vladimir Lossky, *The Mystical Theology of the Eastern Church* (Crestwood, N.Y.: St. Vladimir's Seminary Press, 1976), 38–39, 240.

2. Vladimir Lossky, *In the Image and Likeness of God* (Crestwood, N.Y.: St. Vladimir's Seminary Press, 1974). Timothy Ware, *The Orthodox Church*, new ed. (New York: Penguin Books, 1993), 218–21. John Meyendorff, *Byzantine Theology: Historical Trends and Doctrinal Themes* (New York: Fordham Univ. Press, 1979), 138–43. Greek patristic thought gives particular attention to the theological foundations of the idea of personhood.

3. Jaroslav Pelikan, *The Emergence of the Catholic Tradition (100–600)* (Chicago: Univ. of Chicago Press, 1971), 155, 344–45. Jaroslav Pelikan, *The Spirit of Eastern Christendom (600–1700)* (Chicago: Univ. of Chicago Press, 1974), 10–16, 30–36, 254–70. John Meyendorff, *Byzantine Theology*, 2–3, 32–33, 37–39, 77–78, 163–65, 225–26. Timothy Ware, *The Orthodox Church*, 231–38. Panayiotis Nellas, *Deification in Christ: Orthodox Perspectives on the Nature of the Human Person*, trans. Norman Russell (Crestwood, N.Y.: St. Vladimir's Seminary Press, 1987). Lars Thunberg, *Microcosm and Mediator: The Theological Anthropology of Maximus the Confessor*, 2nd ed. (Chicago: Open Court, 1995).

4. *Russian Religious Thought*, ed. Judith Deutsch Kornblatt and Richard F. Gustafson (Madison: Univ. of Wisconsin Press, 1996), is a fine collection of valuable essays that demonstrate the influence of the Orthodox doctrine of *theosis*, in particular, on late-nineteenth- and early-twentieth-century Russian religious philosophy. A similar case can also be made for an apophatic current in Russian religious thought, apart from Bakhtin (which is not to say that "Russian religious thought" is the best rubric for situating Bakhtin in Russian intellectual history). See Andrzej Walicki, "Catholicism and the Eastern Church in Russian Religious and Philosophical Thought," *Soviet Union/Union Soviétique* 15, no. 1 (1988): 45–59. S. I. Hessen, "Bor'ba utopii i avtonomii dobra v mirovozzrenii F. M. Dostoevskogo i Vl. Solov'eva" ["The Conflict between Utopia and the Autonomy of the Good in the

Weltanschauung of F. M. Dostoevsky and Vl. Solov'ev"], *Sovremennye zapiski* (Paris),
vol. 45 (1931), 283, makes the apophatic connection. He writes that in *The Brothers
Karamazov*, Dostoevsky comes very close to negative theology (in another context
Hessen refers to Bakhtin's polyphonic image of Dostoevsky, 281, note).

5. See, for example, Richard Swinburne, *The Existence of God*, rev. ed. (Oxford:
Oxford Univ. Press, 1991), chapter 9, "Arguments from Consciousness and Morality," 152–79. Both the cosmological and ontological proofs can also be considered
types of argument from consciousness: they turn on the insight that infinitude,
perfection, and necessity are *a priori* ideas, i.e., ideas that are not extrapolations
from the empirical world but are already present as a condition of awareness of
finitude and contingency. As Leszek Kolakowski, in *Religion* (Oxford: Oxford Univ.
Press, 1982), 72, writes, "To assert the priority of infinitude is the same as to assert
the contingency or non-self-sufficiency of the finite world, and the real question
is: where does this idea come from?" Charles Taylor, *Sources of the Self: The Making
of the Modern Identity* (Cambridge: Harvard Univ. Press, 1989), 140–41, makes the
same point in his interpretation of the ontological proof. Alvin Plantinga's classic
defense of the rationality of theistic belief, *God and Other Minds: A Study of the Rational
Justification of Belief in God* (Ithaca: Cornell Univ. Press, 1967), likewise proceeds from
philosophy of mind: belief in God is no less rational than belief in other minds.

6. "I entitle *transcendental* all knowledge which is occupied not so much with
objects as with the mode of our knowledge of objects in so far as this mode of
knowledge is to be possible *a priori*." Immanuel Kant, *Critique of Pure Reason*, trans.
Norman Kemp Smith, unabridged ed. (New York: St. Martin's Press, 1965), 59.
In his well-known "Preface to the Second Edition" of the *Critique of Pure Reason*,
Kant explains that objects must conform to *a priori* concepts of the faculty of
understanding. "For experience is itself a species of knowledge which involves
understanding; and understanding has rules which I must presuppose as being
in me prior to objects being given to me, and therefore as being *a priori*. They
find expression in *a priori* concepts to which all objects of experience necessarily
conform." *Critique of Pure Reason*, 22–23. In short, "it is possible to show that pure *a
priori* principles are indispensable for the possibility of experience" (ibid., 45).

7. Kant, *Critique of Pure Reason*, 152–55, in the "Transcendental Deduction."

8. He was specifically concerned to refute "idealism," in the solipsistic sense
it often had in his time, that nothing exists apart from the self. *Critique of Pure Reason*,
244–47.

9. Kant arrives at his three postulates of practical reason—freedom of the
will, immortality of the soul, and the existence of God—from the nature of
moral experience. Moral consciousness of "what ought to be" (*das Sollen*) is neither
derivative from nor reducible to the empirical world of "what is" (*das Sein*). "Ought,"
the force of which is felt in duty, can determine the will in opposition to natural
causes. "There is in man a power of self-determination, independently of any

coercion through sensuous impulses," writes Kant (*Critique of Pure Reason*, 465). Kant's system is a tightly integrated whole: the epistemology (transcendental idealism) and the ethics mutually corroborate the autonomy or irreducibility of the self. Transcendental idealism, by reconceptualizing nature as the capacity for empirical experience, makes possible or validates duty and free will as authentic (otherwise, they are reduced to psychological illusions), with all the implications this holds for metaphysics. "Ought" is one of Bakhtin's fundamental philosophical categories.

10. Errol E. Harris, *Atheism and Theism* (Atlantic Highlands, N.J.: Humanities Press International, 1993), 64.

11. Katerina Clark and Michael Holquist, *Mikhail Bakhtin* (Cambridge: Harvard Univ. Press, 1984), 43, 103, state that in 1919, Bakhtin ran a study group in Nevel on the *Critique of Pure Reason*, and that in 1925, in Leningrad, he gave a private course of eight lectures on the *Critique of Judgment*. L. V. Pumpiansky's notes from Bakhtin's lectures of 1924–25 contain schematic accounts of six (out of apparently nine) lectures on Kant, which Bakhtin probably delivered in October–November 1924. These lectures are on the *Critique of Pure Reason*, not the *Critique of Judgment*. However, it is possible, as N. I. Nikolaev suggests, that Pumpiansky's notes date from an earlier series of lectures on Kant. The 1924–25 notes were published in Russian as "Lektsii i vystupleniia M. M. Bakhtina 1924–25 gg. v zapisiakh L. V. Pumpianskogo" ["M. M. Bakhtin's Lectures and Speeches of 1924–25, as transcribed by L. V. Pumpiansky"], introduced, edited, and annotated by N. I. Nikolaev, in *M. M. Bakhtin kak filosof*, ed. L. A. Gogotishvili and P. S. Gurevich (Moscow, 1992), 236–44. An English translation of them is included as an appendix to this volume.

12. Bakhtin later gives a succinct statement of the difference between subject and object: "The other always stands over against me as an object: the exterior image of him stands over against me in space and his inner life stands over against me in time. I myself as *subiectum* never coincide with me myself: I—the *subiectum* of the act of self-consciousness—exceed the bounds of this act's content" ("A&H" 109).

13. Clark and Holquist, *Mikhail Bakhtin*, 59, write that Bakhtin wanted to claim Kant for a fuller understanding of lived experience, and that he used Kantian ideas about space and time but took them not as transcendental forms but as forms of the most immediate reality (here they quote Bakhtin's essay, "Forms of Time and of the Chronotope in the Novel"). On subjectivity, they also draw the comparison with Kant's "I think" (71). On these points my own reading of Kant and Bakhtin fully concurs with theirs.

14. In his expert annotation of Bakhtin's *Toward A Philosophy of the Act*, Liapunov stresses Bakhtin's phenomenological approach, 83 n. 19, 94 n. 97. Bakhtin was undoubtedly influenced by the Russian phenomenologist Gustav Shpet, whose book *Appearance and Sense* appeared in 1914.

15. In Bakhtin's own words, "Idealism is a phenomenology of my experience of myself, but not of my experience of the other; the naturalistic conception of

consciousness and of man in the world is a phenomenology of the other. We are not concerned, of course, with the philosophical validity of these conceptions. Our only concern here is the stock of phenomenological experience that underlies them; in themselves, these conceptions are the result of a theoretical processing of that stock of experience" ("A&H" 110).

16. Clark and Holquist, *Mikhail Bakhtin*, 90, on Bakhtin's approach to the apparent paradox of the self's inability to see itself: "That invisibility is neither mysterious nor even metaphoric but rather structural."

17. Susan M. Felch, "'In the Chorus of Others': M. M. Bakhtin's Sense of Tradition," in *Tradition and Literary Study*, ed. Donald Marshall. Forthcoming.

18. Alexandar Mihailovic, *Corporeal Words: Mikhail Bakhtin's Theology of Discourse* (Evanston: Northwestern Univ. Press, 1997), 233.

19. Quite the contrary. In 1961, Bakhtin returned to a theme he first took up forty years earlier in "Author and Hero," that death cannot be a fact of self-consciousness (for the simple reason that I am incapable of experiencing the moment of my own death). "In Dostoevsky's world death finalizes nothing, because death does not affect the most important thing in this world—consciousness for its own sake." Commenting on this, Bakhtin writes: "Dostoevsky gives all this an idealistic cast, draws ontological and metaphysical conclusions (the immortality of the soul, and so forth). But the discovery of the internal uniqueness of consciousness does not contradict materialism. Consciousness comes second, it is born at a specific stage in the development of the material organism, it is born objectively, and it dies (also objectively) together with the material organism (sometimes even before it); it dies objectively" ("TRDB" 290). The irreducibility of the self to nature is—let there be no doubt—an important idea in Orthodox thought and is thus directly relevant to the issue of Bakhtin and theism. John Meyendorff writes that Byzantine theologians often describe man in terms of the trichotomist conception: spirit or mind (*nous*), soul, and body. Bakhtin himself makes extensive use of this trichotomy in his essay, "Author and Hero." In the Byzantine tradition, the spirit (*nous*) most represents the person in the human being (for Bakhtin, the unfinalizable, internal uniqueness of consciousness). "This concept of the person or hypostasis, *irreducible to nature or to any part of it*," Meyendorff writes, "is a central notion in both [Byzantine] theology and anthropology" (*Byzantine Theology*, 142, my italics).

20. Catherine Evtuhov, *The Cross and the Sickle: Sergei Bulgakov and the Fate of Russian Religious Philosophy* (Ithaca: Cornell Univ. Press, 1997).

21. S. N. Bulgakov, *Svet nevechernii* (Moscow, 1994), 88–154.

22. There are other parallels as well between Bulgakov and Bakhtin. Mihailovic, *Corporeal Words*, 37–38, compares Bakhtin's essay from the mid-1930s, "Discourse in the Novel," to Bulgakov's essay, "Was ist das Wort?" published abroad in 1930 (it is the first chapter of Bulgakov's book, *Philosophy of the Name*, written in 1919 but not published as a whole until 1953). Steven Cassedy, *Flight from Eden: The*

Origins of Modern Literary Criticism and Theory (Berkeley and Los Angeles: Univ. of California Press, 1990), 111–14, discusses Bulgakov's *Philosophy of the Name.* Michael A. Meerson, "Sergei Bulgakov's Philosophy of Personality," in *Russian Religious Thought,* 142–43, 150, refers to Bakhtin in the context of Bulgakov's theory of personhood.

23. Robert Slesinski, *Pavel Florensky: A Metaphysics of Love* (Crestwood, N.Y.: St. Vladimir's Seminary Press, 1984).

24. The problem of antinomies is central to Florensky's major work, *The Pillar and Foundation of Truth* (1914), on which Bulgakov relies and which Bakhtin would have known. Apart from the apophatic conclusions that follow from the antinomies of reason, the similarities between Florensky and Bakhtin include the idea that personhood (*lichnost'*) emerges within a multiplicity of consciousnesses (an explicitly Trinitarian context for Florensky) and the idea of kenotic embodiment. For the *lichnost'* comparison, see Meerson, "Sergei Bulgakov's Philosophy of Personality," 143–44; and Mihailovic, *Corporeal Words,* 99–102. For the kenosis comparison, see Clark and Holquist, *Mikhail Bakhtin,* 84–87, 135–37; and Cassedy, *Flight from Eden,* 114–20. The apophatic connection between Kant and Florensky has recently been drawn by T. B. Dlugach, "Problema vremeni v filosofii I. Kanta i P. Florenskogo" ["The Problem of Time in the Philosophy of I. Kant and P. Florensky"], in *Kant i filosofiia v Rossii,* ed. Z. A. Kamensky and V. A. Zhuchkov (Moscow, 1994), 186–211. Dlugach writes that for all the differences between Kant and Florensky, "nonetheless the philosophical reflections of both aspire beyond the limits of scientific reality—to being in itself, and in this sense they move from logic to ontology, to metaphysics. Kant takes being in its negative, apophatic significance, while for Florensky it becomes a symbol of true, Divine existence."

25. Being-as-event, or the event of being, is Bakhtin's most basic category in *Toward a Philosophy of the Act.* One of his clearest uses of it occurs in the specific context of his critique of theoreticism. Theory (philosophy and science) is only one particular moment that participates in being-as-event. Theory is not a detached, separate world, let alone the whole world, "but rather a world that is incorporated into the unitary and once-occurrent event of Being through the mediation of an answerable consciousness in an actual deed. But that once-occurrent event of Being is no longer something that is thought of, but something that *is,* something that is being actually and inescapably accomplished through me and others (accomplished, *inter alia,* also in my deed of cognizing). . . . This Being cannot be determined in the categories of non-participant theoretical consciousness—it can be determined only in the categories of actual communion, i.e., of an actually performed act" (*TPA* 12–13). Being-as-event is the world that phenomenology, Bakhtin's first philosophy, is to disclose (*TPA* 31–32). "Author and Hero," as well, specifies that "[t]he *event* of being is a phenomenological concept, for being presents itself to a living consciousness as an event, and a living consciousness actively orients itself and lives in it as in an event" ("A&H" 188, note).

26. Bulgakov, *Svet nevechernii*, 128–30. More recently, the apophatic moment in Kant has been singled out by Henry E. Allison, *Kant's Transcendental Idealism: An Interpretation and Defense* (New Haven: Yale Univ. Press, 1983), 242; and Don Cupitt, "Kant and the Negative Theology," in *The Philosophical Frontiers of Christian Theology*, ed. Brian Hebblethwaite and Stewart Sutherland (Cambridge: Cambridge Univ. Press, 1982), 55–67. Two Russian scholars have compared Kant to the apophatic currents in Russian religious philosophy: Dlugach (see note 25 above), and A. V. Akhutin, "Sofiia i chert (Kant pered litsom russkoi religioznoi metafiziki)" ["Sophia and the Devil (Kant before Russian Religious Metaphysics)"], in *Rossiia i Germaniia: Opyt filosofskogo dialoga*, ed. V. A. Lektorsky (Moscow, 1993), 207–47. Akhutin, like Dlugach, draws attention to the apophatic or negative quality of Kant's philosophy, comparing it to the "critical antinomism" of S. N. Bulgakov and P. A. Florensky and the "apophatic ontology" of S. L. Frank.

27. On Askoldov, his critique of neo-Kantianism and Bakhtin, see Clark and Holquist, *Mikhail Bakhtin*, 132–33.

28. S. A. Askoldov, "Vnutrennii krizis transtsendental'nogo idealizma" ["The Internal Crisis of Transcendental Idealism"], *Voprosy Filosofii i Psikhologii* 25.5, kn. 125 (1914): 787.

29. Bakhtin writes, "Formal ethics starts out from the perfectly correct insight that the ought is a category of consciousness. . . . But formal ethics (which developed exclusively within the bounds of Kantianism) further conceives the category of the ought as a category of theoretical consciousness, i.e., it theoretizes the ought" (*TPA* 25). Bakhtin levels this criticism against both Kant and the neo-Kantians, but it applies far more to the latter, in their abandonment of Kant's noumenon, transcendent to theoretical reason.

30. For historical development, see Jaroslav Pelikan, *The Emergence of the Catholic Tradition (100–600)*, 344–49; Pelikan, *The Spirit of Eastern Christendom (600–1700)*, 30–36, 254–70; Timothy Ware, *The Orthodox Church*, 62–70; John Meyendorff, *Byzantine Theology*, 11–14, 27–29, 76–78; and Deirdre Carabine, *The Unknown God: Negative Theology in the Platonic Tradition: Plato to Eriugena* (Louvain: Peeters Press, 1995), especially on Gregory of Nyssa.

31. Thunberg, *Microcosm and Mediator.*

32. Deirdre Carabine, *The Unknown God*, 325, concludes as follows: "From an apophatic viewpoint, the only way to cross the distance that is seen to exist between the soul and the One, between the soul and God, is the breakdown and negation of all the normal epistemological categories of subject and object, which are, of course, the basis for all cognition." Raoul Mortley, "What is Negative Theology? The Western Origins," *Prudentia*, Supplementary Number on *The Via Negativa*, (1981), writes: "Predication itself involves a threefold structure, that of subject, verb and object, and so it is impossible that it should ever be able to grasp unitary truth without perverting it in some way. The way in which it perverts will be clear: it will multiply the One" (11).

33. "Our negative theology demands as counterpart a 'negative anthropology.'" Bishop Kallistos of Diokleia [Timothy Ware], foreword to Panayiotis Nellas's *Deification in Christ*, 9.

34. "A&H" 56. According to Vadim Liapunov's note, Tadeusz Zielinski (1859–1944) was a Russian-Polish classical philologist, historian of religion, and philosopher of culture. He was one of Bakhtin's professors at St. Petersburg University. Adolf von Harnack (1851–1930) was, of course, the great German historian of Christian dogma.

35. Ware, *The Orthodox Church*, 232.

36. "Lektsii i vystupleniia M. M. Bakhtina 1924–1925 gg. v zapisiakh L. V. Pumpianskogo," 246. See the appendix to this volume.

37. Ware, *The Orthodox Church*, 208–18, provides a lucid exposition of the theological issues here and in the paragraph above. Also see Meyendorff, *Byzantine Theology*, 91–94, 168–73, 180–86.

38. See note 24 above.

39. Ware, *The Orthodox Church*, 237.

40. Leszek Kolakowski has traced this development—the history of the idea of "self-enriching alienation," the dialectical, eschatological striving for recovery of lost unity between subject and object—with remarkable perspective in his three-volume history of Marxism, *Main Currents of Marxism: Its Origins, Growth and Dissolution*, trans. P. S. Falla (Oxford: Oxford Univ. Press, 1978), especially vol. 1, *The Founders*, chapter 1, "The Origins of Dialectic," 7–80.

41. The critique of utopianism is an obvious implication of the "apophatic Bakhtin" thesis, as of the "prosaics" interpretation advanced by Gary Saul Morson and Caryl Emerson in their *Mikhail Bakhtin: Creation of a Prosaics* (Stanford: Stanford Univ. Press, 1990).

42. See Caryl Emerson's note, *PDP* 6.

43. Cf. John D. Zizioulas, *Being as Communion: Studies in Personhood and the Church* (Crestwood, N.Y.: St. Vladimir's Seminary Press, 1985). "Being as communion" is one of Bakhtin's central concepts (although his context is not necessarily theological).

44. All this clearly relates to one of Bakhtin's most famous passages: "It is quite possible to imagine and postulate a unified truth that requires a plurality of consciousnesses, one that cannot in principle be fitted into the bounds of a single consciousness, one that is, so to speak, by its very nature *full of event potential* and is born at a point of contact among various consciousnesses" (*PDP* 81). This aspiration toward *pravda*, the unitary and unique truth of unity in diversity—the diversity of uniquely valuable persons—is by its nature apophatic.

45. Forty years after *Toward a Philosophy of the Act*, Bakhtin could still write, "And this sole and irreplaceable position in the world cannot be abolished through any conceptual, generalizing (and abstracting) interpretive activity" ("TRDB" 296).

46. Gary Saul Morson and Caryl Emerson, *Mikhail Bakhtin*, 179–96, in their analysis of "authoring a self" (in both art and life) in "Author and Hero," stress the spirit's creative transcendence of the forms that others bestow upon it (a more nuanced understanding than Bakhtin himself offers).

47. Confession is another enduring theme for Bakhtin, which is not surprising in view of his work on Dostoevsky. Of the great Russian novelist, Bakhtin wrote, "He depicts confession . . . to show the interdependence of consciousnesses that is revealed during confession. I cannot manage without another, I cannot become myself without another" ("TRDB" 287). See Paul J. Contino's essay, "Zosima, Mikhail, and Prosaic Confessional Dialogue in Dostoevsky's *Brothers Karamazov*," *Studies in the Novel* 27, no. 1 (1995): 63–86.

48. The best example of the Orthodox practice of the "repetition of prayers" is the Jesus Prayer ("Lord Jesus Christ, Son of God, have mercy on me a sinner"). Ann Shukman, "Bakhtin's Tolstoy Prefaces," in *Rethinking Bakhtin: Extensions and Challenges*, ed. Gary Saul Morson and Caryl Emerson (Evanston: Northwestern Univ. Press, 1989), 137–48, notes that the prayer of the publican is a source of the Jesus Prayer. Shukman writes that the three Gospel episodes that Bakhtin refers to here all relate to the theme of the lack of human self-sufficiency.

49. "Someone" is capitalized in the corresponding passage from "Lektsii i vystupleniia M. M. Bakhtina 1924–25 gg. v zapisiakh L. V. Pumpianskogo," 236: "I am infinitely bad, but Someone needs me to be good" (appendix).

50. The first part of this essay demonstrated that Bakhtin saw nothing mysterious in the "internal uniqueness of consciousness." Now, he maintains that the very fact of self-consciousness testifies to the existence of God. The paradox results from Bakhtin's fear that miracle, mystery, and philosophical argument (such as the transcendental irreducibility of consciousness to nature) all diminish faith. Thus, Bakhtin feels it necessary to stress that the purpose in reading another's confessional self-accounting is not theoretical cognition but reproducing within oneself the inner event of faith ("A&H" 149–50).

51. M. I. Tubiansky, a member of Bakhtin's Leningrad circle (Clark and Holquist, *Mikhail Bakhtin*, 102), provides a good formulation of this set of ideas. Miracle and revelation would lead to the atrophy of moral consciousness and thus of human personhood. They would in fact degrade the human relationship to God, "because if there were the slightest *assurance*, then merit and the possibility of faith would disappear." Tubiansky refers to Kant's postulates of practical reason as one of the links between the human and divine worlds. See Tubiansky's remarks in "Lektsii i vystupleniia M. M. Bakhtina 1924–25 gg. v zapisiakh L. V. Pumpianskogo," 244–45; appendix. In his response to Tubiansky, Bakhtin does not acknowledge the large area of agreement between them. It was Bakhtin, after all, who condemned the "[f]orces that lie outside consciousness, externally (mechanically) defining it: from environment and violence to miracle, mystery, and authority. Consciousness

under the influence of these forces loses its authentic freedom, and personality is destroyed" ("TRDB" 297). It is interesting, however, that Bakhtin objects to Tubiansky for taking a rationalistic approach to religion and for neglecting its personal essence: "thus, *argumentum ad hominem* in religion is fully admissible, as religious logic is not at all philosophical logic." "Lektsii i vystupleniia M. M. Bakhtina 1924–25 gg. v zapisiakh L. V. Pumpianskogo," 246; appendix.

Afterword: Plenitude as a Form of Hope

Caryl Emerson

In a lapidary formulation, Graham Pechey refers to Bakhtin as a "theologically inflected aesthetician." Without a doubt, religious categories helped Bakhtin define the functions, dynamics, and potentials of art (in its ability to transfigure life—as Pumpiansky noted down during one of Bakhtin's lectures—"aesthetics is similar to religion"). But the insights into art and its ethical dimension that Bakhtin develops on this quasi-secularized domain are hardly mainstream. Nor would they have been mainstream in earlier times, when arguments from a position of faith were much less on the defensive in the humanities.

Why this is so has been the burden of the present volume. A sense or "feel" for faith, in Bakhtin's view, is not measured by our baptism, church affiliation, or even by the writ we hold sacred. In Randall Poole's masterful demonstration of Bakhtin's position, this feeling is prior to those rituals and commitments; it is a function of the connection between self-consciousness and the hierarchy of times. The more I seek support and validation for my own (and others') selves in the *future*, the more authentic and durable will my faith prove to be. Orientation is all; doctrine is almost incidental. For as Alexandar Mihailovic points out, a "feeling for faith"—at least as Bakhtin would have us feel it—is a rather formal thing; it testifies to "an interest not so much in the content or religious credo of Orthodoxy" as in its "structural paradigm," a model that values interpenetration and inseparability within an open set of unfused, unrepeating particulars. What each particular turns out to be is of course crucially important for any given individual. But this individual profile resists generalization into precepts, commandments, or articles of faith.

Indeed, "content" itself is understood by Bakhtin in a radically nonessentialist way. According to Pumpiansky's notes, Bakhtin believed that "content is not this or that particular something, but rather is an angle of vision"; as material, "content" is never indifferent, neutral, objective, but is drawn (literally) into being by a personally performed act, or by faith. The content of anything is a provisionally autonomous clump of data brought to our attention because it has been "paralyzed by form." These comments suggest that even had he wished it, and had he lived in a society that permitted it, Bakhtin would not have been inclined to preach a religious platform. By temperament he was not a prophet, proselytizer, or didactic "conqueror of souls." His writings are not burdened by the ethical imperatives and authoritative statements one might expect when religious truth combines with artistic creation to inspire or regulate human behavior. If Bakhtin's "theological inflections" are moral philosophy, then, they fall into none of its customary classifications.

This moral philosophy is not normative, applied, or metaethical. It seeks neither to establish criteria for distinguishing right from wrong, nor to apply such principles in judging complex individual cases. (What does Bakhtin think about capital punishment? War? Medical ethics? Telling lies to protect one's privacy or to ease pain? We have no idea.) Nor does Bakhtin appear to have fretted over the epistemological dilemmas that have defined our time, such as the function of moral discourse, the knowability of moral facts versus empirical evidence, or why ethical, artistic, and religious values should matter to life at all. He either took those realms for granted—the human being is a spiritual being, period, and this spirituality is apophatic—or else he was so taken up by what he considered the inappropriate, but triumphant, models for consciousness and ethical obligation routinely applied to the spiritual realm that he chose to concentrate his energies on correcting those models, not on validating the field or filling in its blanks with specific virtues and vice. One suspects that Bakhtin relegated most judgments of a person's virtues or vices to "small time." Evidence suggests that Bakhtin himself was almost impossible to shock, offend, or surprise. He had a patient and uninsultable mind.

And yet Bakhtin was no moral relativist. He held witnessing and judgment in the highest regard. As one scholar has recently argued, Bakhtin did acknowledge "norms of answerability"—but not norms of the functionalist or theoretical sort, designed in response to the Kantian question "What must I do?" with its echoes of guilt, imputability, and moral failure—but rather norms only in the sense of the more Socratic query "How should I act toward another, so that we both grow in self-knowledge?"[1] Again, the models proposed by the personalist Bakhtin to replace "law" and "norm" are remarkably formal structures. They provide us with a method for building personality *through* them, but prescribe no special content. Although art fulfills an indisputably ethical function, this ethics exists nowhere as a systematic guide for identifying the good. In fact, as Pechey points out in his essay, "aesthetics has for Bakhtin the task of tempting ethics away from 'morality' and toward an ontology of the uniquely situated body." What matters is not so much what I do as whether or not I am willing to answer for what I do (whatever that is); accordingly, "who I am" becomes a function of that string of "signatures" on a series of my acts, not the actual substance of those acts.

We should not be misled, however, by the resemblance between these formal Bakhtinian structures and the idea of the "empty signifier" that has proved so electrifying to structuralist and poststructuralist thought in the West. As I shall argue below, Bakhtin had no truck with emptiness anywhere. But he had a highly subtle feel for the parameters of individual freedom. As Bakhtin phrased it, the concrete givens of my life (its material options and conditions) are rarely mine to choose, but I am always free to craft my own *response* to those conditions. For this reason, my identity can only be "mine"—that is, a product of my own craftsmanship—to the extent that I embody each of my irreplaceable, unrepeatable responses and resolve to stand behind those responses, at least for as long as I have listeners and witnesses. In Bakhtin's interactively personalist cosmos, the human psyche, during its moments of deepest uncertainty, would do best to repair not to legal counsel or to a tablet of laws but rather to a beloved person and ask: knowing me as you do but remaining yourself, what would you do this very minute, were you in my position?

There is every indication that Bakhtin's favorite candidate for this role of beloved interlocutor was the same as Dostoevsky's: the person of Christ. The paradox here is a peculiarly Bakhtinian one: the limitless personality of Christ, understood as a *formal* (an objectively unfilled, unpredetermined, infinitely receptive) structure, confronts my "uniquely situated body," which is defined by its locally grounded needs and limited perspective. Both as ethical philosopher and as Eastern Orthodox Christian believer, Bakhtin begins by embracing the Incarnation. But as Charles Lock reminds us in his penetrating essay, the commonsensical hope embedded in this turn toward embodiment has become difficult to grasp due to "the globalization of Protestant paradigms and anxieties" in modern writing about theologically inflected aesthetics. Can we even imagine a world of the mind without those familiar anxieties, a world in which there is no conflict between faith and reason? Where the sensible and the intelligible are not antagonistic? Where body and spirit naturally belong together, reinforce one another, willingly teach one another mercy and discipline? Where—in Lock's words—"the immediate associations [of theology] would be neither creedal nor ethical but liturgical (bodily presence) and sacramental (the holiness of matter)"? In the opinion of the Marburg and later the Nevel philosophers so important for Bakhtin, only such an environment could guarantee to our frail human being the nourishment necessary for a growth of *otvetstvennost'*. In Pumpiansky's notes, this term is enhanced to encompass not only answerability and responsibility but also "moral being," "actual being," and "serious reality."

In a world according to Bakhtin, religious consciousness is obliged above all to answer to the demands of "serious reality." This obligation cannot be systematized. What is real is always serious because it is always unavoidably right in front of us, requiring a response from us that will not factor out cleanly into a product of the body or the mind, cleanly right or wrong. In my position, at that moment, who can say how *you* would have acted? Thus does N. I. Nikolaev, in his editorial mosaic of Pumpiansky's notes on Bakhtin's lectures, emphasize that moral reality must be described phenomenologically, "in an engaged, participatory manner . . . not by means of theoretical terminology but by means of natural language." In that spirit, this afterword will revisit the preceding entries and expand briefly, in "natural language," on the wisdom they might offer the "uniquely situated body" in its relation to seven absolutely quotidian spiritual states: love, repentant conscience, reverence toward authority, seriousness, silence, plenitude, and fear.

Love

From different perspectives, Alan Jacobs and Randall Poole provide an eloquent gloss on the Bakhtinian case for love. Both are unsentimental and (as was Jesus Himself) unswayed by the argument that outrages against earthly justice are for us to resolve; each values the love relation not necessarily as self-evident, just, or deserving (where in Christ's parables is justice straightforwardly honored?) but as efficient, productive, charitable, cognitively enabling, quite simply the most sensible way to behave. With Augustine as his starting point, Jacobs pursues the "law of love" as a hermeneutic, focusing on the interpretive skills we stand to gain when we adopt charity as our mode of operation. In an angry or loveless mood— however justified—I cease to pay attention and develop careless habits; I become a bad reader of others, who will then project onto me these distorted images of my self. Thus the effects of lovelessness mimic the effects of generalization (what Jacobs properly identifies as Bakhtin's "implicit critique of a generalized ethical humanism," that which paves the way for "universal ethical failure"): when angry, we discern poorly and react imprecisely. When resentful or suspicious, I am thrown back on the one psyche that seems closest and clearest to me, namely, my own; but since self-identity and self-love are structurally impossible in Bakhtin's world, an attitude devoid of love will uncover less and less love-worthy material, in an impoverishing vortex.

At this point, Jacobs draws close to concerns taken up by Randall Poole: kenosis, *apophasis*, the humbling of body and mind through the evacuation of authoritative truth claims. But Jacobs warns against a literalist reading. In any act of humility, the self should never be wholly eradicated, but only chastened; there must always be some concrete attributes remaining within me to offer another, and the shaping of this proactive residue requires uninterrupted will and work. A "selfless" love of the other is impossible. Indeed, a case could be made that selfless love, being relatively free of risk, is cowardly and even grotesque. The hermeneutic that Jacobs outlines here is governed—as is Bakhtin's own—by a demanding, resilient, highly disciplined type of love.

In his discussion of the humble, unsystematizable love relations advocated by Bakhtin, Poole begins from the Eastern Orthodox end, not with the Western fathers of the Church. But Poole too focuses immediately on the seeming paradox of "-less." Apophatic theology might appear to deny and negate, but in fact such an emptying-out of definitions is prelude to the most affirmative plenitude. If God is unknowable, and if human beings are persons by virtue of their likeness to God, then persons are also unknowable, more truly described as carriers of potential rather than of past accomplishment. The fact that complete self-knowledge is impossible is therefore the Good News, not the bad, for charity and hope reside solely in the possibility that we are more than the sum of our available parts. Love among human beings is fueled by the realization that "being a subject means having major real-life inadequacies." Only other persons can remedy this inadequacy. That the other will in fact answer my need must be a matter of "insane" faith, since in Bakhtin's cosmos neither nature nor metaphysical theism offers guarantees.

Here Poole lays bare the apophatic underpinnings of genuine creativity. He gestures toward that subversive fellowship of Russian thinkers (most famously, Vladimir Solovyov) who applied to Plato's theory of love an Orthodox Christian corrective:[2] creation is not emanation from the realm of the already-existing, but authentically new fruit borne of interaction and personal risk, involving persons ultimately unknowable to—because external to—one another. For this reason does Bakhtin insist so mercilessly on the utter uniqueness, utter validity, and unavoidable "oughtness" of each consciousness in its own time and place. Without that confirmation of our uniqueness, arguably we could not bear to expose ourselves to the terrible uncertainty of so many individual moral variables; and we would not, of course, find ourselves so often in need of grace.

The bestowal of grace and the urge to confess, which Poole deduces so eloquently from Bakhtin's apophatic philosophy, helps us to understand Bakhtin's comment in his 1925 lecture on "Grounded Peace." "I am infinitely bad, but Someone needs me to be good," Bakhtin remarks. "In repenting, I specifically establish the One in Whom I posit my sin." What checks our badness, in the first instance, is Someone (or someone) else's need. That needful Other (or other) is then affirmed by an act of trust, quite independent of logical deduction. "What is at issue is more serious than freedom," Bakhtin notes, "what is at issue [in faith] is something more than freedom." What is this greater thing? As so often with Bakhtin, the positive term eludes definition. But when we see the dynamic unfolding in scenarios by his most beloved authors, we recognize it as authentic.

Consider Raskolnikov, still the unrepentant murderer, in part 6 of *Crime and Punishment.* He is confronting his sister Dunya, who has learned of his crime and is horrified by it. Raskolnikov cannot understand why " 'hurling bombs at people according to all the rules of siege warfare' " is necessarily more respectable or defensible than his calculated elimination of a greedy pawnbroker. " 'Now more than ever,' " he exclaims, " 'I fail to understand my crime!' " Dostoevsky does not refute the rightness of Raskolnikov's logic. But he confirms the senselessness of the act all the same. "As he was uttering this last exclamation, his eyes suddenly met

Dunya's, and so great, so great was the anguish for him in those eyes that he came involuntarily to his senses."[3] Repentance begins not because I have been logically persuaded of my error, but because I witness another's anguish in the face of that error. The other *needs* me to be good. A similar dynamic underlies Bakhtin's image of the responsive, humiliated conscience.

Repentant Conscience

How does my "I-for-myself" register a repentant moment, a pang of bad conscience? No theory is necessary here, although—to be sure—I would love to hide behind it: I wince, look about for alibis, scan my horizon for factors that would have made any other action on my part impossible at the time, and when all this fails (which it does with astonishing quickness), I try to thread my way out with words. But underneath, the "infinitely bad" nature of my act thrusts up, out of these evasions and coverings. I could have but did not; I knew better and chose against. At issue here is not "getting caught," nor is it condemnation from the outside; Bakhtin insisted that every act, even a lie, could be understood within its own context. (Consider his generous line: "Even a word that is known to be false is not absolutely false, and always presupposes an instance that will understand and justify it" [*SpG* 127].) Bad conscience is another beast: it makes itself felt when I cannot accept another's proffered justification, when others' words make no difference. The authors in the anthology most concerned with this state of the psyche are Graham Pechey and Ruth Coates.

Coates proceeds in the more literary way, by means of figuration, motif, and metaphor. She begins with the originary biblical scenario of the Fall, hinting at a Manichean side to Bakhtin which she sees in his fondness for binary splits and images of a dichotomous world. In this world, sin and bad conscience are linked to the illusion of autonomy. Redemption begins when I acknowledge my "aesthetic need" of the other—a need, paradoxically, that the other can satisfy either by helping me achieve closure from within an open world, or aperture from within a closed one. In either case, the only acceptable response to another's anguished conscience is a continued effort to provide it with new contexts, talk with it, even if the sinful party adamantly refuses to accept relief. It is in this sense, surely, that the Elder Zosima insists "we are all answerable for all and guilty in front of all." Zosima is not guilty in any ordinary cause-and-effect way, nor does his answerability exonerate me or erase the badness of my act. It simply obligates him to complicate my act by taking it seriously, attempting to understand it, and thereby beneficently re-authoring it.

Pechey takes the broader view, casting all of modernity into a state of "bad conscience." His reasons are Coates's as well: the hubris of intellect, the conceit of self-consummation, the "will to totality" so characteristic of atheistic modern consciousness. Yet modernism also makes available a multitude of secular forms that are in fact transformations of foundational Christian forms of belief. Pechey stresses Bakhtin's partiality for the premodern genres of confession and saint's life— noting that in modern times, only polyphonic writing can aspire to the radical novelty that the Gospels enjoyed within their ancient Roman context. In pursuing these analogies, Pechey raises the awkward issue of authority in Bakhtin's house of value. If Bakhtin in effect "sacralizes the novel," making of it a "talisman" that "we may wear against the idolatrous temptations of our late-modern world," then it is of some import to define the nature of the reverence that the novel would elicit from us. Is a "religious" Bakhtin at odds with the very low marks Bakhtin assigns to "official seriousness," wherever it appears? Is any attempt to rehabilitate the much-maligned "authoritative word" in the novel compatible with that genre's advocacy of freedom—or is this another situation where "what is at issue is more serious than freedom"?

Reverence toward Authority

Recent work on Bakhtin's concept of the author has argued that Bakhtin endorsed the Romantic or Promethean view of the author as a "demiurge with a god-like capability of creation" early in his career; for all his humbling gestures and strategic fragmentations of the authorial image, so this argument goes, he sustained this belief throughout his life.[4] Coates would agree. She maintains that Bakhtin in the 1920s entertained, but then rejected, the idea of the "abusive author." According to her, the possibility of a tyrannical (monologic) authoring force is first confronted in the Dostoevsky book. But so terrible is this possibility for Bakhtin that the problem is evaded, or transcended, through a massive redefinition of authorship. But with that many centers, is there anyone to whom we might pray?

This issue of reverence toward authority, in an otherwise irreverent Bakhtin, is of enduring importance to Bakhtinians. Mihailovic elegantly resolves the problem on theological soil. Where others have seen contradiction or paradox in Bakhtin's writings, Mihailovic sees the uncompromised Chalcedonian ideal of "coinherence": the constant interpenetration, yet nonconvergence, of discrete entities. In his view, Bakhtin is too often put in the false position of seeming to endorse singular authorities that in fact he resisted: the "unimpeded collectivism" of Slavophile *sobornost'*, for example, or his only-apparent tolerance of faceless mass carnival. The unspeakably odd phenomenon of Nikolai Marr and his single-point creationist theory of language provides Mihailovic with the perfect case study in the secular realm. Marr was dethroned on Stalin's orders in 1950; Bakhtin, long adept at Aesopian camouflage for his own ideas but by that time in a responsible (that is, unfree) position as pedagogue to future teachers, had the unenviable task of exploiting a new rising authority against an old falling one—both, it should be said, fraudulent—in the interests of his own utterance. "The Problem of Speech Genres," a product of this exploitation, serves authority by undermining Marr while distancing itself from the freshly authoritative Stalinist alternative. However delicate the balancing act, Mihailovic argues that a juxtaposition of extant authorities was always an active option for Bakhtin. The strategy is validated by a Chalcedonian notion of the word, in which nonconvergent, yet contiguous, interaction between two or more entities is the central paradox governing the dynamics of the whole. But is this yet another way—a deceptively religious way— of writing off our lives to the endlessly ambivalent caprice of carnival? Mihailovic thinks not. For an additional virtue of the essays gathered here is their contribution to a project long underway among Russian Bakhtinians, parallel to their rethinking of Bakhtin's religious roots: a new look at his appreciation of the serious.

Seriousness

For many years, the carnival bias in Bakhtin's thought held undisputed sway. To resent carnival laughter meant to endorse "one-sided" or "official seriousness," clearly an oppressive quality that Bakhtin associated with the worst of secular (and ecclesiastical) authority. Then in 1992, the Russian journal *Voprosy filosofii* published a long narrative written by Bakhtin in 1944 and intended as a guide to his revisions of the recently completed book on Rabelais.[5] It opened on a welcome reassessment of seriousness—fully consonant, as it happens, with the Chalcedonian ideal. The growth of seriousness in the modern world is unfortunate, Bakhtin argues, not because the world has become a cheerful place (any such thought in the Soviet Union of 1944 could only be obscene) but because it leads to "uni-tonality," to "a transfer of the image out of the sphere of ambivalence," to a "hardening of borders" where "the positive and negative are separated out," and to a constancy, stabilization, and canonization that could only increase the weight of "threat, intimidation, and terror" in the world. Bakhtin then went on to distinguish between "official" (bad) and "unofficial" (good) seriousness—sensing, no doubt, the lopsidedness of his own deep preference for the popular laughing forms. In addition to the "seriousness of power," he wrote, there is also

> the unofficial seriousness of suffering, terror, fright, weakness, the seriousness of the slave and the seriousness of the victim . . . Unofficial seriousness in Dostoevsky. This is the ultimate protest of individuality (bodily and spiritual) thirsting for perpetuation, [which struggles] against change and absolute renewal, the protest of the part against its dissolution in the whole, this is

the greatest and most justified claim for the eternal everlasting, for the non-annihilation of everything that once was (the non-acceptance of becoming). The eternity of an instant.

Bakhtin follows this defense of the edifying forms of seriousness with a discussion of carnival in Shakespeare, one considerably more nuanced and literary than the ecstatic paean to mass laughter familiar to us in Bakhtin's writings from the 1930s. It presents a darker, more sober and balanced reading of both the Dostoevskian novel and Renaissance drama. But even with this corrective in place, the realm of the serious cannot be said to receive Bakhtin's overall sympathetic attention; he is not in a loving relation with it. This lack is felt in a volume such as ours, for it reminds us how rare, in Bakhtin's readings of literary works, are those moments associated with sustained, heightened religious experience. Bakhtin does not much value awe; he appears to have little use for the Sublime as conventionally defined; in Randall Poole's deft formulation, the "mystical union of self and other in God is not an idea congenial to Bakhtin's thought"; and when Bakhtin does turn to "true" or "unofficial" seriousness, he does so through motley Shakespeare rather than through ancient tragedy. Why does Bakhtin assign so little creative potential to the elevated, nonlaughing forms? Why is seriousness so often presumed to be "false and hypocritical," "stingy and lenten," an angle on the world that "suppressed, frightened, and fettered" human nature? Very helpful in this regard is Sergei Averintsev's essay on laughter and Christian culture.

As is clear from Bakhtin's 1944 notes toward the Rabelais revisions, such values as constancy, perpetuation, nonannihilation, and the "eternal everlasting" belong to a "serious" (and, we might add, to a sacred) view of the world. Should laughter aspire to such qualities of permanence and endurance, however, it would become not so much serious as demonic and hysterical—because, as Averintsev observes, laughter is by nature transitional, a "burst" and not a state, a bridge from one psychic state to another and freer one. Unexpectedly, both the target and the trajectory can change en route. For to be launched at all, laughter must have a wild side; once set loose, it casts "spiritual caution" to the winds and at times will border on "internal apostasy." Thus sacral beatitude might be *induced* by laughter, but not sustained by it. Steady-state sustenance, in contrast, is dependent upon quiet good humor, on a tolerant or indulging smile. If Christ did not need to laugh, surely it was because He could not be surprised.

The laughing forms are not serious in themselves, then, but the functions they perform are deeply and abidingly so. I laugh down cowardice in myself, I grin and bear my failures, I learn to respond to mockery (another's unkind outsideness) with humility. If successful, these habits serve to clear the path toward Bakhtin's favorite tense: an immediate future for myself that can be different from, and better than, my present. Averintsev intimates that Bakhtin, in his pursuit of the "truth of laughter," cared only for these *functions* (and highly idealized functions at that), not for laughter's crude or abrasive resonance, that which actually issued from Ivan the Terrible's—or Stalin's—crooked mouth. Bakhtin's "absolutization of laughter" and its role in his life as a "talisman" prompt one to speculate further than Averintsev himself was willing to go. Perhaps Bakhtin treasured laughter somewhat as a Christian believer treasures the crucifix on a silver chain around her neck. Elegantly abstracted, with all the dirt and violence of the Roman guillotine stylized away, the cross—like laughter—comes to symbolize a psychological threshold. It is taken onto the body as a resource, for those moments "when the defense of freedom must be conducted at the point of no return." One cannot imagine anything more risk-laden and serious than such moments of unjustified hope. For here as always with Bakhtin, freedom is not the license to change the world but the strength to respond to it creatively and with love.

Silence

When Christ kisses the Grand Inquisitor on his bloodless lips but refuses to utter a word in His own defense, is this dialogue? If so, was it undertaken in the spirit of fair play? Was it not the easy way out, to leave your interlocutor in the position of monologist, with only his own uncountered and unanswered words ringing in his ears? Or perhaps—and this appears to have been the resentful Inquisitor's experience—I need another person not as a source of alternative truths but more as a gravitational field, a block, a focal point (preferably mute) against which my own closed thoughts, piled up for so many years, can be released and become articulate? Such questions have long haunted readers of both Bakhtin and Dostoevsky, for they cut to the core of what is meant by a "dialogic zone."

There are three varieties of silence in Bakhtin, and the contributors to this anthology touch upon them all. The first, while least important to Bakhtin, has seemed most pressing to many of his readers: the silence of the oppressed, of the specifically *silenced*, the nonresponse of the martyred. Averintsev would have Bakhtin account for these victims of political violence. He would have him acknowledge the jeering mob-lynchers of Christ as well as the manipulators of our present day, and confront the fact that laughter not only releases and rejuvenates but also "can be used to plug the mouth." Contemporary Russian critics of carnival, survivors of that fraudulent, officially cheerful chatter that was a trademark of Stalinist culture, have routinely felt honor-bound to point out Bakhtin's naïveté whenever actual historical data are brought into play. Averintsev is no exception. Outsiders to the Soviet experience can only empathize with his frustration.

A second variety of silence, on balance more creative and interesting, is taken up by Charles Lock in his discussion of the foundational tropes of Orthodoxy.

Emphasizing the importance of nonidentity and asymmetry in the Russian church, he arrives at the strong thought that a sacrifice of reciprocity (what might be called "contractual" thinking) and of symmetry (the insistence on justice) makes possible that special Bakhtinian brand of "transgredience" that is specifically distinct from transcendence. The transcendental move is cold, leveling, invasive, imperial, presumptuous. It pretends to a higher position that can encompass all selves in a language that all can speak. Bakhtin's way, Lock argues, is more dangerous because genuinely respectful of exterior placement. It is built on the reality of the "adjacent differential self" that can never know for sure anything other than what it sees from its own limited position. Against conventional wisdom, Bakhtin counsels us to *trust* appearances. Not transcendence and symmetry but contiguity, proximity, and irregular, only provisional fit are what guarantee each of us a mutable private realm.

From this vantage point, Lock presents Bakhtin's case for silent writing—the realm of the novel, which has many voices but is mutely consumed—over the voiced genres. The resemblance to Derrida's project is intriguing and noted in passing, but the immediate precedents invoked are religious. In hesychastic thought, outsideness is linked with silence. Silence in that tradition is not merely a lack, not merely "an unrealized or unfulfilled sound"; it is a "bodily practice" that opens up a space for free differentiation. Spoken utterances rally the crowd and flatten content. But the growth of silent reading, from St. Augustine to the present, must be welcomed as an absolute growth in the number of individuated, uniquely bounded private worlds. What magnificent potential opened up for humanity when discourse entered the realm of the (literally) unspeakable! Again we glimpse the apophatic Bakhtin, far from the book-burning carnival square, alone with the printed page.

The third variety of silence returns us to the Grand Inquisitor. Christ did not see fit to bestow a verbal response on the Inquisitor's confession—but that confession could only have occurred in His presence, oriented toward the palpable fact of His Second Coming. A *dialogic situation* was essential for the utterance to begin; in all likelihood, too, the mournful love that permeates Christ's silent "listening act" is indispensable for the full and honest unfolding of this inspired quest for self-acquittal. Christ is silent in this scenario not only because he has nothing to add (he cannot be surprised) but also because the Inquisitor, like the Underground Man, is in no mood to be interrupted. Such monologists deeply crave a savior from within their zone, but are wholly disinclined to open themselves up to the supplement of others' words. Having spoken their piece, however, they feel themselves irreversibly changed. Does dialogue always require two people actually talking?

The answer, I believe, must be no. "Not being heard" might indeed be equivalent to hell in Bakhtin's view—he suggests as much apropos of Thomas Mann's *Doctor Faustus*[6]—but being left in silence, with no more than a singular, symbolic gesture to decode (the kiss, the slap, the deep bow to the earth) *after* we have been heard out, is a challenge of another sort. As Dostoevsky's more cynical characters are quick to observe, such silent gestures can be both cunning and unkind. Those who practice them escape the vulnerability of the specifically verbal mask, always so ridiculous when resonating in a void. How to understand "dialogic zones with only one speaker" is a task well suited for the student of religious genres, and secular practice has much to learn in this area. Emptying-out or abstinence as regards the answering word is related to another paradoxical fact in Bakhtin's world, addressed by Pechey in his essay: the fact that any attempt to rhythmicize our lives from within, to grasp our own meaning, will impoverish us, whereas acquiescence in nonknowing, nonconsummation—the *refusal* to accept any integrity as definitive—almost always enriches.

Plenitude

The key to this paradox, too, is the apophatic method. But we might extend it further than Poole chooses to do, to that speculative point where it intersects with creative forms of laughter and with beneficial forms of seriousness. "Why," Mihailovic asks in the opening salvo of his essay, "should a 'feeling for faith' be more important than faith itself?" His answer draws on the Trinitarian paradigm of unity within diversity. Faith works with achieved units. It has arrived at its conclusions and is at rest. But a "feeling for" (or a groping toward) faith is restless, engaged, at risk, conscious of being on the boundary with another and different substance. Bakhtin's theologically inflected aesthetics, so wary of finalization, provides little justification for a legitimate "at rest" moment. In his lecture on "Grounded Peace" we are given a hint, however, about a possible proper method. We can avoid tranquil self-complacency—the wrong sort of rest—by transforming our disquietude, by means of repentance, into trust. In what does this trust consist? There is an element of insanity in it, similar to the "insane" conviction that I do not coincide with myself, have never coincided with myself, and so the fullest parts of me are always still to come. To be true to this thought, I must accept the world as a nutritious place. "Trust," in Bakhtin's special feel for the word, is above all the conviction that the goods of the world will *not run out*.

Several of our essays reinforce this hypothesis. In his defense of those compact, oxymoronic carnival constructs so beloved by Bakhtin (praise/blame, revere/curse), Mihailovic stresses that their ambivalence gives rise not to contradiction, and thus to meaninglessness, but to *fullness*. Jacobs, developing a charitable hermeneutics on Bakhtinian foundations, assumes (quite counterintuitively, one could argue) that the slower one moves and the longer one lingers over an object, the more numerous will be the particular forms of good revealed in it—that is, the more likely our attentiveness will eventually turn to love. Similar faith in the heroic persistence and benevolence of matter, even under the most blistering scrutiny, is felt in Coates's discussion of the incarnational principle in Bakhtin and in Lock's defense of the novel as "the incarnation of language," akin to the icon's nonreductive representation of the Holy. With his image of the apophatic Bakhtin, fastidiously eschewing any leap of faith, Poole confronts the issue head on. Personhood is potentially divine because, like Godhood, it is unknowable in its essence and therefore always able to be supplemented by an other, or by grace. As a subject in the world I am insufficient; I must constantly take in. But—here is the paradox—I must not "pile up." The solid fruits of acquisition always risk becoming dogmatic, oppressive, "official," the bad forms of seriousness or the static forms of faith. Thus my copious "filling up" is kept in check by a constant kenosis or emptying-out. As many have remarked, Bakhtin's model of the self has a somewhat ghostly aura about it, the well-trafficked but unlived-in feel of a way station or exchange post. His is the curious paradigm of plenitude without accumulation.

There is only one domain where copious goods are combined with a commitment to transitoriness or change—and that is comedy.[7] Indeed, such is Hegel's view in his aesthetics, where comedy functions as a sort of universal solvent for survivors after tragedy has played itself out; it is the one mode that does not denounce the base, vigorous energies of the sublunary world but significantly does not award that world any permanence. The comedic genres, and by extension carnival laughter, value above all modest intention, a decentering of self-important heroes, unending variety, and the refusal to die. Comedy provokes laughter by its mass of uncoordinated, unexpected details and its crackpot catalogues and lists (consider Rabelais), which are comic precisely because such inventories are so obviously inadequate to describe the richness of the world.

Such an assumption of plenitude is at base a religious commitment, and at its center we find the apophatic ideal. So immense and in flux is the variety of the world that I cannot possibly know it. Contrary to Platonic teachings, Bakhtin would assert, true things change constantly: "It is an unfortunate misunderstanding," he writes in a famous passage, "to think that truth can only be the truth that is composed of universal moments; that the truth of a situation is precisely that which is repeatable and constant in it" (*TPA* 37). What is more, the unknowable variety of the world is our best defense against evil, which, being humorless and single-minded, is slower to adapt. Plenitude—without which carnival cannot exist—does not deny evil or trivialize it; its strategy is to immerse, dilute, outwit, and disorient evil in a mass of metamorphosing things. Laugh at evil, or at one's own fear in the face of evil, and it will shrink. The most persistent enemy of such a worldview is that singularly highlighted sin in the Christian tradition (not an easily targeted behavioral sin like sloth, lust, gluttony, wrath, but a sin of spiritual attitude) which in Russian is called *unynie,* inconsolable despair.

Fear

Why is it so difficult to rid ourselves of despair? In the mid-1920s, as we learn from the notes translated here, Pumpiansky was fascinated by parapsychology and researched deeply into the question of the survival of consciousness after bodily death. By all accounts, his friend and colleague Bakhtin remained more the phenomenologist, lecturing on Kant, on the philosophy of religion, and resisting the temptations of miracle, mystery, and authority as explanations of what men live by. The tone of Bakhtin's lectures, that of a fully engaged intellect categorically denying any necessary contradiction between reason and faith, is of enormous importance for understanding the famous writings on literature to come. Especially telling are Bakhtin's objections to Mikhail Tubiansky's paper, over the question of Revelation.

Revelation, Bakhtin insists, is continual, multifaceted, various—and as characteristic of the world as are natural laws. Faith and definitiveness are quite compatible. The difficulty comes with *trust* (which, as a mental attitude, belongs more in the category of a "feeling for faith") because trust, by definition, makes us so vulnerable. Another open human being is implicated. Trusting others, I must risk seeing and hearing them in all their incoherence and complexity; if instead I allow myself to be guided solely by my own inner moral law, I can act blindly and within a closed loop of certainty. But such an innerly grounded attitude, Bakhtin suggests, is the predictable result of a frightened mind. Reliance on inner law "is not a refusal to accept Revelation but a typical *fear* of Revelation." This fear is of a highly specific sort, compounded with self-confidence, anger, pride, and the quest for internal tranquillity and autonomy. Bakhtin associates this fear with people "who are afraid of accepting a favor, afraid of becoming obligated," with "the fear of receiving a gift." Such is the serious purpose of carnival laughter: not to demonstrate the inherent levity of the world but to get fear out of the way. A frightened person is always helpless, because the outside has ceased to be a source and has become a blank.

A feeling for faith is grounded, then, in a freedom from fear. For Bakhtin that was an important part of the wisdom of Revelation. But it was not the whole of that wisdom—for "freedom from," like every negation of a negative, is only positive in the trivial mathematical sense; without further active work it remains the first step only, a mere preliminary, a clearing that is accomplished so that plenitude becomes a possibility. Recall Charles Lock's observation, that central to Bakhtin's tasks in the 1920s was an Orthodox Christian demonstration that reason and faith are not necessarily in contradiction. To be honest, a life of the mind did not have to be anxious in "Protestant" ways. There are indications, however, that Bakhtin made even more concrete claims for a life in faith. Susan Felch and Paul Contino, in the opening pages of their introduction, remark on Vadim Kozhinov's recollections of discussions with Bakhtin in the 1960s on the nature and necessity of God. Those discussions, looked at in more detail, might provide us with suitable summation and closure for the many issues raised in this anthology, philosophical as well as theological.

"Mikhail Mikhailovich rarely discussed personal religious issues," Kozhinov recalls. "His age (he was sixty-five when I met him) and probably his original spiritual makeup were not disposed to any kind of 'profession of faith.' Nevertheless, a few times he generously dilated on the most sacred things."[8] Kozhinov remembers one long evening of talk "about God and Creation" that so thrilled him he literally could not sleep. Here was Bakhtin, survivor of an atheistic and materialist regime, confirming such convictions as compatible with philosophical speculation! And then Kozhinov made the remark referred to in the introduction to this volume, that according to Bakhtin, religion alone can provide human beings with freedom— not only for the spirit (the usual fruits of faith), but for the mind as well. Thinkers and scholars were better off, better at their professional labors, if religion was part of their lives. "Only religion," Kozhinov recalls Bakhtin saying, "can bring about completely unlimited freedom of thought, because a human being absolutely cannot exist without some kind of *faith*. The absence of faith in God inevitably turns into *idolatry*—that is, faith in something notoriously limited by the boundaries of space and time, and incapable of providing true freedom of thought."

The paradox here is richly productive. All his life, Bakhtin argued for the virtues of modest delimited consciousness, for restricted (and therefore authentic) perspectives, for values that were real because they acknowledged "the boundaries of space and time." His world is one of infinitely differentiated particulars, free in their relations because not prescribed within a system. Even my own self does not coincide with itself and is inaccessible to itself. Yet true freedom of thought can operate only in some envelope more vast, more authoritative than this fragmented and earthbound model suggests; it requires a feeling for faith that is *taken* on faith. Without it we will become, in the root sense of the word, infidels. And if we survive, it will be only by chance.

Love, repentance, reverence, seriousness, silence, plenitude, fear: such is the daily fare of the needy self. But we are so constructed that no human need exists beyond all hope of relief. Since the world is objectively a place of comedic—or carnival—abundance, we are obliged to learn how to receive. Only then "a place for God is opened up." The great challenge of this move must have been felt acutely by Bakhtin, a proud and private man to whom so much was gifted and from whom so much was taken away.

Notes

1. See Greg Nielsen, "The Norms of Answerability: Bakhtin and the Fourth Postulate," in *Bakhtin and the Human Sciences: No Last Words*, ed. Michael Mayerfield Bell and Michael Gardiner (London: Sage Publications, 1998), 214–30.

2. For one illuminating discussion, see Judith Deutsch Kornblatt, "The Transfiguration of Plato in the Erotic Philosophy of Vladimir Soloviev," *Religion and Literature* 24, no. 2 (1992): 35–50.

3. Fyodor Dostoevsky, *Crime and Punishment*, trans. Richard Pevear and Larissa Volokhonsky (New York: Knopf, 1992), 519.

4. Giovanni Palmieri, "'The Author' According to Bakhtin . . . and Bakhtin the Author," in *The Contexts of Bakhtin: Philosophy, Authorship, Aesthetics*, ed. David Shepherd (Overseas Publishers Association/Harwood Academic Publishers, 1998), 45–56, esp. 45.

5. M. M. Bakhtin, "Dolpolneniia i izmeneniia k 'Rable,'" *Voprosy filosofii*, no. 1 (1992): 134–64; reprinted in *M. M. Bakhtin. Sobranie sochinenii*, vol. 5, ed. S. G. Bocharov (Moscow: Russkie slovari, 1996), 80–129. Subsequent citation in the text is from this later edition, 80–81. An English translation by Harold Baker as "Additions and Changes to *Rabelais*" is forthcoming in Harold Baker, ed., *The Unknown Bakhtin* (Dana Point, Calif.: Ardis Publishers).

6. See Bakhtin's parenthetical remark in his 1959–61 essay "The Problem of the Text": cf. "the understanding of the Fascist torture chamber or hell in Thomas Mann as an absolute *lack of being heard*, as the absolute absence of a *third party*" (*SpG* 126).

7. For this idea I am indebted to Robert S. Dupree, "The Copious Inventory of Comedy," in *The Terrain of Comedy*, ed. Louise Cowan (Dallas: Dallas Institute of Humanities and Culture, 1982), 163–94.

8. From Vadim Kozhinov, "Bakhtin i ego chitateli" (1992), translated by Craig Cravens as "Bakhtin and His Readers" in *Critical Essays on Mikhail Bakhtin*, ed. Caryl Emerson (New York: G. K. Hall, 1999), 75–76.

Appendix: M. M. Bakhtin's Lectures and Comments of 1924–1925

From the Notebooks of L. V. Pumpiansky

Introduced, edited, and annotated by N. I. Nikolaev

Preface to the English Edition by Vadim Liapunov

What the reader will be dealing with below is, first of all, a translation of an article by N. I. Nikolaev (St. Petersburg University) in which he argues for the existence of a distinctive school of Russian philosophy—the Nevel school of philosophy, centered around M. M. Bakhtin. (Nevel, a small town north of the city of Vitebsk, was where the "school" came into being, and where Bakhtin lived from 1918 to 1920.) Nikolaev's article is followed by a number of texts that he selected from one of the notebooks (dating from 1923 to 1925) of Lev V. Pumpiansky (1894–1940); all of these texts have the character of lecture notes, and all of them present Bakhtin either as a discussant or a lecturer. Pumpiansky was one of the most active members of the "Nevel school," and when Bakhtin returned in 1924 to St. Petersburg/Petrograd (renamed "Leningrad" that same year), Pumpiansky, who had moved to Petrograd in the fall of 1920, actively promoted there the resumption of the philosophical symposia that had begun in Nevel.

In 1910 Pumpiansky had completed his secondary education in Vilnius, in Russian-ruled Lithuania, and during this time he became a friend of Bakhtin's older brother, Nikolai (1894–1950), a friendship that continued at St. Petersburg/Petrograd University (from 1912). In 1911 Pumpiansky converted to the Russian Orthodox faith, and until at least 1928 he was passionately interested in religion, theology, and the philosophy of religion. His "lecture notes" published below are unique in one particular regard: they include texts that give us access to Bakhtin's thinking about religion. Otherwise, in the works known to us until now, Bakhtin (as a philosopher schooled in the Kantian tradition) is careful in observing the limits of philosophical discourse (secular in character) in distinction to either religious or theological discourse. When Bakhtin speaks about religion, he speaks about it as a philosophical problem, that is, as a problem to be made sense of within the bounds of philosophy as a secular discipline. The particular texts that the reader should consider in this connection are "The Problem of Grounded Peace," Bakhtin's "Objections" to Tubiansky's paper, and his lecture of November 1, 1925, which represents a development of his earlier "Objections."

[Introduction by N. I. Nikolaev]

The present publication of M. M. Bakhtin's 1924–25 lectures and comments not only enriches with new material the heritage of the great Russian thinker but also allows, with greater precision, the evaluation of a very important trend in Russian twentieth-century thought—the Nevel school of philosophy.[1]

The publication of Bakhtin's early works written in the late 1910s and the early 1920s (and later retrieved from the philosopher's papers) was begun in 1975 and has been completed in recent years.[2] During these same years (mainly through the study of Bakhtin's biography), some additional information was obtained about the Nevel school.[3] As a result, it has become possible to define the environment and intellectual atmosphere in which Bakhtin created his early works.

To what extent, however, is the term "the Nevel school of philosophy" justified? I. I. Kanaev attests that I. I. Sollertinsky assigned Bakhtin, L. V. Pumpiansky, M. I. Kagan, and himself to what he called the "Nevel school of philosophers." Thus, at least a younger representative of the Nevel school (Sollertinsky was Pumpiansky's and Bakhtin's disciple) was conscious of belonging to a circle of thinkers with shared views—a fact that represents one of the most important constitutive traits of a philosophical school. What in fact united the Nevel school was not so much unanimity in the resolution of philosophical problems (all of its main representatives were original thinkers in their own right), but rather unanimity in the way they posed and treated philosophical problems, as well as to some extent the fact that they belonged to a shared philosophical tradition. Furthermore, the very format of the school's existence—more or less regular meetings of a group or circle of philosophers who presented and discussed their own works as well as reports on the work of other philosophers—implied polemics, that is, disputation of one's own point of view.

The school's name comes from the town of Nevel where its three main representatives happened to live in 1918: Mikhail Mikhailovich Bakhtin (1895–1975), who had arrived from Petrograd early in the summer of 1918; Lev Vasil'evich Pumpiansky (1891–1940), who had been staying in Nevel already for some time;

and Matvei Isaevich Kagan (1899–1937), who had returned home from Germany where he had studied with Hermann Cohen (1842–1918), the famous head of the Marburg school of neo-Kantian philosophy.

The activity of the Nevel school lasted with interruptions from 1918 through (most likely) 1927, when regular meetings probably ceased. The Nevel period of 1918 to 1919, during which the school's three main representatives apparently developed their original standpoints, was the most important and defining one in the school's history. This was the only time when Bakhtin, Kagan, and Pumpiansky regularly met and communicated with each other. This was also the time when Maria Veniaminovna Yudina (1899–1970), Boris Mikhailovich Zubakin (1894–1937), Valentin Nikolaevich Voloshinov (1896–1934), and a few others participated in the school's meetings. After that, the Nevel school resumed its meetings in Vitebsk, where Pumpiansky moved in the fall of 1919 and Bakhtin in 1920. But this period did not last long because, already in 1920, Kagan was teaching at the University of Orel and Pumpiansky moved to Petrograd in the fall of 1920. It was in Vitebsk that Pavel Nikolaevich Medvedev (1891–1938) and Ivan Ivanovich Sollertinsky (1902–44) joined the circle of philosophers. The energetic cultural and educational activity of the school's representatives in these years is relatively well documented by publications in the Nevel newspaper *Molot* [*The Hammer*], the Nevel periodical *Den' iskusstva* [*The Day of Art*],[4] the newspaper of the Vitebsk Soviet *Izvestiia* [*The News*], and the Vitebsk periodical *Iskusstvo* [*Art*]. A list of public lectures delivered by them in Vitebsk has been found in Sollertinsky's papers.[5] The school's meetings resumed in Petrograd without Bakhtin in 1922–23 after Kagan's temporary move from Moscow to Petrograd, where he actively participated in the work of the Free Philosophical Association [*Vol'naia filosofskaia assotsiatsiia*] along with Pumpiansky. It was from this time on that Mikhail Izrailevich Tubiansky (1893–1943) became a very important participant in the school's philosophical discussions; the poet Konstantin Konstantinovich Vaginov (1899–1934) and the biologist Ivan Ivanovich Kanaev (1893–1983) also began to attend the meetings. The school's activity resumed once again, albeit without Kagan, when Bakhtin, following his friends, moved from Vitebsk to Leningrad in the spring of 1924. Bakhtin's lectures and comments published here belong to this Leningrad period of the school's history. We can get an idea of the format of these philosophical encounters from a letter by Pumpiansky sent in 1926 to Kagan in Moscow:

Dear Matvei Isaevich . . . I am extremely interested in your works on Pushkin. A profound mind like yours will always shed new light even on the most familiar of subjects. We miss you very much (excuse my Gallicism)[6] this year—all these years—but especially this year because we are persistently studying theology. The circle of our current friends is the same: M. V. Yudina, Mikh. Mikh. Bakhtin, Mikh. Izr. Tubiansky, and I. Believe me, we would often exclaim: "What a pity Matvei Isaevich is not here—he would have helped us to unravel this problem!" Not long before Christmas we had a plan to invite you to come for a visit. We wanted to hear you reading your new works, and we wanted to find out your opinion on the theological problems that interested us. Then we learned that because of your job you could not leave suddenly, without prior arrangements. That's fine, we will make up for this later: great disputations and nocturnal conversations still await us. We will revive the memories of those wonderful times ("Ladies and gentlemen, dear Mikhail Mikhailovich") which Maria Veniaminovna recalls with such fondness. ("BiK" 265–66)

It is natural to assume that even during the long intervals between the meetings, and even after the meetings ceased, the members of the Nevel school continued to be united for a long period of time by a shared universe of thought that had come into being in Nevel. An indispensable ingredient in this universe of thought was the members' common interest in each other's opinions, which included an interest in the other's possible disagreement or approbation. The best confirmation for this would have been the presence of mutual references in the works of the school's members, as well as the character of these references. Yet, even though such references do exist, there are far too few of them. This shared universe of thought is attested in a more definite way by the school's members themselves. In his letter of August 7, 1936, M. I. Kagan writes to his wife, S. I. Kagan: "I am going to read right now a work by Mikhail Mikhailovich, 'On Discourse in the Novel' ['O slove v romane']. He gave it to me in manuscript. Judging by the beginning, its idea is similar to the one that I expressed some time ago in my article on Turgenev. . . . In my article this idea is expressed in passing. . . . In Mikhail Mikhailovich's study everything is fully developed, full of significance" ("BiK" 268).[7] It should be noted in this connection that Bakhtin and Kagan had not seen each other for many years, and that Bakhtin's study[8] was written during his banishment to Kustanai, in Kazakhstan, where he lived from 1930 through 1936. In 1972, Bakhtin recommended Pumpiansky's unpublished book on Gogol, which had been written fifty years earlier. Pumpiansky's book on Gogol contains, among other things, the first philosophy of laughter in the history of the Nevel school;[9] the second philosophy of laughter was developed by Bakhtin during the 1930s in his book on Rabelais. Finally, the shared universe of thought is also attested by the presence of "common ideas" in the works of the school's representatives. Thus, for example, Pumpiansky's nontraditional use of the terms 'author" and "hero" in his book *Dostoevskii i antichnost'. Doklad, chitannyi v Vol'noi filosofskoi assotsiatsii 2 oktjabrja 1921 g.* (Petrograd, 1922; *Dostoevsky and Antiquity*)[10]—a use similar to Bakhtin's understanding of the terms—most likely represents an original development (for the purposes of the given lecture) of ideas that Bakhtin was working out methodically in his early works. Neither in the first draft of his Dostoevsky lecture, written in the Nevel period, nor in Pumpiansky's other works of the late 1910s to early 1920s, do we find these terms used in such a way.

Any attempt to outline the overall orientation of the Nevel school of philosophy is, in our view, impossible for the time being, inasmuch as such an outline would consist mostly of negative characterizations. For example: the Nevel school of philosophy contended against metaphysics and positivism, and in particular against the formal method [i.e., the method of the Russian formalists], against unsystematic philosophizing, and so forth. The school's philosophical tradition can be defined more positively (which does not exclude the school's paying close attention to other currents of thought): Kant, neo-Kantianism, and especially the Marburg school of neo-Kantianism, and the head of that school—Hermann Cohen.[11] One could even say that at least until the mid-1920s the school's philosophical activity proceeded within a frame of reference determined by the problematics of Cohen's philosophy. As for the filiation of the school's ideas, and the concrete history of its periods (and in particular that of the most important of them—the Nevel period), all we can do is conjecture about that. This is due to the fact that the works of the school's members have survived to an unequal extent. And finally, the topics of the cultural and educational lectures reported in the press of the time also add very little to our knowledge, since they demonstrate the breadth and depth of the school's interests rather than its overall orientation. Nevertheless, in spite of the unequal extent to which the school's works have survived, one can attempt (by using materials from Pumpiansky's papers as well as from other sources) to (1) gain a clearer understanding of the subject of the Nevel discussions in 1918 to 1919; (2) determine their significance for the subsequent work of each one of the participants; and (3) bring out the relationship of each participant to the general philosophical tradition mentioned above. In the latter case, it might be more fruitful perhaps to compare successively their views with all the main trends of philosophical thought at the beginning of the twentieth century.

In the prefatory note to his article on the philosophy of history ["How is History Possible?"](dated May 21, 1921), Kagan cites evaluations of the article by N. I. Konrad, I. A. Il'in, G. G. Shpet, and Viacheslav Ivanov, and states that "the article was written two years ago."[12] Consequently, the article must have been written in Nevel in 1919, and its first interested audience consisted, in accordance with custom, of the members of the Nevel circle. Kagan's article ["Hermann Cohen"], which is dedicated to the memory of Hermann Cohen, bears the date of 1920,[13] that is to say, it was written at the very end of the Nevel period. The system of concepts used in Kagan's works of this time remained the same for his entire career, judging by Pumpiansky's notes of one of Kagan's lectures delivered at a Petrograd meeting in 1923 and by Kagan's 1937 article on Pushkin's narrative poems.[14] The article on Pushkin cannot be understood fully without taking into account Kagan's works of the Nevel period.

Pumpiansky's small book *Dostoevsky and Antiquity* (1922) contains reflections on the fortunes of Russian literature from the standpoint of a certain philosophy of history, and these philosophical reflections are echoed in all of his subsequent works. The book can be regarded as a summation of his thought during the Nevel period. This is attested by the works he wrote in the summer of 1919 that have survived among his papers: the lecture "Dostoevsky as a Tragic Poet," "A Brief Lecture at the Dostoevsky Debate," a study of *Hamlet*, and "The Meaning of Pushkin's Poetry." The draft of a theory of the comical ["An Essay in Constructing a Relativistic Reality According to *The Government Inspector*"] also dates from the summer of 1919; his 1922–25 book on Gogol goes back to this essay.

Among Bakhtin's early works, only his 1919 piece "Art and Answerability" ["*Iskusstvo i otvetsvennost'* "] belongs to the Nevel period. And although the rest of Bakhtin's early works were written in 1921–24, one can assert with certainty that their ideas go back in many respects to the Nevel period. Clark and Holquist (who perspicaciously entitled their chapter on Bakhtin's early works "The Architectonics of Answerability") are quite justified in analyzing Bakhtin's 1919 piece together with the works of 1921–24.[15]

When Kagan writes that the philosophy of the Marburg school, and therefore that of Hermann Cohen, "meets the needs of philosophy at this point of its historical course,"[16] he is not merely paying tribute to his teacher, Cohen, who appreciated his disciple's first works, and whose comrade-in-arms, Paul Natorp, helped to publish the first two articles by Kagan in German philosophical journals[17] when their author was interned in Germany as a Russian subject during World War I. We can assume that, since Kagan wrote his article on Cohen just after the end of the Nevel period, his assessment of Cohen's philosophy was shared by all members of the Nevel school. Indeed, their real need for Cohen's philosophy is attested by the fact that in his letter of November 1921, Bakhtin asked Kagan to send him Cohen's book on Kant's ethics which he needed to finish his work "The Subject of Morality and the Subject of Law" ("BiK" 262).[18] We can also assume that the fundamental problems of Cohen's philosophy, as they are formulated in Kagan's article, took on definite form precisely during the discussions in Nevel.

The Nevel school's close relationship to Cohen's philosophy is demonstrated above all by the works of its members. The terminological apparatus of the Marburg school, and that of Cohen in particular, is employed in their works as a generally recognized system of concepts, requiring no explanation. This applies to such concepts, for example, as "the given and the posited" [*dannost' i zadannost'*] "problem," "purpose" (teleology), "unity" (of consciousness, knowledge, being, etc.), "act" [*postupok*], "answerability" [*otvetsvennost'*], "the interrelation of I and the Other," "unfinalizability" (of knowledge), and so on.

This assimilation of Cohen's philosophy, however, was a critical assimilation in the process of their working out their own original philosophical positions. Just as Cohen himself performed a revision of Kant, reinterpreting and excluding a number of Kant's notions, Cohen's followers in Nevel revised Cohen. In fact, all of the prominent disciples of Cohen went beyond the bounds of his philosophy. In the case of Cohen's Nevel followers, the departure from Cohen's philosophy, in order to deal with a new set of problems, was equally striking. In his article on the philosophy of history, Kagan seeks to establish the validity of a special kind of reality—historical reality. Bakhtin, in his work entitled by its publisher *Toward a Philosophy of the Act* [*K filosofii postupka*], describes a special reality— the being of the ongoing event of an answerable act. This is the reason why some of the concepts that go back directly to Cohen acquire a new meaning in the works of the representatives of the Nevel school. Thus, Bakhtin's "Art and Answerability," for example, can be regarded as a paraphrase of Cohen's philosophy, or rather, as a paraphrase of a certain theme in his *Ethics of the Pure Will* [*Ethik des reinen Willens*]. At the same time, Bakhtin's special use of the concept of "responsibility" or "answerability" in his other early writings led Clark and Holquist to conclude that it is a key concept in Bakhtin's thought throughout the 1919–24 period. In the Kantian tradition, the legal concept of "responsibility" is linked to the concepts of "imputability" and "guilt." In the late nineteenth and early twentieth centuries, the concept of responsibility gradually gained an independent status and began to be used not only in the philosophy of law but also in ethics. The term is used as a moral category, for example, by Georg Simmel (an important name for Bakhtin): "[E]very Ought in the immediate present has been shaped and conditioned by every constituent moment of the life lived until now. The responsibility for our entire history is already present in the Oughtness of every individual action."[19] In his *Ethics of the Pure Will*, Cohen uses the concept of responsibility both in its legal interpretation, characteristic of his system, and as an ethical category in determining individual responsibility.[20] For Bakhtin, however, the concept of responsibility (answerability) has an exclusively moral meaning. We find a similar interpretation of the concept in Kagan's writings: "[T]he heroism of culture demands individual responsibility [answerability] from us in our work in the face of culture and history. This responsibility [answerability] is possible in our modest self-assertion in a state of need."[21]

Pumpiansky's essays and notes from the summer of 1919 show that the problem of responsibility (answerability) was at the center of the Nevel discussions of that time. More than that, even: the particular way in which Bakhtin posed this problem prompted the appearance of Pumpiansky's essays, which were so important for the work he did throughout his entire subsequent career. In his "Brief Lecture at the Dostoevsky Debate," Pumpiansky asks the question of how Dostoevsky's heroes can become what they are: "In what way can a servant be a servant without becoming a lackey?" And he answers: "By following the way of Grinev,[22] and not that of Karamazov the father: the way of answerability."

In this instance, the concept of answerability is completely devoid of its legal significance. Pumpiansky's "Brief Lecture" concludes with words directly addressed to Bakhtin: "And you, dear Mikhail Mikhailovich . . . examine the course of the argument, analyze, make amendments." This is an important testimony to the fact that Bakhtin's conception of his book on Dostoevsky goes back at least to 1919, that is, to the Nevel period.

The following note by Pumpiansky is directly related to the problem of answerability:

A Response to the Problem Proposed by Mikhail Mikhailovich

1. The logical conditions of moral reality have been established by him irreproachably, and they can be summed up in one word: answerability.
2. But what are the conditions for these conditions, i.e., in what ways, i.e., where (*ubi, quo loco*)[23] does one look for their possible realization?
3. First of all, these ways do exist and moral reality also exists because otherwise . . . Descartes . . .
4. Second, actual being, *qua* being that is founded throughout, cannot *be* without being since the creation of the world. i.e., it is metaphysically *prior* to any other being; therefore, it has always been, it is, and it will be. It is not only the most perfect reality but also the only one; (it existed before the Fall, then passed into an invisible state, and thanks to it, becomes ever more manifest from the middle of the historical process, and will come to reign once again after its end).
5. But where should one seek moral being? Since, as explained above, it is invisible, we cannot see it however hard we try (adequate faith, the one that moves mountains, is excluded), and therefore, we have to look for indirect paths.
6. Since moral reality not only exists but exists in a once-occurrent manner, any other kind of being lives only in correlation with moral reality . . . Even relativism. . . . And this applies to symbolism especially—symbolism lives only as the symbolization of true reality *and not otherwise.* . . . Consequently, in symbols we can find an accessible primer of the real (the Latin transcription of Sanskrit!). Therefore, let us proceed into the world of symbols!
7. What we seek are the conditions of answerability for the real? Let us turn our attention to the conditions of *symbolic* answerability!

Pumpiansky's paper "An Essay in Constructing a Relativistic Reality According to *The Government Inspector*" is linked to the content of the above note. The paper begins as follows:

Everybody remembers the past as established by us. . . . The conditions of serious reality were established by Mikhail Mikhailovich. Paraphrase.—But how do we find a connection? . . . Where are the seeds of the future in the very depths of relativism? The one who is irresponsible can thus become responsible?—This is what I was thinking about after assimilating Mikhail Mikhailovich's views.

The paper concludes with words of profound gratitude to Mikhail Mikhailovich Bakhtin. Pumpiansky returns to these topics in yet another draft:

Introduction

    1. Last time, the analysis of *The Government Inspector* showed us that . . .
    2. You remember Mikhail Mikhailovich's train of thought . . . At a certain stage of the world's history a symbol is born . . . and undergoes the following inevitable fate: I . . . II . . . But what was missing in Mikhail Mikhailovich's train of thought was stage III, which follows inevitably from stage II: the expansion of symbolization is connected with the weakening of the symbolic power . . . That which symbolizes stops submitting to that which is being symbolized and begins to approach the birth of its own independent life. . . . The moment is inevitable when both principles attain equilibrium, come to a standstill ±, reaching period III of the symbolic world. . . . The poet of this period is Pushkin . . .
    3. What was most important from the overall point of view was the characterization of period I, of the immovability of monumental symbols . . . However . . . [. . .].

It is evident from the cited materials that the problems posed by Bakhtin in his brief article "Art and Answerability" (published in the periodical *Den' iskusstva*, September 13, 1919) were actively debated during the summer months of 1919. In the opinion of Clark and Holquist, Bakhtin's brief article (to which we would also add Pumpiansky's materials from 1919) already reflects the topics of that body of his early works on moral philosophy that they treat under the title of "The Architectonics of Answerability."[24] And indeed, the validity of moral reality, as a reality conditioned by answerability,[25] is demonstrated in Bakhtin's *Toward a Philosophy of the Act*. In this work, owing to his avowed fondness for "a diversity of terms for a single phenomenon" (*SpG* 155), moral reality is defined in a variety of ways (which attests, most probably, the difficulty and uncommonness of the subject of his philosophizing). The mechanical union of the three realms of culture—science, art, and life—within an individual person ("A&A" 1) is correlated with judgments about the crisis of contemporary action, about the chasm that has arisen between the motive of an act and its product (*TPA* 54–55). What guarantees the inner connection of an individual person's constituent elements is the unity of answerability ("A&A" 2); and the answer to Pumpiansky's questions—How is the realization of the conditions of moral reality possible? How can someone who is irresponsible become responsible?—consists in the fact that "[t]he individual must become answerable through and through" ("A&A" 2). The possibility of such an "ought" consists in the fact that the once-occurrent nature of present-on-hand being is compellingly binding: that it is a fact of "my non-alibi in Being" (*TPA* 40), inasmuch as "I *am* actual and irreplaceable, and therefore *must* actualize my uniqueness. [. . .] The ought becomes possible for the first time where there is an acknowledgment of the fact of a unique person's being from within that person; where this fact becomes a center of answerability—where I assume answerability for my own uniqueness, for my own being" (*TPA* 41–42).

A particularly important question is Pumpiansky's one about the ways of discovering moral being. Judging by the quoted texts, Pumpiansky himself offers a solution in the spirit of Viacheslav Ivanov's late symbolism. Ivanov's theoretical constructions were, incidentally, highly regarded by all members of the Nevel school: "in symbols we can find an accessible ABC of the real." Most likely, Bakhtin could not agree with such a symbolic interpretation because, according to him, "[t]o orient an act or deed within the whole of once-occurrent Being-as-event does not mean at all that we translate it into the language of highest values, where the concrete, real, participative (unindifferent) event in which the act orients itself immediately is only a representation or reflection of those values" (*TPA* 52). That is why Bakhtin's reflections on the stages of symbolization are probably summarized by Pumpiansky in his own terms.

Kagan answers the question in his own particular way, if we assume that the problem of "subjective awareness" or "ontological subjectivity" that he poses can be correlated with the problem of moral reality, that is, of the world of the act-performing consciousness, in Bakhtin's work. Proceeding from Hermann Cohen's thesis about the unity of the consciousness of culture, Kagan writes that "idealist psychology," which studies subjective consciousness, "must have the system of all of objective culture in view, in order to be able to attain, at the peak of its historical life, the specific problem of subjective consciousness, the problem of the subjective individual."[26] Such an approach to "living consciousness" from the standpoint of cultural values is examined by Bakhtin and found to be inadequate (*TPA* 34–35).

Bakhtin's answer derives from the essential nature of the moral reality he had established. Since the world of unitary and unique Being-as-event "is fundamentally and essentially indeterminable either in theoretical categories or in categories of historical cognition or through aesthetic intuition" (*TPA* 16), one can only describe it in an engaged, participatory manner, one can only provide a phenomenology of it (*TPA* 32). This description, moreover, is accomplished not by means of theoretical terminology but by means of natural language in its entire plenitude, although even in that case "full adequacy is unattainable, it is always present as that which is to *be* achieved" (*TPA* 31). At the same time, one can give a description of "the once-occurrent actual act/deed and its author—the one who is thinking theoretically, contemplating aesthetically, and acting ethically" (*TPA* 27–28), by way of analyzing "the world of aesthetic seeing," which "[i]n its concreteness . . . is closer than any of the abstract cultural worlds (taken in isolation) to the unitary and unique world of the performed act" (*TPA* 61). Such a phenomenological description of the "highest architectonic principle of the actual world of the performed act or deed [which] is the concrete and architectonically valid or operative contraposition of *I* and the *other*" (*TPA* 74) was carried out by Bakhtin with the help of the notions of "author" and "hero" in his work "Author and Hero in Aesthetic Activity."

But could the discovery of moral reality (so different from Hermann Cohen's notion of *sittliche Wirklichkeit*) have taken place within the bounds of Cohen's system, if we put aside for the moment other possible sources of Bakhtin's reflections? (And there should be no doubt that this *is* a philosophical discovery, just as much as the introduction of the concepts of author and hero.) A survey of Cohen's system as summarized in Kagan's 1922 article, "German Kogen" (cited hereafter in this essay as "GK"), is instructive. As regards the possibility of a new kind of being, Cohen does seek to validate, for example, the special being of man and the State ("GK" 118), aesthetic being ("GK" 119), and even a special kind of aesthetic consciousness ("GK" 120). As regards the fundamental problem of philosophical aesthetics, it is constituted, according to Cohen, by "the man of nature and the nature of man in their unity" ("GK" 119). The possibility of using ethical categories in aesthetics is tied up with the fact that the content of aesthetic consciousness is morality (*Sittlichkeit*).[27] As regards the problem of unitary and unique being, Cohen's philosophy (which follows the tradition of Old Testament monotheism) correlates the problem of the unity of the single individual precisely with that unitary and unique being. The single individual is the individual of religion ("GK" 121). The individual who exists in constant correlation with God ("GK" 122) is the individual of the correlation with the one, sole, incomparable religious being ("GK" 123) and not the individual of logic, biology, or ethics; not the social person and not the individual of art ("GK" 121–22). But however stimulating Cohen's ideas may have been, he proves to be, in the end, a representative of that theoretical philosophy which cannot find any way of gaining access to moral reality. And, most probably, Bakhtin meant Cohen (who defined the act as the fundamental problem of ethics in *The Ethics of Pure Will*)[28] when he wrote that "[t]he principle of formal ethics is not the principle of an actually performed act at all, but is rather the principle of the possible generalization of already performed acts in a theoretical transcription of them" (*TPA* 27).

Thus, in the process of reflecting on the problems of neo-Kantian philosophy, Bakhtin creates a Christian anthropology that describes the conditions for the existence of human beings in a world in which "the event of Christ's life and death was accomplished, both in the fact and in the meaning of his life and death" (*TPA* 16). The principles of this world, inaccessible to theoretical ethics, are reflected by "the sense of all Christian morality" (*TPA* 75).

This origin of Bakhtin's philosophy determined his special place in the history of Russian thought. What distinguishes Bakhtin from his contemporary Russian religious philosophers (apart from the latter's well-known wariness toward Kant and neo-Kantianism) is most clearly manifested in their respective evaluations of particular cultural phenomena. If Pavel A. Florensky, proceeding from the conformity of a phenomenon to an acknowledged unconditional value, defined the poetry of Aleksandr Blok (which he loved) as demoniac visions, and A. F. Losev defined Rabelais's laughter as satanism, Bakhtin is characterized in his value judgments by a confiding acceptance (cf. his lecture on Blok in R. M. Mirkina's notes; his book on Rabelais) that derives from the very essence of his philosophy as a whole.

Bakhtin's lectures and comments of 1924–25 (which are closely related to the whole problematics of his early works) are highly important for the characterization of his work after his arrival in Leningrad. But these notes of Bakhtin's lectures and comments are equally important for the history of the Nevel school and for gaining a clearer understanding of the issues addressed in its Leningrad meetings, about which we knew until now only from indirect sources. (We knew, for example, that the participants had studied Kant's second critique.)

Chronologically, the present notes are distributed very unevenly. The larger part of them belongs to 1924, and the last two sets to 1925. What we are publishing are all of Pumpiansky's notes that pertain to the activity of the Nevel school in Leningrad,[29] and all of them are connected with Bakhtin. It should be noted that Pumpiansky's papers contain no notes of the lectures or comments of any persons other than those members of the Nevel school that have been mentioned or are published below. All this testifies to the special attention Pumpiansky paid to Bakhtin's ideas. And if the large number of notes from 1924 could be explained by Pumpiansky's striving to record those works of Bakhtin that were still unknown to him (for the purpose of thinking them over later on and discussing them), then the last two sets of notes, dating from a period when the two men were in constant personal contact, attest the great importance for Pumpiansky of the problems posed in them.

Among the notes, Bakhtin's lectures of the fall of 1924 are particularly important because they contain his only known evaluation of the problems of European philosophy in their historical development, and because Bakhtin formulated this evaluation after he had already produced some of his most important works.

The reliability of these notes in conveying Bakhtin's thought is confirmed by the fact that they use a terminology that corresponds to the terminology of Bakhtin's early works (written within the framework of the Nevel school's activities, and thus well known to Pumpiansky). Kagan's terminology and style of thinking are no less faithfully conveyed in Pumpiansky's notes of Kagan's lecture in 1923.

The Nevel school left a profound mark on Russian culture in the person of Bakhtin, but as a school it had no disciples or followers. That is why the works of its representatives, except for Bakhtin, have not been published and studied. And yet, if we do not take these works into account, Bakhtin's philosophy is deprived of its proper ideational and biographical environment, and the study of that philosophy lacks the proper historico-philosophical perspective. And as long as these works remain unpublished, and there are no studies of Russian Cohenism and of the Nevel school's attitude toward Hermann Cohen, that is, as long as the historical context in which the Nevel school of philosophy and Bakhtin's ideas were engendered remains unexamined—we will continue to make do with premature conclusions about the most superficial facts.

The materials from Pumpiansky's papers were kindly made available to us by the scholar's widow, E. M. Isserlin. We would also like to thank S. I. Kagan [M. I. Kagan's widow] and Iu. M. Kagan [his daughter] for the opportunity to examine and use the materials from M. I. Kagan's papers. We are also grateful to Vadim Liapunov, the American Bakhtin scholar and translator, who read this introductory article and made a number of encouraging and critical observations.[30]

[Comments during the Discussion of Pumpiansky's Report on F. W. H. Myers's Book]

Discussion

Mikh. Izr. Tubiansky:[31] Myers violates Newton's *hypotheses non fingo.*[32] He invokes hypotheses that do not follow from the investigation itself. His approach is a mixture of the scientific and the nonscientific, as is the case in many metapsychical works. Myths are invoked as hypotheses in order to explain the phenomena.— Meanwhile, if he presents a sketch of the occult picture of the world, why then does he not accept the occult restructuring of consciousness? Myers and Lev Vasil'evich [i.e., Pumpiansky] lack philosophical culture. The alternation of occult and philosophical strivings existed in past civilizations, and there is no reason to think that it will not continue.[33]

N. I. Konrad:[34] There is a parallel between Myers's truth and Spengler's truth, in spite of the fact that perhaps *all* their particular assertions are completely in the wrong; all of contemporary civilization is moving toward the affirmation of the metapsychical phenomenon. Myers's book can claim to represent no more than just one of the paths of that movement. Its terminology is excessive; its material (for example, the spiritualist material) has no serious occult significance; its conclusions are arbitrary. An immense reality is known to him only from accidentally discovered facts, from facts that are completely fortuitous and admit of no hypotheses; contemporary German scientists, for example, have renounced now any hypotheses whatsoever when investigating the phenomena of materialization. Thus, the whole book falls apart, but—its direction is quite right and highly significant.

Mikh. Mikh. Bakhtin: One should distinguish in Myers's book between the empirical plane and the value plane.—On the empirical plane, everything depends on the extent to which he has used *all* of the facts, on the extent to which he has correctly established, for example, the connection between what is a matter of genius and what is a matter of hypnotism.—But the main thing for Myers is the second plane. What constitutes the center on this plane is his doctrine of personality; and in this context, a number of moments keep intersecting all the time: sometimes juridical moments, sometimes aesthetic ones, sometimes religious ones, and so on, so that every problem is passed through a number of these moments. Thus, the certainty of continued existence is illegitimately substituted for the religious problem of immortality (a problem of value);[35] the biological *subiectum* declares himself to be the religious *subiectum*, whereas in fact we are dealing here with nothing but biology raised to the highest plane.

Hero and Author in Artistic Creation:
A Series of Lectures by M. M. Bakhtin

1. Methodological introduction.[36] 2.[37]

3. The hero in space (body). 4. In time (soul). 5. The interrelationship of author and hero.

The tendency of *Kunstwissenschaft*[38] to establish a distinct scientific discipline that deals with art and is independent from general philosophical aesthetics. Meanwhile, the scientific character of a branch of knowledge is defined in terms of two exact (constitutive) characteristics: its relation to the empirical and its relation to mathematics; such is the scientific character of the natural sciences. Another type of the scientific (of the two solely existing types) is the scientific character of the human sciences,[39] defined by their relation to empirical reality and their relation to meaning and purpose. The type of experience in the human sciences is quite different; what is important here is its intensiveness.[40] The fact that one kind of experience is fully formed while the other is still in process of formation leads to the attempts to transpose the methods of positive science upon artistic creation. To do this consistently is impossible, whatever one does, and so one transposes them inconsistently. First of all—the orientation toward material that seems to bring together the work an aesthetician does and the work of the positive sciences, and represents a temptation for nonspecialists. Yesterday it was an orientation toward psychological material, today it is toward poetic material. What one ends up with are the results of being rashly "scientific"; one ends up with pretended judgments that are numerous and yet completely disconnected from each other. However, even the "formal method" (in reality, the material method) cannot do without a *telos*,[41] otherwise the Formalists would not have been able, of course, to go beyond the limits of pure linguistics. But they bring in the *telos* in an arbitrary, eclectic way, and they determine their bearings by reference to the given material, i.e., according to the products of conforming with laws.—This accounts for the problem of the *place* of material; the general question of the makeup of the aesthetic object and of the place that material occupies in it, so that we inevitably arrive at a problem in general aesthetics, which is the only discipline competent to deal with that problem.

Chapter 1.

The concept of concrete systematicalness. Every phenomenon of culture is located on a boundary.[42] What cognition finds is not indifferent or neutral material, but being that has been valuated by an act, by faith, and so on.[43] Every phenomenon of culture, in every one of its constituent moments, demarcates itself from contiguous domains of culture.[44] But in this respect, aesthetics differs from other domains of culture: the aesthetic act relates positively[45] [to being], for it relates to being that has already been valuated and identified by a deed; it does not abstract from this identification and valuation but rather introduces their coefficient [into its attitude toward being]. In terms of this positive stance aesthetics is similar to religion.[46] This also gives a meaning to the commonly voiced demands, [such as:] "art must transfigure life," and so on—indeed, the attitude is a positive one. It is this identified and evaluated reality that Mikhail Mikhailovich calls "content."[47] Content is not this or that particular something, but rather is an angle of vision, according to which everything in art can be extended or continued in purely cognitive or purely aesthetic terms. Content is the possible (infinite) prosaic context that, however, is always paralyzed by form;[48] the passivity of all that which comes to know, of all that which takes action.[49] And the problem of aesthetics consists precisely in explaining how it is possible to paralyze the world in this way.

The Problem of Grounded Peace: A Lecture by M. M. Bakhtin

To understand[50] the *form* of the world[51] in which prayer, ritual, hope . . . gain validity—this is the task of the philosophy of religion.[52] Philosophy of religion, inasmuch as it posits problems, must, initially, pose dogma itself as a problem,[53] that is, nondogmatically. But the moment will inevitably arrive when philosophy of religion will itself become dogmatic.—The form in which religious consciousness lives is the event;[54] this is the first step in defining the position of religious consciousness. But the doubleness of the concept of event is revealed by comparing, for example, a historical event with a personal and intimate event. In the intimate event, the most important thing is my own involvement or participation. Now the religious event clearly belongs to this category of personal participation.[55] I find myself in being as in an ongoing event;[56] I participate in the once-occurrent moment of its accomplishment.[57] Religious impenetrability is not at all physical; my ineffaceability, the indestructibility of my unique place in being;[58] in analogy to physical impenetrability, dogmatic metaphysics turns it into substantial impenetrability, whereas it is solely a participation that is an *event*. It is the consciousness of it that constitutes *conscience;* that is, the ought is not a moral ought, but a unique or once-occurring ought: no one in the entire world, besides myself, can accomplish what I myself must accomplish.[59] Meanwhile, the moral ought is an ought conforming with laws.[60] Whereas here the ought proceeds from unrepeatability or uniqueness alone, and one is tormented by conscience not for disobeying a law but as a result of proceeding from my once-occurrent position. Hence the impossibility of generalizing a religious norm; hence, as well, the Christian's demand (which Feuerbach failed to understand)[61] of the cross for himself and happiness for others. Yes, for a Christian, a chasm divides me myself from others; the division is without any remainder: I and Others;[62] this division is irreversible; it is from this absolute division that participatory consciousness proceeds.—Hence it is clear how hopeless is the attempt to understand ritual, prayer, etc., *morally.*—Outside the bounds of this fundamental fact of religion (the isolation of myself) it is impossible to explain any religious phenomenon. Thus, for example, repentance is completely inexplicable in terms of the principles of morality, i.e., properly speaking, juridical principles (which constitute the logic of ethics).[63]

Where, for moral consciousness, there are two people,—for religious consciousness there is a *third* one: a possible someone who evaluates.[64] Consider the Publican, who is right in religious terms, in the parable of the Publican and the Pharisee in Luke 18:9–14.[65] Let us imagine that he would render the justification of himself immanent. If he did so, he would immediately become unrighteous. Thus, his justification is possible only by an incarnated Third One. Meanwhile, the Pharisee absorbed this Third consciousness *into himself*, whereas the Publican unsealed the possible myth about his own personality.—Similarly, a child, in saying "my little hand,"[66] evidently receives his own value from his mother; for he does not possess an autonomous value-oriented self-consciousness. The evaluations of me myself that occur in registration by the State or in everyday life (someone gives me a place at the table)[67] also come from outside. In the case of dogmatic rigidification this produces mythologems of "natural law." The same is true for the way I gain an evaluation of myself in those cases when my soul is in the position of a bride or a bridegroom, i.e., in another's love.[68] In this case, too, mythologems are possible, and they are equally possible in the absorption of authorship into oneself (in the case of the aesthetic double).[69] One could also usurp one's being "written in heaven";[70] what saved one from such a usurpation was, for example, predestination, which transferred the evaluation of me myself to God and left me outside the bounds of [salvation],[71] regardless of whether my name was written down or not.

The true being of the spirit begins only when repentance begins,[72] that is, essential and fundamental noncoinciding:[73] everything that can be of value, *everything* exists outside of me; I am only a negative agency, only a receptacle of evil.[74] Leo Tolstoy's diaries;[75] supplications for the gift of tears.[76] To get a feel of one's being and grasp it, finally, in a real way: to attain, finally,—attain in truth, the reality of one's personhood, rejecting all the mythologems about it. I am infinitely bad, but Someone needs me to be good.[77] In repenting, I specifically establish the One in Whom I posit my sin. And it is this that constitutes grounded peace, which does not make up or fabricate anything. Tranquillity or peace of mind can be either the tranquillity of self-complacency or that of trust; what must free me from the tranquillity of self-complacency,[78] that is, from the tranquillity of an aesthetic mythologem, is precisely disquietude,[79] which will develop, through repentance, into trust.[80]—What is at issue is more serious than freedom, what is at issue (in faith) is something more than freedom, i.e., more than guarantees.[81]

But at certain moments we will inevitably confront the problem of the *incarnated* God.[82]

[M. M. Bakhtin's Lectures]

M. M. Bakhtin's Introductory Lecture

[Let us proceed] problem by problem,[83] following the Transcendental Aesthetic;[84] thus in connection with the problem of space—all of Bergson.

One can evaluate a systematic philosophy only by proceeding from it; the evaluation of it already presupposes in itself the systematic character of one's position. As for the usual correlations, they are muddled, and unconvincing from the standpoint of their method. Even in neo-Kantianism there is a school, the fulcrum of which is outside the bounds of systematic philosophy (Rickert).[85] All approaches of this kind are no more than naive correlations.—Another possibility is to treat systematic philosophy as a cultural *Leistung*,[86] as a historically embodied fact. From this standpoint, one could speak about systematic philosophy nonsystematically; this would be the standpoint of historical or intellectual psychology.[87] The following theme is possible: the problem of a systematic philosophy proceeding from the historical *subiectum*.

The moments that cannot be dissolved in the unity of the *subiectum* (the old man planting a tree) are free even from the presupposition of the existence of all humankind; they are fundamentally and essentially transgredient[88] (it is not for nothing that, for the popular consciousness, philosophy is a matter of meditations on death, immortality, and so on).—Another possibility is to hypostatize[89] metaphysically the moments that are transgredient to a consciousness (classical Platonism); they are rendered substantial, the category of being is attributed to them. But to substantialize a problem is not the same as to resolve it.[90]—As for nihilism, it seeks at all cost to uphold the unity of the natural *subiectum*, repudiating in principle the undissolvable moments. But nihilism as well presents corporeality to a physician; this corporeality differs, of course, from Plato's Ideas, yet it exists, nevertheless, and it has even engrossed the contemporary consciousness.[91] To renounce the corporeality of transgredient moments is a task that may be impossible to accomplish.

Thus, all of the directions of thought proceed (positively or negatively) from an excess;[92] they proceed not from the natural human being, but from the historical one. This is a transposition of everything from the subjective to the objective unity. Of course, the subjective unity is necessary and remains present (memory!), but now object-related unity comes to stand next to it.—Object-related unity has always been present in thinking, but it was present as an image; for example, the human being and—nature. This image, however, is founded, after all, totally on the unity of my own position. We have not moved, [therefore,] even a single step beyond the bounds of the natural human being.—Kant's great achievement consisted in destroying *this* unity, because it is only the unity of the natural *subiectum*.[93] For philosophy, all correlations are equal.—Objectivity (reality)[94] is given in history and culture, and not in nature, not in consciousness; objectivity and continuous objectivization [are given] in the work of culture. Not in an image, not in a substantialization,[95] but in the *work* [of culture]. Side by side with the subjective unity, which is necessary for assimilation [into my own thinking], there exists the objective unity of the theorem itself. It is this that constitutes Kant's problem of the objectivity of consciousness. The subjective unity is only a technical apparatus for bringing about the reality of culture. The unity of thinking should be understood as the unity of science;[96] the unity of will is *Einheit*;[97] the unity of consciousness is only an image of the unity of culture that, in principle, cannot be actualized in the single consciousness. This is part of the definition. As a *subiectum*, I never come to know anything; a scientist[98] immediately ceases to be a scientist the moment he becomes a sage, i.e., someone who wants to create a *subjective* unity of consciousness.[99] The principal danger consists in the image's becoming something more than an auxiliary [means]; forgetting that the unity of consciousness is only an image—that is what constitutes the principal danger for philosophy.

The second danger is the condensation[100] of the unity of culture to the point of becoming an image of culture (for example, in aesthetics, in the social sciences—the objectively real significance of institutions), [that is], a relapse into primitive, pre-Platonic suppositions, which have been vanquished long ago in philosophy itself. The naive objectification of one's own objectivity. The condensation may occur in different constituent moments of an image, but the process remains one and the same everywhere: the image assumes the place of the objective nexus.[101]

Objectivity is only the objectivity of the process of becoming of culture. Kant's achievement consists in replacing natural consciousness (and its loopholes) with historical consciousness.—But where, then, is the guarantee in respect of method for the historical consciousness [?].—The unity of the path and the historical stages [of the path].—The directedness [of the path in a certain direction], which runs through all the stages, is the sole subject of philosophy. In every thought there is a moment constituting a problem and a moment constituting a thesis; in a problem, thought goes beyond its own bounds. In scientific cognition, the distinction [of problem and thesis] is relatively difficult, but in the moral domain a thesis takes on the most seductive forms.—The essential and fundamental equality of all [historical] stages [of the path]. This is contradicted by the philosophy of revelation—discovery—unhoped-for joy—surprise. All this fails to understand the equality of all the [historical] stages [of the path].[102]

This is not even a thesis but deviations from a thesis that has separated itself from a problem; this is [a subjective] arrangement[103] in which a given quantity is dealt with not in the unity of culture, but in the unity of a given consciousness. A stage [of the path] closes the path, and the thesis ceases to be a thesis.—Every thought can be evaluated depending on [the following]: what does the thinker have in mind[104]—the image of a sage or rather the image has only a technical significance for him [?]—This difference affects everything, even the style of thinking.—All philosophemes of the revelational type suppress the presence of problems but cannot forget it; being sure that a judgment is part of some unity must obtain even for a subjective arrangement. Hence the hopelessness (a hopelessness from the outset) of such philosophemes: they lay claim to methodologism yet, on the other hand, seek subjective completion. The *pivot* is unsound—which does not annul, of course, the value of Hegel and Schelling. Should one proclaim oneself to be recognized or proven? Should one demand faith or verification? These philosophemes do not know themselves what the answer is.—The sage has become—not for nothing—skeptical; we no longer have faith in any other form of wisdom. Skepticism is distrust of anything that does not accommodate me.—[There is] one sure principle: to follow on what plane thought is working—on the plane of "achievement" or on that of "proof." Philosophy has always been full of the scraps of revelation; anthroposophy, in a way, did a good thing in gathering together all these scraps.[105]

Mikhail Mikhailovich's Second Lecture

The only possible way[106] of philosophically discussing systematic philosophy is by proceeding from within systematic philosophy itself. But what is also possible is a historico-philosophical characterization of systematic philosophy. Why, then, are other types of doing philosophy possible, besides the systematic type? There are three reasons: (1) Recourse to images, which is peculiar to thought itself. *Plat. Resp.:*[107] thinking as no more than an adjunct to [one's] horizon. Bergson also wishes to return thinking back to primordial imaging, back to the unity of [one's] horizon. The logic of [one's] horizon—that is what constitutes the source of nonsystematic philosophy; the immanent logic of an aesthetic image creates and propels a number of philosophical projects. Aesthetics must construct a typology of such doctrines.[108] (2) Revelation, to which one attempts to impart a philosophical form. In this case, it is no longer aesthetics but philosophy of religion that must show the pure, that is, dogmatic, form of it. The corporeal-psychic human being seeks everywhere to subject philosophy to his own ends, [that is,] to distort the fundamentally and essentially unfinished character of thought.[109] (3) Reality as the ultimate court of appeal for the verification of philosophical views. From this reality one must exclude its authoritativeness; elementary conditional authoritativeness takes on the form of [incontestable] certainty, which leads to the question of that once-occurrent horizon, within which the fact first appeared. [The role of] elementary authority in the service of reality is so great that it was possible to introduce reality into the world of religion (not truly, but verily). But if this authoritativeness were to be removed, all one would be left with is the reality of a performed act; this is only a need for reality. It is this need that leads to metaphysics, all of which is a postulate of the performed act, because a performed act is always in need of reality. For the performed act the whole question consists in the existence and the character of reality (for religion, meanwhile, the question is not whether the kingdom in heaven exists but whether I will get into it). The postulative character of reality, that has fused with imagery and revelation, forms the basis of all philosophemes.[110] Proceeding from this, a number of interesting projects is possible: [for example,] to translate back into image—revelation—morality what a great philosopher has set forth in a theoretical form (for example, Fichte). A typical characteristic of going outside the bounds of pure cognition is the intermixing of what is *a priori* and what is *a posteriori* (which passed from Fichte into German idealism as a whole).

    This is what renders nonsystematic philosophizing persuasive; in it the natural consciousness wants to be the only one (*après nous le déluge*).[111] Another possible danger for pure thought consists in the mythologization of the path; in this case the method becomes the hero of philosophizing and wants to be rewarded straightaway; risk becomes the hero (Freiburg).

    The question of the *right* of science as an institution, as a historical fact. Besides that, Kant's orienting himself in relation to positive science raises the question of the factuality of science itself: will we not be compelled to revise the *Kritizismus* perpetually, in connection with the alteration of science itself?[112] All these doubts are based on a failure to comprehend Kant's *Kritizismus*. Kant's orienting himself in relation to the *fact* of the sciences has the character of a problem pure and simple. Kant did not even assert the existence of science as such, [but] treated science itself as a problem (and *not* as a *basis*). When philosophy deals with facts, these facts are not historical. Proceeding from a fact is not [equivalent to] basing oneself on a fact: Thales already problematized nature.[113] Why, then, does Kant problematize science specifically (and not perception, not "the intuition of *durée*,"[114] and the like)? This problematization is, of course, purely hypothetical; it is not [a matter of] being conditioned by a fact, [for] Kant does not at all want to proceed from the supposedly acknowledged rightness of the natural sciences.—What remains in doubt is the correctness of the fact chosen for problematization: Was science really the best choice . . . ? Would something else have been a better choice . . . ?

But *what kind* of problematization? An immanent problematization, i.e., the kind that is founded in scientific cognition itself, as a result of which philosophy is the reflection of science upon itself; there is no tribunal from outside.

Mikhail Mikhailovich's Third Lecture

The analysis of Kant's orienting himself in relation to science. Three objections: (1) Science as a historical fact—can one orient oneself in relation to a historical fact? (2) In general something is presupposed; philosophy seems to have conditioned itself by something from the very outset; as if philosophy were in a state of dependence on the need for science. Kant, supposedly, chose mathematics and natural science beforehand, and he did so for pragmatic reasons: "We had better stay with mathematics rather than with metaphysics." Consequently, Kantianism is conditioned by a certain extra-philosophical fact. (3) Does not the relativity of science render philosophy relative as well?—All these objections fail to understand that orienting oneself in relation to science is a problematization of science, and not in the least a matter of basing oneself on it. But here an objection is possible: was Kant right in choosing science? The objection has no validity, because all it can offer in opposition is another problematization. This problematization of science is immanent to science itself; Kant does not ask whether science is useful from moral, religious, social, and other standpoints (the representatives of the sciences themselves often fail to understand this—they think that philosophers discuss their particular science from some alien, "philosophical" point of view). Hermann Cohen's error: It is not the cognition of art that is problematical, but art itself; meanwhile, the forgetting of the secondary nature of ethics and aesthetics turns the philosopher into a man who takes the side of one particular party; ethics problematizes the State itself, and so on (and not the science dealing with the State); it does not take possession of the State, but will be itself taken prisoner by the State.—The objection in regard to Kant's philosophy being historically conditioned: All we need to do in order to obtain a problematization in this case is to require a nonconditioned philosophy; philosophy needs nothing more than that.

*   *   *

Only the Marburg school has stayed with the terminology of the *Einleitung*,[115] discarding *Anschauung*[116] and *Begriff*[117]—the former as a psychological moment in a judgment and the latter as an abstract one. Thus, the contraposition of the three—*Anschauung, Begriff,* and *Urteil*[118]—is discarded, and only *Urteil* is left; the proper place for a judgment is only among other judgments, i.e., in a system. A judgment tends toward a system; the proper place for it is not, of course, in my psyche. This company of judgments is innumerable; as soon as the number of judgments is restricted, we find ourselves outside the bounds of science; a judgment is conceivable only in an infinite context of judgments; orienting oneself in relation to science consists in orienting oneself in relation to a fundamentally and essentially open and unlimited system of judgments. But why judgment? Why does Cohen place sensation on the very margin of his system? Because sensation is primary only in the subjective unity; the only way it becomes part of science is by passing through a series of judgments. My own sensation, which may be at the center of my own life, occupies a very modest place in science where it is only a question and not an answer. That is why sensation [occupies a place] at the beginning of philosophy only where the [philosophical] position is not stringent.—The same applies to intuiting in Kant—it is a deviation from the proper position, an illegitimate substitution of scientific consciousness for science; Kant's right and left gloves constitute a subject of psychology, not philosophy. What we reject is the psychological as well as the historical determination of science, and we reject in general any determination of the mode of being to which science belongs; this mode of being we determine ourselves. The theory of cognition creates a special mode of being:[119] philosophical being, culture. This is a specific mode of being that does not coincide with the natural-scientific, historical, psychological [modes of] being. One should beware, however, of the term "ideal being," because of its metaphysical character, [where] the spatio-temporal causes appear to exist in consciousness; [we should beware] in general of ascribing being to that which in principle has *only* special *philosophical* being. We have to be more modest and leave the judgment *only* in science; [we must avoid] putting more into this concept than we need, [avoid] enriching it.

The Fourth Lecture (October 25, 1924)

The psychological makeup of cognition can be found only by proceeding from the fact of science; to meet with the *subiectum* by proceeding from within science is the only right way [of doing it]. At the beginning of philosophy, the problem of sense-perception and other problems of the subjective consciousness cannot even arise. That is why Kant proceeds quite correctly from the judgment; a judgment of physics, and so on, is taken from within physics itself, and so on, and not in the contexture of subjective consciousness that is itself in need of unity. But already in the Transcendental Aesthetic, Kant becomes unfaithful to his own position in the *Einleitung*, engendering a need for the intuition of space and time; the result is that we appear to obtain objective unity from within subjective consciousness, whereas in reality the objective unity is presupposed by the very formulation of the problem. If, on the other hand, we take the course of subjective cognition at the very beginning of our path, we immediately complicate it with ethical, religious, aesthetic adjuncts.—Thus, knowledge is an objective system of judgments; the only possible company for judgments are other judgments; outside [the company of other judgments] a judgment is not a judgment at all; a judgment has life only within the system of other judgments. This prosaism is indispensable at the beginning of the path [followed by] philosophy, because any enrichment of the judgment at the beginning of that path takes place at the expense of its subsequent stages; any premature condensation that deviates from the method can ruin all subsequent work.

The other characteristics of the judgment in Kant are its synthetic and *a priori* nature. "Synthetic" means "nondogmatic," [that is,] it signifies the absence of anything finished and available, where all that is left for us to do is analyze it; "it has turned out to be," "it already exists"—[these expressions] correspond to the basic tendency of cognition to describe itself as something already given, i.e., the tendency [specific to] passivity.[120] The concepts of the synthetic and the analytic need to be broadened; the connection [of the synthetic] with the analytic is not something instituted, but something directly present.[121] Kant meant to say that a revelation that would contain a judgment within itself does not exist. What is at issue in cognition is the birth of a judgment anew; the synthetic judgment is the instituting of a connection that cognition does not find anywhere as something already on hand.[122] Cognition is synthetic throughout, while analysis is only a technique; analysis is not a characterization of cognition; an analytical judgment is not a judgment at all.

In the *Einleitung*, apriority is conceived very purely—*not* as being-prior-to-experience (neither in the temporal—*sic!*—nor in the valuative sense, [i.e.,] apriority is *not* "higher," and so on). In the *Einleitung*, apriority is primary in the system of judgments only in respect of method. In any other sense apriority may also occur but not at the beginning of the path.

And thus, what is problematized is the system of judgments, the interconnection of which is instituted *for the first time*, and this is done in the following way.

Kant's first argument for proving the apriority of space (that space is already necessary for perception, and so on)[123] already attests that he proceeds from the standpoint of subjective consciousness, from the standpoint of the horizon, i.e., not from that of science (geometry, for example). The second argument: one cannot disregard space as intuiting.[124] The disputes [about it] were conducted naively: "Should we not verify whether it really cannot be disregarded . . . ?" But what is at fault here is the very formulation of the problem in Kant: whether one can or cannot *have a presentation* [of it][125] has nothing to do with the question of whether one can or cannot *operate* [with it].—Thus the second argument goes back to the same corporeal-psychic standpoint.

The third argument, which distinguishes between discursiveness and intuition, deteriorated Aristotle's schematism, because Kant's concepts are, evidently, not the concepts that have life in science. Kant is constantly on the verge of a presentation [*Vorstellung*] of space as an object—an aesthetic point of view that demonstrates brilliantly that what Kant has in view all the time is the space of the horizon (a space that has parts, and so on), whereas geometry does not know any space that constitutes a whole, so that the designation "aesthetics" turns out to be unexpectedly justified![126]—In order to contrast the concept "a human being" to a single human being, one would need to turn the concept into a species comprising a single being. The intuition of space, as something that is distinguished from other productive concepts, is not relevant; what remains is only the concept of space.

The fourth argument concerning the infinity of space also goes back to the infinity of any concept. Whether we can or cannot imagine space to be noninfinite is an irrelevant question. There are no grounds for isolating space from everything else. As far as scientific cognition is concerned—all this can enter into it only by way of [introjection from outside].—This is a true description of seeing, but not of the logic of science.

The proposal that we introduce the terms "spatiality" and "temporality" into philosophy, while leaving space and time for aesthetics.[127] A chasm separates the logic of intuiting and the logic of science, and it is impossible to derive one from the other. As for Kant, all he has is the logic of the horizon, i.e., of the *subiectum*.

The Fifth Lecture

Later on, Kant does return to the correct point of view: Here is space—what is its role in science?

The subjectivity of space must be cast aside because geometry does not pose this question at all. It is another matter, however, [when we have to do with] the following proposition: everything that appears in experience is spatially localized. Space is real, because one cannot acknowledge the reality of an object without a univocal space; all that exists in nature is inevitably localized spatially.—The space that is ideal is not the empirical but the transcendental space (what would be empirically ideal is a unicorn, and so on); transcendental ideality, on the other hand, signifies that space is indispensable for experience and knowledge—and only for [them]; that is why that-which-exists-outside-the-bounds-of-space is irrelevant. Space is conditioned throughout by the limits of experience.

Time as well is treated by Kant within the unity of the subjective horizon. The time that Kant deals with is not the time in which one performs a calculation (because it does not presuppose a temporal image). Musical time is another matter entirely—musical time is a temporal image throughout. It is *only with this* (aesthetic) time that the theory of relativity comes into conflict. This is the space and time in which an aesthetic image is constructed.

A mathematical series is not a temporal series; the succession of numbers operates with time only as an image (instrumentally), whereas Kant grounds the interconnection of number with time *not* as an image.

The Sixth Lecture

Bergson's theory leads to the attempt to explain culture in its entirety as a superstructure; even cognition itself turns out to be fortuitous from the standpoint of the philosophical basis he found. This is not yet in itself an objection, of course, but merely a psychological localization of Bergson's theory among other "impoverishing" theories.[128] Bergsonianism starts, of course, with the *subiectum;* the *subiectum*, meanwhile, is an exemplar (productive in biology and psychology) and the *subiectum's* consciousness has the character of an exemplar. It should be clear that such a conception of the *subiectum* will not satisfy Bergson, nor in general a philosophy with [similar] pretensions, i.e., a philosophy that needs a presuppositionless *subiectum*. Bergson needs a disempiricized *subiectum*, and he arrives at such a *subiectum* by way of a highly oversimplified method: by way of an act of empathizing, [i.e.,] by coinciding with this *subiectum*. In Kantian terms this would mean that the cogency of reality is achieved only by identifying with reality. Bergson goes even further; even I and you, I and thing, already constitute a superstructure. Whereas the primordial is a unity of reality that knows no differentiation—which relates Bergson to mysticism (as any intuitivism does), because that act of empathizing no longer belongs to me alone but constitutes a fact either of historical or cosmic life (for example, the everlasting birth of Christ in the soul, in Meister Eckhart).[129] The apprehension of reality by the *subiectum* in such a way that the *subiectum* loses his localization—already constitutes mysticism; whereas returning to the localization—already constitutes a regression. A physicist, meanwhile, without losing his localization and the uniqueness of his place [in being], enters into communion with life through culture and science—which, for Bergson, is a path of regression. The little corner [occupied by] culture is, for him, a distortion of the truly-existent; to discredit this corner (to prove the nullity of our experience) [he uses] the famous example of the *Sphex*, and so on.[130] Intuiting has become the highest value, which is attained by forgetting culture in its entirety,—culture being a small superstructure that disintegrates at its first contact with reality. Bergson's single *subiectum* is not the result of fragmentizing the world for the purpose of pragmatic cognition; it is rather the cosmic *subiectum*. As for reality, it is that which has been experienced by the cosmic *subiectum*, which makes it extremely difficult to argue with Bergson.—A crude anthropocentrism would be the only world-picture for "possible" experience. In determining what reality is, it is impossible to refer to the actual and the possible experience of a fictitious *subiectum*; the only thing we can settle on is time, taken from science, and not on the nonexistent lived-experience of time; time is not an object of lived-experience, time is itself the precondition of scientific experience.

The logical series of successive consequences is free from the presupposition of time; time is not part of the logical series, and it is founded by way of a qualitative evaluation because I am in need of the unity of time in order to be able to evaluate the moments of time.—What is also unconnected with the temporal series is the consequentiality or consistency of the logical succession (the conclusion does not come "after" [in a temporal sense] the premises).—The extra-temporal ethical series of successive values merely *borders on* the temporal series, but, abstractly, the two have to be stringently distinguished (from the lowest level of appeal to the highest or conversely). In the religious domain, the hierarchy of the ethical series [illegible][131] into time (*first* God, and *then* the world). While in the numerical series there is no *gravitation* toward time, the ethical series exhibits an evident gravitation toward taking possession of time; thus, its *bordering on* the temporal series is unquestionable (what is trenchantly distinguished from this [bordering-on] is becoming invested with psychological time, which is of no concern to philosophy).

The Seventh and Eighth Lectures, the Ninth Lecture

[M. M. BAKHTIN'S OBJECTIONS DURING THE DISCUSSION OF M. I. TUBIANSKY'S PAPER]

M. I. Tubiansky's Paper

The critique[132] of the *Wunschtheorie*[133] is outdated, because Schell[134] could not have foreseen psychoanalysis.[135]—The promise of Revelation—as a maternal milieu (Revelation "mitigates" the imbalance between the ideal and the sensuous).—It is precisely this *assistance* that is unacceptable and impossible from the *religious* standpoint. Miracles and Revelation are impossible *not* because they violate the laws of nature, but because the laws of nature exist precisely *in order to* make them impossible. Revelation and miracles are impossible [for the following reasons]:

(1) In order that the world could exist—if miracles exist, the world loses all sense. The meaningfulness and the physiognomy of the world are possible only on the condition that miracles and Revelation be absent. (2) Miracles and Revelation must not exist, in order that the human being could exist; it is true that moral requirements would be observed, but [they would be observed] out of fear and hope, and instead of a moral person there would be a superb marionette, [that is,] the stock of motives would change so much that morality itself would become impossible. Why do souls, according to Proclus,[136] have to drink from the waters of Lethe before becoming embodied? The field of force around human beings would change the whole character of their earthly activity. "The veil of mercifulness conceals . . .":[137] to violate this mercifulness would be both cruel and unwise. (3) Miracles and Revelation must not exist also for the sake of the human being's relationship to God because if there were the slightest *certainty*, then merit and the possibility of faith would be invalidated. In order for religion to be possible, [the darkness of] night is needed between the two worlds. As for the position that demands *assistance*, it is the position of a child, whereas providing such assistance is a maternal position.—Now the positive answer [to the question]: Where *is* the interconnection between the two worlds? The interconnection is threefold: (1) The common revelation in life, in the individual person, in history—"God has divided his worlds with soundlessly lapping Lethes,"[138] divining—"shepherded by Goals that are native to us, . . ." "burn on, o unriscn star!," "we bloom towards them out of darkness." (2) Myths that sing softly of the world beyond, a quiet interconnection—I seek to touch the hem of [his] garment.[139] (3) The postulates of practical reason.

M. M.'s [Bakhtin's] Objections

Why would the world lose its physiognomy only if natural laws did not obtain? Why wouldn't the world also lose its determinateness if the Revelation were absent from it? Revelation characterizes the world just as much as natural laws do. Even more than that: even without the existence of *several* revelations that contend with each other, and of which only one is true, the world and history would also change in their physiognomy.—Faith and certainty[140] can be contrasted only if one takes them abstractly; in their concreteness one does not exclude the other.—Mikhail Izrailevich[141] both trusts and distrusts the human being and puts both too much on the human being's shoulders (taking up the position of the father) and too little (once he has come to know God, the human being cannot be a moral person, and so on . . .). In Christianity, meanwhile, trust and distrust are ideally conjoined—this is a very important point in the Christian religion.[142]—If the moral law can be founded only from within, then any other attitude toward the world becomes invalid, except for the attitude of bare rationality; Mikhail Izrailevich, meanwhile, does accept whisperings or sudden inspirations from above.—This is not a refusal to accept Revelation but a typical *fear* of Revelation. Cf. the people who are afraid of accepting a favor, afraid of becoming obligated; what we are dealing with here is precisely the *fear* of receiving a gift, and thereby obligating oneself too much. What always arises on this basis around religion is the fear of obligating oneself. This is a typical cultural specialization, and it is here (Protestantism) that the fear of being disturbed is engendered. Why would I need the Church, if I have a *Fach?*[143] The tendency to achieve salvation in one's own place in the world.

M. M. Bakhtin [Lecture] (November 1, 1925)

St. Augustine[144] against the Donatists[145] subjected inner experience to a much more fundamental and essential criticism than psychoanalysis does. [The utterance] "Lord, I believe, help thou mine unbelief"[146] finds the same thing in inner experience that psychoanalysis does.—Assistance is needed not for the sake of the object of faith but for the purity of faith itself.—Revelation is characterized not by assistance but by the Person who *wants* to reveal Himself; one of the most important moments in Revelation is its being personal. That is why the problems of Revelation could not be even touched upon in Mikhail Izrailevich's paper. [What characterizes the Revelation is] precisely the relationship of two consciousnesses, [our] being likened to God,[147] and that changes the formulation of the problem radically, because personhood, as the form of God in Revelation, pertains to the *subiectum* as well. What constitutes the *subiectum* of Revelation is not an especially qualified consciousness, not just a single consciousness, but *all* consciousnesses in their singularity; the personhood of God and the personhood of all the believers is a constitutive feature of religion. That is why the *argumentum ad hominem*[148] is perfectly admissible in religion, so that the logic of religion is completely different from that of philosophy: a personal relationship to a personal God—that is the distinguishing feature of religion, but that is also what constitutes the special difficulty of religion, owing to which there may arise a distinctive fear of religion and of Revelation, a fear of the personal orientation, a desire to orient oneself within a single object-related [consciousness], within one single meaning, as within something that is exempt from sinning. It is in relation to this kind of cultural immanentism[149] that contemporary neo-Judaism, fearing the personal God, orients itself. What characterizes this cultural immanentism is the striving to answer *ex cathedra*,[150] and not on one's own behalf, not personally; to answer in a single consciousness, to answer systematically as an ethical, moral, and so on *subiectum.* This is an attempt to enact an event with only one participant; meanwhile, there is a fundamental and essential injustice, a fundamental and essential irrationality in the event as such; the Incarnation in itself has destroyed the unity of the Kantian person.—Owing to the omission of the Person in Revelation in Mikhail Izrailevich's argument, Revelation has assumed a *reified* character, [the character] of something transmitted. [On the one hand,] the reification of Revelation, the forgetting of the gift and of the Giver of the gift, [and on the other,] the state of bald questioning and the absolutization of need—need itself is needed, and nothing more.[151]

Notes

1. This introduction by N. I. Nikolaev was translated by Leonid Livak and revised by Alexandar Mihailovic. It has been extensively revised with additional annotations by Vadim Liapunov. Notes marked with an asterisk are by Vadim Liapunov; additions to Nikolaev's notes are placed in brackets.

2. [The following list of Bakhtin's works translated into English has been ordered in the sequence of the original publication dates in Russian which Nikolaev cites.] (1) "The Problem of Content, Material, and Form in Verbal Art," in *Art and Answerability: Early Philosophical Essays by M. M. Bakhtin,* edited by Michael Holquist and Vadim Liapunov; translation and notes by Vadim Liapunov; translation of "PCMFVA" by Kenneth Brostrom (Austin: Univ. of Texas Press, 1990), 257–325. (2) "Art and Answerability," in *Art and Answerability,* 1–3. (This was Bakhtin's first publication, which appeared in 1919.) (3) "Author and Hero in Aesthetic Activity," in *Art and Answerability,* 4–208; 231–54. (4) *Toward a Philosophy of the Act,* translation and notes by Vadim Liapunov; edited by Vadim Liapunov and Michael Holquist (Austin: Univ. of Texas Press, 1993). (5) "Author and Hero in Aesthetic Activity (Fragment of the First Chapter)," in *Art and Answerability,* 208–31; 254–56.

3. This additional information is for the most part presented in Katerina Clark and Michael Holquist, *Mikhail Bakhtin* (Cambridge: Harvard Univ. Press, 1984). A characterization of the discussions among the friends who made up the Nevel school, as well as some observations about the overall tendency of their thinking, can be found in the preface to "M. M. Bakhtin i M. I. Kagan (Po materialam semeinogo arkhiva)" published by K. Nevel'skaia [a pseudonym of M. I. Kagan's daughter, Iu. M. Kagan] in *Pamiat': Istorichesky sbornik* 4 (1981): 250.

4. *Den' iskusstva* published, in addition to Bakhtin's article "Art and Answerability," three short articles by Kagan; by this time Pumpiansky had already moved to Vitebsk.

5. The list was published in L. Mikheeva, *I. I. Sollertinsky: Zhizn' i nasledie* (Leningrad, 1988), 28–29.

6. *"Vy ochen' nam nedostaete"*: Pumpiansky uses a calque from the French *"vous nous manquez"* (translators' note).

7. Cf. also the review of materials from M. I. Kagan's papers (published in the newspaper *Sovetskaia Mordoviia,* July 24, 1988) in *Voprosy literatury,* no. 7 (1989): 282.

8. M. M. Bakhtin, "Discourse in the Novel," in *The Dialogic Imagination: Four Essays by M. M. Bakhtin*, ed. Michael Holquist, trans. Caryl Emerson and Michael Holquist (Austin: Univ. of Texas Press, 1981), 259–422.

9. L. V. Pumpiansky, "Gogol'," in *Uchenye zapiski Tartusskogo gos. Universiteta*, v. 664 (1984): 125–37; "Vechera na khutore bliz Dikan'ki; O 'Zapiskakh sumasshedshego' N. V. Gogolia," in *Prepodavanie literaturnogo chteniia v estonskoi shkole* (Tallinn, 1986), 100–26.

10. [*Dostoevsky and Antiquity*: a lecture read at the Free Philosophical Association on October 2, 1921.]

11. Clark and Holquist, *Mikhail Bakhtin*, 54–62.

12. M. I. Kagan, "Kak vozmozhna istoriia?" ["How is History Possible?"](Iz osnovnykh problem filosofii istorii), in *Zapiski Orlovskogo gos. universiteta* (1921), 137–92.

13. M. I. Kagan, "German Kogen" ["Hermann Cohen"], in *Nauchnye izvestiia* v. 2 (1922): 110–24.

14. M. I. Kagan, "O Pushkinskikh poemakh," in *V mire Pushkina* (Moscow, 1974), 85–119.

15. Clark and Holquist, *Mikhail Bakhtin*, 54, 63.

16. Kagan, "German Kogen," 123.

17. M. Kagan, "Zur Logik der elementaren mathematischen Rechenoperationen," *Zeitschrift für Philosophie und philosophische Kritik* (1915); "Versuch einer systematischen Beurteilung der Reliogiosität in Kriegzeit," *Archiv für systematische Philosophie* v. 22 (1916): 31–53.

18. The very title of Bakhtin's work could be matched with certain passages in Cohen's writings. For example, cf. H. Cohen, *Ästhetik des reinen Gefühls*, v. 1 (Berlin, 1912), 395.

19. G. Simmel, "Das individuelle Gesetz. Ein Versuch über das Prinzip der Ethik," *Logos* 4 (1913): 159. Nikolaev quotes from the Russian translation of Simmel's essay published in the Russian-language *Logos*: "Individual'nyi zakon: K istolkovaniiu printsipa etiki" (*Logos* [SPb., M.] tom. 1, vypusk 2 [1914], 244–49; cf. 247).*

20. H. Cohen, *Ethik des reinen Willens* (Berlin, 1904), 338–52.

21. Kagan, "Kak vozmozhna istoriia?" 179.

22. Grinev is the main character of Pushkin's *Captain's Daughter.*

23. "*Ubi, quo loco*": Latin, "Where, in what place?"

24. Clark and Holquist, *Mikhail Bakhtin*, 57.

25. "Moral reality": also called moral being, actual being, serious reality.

26. Kagan, "German Kogen," 122–23.

27. Cohen, *Ethik des reinen Willens*, 452.

28. Ibid., 68.

29. All of the texts published here come from one of Pumpiansky's working

notebooks, dating from 1923 to 1925. The bulk of the 1919–25 materials from his papers is found in similar schoolboy notebooks or exercise books filled with minute handwriting (a page of text corresponds to one third of a printer's sheet), containing his own works, summaries of the books he had studied, and detailed outlines of the school courses he had taught. Judging by cross-references, most of the notebooks of this period have survived. However, we were unable to find in Pumpiansky's papers many of the articles and lectures by him about which we know from the periodical press of those years, and including the works mentioned in Bakhtin's letter to M. I. Kagan dated January 18, 1922. The texts with no date of entry are provided with an approximate date according to their location among other works. Pumpiansky's "Lists of Books I Have Studied, Read, or Glanced Through" for particular periods are also helpful in establishing dates. These lists of books, taking into account almost continuously the years 1920–25, and containing scores of titles, allow us to judge unerringly about Pumpiansky's research interests during those years.

The texts of Bakhtin published here are written in ink, in regular handwriting, characteristic of Pumpiansky's book summaries. Bakhtin's lectures, however, are written down in ink of a different color and in pencil, filling the blank spaces left between the entries made in the summer of 1924.

In the present publication, all abbreviations made by Pumpiansky are spelled out. Square brackets contain possible variants of abbreviated words and names, written here in full.

30. Pumpiansky's notes were edited and annotated by N. I. Nikolaev, and are translated here with additional annotations by Vadim Liapunov.

31. Mikhail Izrailevich Tubiansky (1893–1937): Orientalist, a pupil of the eminent Orientalists F. I. Shcherbatskoy and S. F. Ol'denburg; did research in Buddhism and Hinduism. He was the first translator of Rabindranath Tagore from Bengali into Russian. In Pumpiansky's notebooks, Tubiansky's name appears for the first time in the notes of the discussion of Keyserling's book at the beginning of March 1923.

32. *"Hypotheses non fingo"* (Latin: "I do not frame hypotheses or suppositions"): cf. in Sir Isaac Newton's *Principia:* "Hitherto we have explained the phenomena of heavens and of our sea by the power of gravity. . . . But hitherto I have not been able to discover the cause of those properties of gravity from phenomena, and I frame no hypotheses; for whatever is not deduced from the phenomena is to be called an hypothesis; and hypotheses, whether metaphysical or physical, whether of occult qualities or mechanical, have no place in experimental philosophy. In this philosophy particular propositions are inferred from the phenomena, and afterwards rendered general by induction." Sir Isaac Newton, *Mathematical Principles of Natural Philosophy and His System of the World,* translated into English by Andrew Motte in 1729. The translations are revised, and supplied with an historical and

explanatory appendix, by Florian Cajori (Berkeley: Univ. of California Press, 1960), 546–47, and commentary on Newton's stand against hypotheses, 671–76.*

33. Most probably, Pumpiansky made this entry ["Comments during the Discussion of Pumpiansky's Report on F. W. H. Myers's Book"] between the end of May and the beginning of June 1924. From the middle of 1923 to the middle of 1924, he assiduously studied the literature on metapsychic and parapsychological phenomena. His notebooks are filled with summaries of books by Charles Richet, William James, Henri Bergson, and of the *Proceedings* of the Society for Psychical Research, founded in London in 1882. A significant place in the notebook of 1923–25 is occupied by a highly detailed summary of the book *Human Personality and Its Survival of Bodily Death* (London, 1903) by Frederic William Henry Myers (1843–1901), the well-known researcher of psychic phenomena; the book contains a vast quantity of materials concerning supernatural phenomena, as well as an interpretation of these phenomena. [For introductory information on F. W. H. Myers (including a discussion of his posthumous magnum opus), see the *Encyclopedia of Occultism and Parapsychology*, 4th ed., ed. J. Gordon Melton, 2 vol. (Detroit: Gale, 1996).] Fascinated by the subject of psychical research, Pumpiansky wrote two articles at that time—"On the Possible Significance of the Development of Metapsychical Sciences" and "On the Possible Consequences of the Development of Metapsychical Sciences," in which he forecasts the consequences of further progress in the study of metapsychical phenomena for philosophy, culture, and the life of humanity. Pumpiansky presented a number of reports on this subject at the Nevel school meetings that resumed after Bakhtin's arrival in Leningrad in the spring of 1924. Pumpiansky's notes below concern the discussion of one of these reports—a summary of F. W. H. Myers's book. Soon after this discussion, Pumpiansky presented his concluding report on the subject, and from July 1924 on we find no further entries on the subject of metapsychical phenomena. These studies, however, were not fruitless. At the end of the 1920s, Pumpiansky applied his knowledge brilliantly in the analysis of [what are known as] Turgenev's "mysterious" novellas of 1860–70 (L. V. Pumpiansky, "Gruppa 'tainstvennykh' povestei," in I. S. Turgenev, *Sochineniia*, vol. 8 [Moscow-Leningrad: GIZ, 1929)], v–xx). Pumpiansky's notes of the discussion published here also indicate the format of these discussions of reports and papers. One more example of such a discussion dates from the beginning of March 1923, when Pumpiansky presented a report on Count Hermann Keyserling's book, *Das Tagebuch eines Philosophen* (1919). The participants of the discussion of that report included M. I. Kagan and M. I. Tubiansky.

34. Nikolai Iosifovich Konrad (1891–1970): outstanding Orientalist and member of the Academy of Sciences. Kagan became friends with Konrad in 1920–21 when he was teaching at Orel University, where Konrad served as a rector. It is possible that in the fall of 1922, when Kagan came to Petrograd, he and Pumpiansky made the acquaintance of Tubiansky through Konrad.

35. The value aspect of the problem of immortality is examined by Bakhtin in his "Author and Hero in Aesthetic Activity" ("A&H" 100–1, 110–11): "It [the problem] concerns the soul as situated on one and the same plane with the other's outer body and as indissociable from it in the moment of death and immortality (resurrection in the flesh)" (101).

36. Most probably, Pumpiansky made this entry, "Hero and Author in Artistic Creation: A Series of Lectures by M. M. Bakhtin," in July 1924. The title of the series of lectures, "Hero and Author in Artistic Creation," its plan and content, allow us to say that this is an exposition of Bakhtin's work written in Vitebsk, "Author and Hero in Aesthetic Activity" [both the long text and the fragment of the first chapter], whose title, provided by its editor, was, as we can see now, very close to the original one. Since the beginning of "Author and Hero in Aesthetic Activity" has been lost, we can suppose that the lecture notes published here give us an idea about the missing part. At the same time, these lecture notes can be regarded as an exposition (cf. notes 39–48) of the 1924 article "The Problem of Content, Material, and Form in Verbal Art." Thus, one can pose the question of the sources of "The Problem of Content, Material, and Form in Verbal Art" and the question of a possible reconstruction of the missing beginning of "Author and Hero."

On the one hand, we can suppose that the article "The Problem of Content" is a reworked version of the missing beginning of "Author and Hero." "Author and Hero," in which we find a "phenomenological description of the axiological consciousness of oneself and of one's consciousness of the other in the event of being" ("A&H" 188), continues the investigation of moral being discovered in *Toward a Philosophy of the Act,* but does so within the framework of philosophical aesthetics and by means of the concepts of "author" and "hero"; whereas in the article "The Problem of Content" (written especially for the periodical *Russkii sovremennik*), Bakhtin sets forth from the standpoint of philosophical aesthetics his understanding of fundamental concepts in poetics, paying special attention to the Russian "formal method" as one of the trends in "material aesthetics." That is why one can isolate in the text of "The Problem of Content" those layers that go back directly to the lost beginning of "Author and Hero," those that represent the reworked and expanded parts of "Author and Hero," as well as newly written sections. What should be assigned to the layers going back to the missing beginning are the following segments of the article's text: in the chapter "The Problems of Content," from the chapter's beginning on page 274 to the end of the fourth paragraph on page 282; and from the beginning of the second paragraph on page 285 to the end of the chapter on page 291; in the chapter "The Problem of Material," from the beginning of the second paragraph on page 296 to the end of the second paragraph on page 303; in the chapter "The Problem of Form," probably from the beginning of the second paragraph on page 304 to the end of the fifth paragraph on page 307. The text of the first chapter of "Hero and Author in Artistic Creation" in Pumpiansky's lecture notes finds its analogues in the article "The Problem of Content" precisely in the layers we isolated (cf. notes 40–44). The legitimacy of isolating these layers is confirmed by a loose end that was not removed in the article "The Problem of Content." In the article Bakhtin writes that, "Later on we shall have to consider in greater detail the so-called aesthetics of empathy" ("PCMFVA" 286, note h). The "aesthetics of empathy" is analyzed by him, however, in the treatise "Author and Hero in Aesthetic Activity" ("A&H" 61–92). Finally, the text that in Pumpiansky's lecture notes corresponds to the introduction was probably expanded and reworked into the chapter "The Study of Art and General Aesthetics" ("PCMFVA" 257–74).

The following segments from the first chapter of "Author and Hero" were reflected in a reworked form in the article "The Problem of Content": on the thematic aspect of content (cf. "PCMFVA" 301 and "A&H (FFC)" 220–22); on the ordering of meaning (cf. "PCMFVA" 310–11 and "A&H (FFC)" 209–10); on intonation (cf. "PCMFVA" 311–12 and "A&H (FFC)" 215–19); and on realistic intonation in particular (cf. "PCMFVA" 312 and "A&H (FFC)" 216); on the interrelationship of author and hero; and on the human being as the subject of aesthetic vision (cf. "PCMFVA" 316–18 and "A&H (FFC)" 222–30).

Another part of "Author and Hero," which deals with the problem of overcoming language as a linguistic *determinatum*, is also reflected in "The Problem of Content" (cf. "PCMFVA" 292–97, 307–10, and "A&H" 192–94). In his detailed discussion of this problem in the article "The Problem of Content," Bakhtin introduces for the first time such concepts as "utterance," "utterances from everyday life," "linguistic construction," and "the unity of cognitive utterance" ("PCMFVA" 292–93, 309–10) that played such an important role in his subsequent works. Bakhtin's reflections in "Author and Hero" on the possible substitution of a literary context for the author's valuative context also find their analogue in "The Problem of Content" (cf. "PCMFVA" 282–84 and "A&H" 195–98). Thus, the only sections not linked to Bakhtin's previous work are the short segments of "The Problem of Content" devoted to the analysis of such concepts of the Russian "formal method" as image or figure ("PCMFVA" 298–300) and "defamiliarization" [*ostranenie*] ("PCMFVA" 306–9).

On the other hand, even if the supposition that the lost beginning of "Author and Hero" was directly integrated into the article "The Problem of Content" were to turn out to be invalid, Bakhtin's 1924 article would still remain the first work of his openly expressed philosophy in which he presented (to satisfy the requirements of a particular occasion) a synthesis of all the main ideas of his previous works.

If we assume that Pumpiansky's lecture notes reflect the Nevel school's first exposure to Bakhtin's Vitebsk work, then we can also make a judgment about the time when "The Problem of Content" was written: most probably, it was written in July–September. Besides the fact that the periodical *Russkii sovremennik* was banned in the fall of 1924, October–November 1924 is the indicated date of the article "Uchenyi sal'erizm: o formal'nom (morfologicheskom) metode" ["Learned Salierism: On the Formal (Morphological) Method"] (*Zvezda*, no. 3 [1925]: 264–76), signed by P. N. Medvedev, but written undoubtedly by Bakhtin, because it reproduces the same critical argumentation for the inadequacy of the "formal method" as in "The Problem of Content," and also uses Bakhtin's philosophical terminology.

37. Followed by a blank in the manuscript.

38. *"Kunstwissenschaft"*: German, "the scientific study (science) of art."

39. Bakhtin treated the problem of special methods in the humanities throughout his entire career (cf. *SpG* 144–45; 159–72).

40. Jonas Cohn deals with the special intensiveness of aesthetic value, in comparison to other cultural values, in his *Allgemeine Äesthetik* (Leipzig, 1901).

41. Cf. "PCMFVA" 267–68. The category of purpose, or end, is one of the most important categories in the philosophy of neo-Kantianism, including the philosophy of Hermann Cohen.

42. Ibid., 274–75.

43. Ibid., 275–76.

44. Ibid., 276–77 (knowledge), 278 (ethics), 278–80 (aesthetics).

45. Ibid., 275–76, 278; also "A&H" 190.

46. Cf. "PCMFVA" 278–79. Due to the circumstances of that time, the term "religion" was replaced in the article "The Problem of Content" by the phrase "all of the kind, accepting and enriching, optimistic categories of human thinking about the world and man" (279). In the same segment, we read that reality is transfigured in aesthetic activity.

47. Ibid., 281.

48. Ibid., 286; on the problem of isolation, cf. "PCMFVA" 306–7.

49. Ibid., 370, 315–16.

50. Pumpiansky made this entry, "The Problem of Grounded Peace," most probably in June 1924. It is located on the same page with the preceding entry, and this location is, apparently, not accidental. "The Problem of Grounded Peace" can be seen as a kind of extract from "Author and Hero" for the construction of a philosophy of religion. As regards the notion of "grounded peace" ["peace" for the Russian word *pokoi*], along with its usual usage, the word *pokoi* is used as a physical concept ["rest"] and can also be used in ethics to describe moral states of being (cf., for example, Hermann Cohen, *Ethik des reinen Willens*, 165; Cohen, *Äesthetik des reinen Gefühls*, vol. 1, 208). Unlike Cohen's marginal use of this concept, Bakhtin uses "grounded peace" to designate a highly important category of religious experience. It should also be noted that in describing different spheres of reality, Bakhtin gives different meanings to the same concepts and determinations. Thus, in "Author and Hero," "grounded peace" is determined as a condition for aesthetic activity

("A&H" 205). In his moral philosophy, Bakhtin describes the answerable act as the "act which is performed on the basis of an acknowledgment of my obligative (ought-to-be) uniqueness" (*TPA* 42), whereas in the philosophy of religion, as the published account shows, he defines the consciousness of ought-to-be uniqueness as conscience.

51. For a helpful introduction to the notion of "world," see William E. Paden, *Religious Worlds* (Boston: Beacon Press, 1988), chap. 3.*

52. Kagan notes that, according to Hermann Cohen, "prayer, lyrical speaking to God, is a problem of religion" (Kagan, "German Kogen," 122).

53. According to Hermann Cohen, the posing of problems is a highly important characteristic of cognition: "The fact of the sciences and of science is posed as a problem"; "being is always problematic, it is always an unsolved riddle" (Kagan, "German Kogen," 114, 116).

54. "Event" is the fundamental concept of Bakhtin's moral philosophy (*TPA* 12–13, 15–16, 44–45; "A&H" 79).

55. Cf. *TPA* 16, 44.

56. Ibid., 15, 44–45; "A&H" 187–88.

57. Cf. *TPA* 40–42; "A&H" 118, 159.

58. Cf. *TPA* 16–17, 40–43; "A&H" 23. Cf. also the application of the notion of "impenetrability" in *Toward a Philosophy of the Act* (*TPA* 3–4, 6, 33–34, 40).

59. Cf. *TPA* 5–6, 12–13, 24–25, 39–42, 44–45, 56–57; "A&H" 118.

60. For the difference between the "ought" expressed in universally valid moral laws and the "ought" in Bakhtin's philosophy of the act, see *TPA* 5–6, 22–27; "A&H" 48–49; "PCMFVA" 278.

61. Ludwig Feuerbach (1804–1872): German philosopher. Bakhtin is referring to Feuerbach's critical writings against religion and Christianity, such as *Das Wesen des Christentums* (1841) or *Das Wesen der Religion* (1845).*

62. Here, in the philosophy of religion, Bakhtin illuminates in a new way the fundamental architectonic principle of his moral philosophy—the interrelationship of I and the other (*TPA* 41–42, 45–47, 53–54, 72–75; "A&H" 38, 86, 128–29, 148–49, 187–88)—just as he does other concepts. The correlation of I and the other is an element of Hermann Cohen's ethics. Cf. Hermann Cohen, *Ethik des reinen Willens*, 201–2. On the problem of the correlation between I and the other in European philosophy of the nineteenth and early twentieth centuries, see Tzvetan Todorov, *Mikhail Bakhtine: Le principe dialogique* (Paris, 1981), 151; and Nina Perlina, "Mikhail Bakhtin and Martin Buber: Problems of Dialogic Imagination," *Studies in Twentieth Century Literature* 9 (1984): 13–18.

63. On the impossibility of expressing and explaining moral reality in theoretical terms, cf. *TPA* 7–8, 24–25; "A&H" 79; "PCMFVA" 266, 289.

64. "A&H" 127–28.

65. Ibid., 145.

66. "My little hand" translates the Russian word *ruchka*, which is a form of the word "hand" specific to a child's language.*

67. Cf. Dennis E. Smith's article, "Table Fellowship," in *The Anchor Bible Dictionary*, vol. 6 (New York: Doubleday, 1992), 302–4; p. 303 (first column): "Meals as social institutions are characterized by the ways in which they define social boundaries in terms of who is excluded and who is included."*

68. Cf. "A&H" 47–48, 50–51, 111, 153–54. [The bridehood of the soul or the soul in the position of a bridegroom: Bakhtin uses biblical metaphors to characterize the loving relationship between myself and another. In both the Old Testament and the New Testament, the loving relationship between bride and bridegroom is invoked to express the spiritual relationship between God and his people (Isa. 54:1–6; 62:5) and between Christ and his church (2 Cor. 11:2); in Eph. 5:21–33 the relationship between husband and wife is explained in terms of the relationship that exists between Christ and his church.]

69. Cf. *TPA* 49; "A&H" 121–22, 152. Pumpiansky's attention was drawn to the problem of doubles and impostors as early as the Nevel period; cf. L. V. Pumpiansky, *Dostoevsky i antichnost'* (Petrograd, 1922).

70. Jesus told his disciples that they should rejoice because their names are "written in heaven" (Luke 10:20). "Written in heaven" goes back to the Old Testament "book of the living" (Ps. 69:28) in which God recorded the names of the living, specifically those who desire to be of his people (Ps. 87:6) and those who are in his special favor (Ps. 139:16). On the contrary, those who sinned are blotted out of his book (Exod. 32:33).*

71. This is a conjectural reading; in the manuscript this word is illegible. [In the Russian text, Nikolaev reconstructs the word as *spa[se]niia*, "of salvation."] The word could also be read as *znaniia* ["of knowledge"].

72. Repentance is one of the most important concepts of Bakhtin's moral philosophy. Cf. "A&H" 54–55, 56–57, 114–16, 119, 123, 126–27, 140–41, 143–44, 179–80.

73. Ibid., 16, 127–28, 143.

74. Ibid., 56–57, 101, 114.

75. Ibid., 142.

76. Ibid., 128.

77. Ibid., 144.

78. Ibid., 101–2, 143–44.

79. Ibid., 121–22, 123–24, 125–26; *TPA* 43 (absolute inability to achieve peace or rest contentedly).

80. Cf. "A&H" 144–45.

81. On faith, freedom, and their correlation, cf. "A&H" 127–28, 140–41, 144–45.

82. Ibid., 55–57, 128–29, 143–44.

83. These lecture notes (judging by the dates in the lecture notes of two of Bakhtin's lectures) date from October–November 1924. There are no records of the seventh, eighth, and ninth lectures. The surviving lectures are based on a discussion of the opening sections of Kant's *Critique of Pure Reason*. According to Kanaev's recollections, Bakhtin once delivered a series of lectures on Kant. It is possible that Pumpiansky's notes were taken during these lectures. In these lectures, Bakhtin gives a critical overview of the fundamental problems of European philosophy. Since in these years Bakhtin constantly takes into account the achievements of the Marburg school, all instances of agreement and disagreement with Cohen in these lectures are important. What deserves special attention in these lectures is the typology of philosophical systems, in the construction of which Bakhtin uses the experience gained in investigating the logic of the horizon of an act-performing consciousness in *Toward a Philosophy of the Act*, and in the investigation of the life of aesthetic consciousness in "Author and Hero" and "The Problem of Content."

84. Bakhtin is referring to Kant's *Critique of Pure Reason*, part 1: "Transcendental Aesthetics."

85. Heinrich Rickert (1863–1936): a distinguished German philosopher and one of the founders of the Heidelberg school (also the Baden school or Southwestern school) of neo-Kantianism.*

86. *"Leistung"*: German, "the result or product of work"; "something produced or effected." For other possibilities, see Dorion Cairns, *Guide for Translating Husserl* (The Hague: M. Nijhoff, 1973).*

87. Historical or intellectual psychology was developed in the works of Wilhelm Dilthey (1833–1911), [an eminent German philosopher who exerted considerable influence on the development of the *Geisteswissenschaften* ("the sciences of the spirit or mind," the human sciences, as opposed to the natural sciences). The word "intellectual" in "intellectual psychology" is a stopgap here. Bakhtin uses the Russian equivalent of the German *geistig* (from *Geist*, "spirit" or "mind"). In German, Dilthey's new psychology is usually called *geisteswissenschaftliche* or *verstehende Psychologie* (*verstehende* from *verstehen*, "to understand").]

88. Transgredience, i.e., being-situated-outside of, is one of the fundamental categories of Bakhtin's analysis of aesthetic consciousness in "Author and Hero."

89. "To hypostatize": according to Kant, to assume "as an actual object outside the thinking subject" "what exists merely in thoughts" (*Critique of Pure Reason* A 384); to turn one's "thoughts into things" (A 395); to posit mere presentations [*Vorstellungen*] outside oneself "as true things" subsisting by themselves (A 392); to reify, objectify, substantialize.*

90. "To substantialize": to render substantial. In the original, the word is the Russian equivalent of "to fix or fixate" (French *fixer*, German *fixieren*).*

91. Cf. *TPA* 52–53.

92. See "A&H" 12.*

93. Cf. *TPA* 52–53.

94. The clarification in parentheses belongs to Pumpiansky.

95. See note 90.

96. "Science" in the comprehensive sense of the German *Wissenschaft*, i.e., the natural sciences as well as the social sciences and the cultural or human sciences.*

97. *"Einheit"*: German, "unity."

98. "Scientist" here also includes "scholar."*

99. What is meant here and below is also a "historically nonactual *subiectum*— a universal consciousness, a scientific consciousness, an epistemological *subiectum*" (*TPA* 6) of modern European theoretical philosophy; cf. also "A&H" 88–90.

100. "Condensation" in the sense of "becoming more dense or compact in consistency," "becoming embodied."*

101. "Nexus": "contexture," or "interconnectedness." Cf. German *Zusammenhang*.*

102. The personification of "All this" occurs in the original.*

103. "A subjective arrangement": the use of the Russian word *ustroenie*, translated as "arrangement," is not entirely clear here. ("Subjective" is added from the way *ustroenie* is used several lines later.) Besides "arrangement" (an ordering of matters to suit me), one might also consider "accommodation," "adaptation."*

104. A more literal translation would be: "what hovers before the mind of the one who is thinking," i.e., what presents itself to him in an unsettled, undecided way. The uncommon Russian verb *prednosit'sia* is, most likely, a calque of the familiar German verb *vorschweben*.*

105. On Rudolf Steiner's anthroposophy, see R. von Maydell, "Anthroposophy in Russia," in *The Occult in Russian and Soviet Culture*, ed. Bernice Glatzer Rosenthal (Ithaca and London: Cornell Univ. Press, 1997), 153–67.*

106. "Mikhail Mikhailovich" is the name and patronymic of Bakhtin. This is a personal and respectful form of addressing or referring to a person in Russian.*

107. Plato's *Republic*.

108. Cf. "A&H" 38–40, 109–10; "PCMFVA" 280–81.

109. Cf. "A&H" 88–90.

110. Cf. *TPA* 11; "A&H" 134–35, "PCMFVA" 278–79.

111. The French phrase means: "When we are gone let happen what may!" That is, it does not matter what happens after we are gone—even if it is a disaster that destroys all life on earth, like the universal deluge.*

112. *"Kritizismus"* (German; Bakhtin uses the Russian adaptation of the German word): since Kant himself, this term has been used to designate Kant's critical philosophy in general, and in particular the requirement that, before constructing a system of knowledge, one must investigate the "possibility" of what is used and presented as knowledge, thus providing the methodical principles and means whereby we should achieve valid knowledge.*

113. Thales of Miletus (625?–547? B.C.): a famous Greek philosopher, astronomer, and geometer; the earliest of the Ionian natural philosophers.*

114. *"Durée"* (French, "duration, perduration"): a special term of Bergson's philosophy. *Durée*, as the immediately and qualitatively felt or lived time, is opposed to "time" (*temps*), as the mathematical time of science that we create by translating it into spatial images.*

115. *"Einleitung"*: German for "introduction." The reference is to the introduction to Kant's *Critique of Pure Reason.**

116. *"Anschauung"*: German for "intuition." Cf. A. C. Ewing, *A Short Commentary on Kant's Critique of Pure Reason* (1950; reprint, Chicago: Univ. of Chicago Press, 1938), 17–18: "The term *Anschauung* which occurs in B 8 [i.e., in the introduction to the second edition of the *Critique*] and in a vast number of other passages in the *Critique* is usually translated 'intuition,' but it has no connection with the sense in which this word is most commonly employed in English to-day as meaning *a priori* insight not based on reasoning. By derivation it is really 'a looking at,' and though this is also what 'intuition' should mean by derivation (*intueor*), *Anschauung* in Kant keeps much more closely to its etymological meaning, though intended to cover other senses beside sight. It means for Kant *awareness of individual entities*. In human beings this awareness can only occur in sense-perception (including introspection) [i.e., *Wahrnehmung*] . [. . .]."*

117. *"Begriff"*: German, "concept."

118. *"Urteil"*: German, "judgment."

119. Cf. Kagan, "German Kogen," 118–22.

120. Passivity in contrast to spontaneity, in the Kantian sense.*

121. "Something directly present" translates the Russian calque of the German *vorliegen.**

122. "Find as something already on hand" translates the Russian calque of the German *vorfinden.**

123. Space and time are dealt with in the two "sections" that make up the "Transcendental Aesthetic" in the *Critique of Pure Reason.*

124. "To disregard" translates the Russian equivalent of the German *abstrahieren von etwas*, "to leave something out of account or consideration."*

125. "To have a presentation" translates Kant's *vorstellen.**

126. Just as in German, the Russian form of the word "aesthetics" (German *Aesthetik*) in its current sense coincides with the form of the word Kant used to designate the transcendental doctrine of sense-perception—the Transcendental Aesthetic (German *Aesthetik*, from the Greek word *aisthesis*, "sense-perception").*

127. In analyzing aesthetic consciousness, Bakhtin, like Cohen in his ethics and aesthetics, uses the concepts of "space" and "time" not in their primary scientific sense but metaphorically.

128. On Bergson, see also *TPA* 13–14, 21; "A&H" 43, 62.

129. Meister Eckhart ("Meister" means "master"—that is how he was generally styled): the founder of German mysticism. Born about 1260; died about 1328.*

130. Bergson demonstrates the intuitive vision of life with the example of how the female wasp of the yellow-winged *Sphex* behaves. [*Sphex*—a notable genus of large digger-wasps, typical of the family Sphegidae (or Sphecidae).] See H. Bergson, *Sobranie sochinenii*, vol. 1 (St. Petersburg, 1913), 151–53.

131. A possible reading is "spills over."

132. Most probably, Pumpiansky made this entry, ["M. M. Bakhtin's Objections during the Discussion of M. I. Tubiansky's Paper"], in October 1925, because its content is related to the following published entry of November 1, 1925. Both entries belong to the period when the Nevel school studied theology during the winter of 1925–26. These studies are attested by the books on theology, including some by Russian Orthodox theologians, as recorded in Pumpiansky's "List of Books Studied, Read, or Glanced Through from April 20 to December 20, 1925." Pumpiansky mentions these studies in his 1926 letter to Kagan: "This year, my theological worldview has been established quite precisely and clearly: the Eastern Orthodox Church. Especially important was my study of H. Schell's *Apologie des Christentums* and my conviction that Kant's and Cohen's philosophy of religion was completely unsound.—But the deepening of my own views, as it always happens, brought me to a serious and considered tolerance based on respect for thought, for the labor of thought, for the personal being of the bearers of thought. Polemics yields to criticism. And in this regard as well, Schell is a great teacher" ("BiK" 266). The discussion of the problem of Revelation may have arisen during the study of Cohen's philosophy of religion, in which this problem occupies an important place. However, it is possible that there were also other sources for posing this problem (for instance, Schell's works). Both entries also represent an example of polemics that could flare up during the meetings of the Nevel school. Bakhtin's approach to the solution of this problem (the approach is in accord with the tradition of Eastern Christianity) follows from the core of his earlier works.

133. "*Wunschtheorie*" (German, "theory of wishes or wishing"): a particular theory (the wish-theory) of the nature of religion [belief in God or gods is a projection of human wishes]. Cf., for example, Ludwig Feuerbach's *Lectures on the Essence of Religion,* trans. Ralph Manheim, 22nd lecture (New York: Harper and Row, 1967), 199 (I have modified Manheim's translation by restoring the verb "to wish" or the noun "wishes" wherever they appear in the original): "Man believes in gods not only because he has imagination and feeling, but also because he has the striving to be happy. He believes in the existence of happy beings, not only because he has a conception of happiness, but because he himself wishes to be happy; he believes in a perfect being because he himself wishes to be perfect; he believes in an immortal being because he himself does not wish to die. What he himself is not but [wishes] to be, he conceives of as existing in his gods; the gods

are men's [wishes] conceived as realities, transformed into real beings. A god is man's striving for happiness, fulfilled in his imagination. For all man's imagination and feeling, he would have [no religion], no gods if he had no [wishes]. Gods are as varied as [wishes], and [wishes] as varied as men." The *Wunschtheorie* of religion belongs to those theories that Van A. Harvey treats as "projection theories" in his *Feuerbach and the Interpretation of Religion* (Cambridge: Cambridge Univ. Press, 1995).

Hermann Schell, in his *Apologie des Christentums*, 2 vols. (Paderborn, 1901 and 1905; reprint, 1967), criticizes Feuerbach's theory of "wish as the basis for explaining religion" at three points in the first volume (*Religion und Offenbarung*): 36, 49, 129.*

134. [Hermann Schell (1850–1906): an original and controversial German Catholic theologian.] One of Pumpiansky's notebooks contains a brief summary of Schell's life and work. Almost all of Schell's works are in Pumpiansky's list of books he had read from April 20 through December 1925.

135. If in the winter of 1925–26 the Nevel school members studied theology, they devoted the winter of 1924–25 to a discussion of psychoanalysis, as confirmed by the presence of Freud's major works and the works of other theoreticians of psychoanalysis in Pumpianksy's "List of the Books Studied, Read, or Glanced Through" from July 1, 1921, through December 20, 1925. At the same time, probably in January 1925, Pumpiansky wrote the article "On the Critique of [Otto] Rank and Psychoanalysis." Some materials, pertaining to the study of psychoanalysis during the same period, have survived among Sollertinsky's papers (cf. Mikheeva, *I. I. Sollertinsky*, 51–55). Another result of these discussions was the following works written by Bakhtin and published under V. N. Voloshinov's name: the article "Po tu storonu sotsial'nogo" ["On the Far Side of the Social"], *Zvezda*, no. 5 (1925): 186–214; and the book *Freidizm* [*Freudianism*] (Leningrad, 1927).

136. Proclus (about A.D. 411–485): the chief exponent of Neoplatonism in late antiquity.*

137. The quotation was identified by Nikolaev: it comes from the opening line of the prefatory sonnet "To the Reader" ["Chitateliu"] of the narrative poem in nine sonnets called "A Dispute" ["Spor," 1908] by the great Russian Symbolist poet, scholar, and philosopher Viacheslav Ivanovich Ivanov (1866–1949). Since Tubiansky, most likely, quoted the entire sonnet (or assumed that his listeners knew it), I provide a prose paraphrase:

To the Reader

The veil of mercifulness conceals God's secret:
Thirst quenched would kill the avid.
The attainment of full knowledge maddens the mind . . .
Let, then, the old world stay young through oblivion—and lies!
And let fear of Death, through saving shudders,

teach us that in the forges of heaven the fire has gone out,
in order that your mind, o guest on Earth, would not be sundered
and the wayfarer, astray, would not wander about the wayside.
And let the meanly closed-up hearts
know not that Death is an incestuous mixer of blood
and that the name of Death is—the Loving Cup.
And let the repining hearts, suffering because of separation
in the prison of a living corpse, let them
meet you, O Resurrector, you whom they did not expect!*

138. This quotation and the ones that follow were identified by Nikolaev:
they all come from various lines in another poem by Viacheslav Ivanov—"The
Eternal Gifts" ["Vechnye dary"], the penultimate poem in the fourth section
(entitled "The Flowers of Twilight") of Ivanov's 1902 book of poetry, *The Lodestars*
[*Kormchie zvezdy*]. Again, I am providing a prose paraphrase of the poem:

The Eternal Gifts

Believe in what your heart tells you:
There are no sureties from heaven.
—Zhukovsky (after Schiller)

"Walking across the pastures of oblivion—
Where do you come from, pilgrims? And where are you going? . . ."
"Blow on gently, o holy breezes!
Burn on, o unrisen star!

Shepherded by Goals that are native to us,
we travel, trembling, towards them—
and, as if beneath invisible suns,
we bloom towards them out of darkness.

God divided his worlds
with soundlessly lapping Lethes.
But the eternal gifts are kept safe by our heart's prophetic signs.

The one who knew you, o skiff of despair!—
for him love prophesied:
'I'll be yours once again on the shore of hope—
Surmised by you once again!' "

The quotation Ivanov uses as a motto to his poem comes from a poem by the great
Russian poet of the first half of the nineteenth century, and a genius of translation,

V. A. Zhukovsky (1783–1852). The poem is "Longing" ("Zhelanie," published in 1813); it is a translation of Schiller's poem "Sehnsucht" ("Ach, aus dieses Tales Gründen . . .", 1803). The lines quoted are the two penultimate lines of the poem both in Schiller and in Zhukovsky. Schiller's lines might be rendered as follows: "You must believe and you must dare, for the gods give us no surety." Bakhtin invokes the lines quoted by Ivanov in "Author and Hero."*

139. Tubiansky's example of "a quiet interconnection" between the two worlds, namely—"I seek to touch the hem of [his] garment," goes back to Matt. 9:20–22: "And behold, a woman, who had suffered from a hemorrhage for twelve years came up behind him and touched the fringe of his garment; for she said to herself, 'If I only touch his garment, I shall be made well.' Jesus turned, and seeing her he said: 'Take heart, daughter; your faith has made you well.' And instantly the woman was made well" (RSV). This same phrase as an expression of faith occurs also in Matt. 14:36.*

140. "Faith," "certainty," and also "trust" and "distrust," all have the same root in Russian, namely, "faith, belief." "Certainty," therefore, is the fact of being totally convinced or believing that something is the case indubitably. "Trust" is believing someone, having complete faith or confidence in someone. Note that faith and trust (fides) are part of the English word "confidence."*

141. "Mikhail Izrailevich" is the name and patronymic of Tubiansky. This is a personal and respectful form of addressing or referring to someone in Russian.*

142. Cf. "A&H" 201–3, 206.

143. "Fach": German, field of professional specialization, one's specialty (special field of study).*

144. Like the preceding one, this entry, ["M. M. Bakhtin's Lecture, November 1, 1925"], is located on different sheets of the 1923–25 notebook among materials belonging to an earlier period.

145. For a translation of St. Augustine's writings against the Donatists, see A Select Library of the Nicene and Post-Nicene Fathers of the Christian Church, ed. Philip Schaff, vol. 4 (Grand Rapids: Eerdmans, 1956). The Donatists were a Christian schismatic movement that developed after 311 and was active until the beginning of the fifth century.*

146. Mark 9:24. Cf. "A&H" 145.

147. Bakhtin's phrase "[our] being likened to God" recalls "Let us make man in our image, after our likeness" (Gen. 1:26, RSV). Cf. Greek homoiosis, Latin assimilatio. Cf. also the traditional way of understanding Revelation as that disclosure which God makes of himself and of his will to his creatures; hence, as containing such Revelation, the Bible.*

148. "Argumentum ad hominem" (Latin, argument addressed to a particular person): "an argument drawn from premises which, whether true or not, ought to be admitted by the person to whom they are addressed, either on account of his

peculiar beliefs or experience, or because they are necessary to justify his conduct or are otherwise conducive to his interest." *The Century Dictionary and Cyclopedia,* vol. 1 (New York: The Century Co., 1906), s.v. *"ad hominem."**

149. "Cultural immanentism": enclosing oneself within the bounds of a culture, and refusing to go beyond them.*

150. *"Ex cathedra"*: Latin, from the throne of a bishop in a cathedral; from the seat of high authority; with the authority that derives from one's rank or office.*

151. Cf. the use of the words "gift" and "need" in "Author and Hero" ("A&H" 100, 142–43; "A&H" 46–47, 123, 127–28, 142–43, 143–45).

Index

Act, answerable. *See* Answerability
Aesthetics: aesthetic double, 209; aesthetic
  sphere, 31; of author, 65, 70, 203, (aesthetic
  event) 51; Bakhtin's theology in form of, 5,
  47, 48, 56, 59, 212, (as ontology) 52, 54,
  57; Bakhtin's use of term, 42n5; in context
  of modernity, 48–50; ethical, *see* Ethics;
  gender bearings of, 57–58; and I/other, 50;
  philosophical, 206; religious aspect of, 2,
  207, (and theology) 5, 40, 50, 51; rhythm
  in, 51, 55, 60; transcendental, 104, 209,
  215, 232n126
"Agelasts," 83, 84
Akhmatova, Anna, 135
Alibi for Being. *See* Loophole
Alphonsus Liguori, St., 83
Ambivalence, 97, 126, 188; and laughter, 86–87,
  88, 134, 184
Ambrose, St., 7
Anagogy, 55. *See also* Metaphor
Andropov, Yuri, 98
Angel of History, 57
Answerability, 15, 18, 47, 77n4, 179, 198–201
  passim; answerable act, 7, 33, 43–44n15,
  182; I-for-myself and, 34, 36, 38; unity of,
  35, 42n6, 202
Anthony the Great, St., 93n11, 116n24
Anthropocentrism, 68, 218
Antinomic thought, 156–57
Apocalypse, 57
Apophaticism, 13, 14, 16, 151–67, 180–81,
  187–89 *passim*
Aquinas. *See* Thomas Aquinas, St.
Archaic period, 86
Architectonics, 19, 33, 198, 203
Aristophanes: *The Frogs*, 85
Aristotle, 111, 216
Asceticism, 38, 41, 93n11
Askoldov, Sergei A., 157

Asymmetry, 12, 102, 104–5, 107, 118n39, 187
Atheism. *See* Naturalism
Attentiveness, loving. *See* Love
Auerbach, Erich, 7, 49, 53; *Mimesis*, 112
Augustine, St., 7, 30, 108, 111–12, 123, 180,
  187, 220; and charitable interpretation, 5,
  27, 40; *On Christian Doctrine*, 25–26
Author: aesthetic activity of, *see* Aesthetics;
  authority of, 48–49; author/self, 17, 60, 70,
  74; Bakhtin's concept of, 183; -hero dyad, 9,
  50–51, 60, 65–67, 203; and outsideness, 9
Authoritarianism, political, 6, 85, 87. *See also*
  Totalitarianism
Authoritativeness, 212; authoritative word, 19,
  183
Authority: of author, 48–49; reverence toward,
  180, 183–84; totalitarian, *see* Totalitarianism
Autobiography, 40
Auto da fé, 85
Autonomy: false/semantic (of Adam and Eve), 8,
  65, 67; of hero, 7–8, 11, 48, 75; illusion of,
  68; negative evaluation of, 65, 66, 70, 74,
  182
Averintsev, Sergei S., 10, 97, 116n24, 185–86

Bakhtin, Mikhail M.: binary oppositions in
  thought of, 63, 182; biography, 1–3; debate
  over, 1; in exile, 90, 196; and feeling
  for faith, *see* Feeling for faith; and the
  hermeneutics of love, 25–41; lectures of, 3,
  15, 181, 188, 190–97 *passim*, 204, 206–21,
  230n83; and the novel, *see* Novel, the;
  opponents of, 15; Russian vs. Western
  views of, 97–102; WORKS OF: "Art and
  Answerability" ("A&A"), 42n6, 100, 136,
  198, 199, 201–2; "Author and Hero in
  Aesthetic Activity" ("A&H"), 4–10 *passim*,
  14–20 *passim*, 27–32 *passim*, 36, 38–39,
  47–60 *passim*, 63–75 *passim*, 100, 153–55,

discourse, 12, 13, 111, 115; and dual nature of Christ, 78n11, 110, 125–26, 133, 141
Charitable interpretation. *See* Augustine, St.
Charity. *See* Love
Chesterton, G. K., 82
Chikobava, Arnold, 134
Christ: Bakhtin's treatment of figure of, 68–71, 73, 112, 159; body of, 54, 73, 113; central role of, 17–18; and the commandments, 25–26, 27; Crucifixion of, 1, 77n1, 204; descent into hell, 38; dual nature ("duophysitism") of, 5, 11–13, 77, 102, 105, (in Chalcedonian thought) 78n11, 110, 125–26, 133, 141; image of, 17, 20, 72, 76; Incarnate, *see* Incarnation; and kenosis, 1, 6, 7, 9, 16, 35–40, 68–71; kisses Grand Inquisitor, 8, 15, 16, 19, 186, 187; and laughter, 10, 79, 80, 81, 185; mocked, 11, 86, 186; parables of, 180; personality of, 179; as Word, 4, 7, 11, 38, 39, 100, 105, 113, 123
Christianity: central ideas of, 13, 27, 30, (good vs. evil) 63; Christian ethics, *see* Ethics; Christian martyrs, 82 (*See also* Joan of Arc); Christian theology, 26, 38–40; Christian tradition, 28, 81, 189, (Augustinian) 27, 30, (Bakhtin immersed in) 4–5, 16–20, 204, (German) 45n26, 53, (Pauline-Augustinian) 30, (Russian) 1, 45n26, 57–58, 76; Creation dogma, 161–62 (*See also* Creation); Greco-Eastern, 102, 233n132; heteroglossia of, 53; "inner," 101, 107; I/other division, 208; and laughter, 10; and modernity, 49, 59; and personhood, 151; trust and distrust in, 219; Western, 108, 123–24, (and European culture) 61n5. *See also* Orthodoxy
Christology, 5, 126; asymmetrical, 12, 104–5; Orthodox, 123–24
Christ Pantocrator (icon), 21, 24n41
Chronotope, 12, 103, 104
Church: as community of souls, 14, 99; as image, 73, 101
Cicero, 111
Circumscription, 112
Clark, Katerina, 1–3, 15, 39, 97, 123, 135, 198–201 *passim*
Clement of Alexandria, 158
Coates, Ruth, 8–10, 182, 183, 189; *Christianity in Bakhtin*, 5
Cognition, 212, 214–15, 217; of art, 213; and

being, 207; cognitive discourse, 50; dualism of, 64; event of, 51
Cohen, Hermann, 195–99 *passim*, 202, 205, 212n127, 213–14, 227nn41, 50, 228nn52, 53, 82, 230n83, 233n132; *The Ethics of Pure Will*, 199, 203. *See also* Marburg school
Cold War, 135
Collective unconscious, 6, 130
Collectivism, 125, 183
Comedy, 189, 191. *See also* Humor; Laughter, culture of
Communion, Being as, 163
Communism, 144; world, 13, 129
Community, problem of, 74
Concise Oxford Dictionary, 67
Condorcet, Marquis de, 10, 87
Confession, 14, 59–60, 164, 165, 181; confessional self-accounting, 10, 15, 59, 165, 166
Conscience, 16, 18, 83, 208; repentant, 182–83 (*see also* Repentance)
Consciousness, 52, 103, 156–57, 161; aesthetic, 203; answerable, 37; Cartesian, 7; after death, 190; dialogical, 33; incarnated, 29; "internal uniqueness of," 155; Kant's theory of, 14, 211; language and, 130; "living," 202; moral, 19, 168n9, 208; multiplicity of, 125, 162–63, 171n24; objectivity of, 210; participatory, 163, 208; philosophy of, 151, 152, 155, 163–67; religious, 16, 179, 208; self-consciousness, 15, 20, 152, 165–67, 208; subjective, 215–16; unity of, 72
Content, 177–78, 207
Contino, Paul, 190
Convergence, 13, 129, 137, 142; nonconvergence, 122, 183, 184
Copernican revolution, 152
2 *Corinthians* 11:2, 229n68
Cosmic Academy of Sciences, 25
Cosmology, 57–58, 126
Creation, 16, 161–62, 181, 191; Creator and, 12, 18, 102–3, 104–5; doctrine of, 30
Creativity, 161, 181
Crowning/discrowning, 11, 86, 87
Crucifixion, the. *See* Christ
Culture, 207, 218; art, 65; crisis of, 64; European, Christianity and, 61n5; folk, 82, 86, 90–91;

Outsideness, 50–54, 59, 70, 98, 110, 113, 122;
the author and, 9; concepts replaced by,
105; distrust of, 162; Dostoevsky and,
74, 76; of God, 12; importance of, 17; of
Incarnation, 107, 108, 109, 114; "inward,"
55; and language, 106–7, 109; principle of,
36; Russian, and the West, 48; and silence,
113

Palamas. *See* Gregory of Palamas, St.
Panegyric. *See* Praise-blame dichotomy
Parapsychology. *See* Metapsychic works
Parmenides, 104
Participatory consciousness. *See* Consciousness
"Passive activity." *See* Self-activity
Pasternak, Boris, 82
Paul, St., 6, 30, 35–38 *passim*, 42n7, 67, 69
Pavlov, Ivan Petrovich, 101
Pechey, Graham, 7–8, 11, 12, 177, 178, 182–83,
188
Pelikan, Jaroslav, 19
Pellicciari, Nick, 23n33
Penetrative (or penetrated) word, 9–10, 19;
Bakhtin's definition of, 75–76; incarnation
as, 71–77
Penitence, 11, 14, 164. *See also* Repentance
Perichoresis (interpenetration), 13, 32, 78n11, 83,
123–26, 140–41
Personhood (*lichnost*), 151, 155, 162, 163, 189,
209; in image of God, 14, 220; and the
Trinity, 159–60
2 *Peter 1:4*, 159
Phenomenology, 14, 52, 70, 154–55, 179, 190,
202–3; European movement, 64; of laughter,
84; as term, 117n39
Philippians, 6, 38; *2:5–7*, 35; *2:5–8*, 69
Philokalia, 39
Philosophy: of consciousness, 151, 152,
155, 163–67; as discourse, 47; German/
European, 14, 53, 204, 230n83, 231n99;
Ideal in, 4, (and idealism) 72, 73; Kantian,
see Kant, Immanuel; and language, 107; of
law, 199; modern, 58, 60, (concern for)
64, (postmodern) 55; moral, 33, 164, 178,
201, 228n50; Nevel school of, 197 (*see also*
Bakhtin Circle); "primary," 65; of religion,
207–9; systematic, 209–14; theology and,
47, 100; Western, 48, 103, 106; of the
Word, 19, 123. *See also* Aesthetics

Piehl, Mel, 23n33
Pinsky, Leonid, 77n1, 97
Plato, 57, 103, 106, 108, 181, 189, 210; anti-
Platonic resistance, 108; and Neoplatonism,
52, 53, 113, 162, 234n136; pre-Platonic
thought, 211; *Republic*, 212
Plautus, 85
Plenitude, 151, 180, 181, 188–89, 190
Plotinus, 108
Polyphony, 5, 112, 140, 183; monologism vs.,
63, 73, 74; novelistic, 48, 50, 60, 73, 122
Poole, Randall, 13, 14–15, 20, 177, 180–81, 185,
188, 189
Positivism, 108, 197
Praise-blame dichotomy, 125–26, 134, 141, 188
Pravda, 134
Prayer, 3, 14, 28, 51, 97, 164; of the Publican,
165; silent (hesychastic), 112–13, 158
Predestination, 209
Problematization, 49, 213–14, 215
Proclus, 219
Promethean view, 183
Protestantism, 86, 100, 108, 179, 190, 220;
German pietistic, 45n26, 101–2, 107
Proverbs 8, 57
Psalms 69:28, 87:6, 139:16, 229n70
Pseudo-Dionysius the Areopagite, St., 36, 158
Psychical. *See* Metapsychical works
Psychoanalysis, 218, 220
Psychology: deplored, 43n12; "idealist," 202
Publican: and Pharisee, parable of, 208; prayer
of, 165
Pumpiansky, Lev V., 3, 15, 131, 177, 179, 190;
Dostoevsky and Antiquity, 196, 198; Notebooks
of, 193–205, (comments on) 205–6
Puritans, the, 92n10
Pushkin, Aleksandr, 195, 197, 198, 201

Rabelais, François, 79, 82, 86, 93n14, 141, 189,
204; Bakhtin on, *see* Bakhtin, Mikhail M.;
Gargantua, 87
Rationalism, 162, 163
Reality, 82, 89, 212, 217, 218; divine, 156, 157;
moral, 200, 201–3; "serious," 179. *See also*
Objectivity, objectification
Reason, 156, 157–58, 190
Redemption, 9, 183; Christ's kenosis as model of,
9, 68
Reed, Natalia, 24n38

Notes on Contributors

Sergei Averintsev is a philosopher, an academician of the Russian Academy of Sciences, and a professor at Vienna University.

Ruth Coates is a lecturer in the Department of Russian Studies at the University of Bristol, England. She is cotranslator and editor of *The Emancipation of Russian Christianity* and the author of *Christianity in Bakhtin: God and the Exiled Author*.

Paul J. Contino is an associate professor of humanities at Christ College (Valparaiso University) and the author of articles on Dostoevsky.

Caryl Emerson is A. Watson Armour III University Professor of Slavic Languages and Literatures at Princeton University. She is the author of numerous works on Bakhtin, including *The First Hundred Years of Mikhail Bakhtin*, and is a primary translator of Bakhtin into English.

Susan M. Felch is an associate professor of English at Calvin College. She is the editor of *The Collected Works of Anne Vaughan Lock* and the author of articles on sixteenth-century British writers and Bakhtin.

Alan Jacobs is a professor of English at Wheaton College in Illinois. He is the author of *What Became of Wystan: Change and Continuity in Auden's Poetry* and numerous essays on religion, literature, and literary theory.

Vadim Liapunov is an associate professor of Russian literature and language at Indiana University in Bloomington. He has written on Pushkin, Boratynsky, Solzhenitsyn, and Bakhtin, and he is the translator of Bakhtin's early philosophical works, *Art and Answerability: Early Philosophical Essays by M. M. Bakhtin* and *Toward a Philosophy of the Act*.

Leonid Livak is an assistant professor of Russian at Grinnell College.

Charles Lock is a professor of English literature at the University of Copenhagen. He is the author of numerous articles on Eastern Orthodoxy and Bakhtin.

Alexandar Mihailovic is an associate professor of Russian and comparative literature at Hofstra University. He is the author of *Corporeal Words: Mikhail Bakhtin's Theology of Discourse* and the editor of *Tchaikovsky and His Contemporaries: A Centennial Symposium*.

Graham Pechey is a visiting research fellow in English at the University of Hertfordshire in England. Besides his work on Bakhtin, he has written a number of articles in the fields of Romantic writing, literary and cultural theory, and postcolonial topics.

Randall A. Poole is an assistant professor of general studies at Boston University. His work in Russian intellectual history focuses on idealist philosophy during the Silver Age.

RETHINKING THEORY

GENERAL EDITOR

Gary Saul Morson

CONSULTING EDITORS

Robert Alter
Frederick Crews
John M. Ellis
Caryl Emerson